Pontotoc County, Mississippi Marriage Book 1849-1891

Hazel Boss Neet

HERITAGE BOOKS
2008

HERITAGE BOOKS
AN IMPRINT OF HERITAGE BOOKS, INC.

Books, CDs, and more—Worldwide

For our listing of thousands of titles see our website
at
www.HeritageBooks.com

Published 2008 by
HERITAGE BOOKS, INC.
Publishing Division
100 Railroad Ave. #104
Westminster, Maryland 21157

Copyright © 2002 Hazel Boss Neet

Other books by the author:

Enumeration of Educatable Children in Pontotoc County, Mississippi, 1894
Enumeration of Educatable Children in Pontotoc County, Mississippi, 1892

All rights reserved. No part of this book may be reproduced or transmitted in any form or by any means, electronic or mechanical, including photocopying, recording or by any information storage and retrieval system without written permission from the author, except for the inclusion of brief quotations in a review.

International Standard Book Numbers
Paperbound: 978-0-7884-2034-4
Clothbound: 978-0-7884-7088-2

TABLE OF CONTENTS

	PAGE
PONTOTOC COUNTY, MISSISSIPPI MARRIAGE BOOK 1849 – 1856	1 – 23
BRIDES 1849 – 1856	24 – 33
PONTOTOC COUNTY, MISSISSIPPI MARRIAGE BOOK 1856 – 1867	34 – 67
BRIDES 1856 – 1867	68 – 84
PONTOTOC COUNTY, MISSISSIPPI "MISSING MARRIAGES" 1867 – 1880	85 – 115
BRIDES 1867 – 1880	116 – 130
PONTOTOC COUNTY, MISSISSIPPI MARRIAGE BOOK 1880 – 1886	131 – 145
BRIDES 1880 – 1886	146 – 151
PONTOTOC COUNTY, MISSISSIPPI MARRIAGE BOOK 1887 – 1891	152 – 165
BRIDES 1887 – 1891	166 – 171

PONTOTOC COUNTY, MISSISSIPPI

MARRIAGE BOOK 1849 - 1856

THE EARLIEST MARRIAGE BOOK ON RECORD IS THE 1849 - 1856 BOOK WITH A FEW EARLIER ONES. BE SURE TO CHECK ALL POSSIBLE SPELLINGS. THE L'S, T'S S.'S AND O'S, A'S LOOKED VERY MUCH ALIKE IN THE OLD HANDWRITING, ALSO SOME OF THE HANDWRITING WAS FADED, VERY DIFFICULT TO READ.

INDEXED BY: HAZLE BOSS NEET
207 NORTH MAIN
PONTOTOC, MISSISSIPPI 38863

PAGE	GROOM	BRIDE		DATE	
124	Abernathy, James F.	Porter, Emaline		12 Nov	1851
208	Abernathy, Marion Z.	Wilson, Martha		23 Nov	1851
219	Abernathy, Rufus T.	Long, Sarah E.		6 July	1852
481	Abernathy, Samuel	Stegall, Elizabeth		15 Nov	1855
420	Adams, D.W.	Davis, Cynthia E.		8 Dec	1854
289	Adams, George M.	Trewett, Matilda C.		6 Feb	1853
303	Adams, James W.	Norris, Sarah A.		8 May	1853
34	Albritton, William	Gambrell, Miss Sarah		8 Nov	1849
74	Alexander, Daniel M.	Bridges, Elizabeth Ann		24 Feb	1850
103	Alexander, Isaac D.M.	Golding, Louisa		23 July	1850
5	Alexander, J.W.	Wardlaw, Miss Nancy V.		22 Feb	1849
449	Alexander, Thomas	South, Sarah		19 June	1855
17	Allbaugh, Jeremiah	Perry, Miss Rosalie		24 Aug	1848
398	Allen, James S.	Mauldin, Jane		28 Sept	1854
38	Allen, Lafayette	Hickman, Miss Lucy		28 Oct	1849
12	Allen, M.C.	Shuttles, Miss Nancy		25 Nov	1848
478	Allen, William	Malone, Julia		25 Oct	1855
80	Allman, Albert G.	Dansby, E.C.		28 Mar	1850
129	Alsup, Franklin C.	Singleton, Nancy E.		4 Jan	1851
572	Anderson, Eldridge N.	Orr, Harriet E.		3 Apr	1856
109	Archy, George	Shears, Lena		28 Apr	1850
339	Arnold, H.C.	Gamble, Jane		24 Nov	1853
86	Ashby, Wm. T.S.	McKinney, Mildred T.		28 May	1850
230	Aston, Archibald H.	Bell, Mary J.		4 Feb	1852
507	Austin, Samuel	Real, Margaret	(B)	27 Feb	1856
490	Austin, William G.	Howard, Nancy H.		23 Dec	1855
160	Autrey, Absolem	Smith, Miss Frances		21 Aug	1850
347	Aycock, Augustus T.	Beckham, Rebecca	(B)	20 Dec	1853
50	Aycock, John M.	Connelly, Martha Ann		9 Oct	1849
492	Armstrong, W.J.	Privitt, Margaret		3 Jan	1856
48	Babb, Joseph P.	Willard, Miss Jane		30 May	1849
129	Babb, Messer (?)	Babb, Stacy Ann		30 Oct	1850
373	Bagwell, Patillo F.	Staten, Lucinda	(B)	28 Mar	1854
509	Bailey, Aaron	Gilmore, Edy		4 Mar	1856
228	Bailey, Alsey	Cromeans, Sarah		12 Feb	1852
351	Bailey, Moses	Shepherd, Isabella		22 Dec	1853
114	Baily, Larkin	Clardy, Jane B.		1 Oct	1850
446	Baily, Robert	Leverett, Amanda C.		29 May	1855
229	Baity (Baily?), Wm C.	Black, Mary E.		5 Jan	1852
65	Baker, Daniel	Jackson, Elizabeth		15 Jan	1850
175	Baker, Davidson	McWilliams, Mary		23 Dec	1844
154	Baker, James	Crane, Louisa		20 Nov	1850
113	Baker, John F.	Shelton, Irena C.		23 Sept	1850
217	Baker, Thomas A.	Mitchell, Lucy C.		23 Dec	1851
489	Ball, Benjamin J.	Saddler, Jane F.A.		27 Dec	1855
299	Ball, Willis	Hill, Sarah W.		14 Apr	1853
82	Bandy, Jesse A.	Nix, Artha E.		7 Apr	1850

(B) - Bond Only

PAGE	GROOM	BRIDE	DATE	
198	Banks, C.C.	Johnson, M.J.	16 Oct	1851
346	Barbee, James D.	Alsup, Dorthula	22 Dec	1853
71	Barber, (Barbee?), John	Cole, Priscilla	27 Nov	1845
349	Barden, Henry H.	Phillips, Charlotte	25 Dec	1853
71	Bardin, Wm. E.	Meador, Jane	24 Dec	1845
400	Barkely, William	Swafford, Sarah A.	3 Oct	1854
425	Barmon, B.B.	Davis, Mary E.	1 Feb	1855
211	Barr, Hugh A.	Hodges, Mary E.	9 Dec	1851
302	Barton, Elias	Wilson, Adaline E.	14 Apr	1853
316	Bass, B.C.	Moore, Martha Ann	31 Aug	1853
325	Bass, William	Waite, Elizabeth	28 Sept	1853
301	Bassham, Henry	Warren, Martha	12 Apr	1853
55	Baugh, David L.	Ussory, Margarette J.	22 Nov	1849
459	Beaver, John	Procter, Josphine	23 Aug	1855
409	Beavers, J.M.	Ware, Martha M.	28 Nov	1854
165	Beckham, John G.	Ward, Martha A.	22 May	1851
97	Bell, James W.	Pannell, Rosanna	4 June	1850
265	Bell, Robert W.	Chancellor, Margarette W.	4 Nov	1852
112	Bell, Wm W.	Carr, Mary A.	17 Oct	1850
406	Bell, Z.S.	Stokes, Elizabeth J.	16 Nov	1854
385	Belyew, William	Barker, Rebecca J.	22 June	1854
100	Bennett, H.P.	Hamilton, Elizabeth	12 Sept	1850
311	Bennett, Pleasant M.	Snider, Barbary T.	14 July	1853
200	Bennett, Wiley M.	Frazier, Martha J.	23 Oct	1851
486	Bensen, Obadiah	Rowe, Elender A.	9 Dec	1855
508	Benson, W.C.	Vaughan, Ann E.	4 Mar	1856
168	Berry, H.P.	Stephens, Penelope J.	15 May	1851
390	Berry, Jarret L.	Tippah, Almeda	18 July	1854
131	Berry, Nathan M.	Ball, Jemima F.	15 Jan	1851
218	Berry, Reason B.	Warren, Christian	1 Jan	1852
444	Betts, James	Hearston, Nancy E.	24 May	1855
462	Betts, Jas. H.	Lockard, M.L.	6 Sept	1855
394	Betts, Phillip H.	Barrett, Elizabeth	2 Sept	1854
92	Bevill, Alexander D.	Johnson, Della	20 June	1850
301	Bevill, Ellison	Shepherd, Mary P.	13 Apr	1853
76	Bice, Thomas J.	West, Emily	27 Dec	1850
40	Bigham, Columbus A.	Mahon, Miss Mary M.	16 Aug	1849
41	Black, Oliver	Winston, Miss Nancy	31 Oct	1849
304	Black, Robert	Long, Charity	28 Apr	1853
418	Black, U.B.	Howard, N.J.	30 Dec	1854
213	Blackburn, Jessie D.	Shelton, Naoma M.	9 Dec	1851
338	Blackburn, Leroy	Tucker, Mary A.	20 Nov	1853
514	Blocker, William G.	Arnold, Malissa Elvira	24 Apr	1856
149	Boatman, Robert M.	White, Rebecca	2 Feb	1851
11	Bolding, James P.	Fisher, Elizabeth	22 May	1849
492	Bolen, William W.	Sweeten, Jane E.	1 Jan	1856
317	Bolt, Lewis A.	Rogers, Elizabeth	22 Aug	1853
13	Bolt, William	Jones, Miss Martha	21 Jan	1849
205	Bond, C.T.	Prewett, Rhoda	26 Oct	1851
449	Bond, William W.	Dansby, Jane C.	8 July	1855

PAGE	GROOM	BRIDE	DATE	
272	Boothe, James M.	Burk, Martha C.		8 Dec 1852
95	Boothe, Warren J.	Campbell, Mary Ann		4 July 1850
223	Bost, Solomon	Cole, Martha C.		20 Jan 1852
186	Bouland, Daniel	Stephens, Elvira S.		31 July 1851
275	Bowen, James A.	Wood, Martha A.		21 Dec 1852
381	Bowen, James E.	Carter, Lucinda F.		18 May 1854
447	Bradley, J.A.W.	Waldrop, Nancy A.	(B)	9 June 1855
313	Braden, James	Fortune, Harriet		19 July 1853
493	Brady, Daniel	Donavan, Mary		3 Jan 1856
361	Bramblett, John W.	Turner, Eliza		6 Feb 1854
13	Bramlette, Hughes A.	Cole Martha		25 Aug 1848
53	Brandon, Christopher	Forbes, Sarah Ann		6 Aug 1849
39	Brandon, Washington	Forbes, Miss Mary M.		25 Oct 1849
480	Brassfield, Wiley	Morgan, Sarah		15 Nov 1855
429	Brewer, B.D.	Young, Martha K.	(B)	13 Feb 1855
458	Brewer, Joseph	Langley, Laura Ann		15 Aug 1855
110	Bridges, Joshua C.	Reid, Nancy G.		15 Aug 1850
148	Bridges, Meredith	Frazier, Margaret C.		10 Jan 1851
14	Bridges, Solomon S.	McCraw, Miss Lucretia		22 Oct 1848
455	Bridges, William E.	White, Mary		1 Aug 1855
147	Bridges, Wm E.	Bridges, Elizabeth	(B)	11 Sept 1850
217	Bridges, Wm E.	Evans, Mary Ann		6 Dec 1851
386	Brock, Jeremiah	Jones, Mary		29 June 1854
317	Brogden, James H.	Ross, Nancy		22 Aug 1853
319	Brookshire, A.J.	Oliver, Mrs. C.E.		12 Sept 1853
281	Brown, Alexander	Chamberlin, Mary		6 Jan 1853
371	Brown, Elijah G. (V.?)	Casey, Delphia		19 Mar 1854
415	Brown, Henry	Abernathy, Eliza E.		21 Dec 1854
478	Brown, James C.	Walker, Emily		1 Nov 1855
355	Brown, James D.	Smith, Louisa		12 Jan 1854
410	Brown, William R.	Maffett, Margaret L.		30 Nov 1854
162	Brown, Wm	Rogers, Frances C.		8 Mar 1851

(Frances C. Rogers on bond, Clementine F. Rogers on ministers return)

PAGE	GROOM	BRIDE	DATE
429	Browning, William H,	Harden, Samantha	15 Feb 1854
510	Brummit, Joab Orren	Robbins, Rhoda CAtharine	18 Mar 1856
353	Bryant, L. Johnston	Murphy, Winny	5 Jan 1854
147	Buchanan, Elijah	Shuttleworth, Mary	7 Nov 1850
15	Buchanan, John H.	Rogers, Miss Elsamena	22 Oct 1848
294	Bugg, James M.	Seymore, Rhoda C.	10 Mar 1853
62	Burch, August O.	Johnson, Minney A.	11 June 1849
438	Burk, R.H.	Williams, Sarah	8 Apr 1855
15	Burke, Alvin	Keel, Miss Etha L.M.	27 July 1848
162	Burks, Calvin	Howard, Mary	9 Mar 1851
311	Burlasen, Jefferson	Glidewell, Martha	5 July 1853
223	Burns (?), Calvin	Gragg, Elizabeth	25 Jan 1852
246	Burns, Wm	Pollock, Irena	15 July 1852
252	Burten, Daniel	Cornell, Mary	9 Sept 1852
369	Burten, James	Downing, Martha	15 Mar 1854
111	Burton, James M.	Fears, Elizabeth F.	7 Nov 1850

PAGE	GROOM	BRIDE	DATE		
136	Busby, James	Sears, Margaret I.		1 Dec	1850
348	Butler, E.F.	Johnston, Mariah C.		21 Dec	1853
174	Butler, John D.	Nelson, Nancy Bell	(B)	11 Nov	1843
14	Byers, James M.	Knox, Miss Newanna		3 Nov	1848
315	Byers, T.A.	Magee, A.E.		18 Aug	1853
188	Byrd, Nazrea	Morgan, Carmilla R.		17 Aug	1851
305	Byrd, Octavias	Justice, Eliza W.		5 May	1853
406	Caldwell, B.J.	Mounts, Sarah R.		9 Nov	1854
338	Caldwell, Charles H.	Stephenson, Jane C.		24 Nov	1853
326	Caldwell, John	Dyer, Nancy		13 Oct	1853
274	Caldwell, John P.	Carlisle, Eliza M.		23 Dec	1852
431	Caldwell, Joseph D.	Reed Cyntha		22 Feb	1855
131	Caldwell, Robert	Goggins, Nancy		14 Jan	1851
342	Caldwell, William P.	Wilkison, Jane T.		8 Dec	1853
232	Calloway, James G.	Strong, Nancy M.		17 Feb	1852
337	Calloway, Jefferson H.	Good, Araminta H.		16 Nov	1853
125	Calvin, Wm	Vineyard, Mary Ann		10 Dec	1850
385	Campbell, John W.	Franklin, Mary F.		27 Aug	1854
272	Campbell, William A.	Jones, Margaret R.		7 Dec	1852
441	Cannon, Christopher	Milam, Jane		2 May	1855
248	Cariker, Martin W.	Jourdan, Sarah		19 July	1852
373	Carpenter, John	Thompson, Sarah E.		28 Mar	1854
499	Carr, John H.	Drake, S.R.		22 Jan	1856
431	Carruth, A.B.	Brown, Amanda C.		26 Feb	1855
185	Carter, John	Johnson, Martha		26 July	1851
408	Carter, Nelson	Free, Mournin C.		19 Nov	1854
335	Cary, Joseph	Staggs, Elizabeth		15 Nov	1853
128	Chapman, R.F.	Whitehurst, Amanda M.		18 Dec	1850
130	Christian, Elijah G.	Robertson, Emeline		12 Jan	1851
500	Christman, James J.	Miller, Cytha A.E.	(B)	29 Jan	1856
143	Clary, Wm N.	Jones, Elizabeth		21 Jan	1851
341	Cobb, H.C.	Baxter, Elizabeth J.		1 Dec	1853
84	Cobb, Isaac W.	Campbell, Nancy		24 Feb	1850
357	Cobb, Rufus J.	Ward, Sarah E.		24 Jan	1854
105	Coe, John J.	Caraker, Martha		6 Nov	1850
	[Thomas J. Coe on bond. John J. on ministers return]				
169	Coffin, Charles P.	Allen, Sarah P.	(B)	18 June	1840
153	Coker, E.M.	Barden, Jane		24 Dec	1850
111	Coker, James T.	Frazier, Frances L.		26 Nov	1850
269	Coker, William G.	Taylor, Elizabeth		7 Dec	1852
389	Cole, Wm P.	Martin, Vina M.		2 July	1854
370	Coleman, H.L.	Potter, E.A.		16 Mar	1854
135	Coleman, Madison B.	Wells, Martha		2 Oct	1850
327	Coley, James M.	Vinyard, Margarett M.		18 Oct	1853
358	Coley, W.G.W.	Vinyard, Nancy		25 Jan	1854
278	Collins, Abraham	Haren, Adaline		30 Dec	1852
60	Collins, Hardy	Wood, Mary F.		28 Dec	1849

PAGE	GROOM	BRIDE		DATE	
436	Collins, J.R.	Collins, Nancy		29 Mar	1855
244	Collins, James	Phillips, Elander Ann		29 June	1852
256	Collins, Moses A.	Rowland, Narcissa E.		7 Oct	1852
144	Cook, Silas	Parton, Malinda	(B)	17 Oct	1848
452	Coon, John A.	Kelly, Mary F.		5 July	1855
143	Cooper, Benjamin N.	May, Zelphia	(B)	14 Aug	1849
142	Cooper, James F.	Knight, Elizabeth	(B)	1 Feb	1851
89	Cooper, Marcus D.	Kough, Sarah Ann		16 May	1850
119	Corey, George W.	Carter, Nancy		4 Feb	1851
190	Cornel, Nathan	Orr, Clarinda		22 Aug	1851
66	Cornelious, Charles B.	Stone, Amelia		13 Dec	1849
282	Cornelious, James	West, Mary		11 Jan	1853
476	Cotton, William	Vincent, Matilda		19 Oct	1855
384	Couch, J.M.	Bevill, Nancy		11 June	1854
473	Cox, David	Crippen, Mary		9 Oct	1855
378	Cox, J.J.	Montgomery, Jane		22 May	1854
289	Cox, James E.	Payne, Nancy E.		10 Feb	1853
355	Cox, James W.	Kidd, Nancy		12 Jan	1854
201	Cox, John	Turner, Malinda		2 Nov	1851
403	Cox, John H.J.	Brown, Sarah		26 Oct	1854
16	Craft, James A.	Barbee, Miss Elizabeth		30 Mar	1849
185	Crague, James M.	Reed, Nancy	(B)	26 July	1851
228	Crim, Samuel T.	Price, Caroline S.		1 Feb	1852
156	Crockett, John F.	Saunders, Elizabeth B.		20 Feb	1851
401	Crosby, David	Salmon, Zembly		15 Oct	1854
312	Crumpton, John B.	Guess, Elizabeth		17 July	1853
114	Cruse, Daniel M.	McGregor, E.J.		25 Feb	1851
424	Cunningham, J.G.	Ramage, Cynthia E.		23 Jan	1855
360	Cunningham, James	Sanders, C.C.		7 Feb	1854
447	Cunningham, R.C.	Rowland, Sarah F.		20 June	1855
513	Dandridge, Thomas R.	Ward, Susannah J.		3 Apr	1856
161	Daves, Elisha G.	McCraw, Susanna C.		5 Mar	1851
483,	Davis, Anderson	Vincent, Rebecca	(B)	24 Nov	1855
253	Davis, Andrew J.	Burnell, Emily A.		9 Sept	1852
405	Davis, James A.	Miller, Elizabeth C.		8 Nov	1854
391	Davis, Jasper C.	Gregory, Martha C.		19 July	1854
513	Davis, Jonathan	Massey, Julia Ann		8 Apr	1856
396	Davis, Thomas C.	Bridges, Lifalet		10 Sept	1854
88	Davis, Warler	Godfrey, Ann L.		10 Jan	1850
120	Davis, Wm D.	Hardy, Mary E.		7 Jan	1851
43	Deason, John C.	Hawkins, Catharine		21 Oct	1849
362	Deason, Josian	Duke, Mary A.		9 Feb	1854
265	Desmond, Council	King, Mary L.		15 Nov	1852
363	Dickson, George	Stone, Elizabeth		12 Feb	1854
421	Dickson, Joseph C.	Payne, Mary E.		9 Jan	1855
99	Dickson, Virgil E.F.	Reed, Nancy		26 Aug	1850
423	Dillard, J.H.	Nowland, Jane		21 Jan	1855
57	Donaldson, Andrew Y.	Waldrop, Rebecca E.		12 Dec	1849
58	Dodson, Richard B.	Stroud, Rosanna		6 Oct	1849

PAGE	GROOM	BRIDE	DATE
453	Donavan, Bartholomew	Long, Julia	6 July 1855
285	Dozier, Calvin	Raby, Judy Ann	18 Jan 1853
150	Draper, Thomas J.	Williams, Mary Ann	30 Nov 1849
207	Duff, Joseph P.	Houston, Mary E.	12 Nov 1851
37	Duff, Walter R.	Walls, Miss Sarah J.	28 Aug 1849
138	Duke, James M.	Spence, Martha Jane	20 Mar 1851
309	Duncan, Jerremiah W.	Wiley, Martha J.	28 June 1853
43	Duncan, Jesse J.	Cole, Miss Nancy E.	19 Oct 1849
12	Duncan, Thomas L.	Maston, Miss Mary	5 June 1849
428	Durham, Samuel	Ramsey, Martha J.	8 Feb 1855
210	Dye, Alfred	Young, Susan	4 Dec 1851
92	Dyson, Lafayette	Jamison, Clarisa	30 June 1850
337	Dyson, John B.	Wray, Sarah	16 Nov 1853
332	Eaves, C.C.	Boothe, Susan Ann	9 Nov 1853
305	Edens, James A.	Morris, Epsy	25 Apr 1853
170	Edrington, James M.	Wilson, Mary Jane	26 Nov 1846
10	Elder, James C.	Nowlan, Miss Caroline	22 May 1849
178	Elder, John	Gwin, Elizabeth J.	18 June 1851
333	Ellis, John W.	Hamelton, Eveline E. (B)	5 Nov 1853
169	Epperson, John	Jones, Louisa Caroline (B)	15 Aug 1837
413	Evans, William	Monk, Jane	19 Dec 1854
472	Evetts, Neal P.	Brown, Harriet E.	9 Oct 1855
199	Falkner, W.C.	Vance, Elizabeth H.	14 Oct 1851
434	Farmer, Robert T.	Johnson, Margaret J. (B)	17 Mar 1855
287	Ferrell, B.D.	Moseley, Julia F. (B)	29 Jan 1853
419	Filgo, Geo W.	Gill, Susan J.	27 Dec 1854
256	Fincher, William C.	Lansdale, Parthena P.	3 Oct 1852
295	Findley, Henderson L.	Ritchey, Clemantine C.	9 Mar 1853
193	Finley, W.W.	Bell, Martha Ann	18 Sept 1851
174	Flarity, Thomas C.	Edwards, Mahala (B)	10 Feb 1843
439	Fortner, John	Hammer, Sarah W.	16 Apr 1855
224	Fortune, R.C.	Malone, Susan C.	23 Jan 1852
104	Foster, Booker	Russell, Elizabeth	29 Sept 1850
398	Foster, Samuel	Vaughan, Caroline	28 Sept 1854
7	Foster, Wm C.	Smith, Clarinda S.	27 Feb 1849
326	Franklin, John I.G.	Allbritton, Amanda S.	6 Oct 1853
366	Franklin, Thomas	Mabry, Frances E.	21 Feb 1854
309	Franklin, Thomas N.	Duke, Jane	29 May 1853
470	Frazier, James L.	Hurley, Martha C.	3 Oct 1855
150	Frazier, James W.	Wiley, Margaret A.	1 Jan 1850
212	Frazier, John D.	Shelton, Elmira	11 Dec 1851
82	Frazier, Willis L.	Scott, Permelia	14 Mar 1850
108	Freeman, Thomas H.	Bramlett, Jane K.	8 Oct 1850
280	Freeman, Wesley	Hadden, Elizabeth	2 Jan 1852
281	Fuller, Henry	Hughes, Nancy (B)	7 Jan 1853
31	Fuller, Wm M.	Reid, Miss Susan C.	22 Oct 1848

PAGE	GROOM	BRIDE		DATE	
81	Fullerton, Geo W.	Pannell, Malinda		28 Oct	1849
368	Fulton, John	Vaughan, Elizabeth		3 Mar	1854
344	Fulton, Samuel C.	Deel, Mary J.E.		7 Dec	1853
329	Fuqua, R.H.	Jenkins, Sarah J.		12 Oct	1853
44	Fuqua, Wm M.	Johnson, Miss Mary Ann		22 Oct	1849
75	Furgeson, Samuel H.	Gilliam, Martha A.		6 Mar	1850
282	Furgison, Milton A.	Morgan, Nancy		11 Jan	1853
225	Furguson, J.R.	Freeman, Salina		27 Jan	1852
244	Gafford, Wm L.	Tyer, Susan E.		8 July	1852
191	Gafford, Joel	Taylor, Lucretia		4 Sept	1851
335	Gaines, Joseph	Guess, Dosia		13 Nov	1853
469	Galaspie, John	Briant, Ann		30 Sept	1855
323	Gallaway, L.B.C.	Price, Elizabeth C.		25 Sept	1853
273	Gamble, R.K.	Herring, Mary M.		21 Dec	1852
197	Gandy, Rose	Ragsdale, Martha P.		8 Oct	1851
318	Garner, A.T.	Brown, Lucy		31 Aug	1853
496	Garrett, D.C.	Muffett, Rosannah B.		10 Jan	1856
	[On marriage the name is Muffett, but should be Maffett]				
370	Garrett, Seaburn	Irby, Sophia M	(B)	18 Mar	1854
242	Gassaway, John W.	Card, Frances		24 June	1852
27	Gates, Joseph N.	Moore, Miss Susanna		10 May	1849
16	Gathright, O.F.	Orr, Miss Mary Jane		5 Oct	1849
464	Gent, Obadiah	Paine, Birchett		19 Sept	1855
259	Gentry, David H.	Holly, Mary J.		21 Oct	1852
115	George, Thomas F.	Herron, Rhoda M.		17 Oct	1851
55	Gibbs, John L.	Haws(?), Pheby H.		13 Nov	1849
349	Gibson, John E.	Worthington, Sophia		25 Dec	1853
428	Gideon, Joseph	Headly, Catharin		20 Feb	1855
285	Gilder, Philip N.	Wright, Permina		19 Jan	1853
291	Gill, George W.	Shaw, Jennette J.		17 Feb	1853
382	Gill, J.J.	McPherson, Martha A.		24 May	1854
510	Gillian, Samuel	Truit, Mary J.		11 Mar	1856
52	Givhan, Wm P.	Prude, Martha B.		6 Sept	1849
323	Glazener, G.R.	Sadler, Mary		25 Sept	1853
503	Glenn, J.J.	Owen, Narcissa		12 Feb	1856
316	Glenn, James M.	Hudson, Mary F.		18 Aug	1853
277	Goen, Thomas	Beal, S.A.A.		29 Dec	1852
67	Golding, Anthony F.	Mitchell, Dorothy H.		13 Dec	1849
404	Goldman, Andrew	Sauceman, Cynthia		26 Oct	1854
70	Goodrich, Harvey	McKinyon, Issabella		1 Aug	1839
297	Graddy, James O.	Gholson, Matilda		30 Mar	1853
310	Grady, W.D.	Moore, Eliza	(B)	27 June	1853
191	Gray, Edward	Morgan, Sounda		4 Sept	1851
296	Gray, Isaac	Swindoll, Jane		16 Mar	1853
336	Gray, William	McClelland, Sarah		17 Nov	1853
145	Gray, Wm P.	Payne, Margaret	(B)	11 Jan	1850

PAGE	GROOM	BRIDE	DATE	
488	Green, George Washington	Mahon, Nancy B.	18 Dec	1855
88	Green, Hiram	Walton, Mary Ann	7 May	1850
396	Greene, Edward A.	Guthrey, Sarah A.	10 Sept	1854
495	Greene, Josiah	Sheppard, Ann V.	4 Jan	1856
34	Gregory, Willis	Billingsly, Miss Amanda	5 Dec	1848
451	Griffin, James A.	Walker, Elizabeth	27 June	1855
90	Griffin, James B.	Griffin, Martha H.	26 June	1850
125	Griffin, James M.	Smith, L.J.	14 Mar	1851
504	Griffith, Richard D.	Gocher, Margaret (B)	13 Feb	1856
99	Griffith, Samuel M.	McClintock, Rachael P.	25 July	1850
445	Grisham, Allen	Markley, Eliza J.	31 May	1855
188	Grisham, J.M.	Johnson, Elizabeth J.	21 Aug	1851
96	Grisham, Littleberry	Myres, Brittania	9 May	1850
157	Grisham, R.H.	Weatherall, Emma C.	2 Apr	1849
118	Grisham, Y.I.M.	Scott, Ellen	11 Jan	1851
86	Grissell, Benjamin S.	Galaspie, Sarah L.	25 June	1850
84	Grissel, Daniel M.	Donaldson, Lucinda	24 May	1850
102	Grizzard, James	Cox, Salina	11 Sept	1850
69	Guinn, Wilson H.	Sullivan, Mary	23 June	1847
184	Gullett, Thomas F.	Betts, A.A.	29 July	1851
149	Guthrie, J.T.	Morris, Susan (B)	3 Oct	1848
10	Guttry, William	Helms, Elizabeth Jane	24 Aug	1848

[Elizabeth Jane Helms name appears as Elizabeth Jane Williams on ministers return]

PAGE	GROOM	BRIDE	DATE	
170	Hagler, George W.	Brown, Rosaline	25 Mar	1851
489	Hagler, Marion J.	Smith, Elmira G.	20 Dec	1855
203	Hale, N.B.	Petty, Rebecca	28 Oct	1851
258	Hale, William	Churchwell, Susanah	16 Oct	1852
90	Hall, Richard C.	Shelton, Adaline	9 July	1850
321	Hall, Thomas S.	Speck, Nancy C.	15 Nov	1853
155	Hulsey, Francis E.	Cole, Cynthia	26 Dec	1850

[Halsey and Hallsell all 3 surnames written for Francis]

PAGE	GROOM	BRIDE	DATE	
387	Hamaker, Joshua	Boatman, Sharlotte	2 July	1854
78	Hambrick, Uriah	Woodward, Martha	18 Mar	1850
368	Hammer, Andrew J.	Phillips, Sarah A.	5 Mar	1854
8	Hamner, Edward F.	Russell, Miss Dorcus	17 Jan	1849
243	Hamner, Joseph	Russell, Elender	29 June	1852
383	Hampten, John W.	Hudson, Louisa F.	1 June	1854
239	Hampton, John C.	Duncan, Georgia Ann	1 Apr	1852
235	Hancock, Hugh B.	McFall, Elizabeth D.	3 Mar	1852
155	Hancock, Loyd	Aycock, Susan E.	25 Dec	1850
260	Hancock, Samuel	Duke, Sarah A. (B)	18 Oct	1852
402	Handley, S.F.	Davis, J.W.	18 Oct	1854
219	Hannell, Wm C.	Sanders, A.C.	7 Jan	1852
342	Harden, Mark	Dillard, Letha	7 Dec	1853
264	Harden, T.W.	Smith, Susan J.	20 Nov	1852
357	Harder, John	Cosby, Martha	22 Jan	1854
157	Hardwick, G.J.	Pippin, Selina	23 Sept	1849
415	Hardy, F.L.	Maddox, Elizabeth	21 Dec	1854
195	Harkey, Daniel D.	Hamlin, Nancy L.	25 SEpt	1851

PAGE	GROOM	BRIDE	DATE	
28	Harris, James M.	Duvall, Ann	14 Feb	1849
87	Harris, John	May, Dianna	26 Apr	1850
286	Harris, John L.	Keys, Martha Ann L.	20 Jan	1853
9	Harris, M.	Cornelius, Miss Mary	24 Jan	1849
389	Harris, William H.	Dorsey, Martha C.	17 July	1854
186	Harrison, Headly	Walpool, Arvagine	29 July	1851
	[Hadley Harrison and Hendly Harrison also given for groom]			
372	Harrison, T.S.	Hampton, Elizabeth Ann	21 Mar	1854
310	Harwood, John M.	Worsham, Mary A.	8 July	1853
483	Hathcock, W.N.C.	Williamson, Mary E.	2 Dec	1855
515	Hattox, G.H.	Norwood, Sarah R.E.	4 May	1856
203	Hattox, James	Hunter, Sarah A.E.	6 Nov	1852
439	Hawes, Erasmus B.	Duff, Mary A.	19 Apr	1855
29	Hawkins, R.N.	Deason, Miss Caroline	12 Jan	1849
412	Haynes, Robert B.	Drake, Signora	17 Dec	1854
511	Hays, James M.	Hunter, Mary F.	1 Apr	1856
49	Head, Elijah B.	Brand, Miss Elizabeth	3 July	1849
505	Heard, William J.E.	Glass, Esther	18 Feb	1856
461	Hellums, L.J.	Douglass, Matilda Mary	9 Sept	1855
1	Helms, Wilson	Price, Martha Jane	7 Sept	1849
320	Henry, James F.	Tally, Lucy Ann	12 Sept	1853
443	Hensley, Mark	Pitts, Mary	21 May	1855
137	Herron, James M.	McCord, May L.A.	11 Dec	1850
420	Herron, Joseph M.	Hardon, Mary (B)	28 Dec	1854
164	Herron, Wm	Morrison, Emeline	27 Oct	1849
29	Hester, Joseph	Dunn, Miss Mary Ann	11 Jan	1849
234	Hickman, Robert	Akins, Susan	28 Feb	1852
298	Hickman, Robert H.	Aikins, Lucy Ann	3 Mar	1853
9	Hiler, John	Hiler, Miss Eliza Jane	10 Sept	1848
437	Hill, Allen	Bailey, Hepsiba	4 Apr	1855
181	Hill, Burton	Williams, Mary E.	8 July	1851
83	Hill, Crawford	Henry, Martha O.	21 Feb	1850
502	Hill, George W.	Sledge, Elizabeth	7 Feb	1856
474	Hill, Henry	Hattox, Martha A.	14 Oct	1855
35	Hill, James A.	McAlister, Miss Claricy C.	16 June	1848
196	Hill, Thomas	Randle (Randol), Amanda	30 Sept	1851
358	Hill, Thomas J.	Lyon, Martha F.	22 Jan	1854
435	Hitt, Peter C.	Williamson, Elizabeth F.	22 Mar	1855
56	Hodges, Jacob M.	Rutherford, Mary Ann	18 Nov	1849
462	Holcomb, John	Moore, Sarah Ann	9 Sept	1855
270	Holditch, S.F.	Smith, F.C.	7 Dec	1852
166	Holditch, W.B.	Long, Martha June	19 May	1851
320	Holly, James B.	Billingsly, Mary Ann	15 Sept	1853

PAGE	GROOM	BRIDE	DATE	
32	Holmes, James L.	Hosford, Miss Frances E.		16 Sept 1848
461	Holmes, William G.	Hurley, Eliza J.		4 Sept 1855
363	Holt, Thomas	Easterwood, Sarah E.		12 Feb 1854
251	Hooper, James	Henry, Sarah M.		10 Aug 1852
64	Hooper, Robert B.	Ruder, Eliza J.		17 Jan 1850
184	Hopkins, A.S.	Hiler, Nancy E.		24 July 1851
230	Horton, D.A.	Gammell, Mary Ann		5 Feb 1852
340	Horton, S.N.	Moore, Mary J.		12 Dec 1853
42	Houlditch, John F.	Mays, Miss Caroline E.		4 Nov 1849
431	Howell, John H.	Revell, Lucy E.		9 Mar 1855
164	Howerton, James M.	Roberts, Emily F.		3 Jan 1850
132	Hoyl, Solomon	Payne, Eliza		9 Jan 1851
200	Hubbard, Anderson	Kennedy, Louisa		16 Oct 1851
197	Hubbard, Wiley	Griffin, Amanda		7 Oct 1851
216	Huckabee, Abraham	Haddox, Elenor		1 Jan 1852
	[Abraham Huckaby and Nelly Haddox also appear on bond]			
243	Huckbee, Benjamin	Warren, Mary		2 Nov 1852
409	Huckabee, Thomas	Evans, Mary		30 Nov 1854
89	Hudaburg, L.C.	Haynes, Miss G.M.		7 May 1850
334	Hudeburg, Thomas	Wilks, Amanda		9 Nov 1853
300	Hudson, John	Mauldin, Mary J.		10 Apr 1853
144	Huff, John	Morgan, Mary	(B)	20 Sept 1847
340	Huffstickler, Lawson	McReynolds, Drucilla		27 Nov 1852
262	Hughes, C.M.	Graddy, Catharine		7 Nov 1852
123	Hulsey, Jacob	Taylor, Martha		19 July 1851
482	Humphreys, David W.	Johnston, Sarah E.	(B)	18 Nov 1855
101	Humphries, George	Vaulter, Elizabeth R.		18 Sept 1850
294	Hunt, A.J.	Hattox, Mary	(B)	7 Mar 1853
352	Hunter, John J.	Mosley, Margaret		5 Jan 1854
48	Hunter, Wm A.	Camp, Miss Hyburnia		4 Sept 1848
148	Ivey, Cyrus	White, Ally		2 Feb 1851
402	Jackson, E.F.	Mallett, Sarah J.		17 Oct 1854
93	Jackson, James	Lisle, Elizabeth Ann		25 Mar 1850
328	Jackson, William	Davis, Elizabeth		19 Oct 1853
116	Jacobs, Clinton W.	Conn, Jane		2 Jan 1851
356	Jacob, Edward L.	Conn, Sarah A.		17 Jan 1854
104	Jones, Robert J.	Harris, Mary H.A.		12 Sept 1850
245	Jamison, Jesse R.	Lankford, Sarah C.		10 July 1852
255	Jarvis, Levi	Meador, Ally Ann		19 Sept 1852
465	Jeffcoat, James	Lee, Martha		20 Sept 1855
486	Jernagan, Wiley H.	Newell, Harriet J.		11 Dec 1855
51	Jimeson, Shederick	Fuqua, Sarah		16 Sept 1849
134	Jobe, Samuel B.	Vaughn, Amanda C.		29 Dec 1850
105	Johnson, Geo W.	Cunningham, Jane		7 Nov 1850
290	Johnson, George W.	White, Polly A.		9 Feb 1853

PAGE	GROOM	BRIDE	DATE		
333	Johnson, J.F.	Maddox, Leah		11 Dec	1853
62	Johnson, James	Ayres, Amelia E.		25 Oct	1849
117	Johnson, James H.	Hall, Sarah		19 Dec	1851
306	Johnson, William	Hale, Mary J.		4 May	1853
127	Johnson, Wm R.	Gambrell, Martha S.		4 Dec	1849
488	Johnston, Joseph	Langum, Verlinda		23 Dec	1855
6	Joiner, E.H.	Courson, Miss Mary M.		4 Apr	1849
417	Jolly, Alvis J.	Brookshire, Elendor J.		24 Dec	1854
273	Jones, Alexander	Kelly, Martha E.		16 Dec	1852
414	Jones, E.W.	Harris, M.E.		21 Dec	1854
512	Jones, F.A.	Hellums, Mary E.		14 May	1856
448	Jones, James	Dyson, Mary	(B)	18 June	1855
459	Jones, James R.	Miller, R. Raney		25 Aug	1855
121	Jones, Jefferson	Bailey, Martha E.		8 Jan	1851
18	Jones, John C.	Calhoun, Miss Elizabeth		14 Aug	1849
103	Jones, Wm C.	Hunt, Nancy		15 Sept	1850
104	Jones, Robert J.	Harris, Mary H.A.		12 Sept	1850
364	Jordain, M.C.	Pollard, Nancy		16 Feb	1854
206	Jordan, A.H.	Strowd, Mary C.		6 Nov	1851
8	Jordan, Jackson	Self, Miss Elizabeth		6 May	1849
291	Jordan, M.C.	Mann, Nancy D.		15 Feb	1853
394	Julian, Thos J.	Chambliss, Matilda B.D.		6 Sept	1854
135	Kavanaugh, Wm W.	Brewster, Nancy		1 Nov	1850
42	Kellum, Wm	Hopkins, Miss Elizabeth		26 Sept	1849
336	Kelly, Azariah	Bailey, Elizabeth J.	(B)	15 Nov	1853
379	Kelly, Azarah	Norwood, Elizabeth J.		10 May	1854
152	Kelly, J.W.	Russell, Elizabeth	(B)	22 Nov	1850
146	Kelly, John W.	Knowls, Mary	(B)	11 Jan	1850
275	Kendrick, Robert	Churchill, Tabitha		23 Dec	1852
118	Kennedy, Robert B.	Rawly, Jemima		4 Jan	1851
347	Kerr, J.H.	Collins, Elizabeth C.		20 Dec	1853
132	Kilpatrick, J.S.	Mallory, Martha F.		10 Dec	1850
218	Kimball, Wiley J.	Wood, Emaline		30 Dec	1851
498	Kimmons, John A.	Wiley, Ellen M.		22 Jan	1856
216	King, Julius A.	Saunders, T.		23 Dec	1851
300	King, C.H.	Rivers, Nancy Ann	(B)	6 Apr	1853
471	King, Green	Morrow, Mary		4 Oct	1855
440	Kennedy, James	Pruitt, Elizabeth A.		29 Apr	1855
279	Knight, Charner	Coker, Jane		30 Dec	1852
283	Knowles, F.W.	Edrington, Charity C.		26 Jan	1853
412	Knowles, Thomas	Wester, Missouri C.		27 Apr	1855
319	Lackey, J.E.	Plant, Sarah M.		7 Sept	1853
33	lackey, R.W.	Coker, Miss Elizabeth		1 Nov	1848
391	Lamar, Stephen E.	Bryant, Florina		27 July	1854
108	Lambert, John T.	Cole, Mary Ann		18 July	1850
32	Laney, R.W.	Wages, Miss Susan		27 Dec	1848
	[Wages, Myres and Marris listed for Miss Susan on bond, license and ministers return]				
236	Loftis, Richard T.	Hardy, Emily A.		14 Mar	1852

PAGE	GROOM	BRIDE		DATE	
481	Lankford, John	Huffstickler, Mary A.		14 Nov	1855
469	Larue, Jacob	Perry, Rhody F.		26 Sept	1855
50	Lauderdale, Benjamin M.	Griffin, Miss Sophia G.		9 Sept	1849
73	Lauderdale, James B.	Lamb, Martha Ann		17 Jan	1850
419	Layton, Thomas	Gill, Hannah C.		27 Dec	1854
33	Leathers, Tilmon	Maddox, Miss Nancy		26 Sept	1848
179	Ledbetter, Laban L.	Thomas, Mary S.	(B)	18 June	1851
167	Liggon, Edwin	Weatherall, Jane		13 May	1851
295	Lile, Marion W.	Coursey, Sarah Ann		15 Mar	1853
77	Lindsey, Newton	Downs, Malinda		12 Apr	1848
479	Lindsey, William R.	Wilson, Margaret M.		11 Nov	1855
407	Long, John H.	Desmakis, Victoria J.		17 Nov	1854
249	Long, Wm A.	Billingsly, Elizabeth E.		28 July	1852
115	Looney, Moses	McLendon, Mary Jane		20 Feb	1851
321	Love, Rufus C.	Blake, Rebecca A.		14 Sept	1853
208	Lower, Andrew J.	Province, Mary E.		19 Nov	1851
463	Lyon, Thomas C.	Lyon, V.F.		9 Sept	1855
327	McBride, Thos J.	Davis Lettie		11 Oct	1853
215	McBride, S.O.	Collins, Martha E.		18 Dec	1851
401	McCarty, John L.	Bailey, Anna J.		12 Oct	1854
328	McCord, Simeon M.	Rowland, Hannah S.		23 Oct	1853
262	McCoy, Abraham S.	Goggins, Rebecca		24 Oct	1852
128	McCoy, Nathaniel	Reader, Mary Ann		1 Aug	1850
100	McCraw, James W.	Holiday, Martha		11 Sept	1850
19	McCurley, John	Blackburne, Miss Martha		1 Sept	1848
460	McDodd, Thomas	Evetts, Sarah Ann		31 Aug	1855
154	McDonald, R.H.	Martindale, Mary		14 Jan	1850
94	McDowell, Wm M.	Scott, Mary		21 July	1850
502	McFall, John W.	Falkner, Martha		10 Feb	1856
379	McFarland, John	Hurley, Szllar (Syllar?)		11 May	1854
471	McGill, Calvin	Hadley, Nancy		9 Oct	1855
487	McGill, John	Stanford, Elizira	(B)	10 Dec	1855
387	McGill, Thos	Stanford, Abigail		2 July	1854
302	McGreger, James	Davis, Celia		13 Apr	1853
395	McGregor, V.J.	Wallis, Mary E.		5 Sept	1854
463	McGreger, Wm	Beard, Martha M.		12 Sept	1855
117	McLarty, Thomas P.	Simpson, Catherine J.		2 Jan	1851
298	McLelland, Isaac C.	Gray, Drucilla M.		6 Apr	1853
350	McMahan, E.L.	Whitten, E.C.C.		22 Dec	1853
231	McNeely, Jesse	Harper, Mary J.		17 Feb	1852
437	McNeely, William	Swafford, Nancy J.		5 Apr	1855
515	McNutt, John	Wilson, Eliza		29 Apr	1856
80	McWhirter, Wm S.	Courson, Sarah A.		15 Jan	1850
142	McWhorter, Geo W.	Huston, L.N.		14 Feb	1851
468	McWhorter, J.H.	Wells, Eliza P.		26 Sept	1855
334	McWhorter, Samuel	Duff, Nancy Belzora		11 Nov	1853

PAGE	GROOM	BRIDE		DATE	
452	Mahon, John C.	Freeman, Julyann F.		15 July	1855
475	Majors, Oliver P.	McKinney, Mary Jane		18 Oct	1855
364	Malan, Sampson	Conley, Christianna		13 Feb	1854
308	Mallett, J.G.W.	Gale, Eliza		19 May	1853
467	Mallett, J.M.	Merrett, Martha A.	(B)	20 Sept	1855
423	Malone, A.W.	Norwood, Mary		11 Jan	1855
47	Malone, C.H.	Shelton, Miss Helen		20 Sept	1849
450	Malone, G.W.	Free, Nancy C.		21 June	1855
271	Malone, George W.	Free, Susanna		8 Dec	1852
19	Malone, Thompson	Alexander, Miss Martha		13 Aug	1848
67	Manahan, Wm L.	Heard, Jane		31 Jan	1849
590	Mann, John C.	Mann, Elizabeth		11 Feb	1853
331	Manning, P.C.	Thomas, Louisa E.		1 Nov	1853
180	Mark, Johnathan	Walker, Cordelia		9 July	1851
426	Marshall, John H.	Benson, Ursula		31 Jan	1855
448	Martin, B.B.	Dison, Jane	(B)	19 June	1855
292	Martin, Reuben	Gladwell, Mary Ann	(B)	16 Feb	1853
288	Martin, Samuel	Johnston, Emeline		3 Feb	1853
418	Massey, Constantine	Frost, Mary J.		25 Dec	1854
225	Massey, Wm J.	Faught, Sarah Ann		25 Jan	1852
253	Masterson, Hance H.	Rucker, Susan		9 Sept	1852
161	Mathews, Robert E.	Gaily, Nancy G.		26 Mar	1849
3	Maulden, William	Pollock, Miss Jane C.		14 Aug	1848
133	Maxey, Robert B.	Oneil, Elizabeth Ann		19 Jan	1851
192	Mayberry, James M.	Hedeburg, Ann C.		8 Sept	1851
257	Mayfield, E.C.	Beckham, Eliza E.		12 Oct	1852
233	Mayfield, Wm	Morgan, Jane		26 Feb	1852
346	Maza, Solomon	Vernon, Cintha		22 Dec	1853
213	Mead, S.M.	Mobly, Mary F.		14 Dec	1851
187	Meadow, Alfred J. (I.?)	Scott, Sarah E.		11 Aug	1851
59	Measles, Starca	Strowd, Lucinda Dianna		6 Oct	1849
47	Medford, Zacariah	Ward, Miss Elizabeth		7 Oct	1849
18	Medlock, John	Gambrell, Miss Martha		6 May	1849
371	Meek, James L.	Long, Mary S.		23 Mar	1854
122	Melton, Elijah	Nabors, Susan C.		29 Feb	1851
126	Milam, Bartlet	Milam, Miss Elizabeth		21 Dec	1848
199	Milam, John L.	Pounds, Sarah		13 Oct	1851
485	Milam, John W.	Anders, Permelia		6 Dec	1855
231	Miller, John H., Jr.	Vasser, Caroline R.		5 Feb	1852
58	Miller, John M.	Miller, Nancy P.		21 Dec	1849
	[Nancy P. Miller on license. Nancy P. Walker on bond and minister's return]				
181	Miller, Robert A.	Feemster, Elizabeth		8 July	1851
77	Milton, Thompson	Bardin, Sarah E.		20 Dec	1849
17	Mitchell, Daniel E.	Potter, Miss Nancy E.		22 Mar	1849
276	Mitchell, David	Nichol, Jane C.		28 Dec	1852
498	Mitchell, John A.	Tuter, Martha		21 Jan	1856
79	Mitchell, Robert S.	Johnson, Martha		19 Mar	1850
179	Mitchell, Thomas A.	Doxey, Ann W.	(B)	20 June	1851

PAGE	GROOM	BRIDE		DATE	
35	Montgomery, Andrew W.	Hubbard, Elizabeth		1 Nov	1849
242	Montgomery, James E.	Alexander, Cynthia A.		27 May	1852
490	Montgomery, Samuel	Cox, Sarah A.		23 Dec	1855
416	Montgomery, William	Cruse, Julia C.		21 Dec	1854
434	Moody, Francis A.M.	Keys, Mary S.		13 Mar	1855
403	Moody, Thomas	Jarrett, Abigail		22 Oct	1854
404	Moore, L.D.	Robison, S.H.		2 Nov	1854
233	Moore, John T.	Morris, H.A.		25 Feb	1852
491	Moore, John W.	Camp, Elizabeth		26 Dec	1855
374	Moreland, A.	Hays, Eliser	(B)	1 Apr	1854
136	Morgan, Ebenezer F.	Jones, Martha E.		22 Dec	1850
509	Morgan, Edward	Armstrong, Nancy A.	(B)	10 Mar	1856
78	Morgan, Hardy	Pilcher, Elizabeth L.		7 Feb	1850
240	Morgan, Wm	Mayfield, Sarah J.		2 Apr	1852
163	Morris, James W.	Potts, Mary A.		12 Feb	1851
194	Morrison, John	Duke, Mary		23 Sept	1851
444	Morrison, R.H.	Hayes, Caroline		10 May	1855
41	Morrow, John B.	Miller, Sarah J. (I.?)		3 Sept	1849
258	Morrow, John C.	Eubank, Margarett, M.		20 Oct	1852
54	Morrow, Thomas T.	Eubanks, Julia E.		15 Sept	1849
427	Mounce, John W.	Smith, Mary E.		7 Feb	1855
411	Mounce, R.T.	Caldwell, Emily J.		19 Dec	1854
109	Munn, James	Hardwick, Cynthia		23 Sept	1850
249	Murphy, Wm	Hawthorn, Emily		29 July	1852
160	Murray, W.P.	White, M.E.		31 Aug	1850
153	Nabors, Bolton O.	Reid, Mary J.C.		9 Jan	1851
211	Nabors, John L.	Brown, Frances C.		11 Dec	1851
422	Nabors, John S.C.	Pitts, Rachael		10 Jan	1855
299	Neblett, George W.	Garland, Nancy Ann		7 Apr	1853
493	Neely, John L.	Chisholm, Martha Jane		1 Jan	1856
138	Neil, Jeremiah J.	Caldwell, Mary		18 Mar	1851
240	Neil, Samuel J.	Jennings, Mary J.		13 Apr	1852
354	Nelson, Samuel	Vaughan, Frances		10 Jan	1854
250	Nelson, Wm C.	Cotton, Delany A. [also Delina Cotton]		8 Aug	1852
381	Newby, William R.	Stone, Clairissa		14 May	1854
36	Newman, George	Snider, Miss Mary H.		23 Sept	1847
193	Nibblett, Samuel	Ferrell, Margaret J.		18 Sept	1851
177	Night, Henry	Curray, Catharine	(B)	15 Jan	1848
159	Nolen, Henry	Robbins, Rebecca		22 Feb	1851
296	Norris, James A.	Abernathy, Amanda E.		14 Mar	1853
36	Norwood, Wm J. (I.?)	Staples, Ruth M.		30 Aug	1849
60	Ocallahan, James P.	Wade, Elizabeth A.		29 Oct	1849
98	Onley, Marcus	Hambrick, Martha A.		17 June	1850
180	Orear, Franklin	Jamison, Elizabeth		21 June	1851

PAGE	GROOM	BRIDE		DATE	
20	Orne, Henry A.	Orne, Anna F.		25 Jan	1849
159	Orr, David	Summers, Nancy		13 Dec	1850
158	Orr, H.C.	Weatherall, Mary E.		27 Mar	1849
202	Orr, Jefferson	Payne, Martha		25 Oct	1851
268	Orr, V.B.	Mauldin, Mary J.		24 Nov	1852
171	Owen, D.G.	Calloway, C.C.		25 Mar	1851
485	Owen, John H.	Read, Mary		4 Dec	1855
274	Owen, William J.	Read, Huldah		21 Dec	1852
189	Owens, Gabriel	Nelson, Mary		18 Aug	1851
392	Owens, M.F.	Newby, Nancy F.		2 Aug	1854
106	Palmer, G.B.	Norvill, Mary F.		13 Nov	1850
345	Pannell, Israel S.	Mobley, Sarah Ann		20 Dec	1853
23	Pannell, J. (I.?) W.E.	Pannell, Miss Elizabeth		19 Apr	1849
22	Pannell, Jonathan	Jones, Miss Anne		13 Sept	1848
451	Pannell, Marion	Dye, Elizabeth		24 June	1855
101	Pannell, Minor W.	Coleman, E.R.		15 Sept	1850
95	Pannell, Philip	Pannell, Elizabeth		26 May	1850
20	Pannell, Wm J.	McCraw, Emaline		1 June	1849
126	Pannell, Zachariah	Morgan, Julia Ann		27 Nov	1850
464	Parchall, A.S.	Fletcher, Clara M.	(B)	18 Sept	1855
445	Parish, A.J.	Dickson, A.M.		31 May	1855
332	Parker, Thomas J.	Greene, Mary A.		4 Nov	1853
56	Paschell, Wm M.	McDonald, Sarah L.		20 Dec	1849
376	Pass, M.J.	Houston, S.E.T.		30 Apr	1854
426	Pate, Charles	Nix, Edy		16 Feb	1855
345	Patterson, Joel B.	Dillard, Martha E.		17 Dec	1853
93	Patterson, Nelson G.	Newell, Mary E.		22 Aug	1850
163	Patterson, R.P.	Payne, Sarah M.		20 Aug	1850
22	Patton, B.P.	Flanekin, Miss Nancy H.		18 Apr	1848
227	Patton, Franklin	McCord, Martha		29 Jan	1852
221	Patton, Hilliard J.	Boyd, Martha J.	(B)	9 Jan	1852
265	Payne, Alfred	Liles, Martha		8 Nov	1852
377	Payne, George W.	Gray, Mary J.		4 May	1854
382	Payne, John G.	Beene, Nancy		18 May	1854
158	Payne, Jonathan	Payne, Ladusky		12 Nov	1850
175	Payne, John G.	Payne, Maria	(B)	22 Jan	1846
73	Payne, Joseph	Bean, Sarah Ann		23 June	1849
383	Payne, R.H.	Porter, Martha D.		25 May	1854
46	Payne, Richmond	Gray, Miss Nancy		30 Sept	1849
236	Payne, Robert M.	Brown, Amanda		14 Mar	1852
303	Payne, Samuel	Cheek, Elizabeth		19 Apr	1853
45	Payne, Wm	Collin, Miss Mary		2 Aug	1849
215	Payton, C.L.	Hale, Louisa		18 Dec	1851
182	Pearsall, E.J.	Gilliam, Kesiah E.		16 July	1851
278	Pearson, Gideon O.	Rodgers, Nancy		29 Dec	1852
444	Pearson, Charles D.	Edwards, Ann		27 May	1855
121	Pearson, Emory S.	Morris, Ellin		21 Nov	1850

PAGE	GROOM	BRIDE	DATE	
261	Perkison, William H.	Brock, Mary E.	24 Oct	1852
172	Petty, Lewis	Swenney, Elizabeth	20 Mar	1851
380	Phillip, E.T.	Wade, L.J. (B)	10 May	1854
392	Phillips, Athel	Payne, Canzada	27 July	1854
360	Phillips, C.C.	Childers, Lucinda	7 Feb	1856
407	Phillips, David, M.	Payne, Margaret	10 Nov	1854
292	Phillips, Melmouth G.	McFarland, Sarah	22 Feb	1853
232	Philpot, Micajah	Harris, Sarah E.	24 Feb	1852
411	Pickens, James	Young, Nancey	12 Dec	1854
21	Pilcher, Franklin	Pilcher, Miss Adeline A.A.	4 Jan	1849
432	Pilcher, Stephen	Staggs, Rosanna	4 Mar	1855
460	Pilcher, William	Todd, Polly	30 Aug	1855
173	Pilcher, Wm	Bascom, Catharine	5 Apr	1851
433	Pitts, A.P.	Harget, Louisa	7 Mar	1855
221	Pitts, Cullin L.	Seals, Martha J.	15 Jan	1852
458	Pitts, Hillory	Level, Sarah F.	16 Aug	1855
422	Pitts, Judson	Waldrop, Mary A.	11 Jan	1855
325	Pitts, Noah L.	Rodgers, Matilda C.	3 Oct	1853
205	Pool, Francis M.	Pannell, Savilla	6 Nov	1851
123	Pool, George W.	Pippins, M.A.	7 Jan	1851
21	Pool, James	Jones, Miss Emaline	26 Oct	1848
260	Pool, James	Carter, Elizabeth	24 Oct	1852
54	Pool, Robert A.	Young, Elizabeth	22 Nov	1849
152	Porter, John O., Jr.	Bourland, Unity	19 Mar	1851
11	Potter, Daniel	Smith, Miss Mary R.	23 Nov	1848
487	Potter, J.F.	Andrew, Margarett E.	25 Dec	1855
442	Potts, William	Pogue, Lucinda M.	2 Aug	1855
139	Potts, Wm, Sr.	Morris, Isabella H.	18 Mar	1851
119	Pound, George H.G.	Neely, Eleanor	24 Dec	1851
287	Prather, Josiah	Norvell, Sarah E.	25 Jan	1853
189	Pratt, Anderson L.	Norris, Angeline	24 Aug	1851
446	Pratt, William	McRory, Mary J.	7 June	1855
362	Price, James L.	Williams, Mary A.	9 Feb	1854
351	Price, Joel A.	Sanders, Elizabeth	25 Dec	1853
359	Price, R.J.	Mitchell, S.B.	31 Jan	1854
23	Proctor, Harris J.	Ware, Miss J.P.	31 Aug	1848
246	Pruitt, Joseph	Blackwell, Sarah	15 July	1852
151	Pruitt, Joseph J.	Holditch, Emma E.	9 May	1851
506	Puckett, W.G.	Ivy, Mary J.	20 Feb	1856
315	Purvis, Cullin	Paschall, Jane A.	7 Aug	1853
146	Purvis, John P.	Baker, Caroline	14 Jan	1851
377	Putt, Jonathan	Nix, Mary J.	4 May	1854
61	Quinlan, Michael	Galaspie, Margaret	1 Jan	1850

PAGE	GROOM	BRIDE	DATE
39	Raby, Wm. H.	Smith, Susan E.	21 Oct 1849
271	Ragan, W.S.	Gary, Susan E.	9 Dec 1852
277	Ragland, Evan	Orr, Elizabeth	4 Jan 1853
330	Rains, H.G.	McFarland, Elizabeth M.	20 Oct 1853
318	Rains, P.B.	Billingsly, Sarah C.	31 Aug 1853
46	Rakerstraw, Joseph F.	Bridges, Miss Elizabeth C.M.	2 Sept 1849
442	Ramsey, Martin	Ceplinger, M.J.	14 May 1855
367	Rankin, Robert	Ecton, Eveline	2 Mar 1854
497	Rankin, Theophelus	Kirkwood, Rebecca H.	24 Jan 1856
491	Ratliff, S.C.	Knowles, Malinda	27 Dec 1855
514	Ray, Henry C.	Cannon, Unity B.	10 Apr 1856
59	Ray, Thomas J.	Payne, Jane	27 Dec 1849
475	Rea, John M.	Fuller, Malinda	26 Oct 1855
496	Real, Edward B.	Miller, Jane (B)	14 Jan 1856
140	Reasons, James S.	Freeman, Julia A.B.	3 Apr 1849
453	Reed, James	Shubert, Mary J.	3 Sept 1855
372	Reed, Robert S.	Goode, Sarah E.	23 Mar 1854
134	Reeder, Isaac	Abernathy, Emeline L.	7 Dec 1850
270	Reeder, Thomas	Goggins, Hannah	2 Dec 1852
107	Reeves, Edward Y.	Pitts, Lucinda J.	29 Oct 1850
359	Regan, Peter L.	Griffin, Manerva A. (B)	28 Jan 1854
139	Reid, Wm. C.	Jones, Melissa (B)	6 Nov 1840
7	Reidling, A.B.	Purdon, Miss Abegail	24 Oct 1848

[Reilding and Redding appears on bond]

PAGE	GROOM	BRIDE	DATE
173	Reynolds, M.L.	Hill, Hannah C.	13 Apr 1851
140	Rhodes, Andrew	Johnson, Mary C. (B)	17 July 1849
24	Rhyne, Henry W.	Johnson, Miss Sarah	29 Nov 1848
470	Richey, James M.	Price, Martha	4 Oct 1855
506	Richey, Jeptha	Kelly, Mary F.	28 Feb 1856
237	Richey, Samuel H.	Donaldson, Mary E.	18 Mar 1852
98	Riggins, John J.	Duncan, Mahala	15 Aug 1850

[Mahala Duncan on bond and ministers return. Martha Duncan on license]

PAGE	GROOM	BRIDE	DATE
25	Ritchey, Albert F.	Wood, Miss Martha J.	25 Jan 1849
112	Ritherford, Shelton L.	Billingsly, Parthena A.	10 Sept 1850
279	Robbins, Arren S.	Nelson, Margarett	4 Jan 1853
72	Robbins, Joseph A.	Young, Adaline	22 Sept 1847
24	Roberts, Spencer	Beasly, Miss Catherine	15 Nov 1848
306	Robertson, George C.	Purvine, Deborah	13 May 1853
257	Robertson, Samuel M.	Dale, Sarah Ann	6 Oct 1852
79	Robertson, Thomas W.	Foster, Martha	30 Jan 1850
374	Robinson, James D.	Johnston, Christianna	13 Apr 1854
477	Robison, William	Tomblen, Nancy E.	24 Oct 1855
214	Rodgers, Thomas A.	Garrett, Mary Ann	18 Dec 1851
416	Roe, John T.	Furguson, Nancy M.	29 Dec 1854
107	Rogers, Henry F.	Allen, Caroline	29 June 1850

PAGE	GROOM	BRIDE	DATE
25	Rogers, Isaac S.	Barton, Sarah R.	14 Sept 1848
31	Rogers, J.W.	Mitchell, Miss Mary Anne	21 July 1848
304	Rogers, John W.	Allen, Susan J.	27 Apr 1853
110	Rogers, Wm. S.	Alexander, Rachael O.F.	24 July 1850
436	Rootes, Edmund W.	Handly, Grizella A.	29 Mar 1855
417	Rowan, Samuel	Stone, Sophrona A.C.	24 Dec 1854
324	Roy, Samuel	King, Hulda (B)	22 Sept 1853
466	Rucker, James M.	Ward, Amanda A.	21 Sept 1855
168	Rush, W.H.	Singleton, S.F.	18 May 1851
81	Ruth, Jackson	Ellis, Martha	27 Feb 1850
438	Sadler, Martin	Stocker, Rachel	26 Apr 1855
238	Sample, Hugh M.	Westmoreland, Francis	1 Apr 1852
251	Sanders, B.F.	Redus, M.C.	12 Aug 1852
314	Sanders, E.D.	Henry, Eliza L.	26 July 1853
141	Sanders, Elijah Simpson	Whitten, Harriet Rebecca (B)	11 July 1848
375	Sanders, G.W.	Mitchell, Martha	23 Apr 1854
472	Sanders, H.K.	Foster, Agnes V.	10 Oct 1855
425	Sanders, John T.	Beard, Nancy	1 Feb 1854
410	Sartin, John	Booth, Eliza	3 Dec 1854
187	Scott, H.A.	Baker, Mary E.	3 Aug 1851
443	Scott, John	Wait, Virginia	17 May 1855
137	Scott, Robert B.	Hunt, Manerva A.	10 Dec 1850
455	Sewell, William	Bright, Martha M.	9 Aug 1855
40	Sexton, James E.	Raby, Miss Mary	28 Oct 1849
248	Shannon, James L.	Boswell, Mary Jane	22 July 1852
356	Shaw, Dushee	Camp, Elizabeth (B)	16 Jan 1854
226	Shelton, Doctor G.	Strait, Margaret S.	27 Jan 1852
284	Shelton, J.L.	Scott, S.A.	18 Jan 1853
30	Shelton, John	Collins, Miss Mary	4 Jan 1849
424	Shelton, Patrick	Johnson, Mary E.	21 Jan 1855
4	Shelton, Whiten	Pollock, Miss MInerva J.	14 Dec 1848
183	Sheppard, Thomas H.	White, Matilda C.	20 July 1851
376	Shepherd, William L.	Chanceller, Georgianna	25 Apr 1854
142	Sheppard, Wm.	Galy, Rebecca G. (B)	7 Feb 1850
97	Sherrod, Redman	Henry, Elizabeth J.	18 July 1850
194	Short, James H.	Caststull, Narcissa	22 Sept 1851
259	Shultz, William	O'Briant, Sarah	21 Oct 1852
	[Sarah O'Bryant on minister's return]		
30	Sigman, Richard	Griffin, Mary	11 May 1853
307	Sikes, William	Griffin, Mary	11 May 1853

PAGE	GROOM	BRIDE	DATE	
473	Simmons, Alexander	Combs, Sarah A.	9 Oct	1855
375	Simmons, G.W.	McKinney, Rebecca	25 Apr	1854
313	Simpson, Samuel E.	Procter, Jane	21 July	1853
234	Sims, Wm S.	Mayo, Sarah	29 Feb	1852
52	Sitton, Philip	Walker, Celia	17 May	1849
477	Skinner, John B.	Reid, Martha J.	30 Oct	1855
247	Skinner, Wm F.	Miers, Martha M.	22 July	1852
183	Sledge, E.W.	Stroube, Margaret E.	22 July	1851
	[Margaret E. Haney on minister's return]			
365	Sledge, T.F.	Elder, Paney	14 Feb	1854
343	Sloan, John N.	Coleman, Susan P.	15 Dec	1853
51	Sloan, Wm D.	Houlditch, Miss Margaret E.	9 Aug	1849
354	Smith, Y.J.	Stephens, M.C.	12 Jan	1854
494	Smith, G.T.	Todd, Charlotte	3 Jan	1856
386	Smith, Isaiah	Brock, Frances	29 June	1854
457	Smith, J.W.	Crum, Maturn A.	11 Aug	1855
339	Smith, John W.	Winbush, Sarah F.	8 Dec	1853
378	Smith, John W.	Bray, Martha J.	6 May	1854
400	Smith, James W.	Pitts, Margaret C.	10 Oct	1854
245	Smith, James	Smith, Mahala	18 July	1852
229	Smith, Jerome D.	Burnes, Mary E.	10 Feb	1852
65	Smith, Jesse T.	Smith, Ellen	25 Nov	1849
196	Smith, Thomas H.	Warren, Mary	28 Sept	1851
5	Smith, Thomas R.	Honnell, Margaritte J.	27 July	1848
284	Smith, William J.	Gambrell, Susan M.E.	13 Jan	1853
68	Smith, Wm H.	Weir, Priscilla C.	12 Feb	1850
85	Sneed, Benjamin C.	Pippins, Martha	24 Jan	1850
91	Sneed, Jasper L.	Pippin, Sarah E. (L.?)	21 May	1850
167	Snider, Cary	Fincher, Elizabeth	9 May	1851
393	Snipes, Mathew F.	Colvin, Susan A.J.	13 Aug	1854
166	Sossaman, David L.	Cruse, Mary A.E.	15 May	1851
503	Souter, Henry B.	Jones, Agnes	14 Feb	1856
266	Souter, William	Levell, Rebecca	19 Nov	1852
427	Souter, Wm L.	Golding, Jane	7 Feb	1855
37	Spencer, Samuel A.	Cox, Miss Lavina	11 Nov	1847
367	Spence, William	Smith, Nancy J.	23 Feb	1854
239	Staggs, Eli	Berry, Mary	4 Apr	1852
227	Staggs, Ezekiel	Chaney, Sarah G.	6 Apr	1852
247	Staggs, Exekiel	Smith, Rosanna	22 July	1852
190	Stanford, George B.	Cornell, Rebecca [Connell?]	26 Aug	1851
2	Stanford, John F.	Lauderdale, Mary J.	10 Sept	1849
269	Stanford, Joseph P.	Thomas, Sarah E.	9 Dec	1852
2	Stanford, William A.	Saunders, Miss Lidia C.	22 Feb	1849

PAGE	GROOM	BRIDE		DATE	
399	Stegall, James M.	Griffin, Mary		2 Oct	1854
204	Stegall, Thomas M.	Grizzard, Mary F.		30 Oct	1851
283	Stephen, E.M.	Reader, Mary Frances		13 Jan	1853
500	Stephens, R.M.	Smith, R.E.		3 Feb	1856
408	Stephens, Robert F.	Watley, Mary	(B)	23 Nov	1854
266	Stephenson, Andrew J.	Reid, Elizabeth		18 Nov	1852
38	Stewart, George	Bevill, Miss Priscilla		3 Nov	1849
141	Stockstill, Thomas	Beckham, Brazilla F.		23 Dec	1849
102	Stocton, Richard A.	Bugg, Sarah		20 Aug	1850
501	Stone, James P.	Walker, Emily		7 Feb	1856
350	Stone, W.G.	Mobley, L.E.		21 Dec	1853
4	Stone, Wm J.	Orr, Miss Emaline		31 Dec	1848
69	Stone, Wm J.	Davidson, Harriet		5 Nov	1845
505	Stovall, Columbus	Davis, Eveline	(B)	16 Feb	1856
397	Stovall, Peter V.	Camp, Nancy M.		27 Sept	1856
241	Strickland, Effington	Barrett, Arrena		9 May	1852
467	Stringfellow, J.C.	Wesson, Frances		25 Oct	1855
431	Suggs, A.J.	Payne, Mary M.		1 Mar	1855
511	Sullivan, Dennis	McNutt, Louisa C.		20 Mar	1856
142	Summers, John B.	Sanders, Martha	(B)	18 Feb	1850
3	Swaim, Charles	McKeown, Miss Ellen		11 Feb	1849
484	Swann, Alexander	Bradley, Lettia	(B)	28 Nov	1855
344	Swindoll, Wm C., Jr.	Harris, Cynthia		22 Dec	1853
222	Sword, Andrew J.	McCarver, Margaret D.		11 Jan	1852
178	Tackett, Lewis	Cook, Anna	(B)	10 Mar	1846
66	Tardy, Alexander B.	Mays, Sarah B.		8 Jan	1850
405	Tardy, Alexis J.	Allen, Eliza W.		8 Nov	1854
293	Tardy, Wm D.	Loving, Mary M.		3 Mar	1853
83	Tallant, James G.	Tallant, Eliza S.		2 July	1850
206	Tally, Gilford	Henry, Unich		9 Nov	1851
482	Tate, Thomas	Phillips, Catharine		18 Nov	1855
124	Taylor, Charles W.	Rowe, Sarah E.		6 Jan	1851
252	Taylor, John M.C.	Stewart, Susan		22 Aug	1852
120	Taylor, Thomas W.	Rivers, Jane F.		4 Feb	1851
63	Teddy (Terry?), James W.	Davis, Margaret E.		13 Jan	1850
195	Terry, Ezekiel	Clements, Martha Ann		9 Oct	1851
26	Terry, Jesse	Sledge, Miss Sarah		3 Aug	1848
261	Terry, John	Lyen, Matilda L.		10 Oct	1852
255	Thompson, William M.C.	Burk, Nancy		22 Sept	1852
288	Thompson, Wm B.	Garrison, Louisa A.		3 Feb	1853
435	Thorn, Nelvin	Shurbert, R.A.T.		20 Mar	1855
209	Thrasher, Joseph A.	Brock, Manerva		27 Nov	1851
26	Tindall, G.A.	Whitesides, Miss Elizabeth		10 Dec	1848
72	Tindall, Robert	Barksdale, Harriet C.		18 Dec	1845
237	Tombalin, Wm	Perry, Nancy D.		16 Mar	1852

PAGE	GROOM	BRIDE		DATE	
76	Tompkins, W.B.	Weldon, Modena		7 Sept	1848
286	Trulove, Francis	Pearsall, Susan A.	(B)	22 Jan	1853
64	Tucker, Calvin M.C.C.	Smith, Sarah J.		10 Jan	1850
171	Turner, Allen	Beard, Malvina		30 mar	1851
133	Turner, E.R.	Cruse, Susanna C.		26 Dec	1850
421	Turner, William D.	Porter, Amanda W.		2 Jan	1855
454	Twaddell, Archey	Box, Mary A.		24 July	1855
353	Tye, Cullen	Murphy, Mary		5 Jan	1854
331	Vaughan, James M.	Guess, Catharine		27 Oct	1853
508	Vaughan, M.D.	Benson, C.M.J.		4 Mar	1856
384	Vaughan, William C.	Smith, Sarah		4 June	1854
127	Vaughn, John	Milam, Mary A.		18 Feb	1851
151	Vaughn, Milus M.	Vaughn, Malvina	(B)	3 Oct	1848
113	Vaughn, Thompson W.	Harris, Narcissa		1 Oct	1850
325	Vernon, Richard	Scott, Sarah E.	(B)	5 Oct	1853
499	Vincent, W.M.	Wilson, Amanda		22 Jan	1856
226	Wade, Henderson	Shelton, Rebecca Jane		27 Jan	1852
390	Waite, James	McKnight, Louisa J.		13 July	1855
44	Waldo, John M.	McDaniel, Miss E.M.		20 Oct	1849
468	Walker, A.J.	Mitchell, Sarah Ann		26 Sept	1855
433	Walker, James T.	Moore, Elizabeth J.		8 Mar	1855
70	Walker, Japheth	Kidd, Susan		10 Dec	1845
480	Walker, Joseph H.	Billingsly, Nancy M.		14 Nov	1855
74	Walker, Josiah J.M.	Kennedy, Mary		2 July	1848
308	Walker, Samuel	Jones, Eliza		24 May	1853
222	Walker, Wm B.	Wiley, Mary H.		13 Jan	1852
479	Wallis, Jerrymiah	Bledsoe, Jane A.		4 Nov	1855
172	Wallis, S.M.	Robertson, Nancy C.		18 Apr	1851
297	Wallis, Thomas D.	Raby, Sarah F.		17 Mar	1853
45	Walton, Zacariah	Green, Miss Francis		11 Oct	1849
366	Walsworth, Francis	Anderson, C.J.		19 Feb	1854
361	Ward, Kenney	Rucker, Martha		9 Feb	1854
440	Wardlaw, David H.	Smith, Malissa		17 Apr	1855
322	Ware, William Z.	Crocker, Margarett S.	(B)	20 Sept	1853
204	Warren, Arthur	Barkley, Elizabeth		2 Nov	1851
145	Warren, Zachariah	Martin, Rosanna		9 Jan	1851
399	Warrington, John S.	Nalley, Martha		3 Oct	1854
504	Waters, John W.	Doxey, Pariley C.		3 Apr	1856
182	Watson, James	Alsup, Elizabeth	(B)	10 July	1851
456	Watts, Malachi	Bright, Drucilla A.		14 Aug	1855
27	Wear, Archibald W.	Scales, Miss Rosemond S.		1 may	1849
220	Weatherall, George H.	Threldkell, Virginia		8 Jan	1852
507	Weatherall, John H.	Barry, Margarett A.	(B)	26 Feb	1856
214	Weatherall, Joseph E.	Mallory, Ann H.J.		17 Dec	1852
254	Weatherall, LaFayette	Neely, Margaret J.		14 Sept	1852
397	Weatherall, Saml W.	Ware, M.A.H.		14 Sept	1854

PAGE	GROOM	BRIDE		DATE	
280	Weatherington, John A.J.	Ward, Martha Ann		13 Jan	1853
307	Wells, Harrison H.	Casteel, Louisa		14 May	1853
314	Wells, Robert J.	Buse, Mary C.		4 Aug	1853
202	Wells, Robert S	Head, Elizabeth		26 Oct	1850
497	Wessen, T.F.	Coker, Milley E.	(B)	14 Jan	1856
414	West, William	Swindoll, Eliza M.		27 Nov	1855
235	Wester, Jonathan	McClary, Ellen	(B)	6 Mar	1852
380	Westmoreland, E.P.	Beard, Mary J.		16 may	1854
250	Westmoreland, F.W.	Marrs, Frances A.		5 Aug	1852
91	Whatley, Seborn S.	Maddox, Manerva		16 May	1850
494	Wheatley, Jesse B.	Vaughan, Jennetta		3 Jan	1856
207	White, A.W.	Bigger, Jane E.		20 Nov	1851
348	White D.C.	Pearson, Cynthia E.V.		25 Dec	1853
209	White, David	Wells, Sarah		25 Nov	1851
224	White, G.W.	Steed, Eliza		22 Jan	1852
267	White, I.N.	Lankford, E.M.		25 Nov	1852
276	White, Samuel H.	Cain, Martha Ann	(B)	28 Dec	1852
176	White, Stephen C.	Higginbottoms, Mary	(B)	12 Feb	1845
28	White, William M.	Gilmer, Miss Sarah A.		17 Nov	1848
176	Whitehead, Ezekiel	Blackburn, Eliza	(B)	26 Aug	1844
220	Whitehurst, Eli	Hensley, Emaline		6 Jan	1852
267	Whiteside, Samuel A.H.	Simpson, Elizabeth J.		18 Nov	1852
474	Whitesides, William H.	Simpson, Margaret C.		11 Oct	1855
96	Whitten, James M.	Cook, Sarah Ann		14 June	1850
49	Whitten, John J. (I.?)	Price, Miss Rebecca Jane		5 Sept	1849
130	Wilder, LeRoy F.	Brock, Elviny (?)		28 Jan	1851
198	Wilder, N.A.W.	Jones, Elizabeth S.		9 Oct	1851
466	Wilder, Spencer B.	Whitesides, Martha G.		20 Sept	1855
165	Wilder, W.F.	Russett, Mary Ann		22 Nov	1850
57	Wilder, Wm P.	Whitesides, Clemantine		13 Dec	1849
495	Wiley, Francis M.	Hattox, Nancy		8 Jan	1856
177	Wilhoit, Mathew	Gammel, Caroline	(B)	12 Jan	1848
94	Wilie, Isaac E.	Wray, Dianna		1 Apr	1850
343	Wilkins, G.W.	Holditch, L.F.		5 Jan	1854
68	Wilkins, John L.	Myers, Mary H.		26 Sept	1847
395	Wilkins, Samuel	Harris, Charlotte		2 Sept	1854
210	Williams, Arthur	Cotton, Susanna		4 Dec	1851
312	Williams, C.B.	Miers, Matilda		17 July	1853
63	Williams, Charles H.	McDaniel, Mary E.		20 Dec	1849
352	Williams, Elijah	Nelson, Lucinda J.		1 Jan	1854
450	Williams, Isaac	Herron, Jane C.		21 June	1855
456	Williams, Lewis	Tiner, Mary		8 Aug	1855
413	Williams, W.G.	Haynes, Margaret C.		18 Dec	1854
53	Williamson, James H.	Cullins, Martha S.		24 May	1849
85	Williamson, Thomas C.	Wiley, Miss M.F.		4 Apr	1850
75	Wilson, Dudley	Wilson, Martha Ann		20 Jan	1850
330	Wilson, Elezer	Myers, Mary Ann		30 Oct	1853
365	Wilson, James W.	Horen, Elizabeth N.		16 Feb	1854

PAGE	GROOM	BRIDE	DATE	
212	Wilson, Jefferson	Pinson, Theodocia O.	9 Dec	1851
293	Wilson, Leonard	Parks, M.S.J.	8 Mar	1853
484	Wilson, Robert	Richardson, Elizabeth F.	2 Dec	1855
106	Wilson, W.H.	McCarty, Hannah B.	18 Nov	1850
454	Wilson, W.L.	Raley, Martha A.	29 July	1855
341	Wilson, William	Huckeby, Charlotte	1 Dec	1853
329	Wilson, William F.	White, Julia A. (B)	18 Oct	1853
501	Windem, William E.	Stack, Elizabeth	7 Feb	1856
201	Wisdom, Joseph	McRary, Rachael (B)	20 Oct	1851
476	Wisinger, Wiley B.	Herron, Mary A.	18 Oct	1855
393	Witcher, William	Forbes, Margaret A.	15 Aug	1854
465	Wolf, Robert H.	Pollard, Sarah	19 Sept	1855
432	Wood, David	Dorsey, Amanda	15 Mar	1855
238	Wood, James F.	McCarter, Nancy	25 Mar	1852
122	Wood, John	Ivey, Mary J.	26 Nov	1850
241	Wood, Moses	Abernathy, Mary J.	13 May	1852
61	Wood, Stanhope	Cooper, Frances	3 Jan	1850
192	Wood, Washington M.D.S.	Wood, Sarah M.	25 Sept	1851
6	Wood, William R.	Criswell, Miss Francis H.	25 Jan	1849
268	Wray, John	Dysen, Carolin M.	1 Dec	1852
457	Wray, John	Brown, Martha J.	14 Aug	1855
87	Wray, Wm	Harris, Elizabeth	17 Jan	1850
116	Wray, Wm	Jordan, Elizabeth	25 Dec	1851
369	Wright, James	Rabey, Elizabeth	12 Mar	1854
322	Wright, John C.	Griffin, Nancy E.E.	25 Sept	1853
1	Wright, Wiley J.	Jordan, Martha Ann	18 Jan	1849
156	Young, Kenny	Cypert, Sarah A.E.	6 Feb	1851
254	Zinn, William S.	Goode, Sophia	9 Sept	1852

BRIDE INDEX
GROOM SURNAME IN BRACKETS

Abernathy, Amanda E. (Norris)
Abernathy, Eliza E. (Brown)
Abernathy, Emeline L. (Reeder)
Abernathy, Mary J. (Wood)
Aikins, Lucy Ann (Hickman)
Akins, Susan (Hickman)
Alexander, Cynthia A. (Montgomery)
Alexander, Miss Martha (Malone)
Alexander, Rachael O.F. (Rogers)
Allbritton, Amanda S. (Franklin)
Allen, Caroline (Rogers)
Allen, Eliza W. (Tardy)
Allen, Sarah P. (Goffin)
Allen, Susan J. (Rogers)
Alsup, Dorthula (Barbee)
Alsup, Elizabeth (Watson)
Anders, Permelia (Milam)
Anderson, C.J. (Walsworth)
Andrews, Margaret E. (Potter)
Armstrong, Nancy A. (Morgan)
Arnold, Malissa Elvira (Blocker)
Aycock, Susan E. (Hancock)
Ayres, Amelia E. (Johnson)

Babb, Stacy Ann (Babb)
Bailey, Anna J. (McCarty)
Bailey, Elizabeth J. (Kelly)
Bailey, Hepsiba (Hill)
Bailey, Martha E. (Jones)
Baker, Caroline (Purvis)
Baker, Mary E. (Scott)
Ball, Jemima F. (Berry)
Barbee, Miss Elizabeth (Craft)
Barden, Jane (Coker)
Bardin, Sarah E. (Milton)
Barker, Rebecca J. (Belyew)
Barkely, Elizabeth (Warren)
Barksdale, Harriet C. (Tindall)
Barrett, Arrena (Strickland)
Barrett, Elizabeth (Betts)
Barry, Margaret A. (Weatherall)
Barton, Sarah R. (Rogers)
Bascom, Catharine (Pilcher)
Baxter, Elizabeth J. (Cobb)
Bean, Sarah Ann (Payne)
Beal, S.A.A. (Goen)
Beard, Malvina (Turner)
Beard, Martha M. (McGreger)
Beard, Mary J. (Westmoreland)
Beard, Nancy (Sanders)

Beasley, Miss Catherine (Roberts)
Beckham, Brazilla F. (Stockstill)
Beckham, Eliza E. (Mayfield)
Beckham, Rebecca E. (Aycock)
Beene, Nancy (Payne)
Bell, Martha Ann (Finley)
Bell, Mary J. (Aston)
Benson, C.M.J. (Vaughan)
Benson, Ursula (Marshall)
Berry, Mary (Staggs)
Betts, A.A. (Gullett)
Bevill, Nancy (Couch)
Bevill, Priscilla (Stewart)
Bigger, Jane E. (White)
Billingsly, Amanda (Gregory)
Billingsly, Elizabeth E. (Long)
Billingsly, Mary Ann (Holly)
Billingsly, Nancy M. (Walker)
Billingsly, Parthena (Ritherford)
Billingsly, Sarah C. (Rains)
Black, Mary E. (Baity)
Blackburn, Eliza (Whitehead)
Blackburne, Martha (McCurley)
Blackwell, Sarah (Pruitt)
Blake, Rebecca A. (Love)
Bledsoe, Jane A. (Wallis)
Boatman, Sharlotte (Hamaker)
Booth, Eliza (Sartain)
Boothe, Susan Ann (Eaves)
Boswell, Mary Jane (Shannon)
Bourland, Unity (Porter)
Box, Mary A. (Twaddell)
Boyd, Martha J. (Patton)
Bradley, Lettia (Swann)
Bramlett, Jane K. (Freeman)
Brand, Elizabeth (Head)
Bray, Martha J. (Smith)
Brewster, Nancy (Kavanaugh)
Briant, Ann (Galaspie)
Bridges, Elizabeth (Bridges)
Bridges, Elizabeth Ann (Alexander)
Bridges, Elizabeth C.M. (Rakerstraw)
Bridges, Lifalet (Davis)
Bright, Drucilla A. (Watts)
Bright, Martha M. (Sewell)
Brock, Elviny (?) (Wilder)
Brock, Frances (Smith)
Brock, Manerva (Thrasher)
Brock, Mary E. (Perkison)
Brookshire, Elendor J. (Jolly)

Brown, Amanda (Payne)
Brown, Amanda C. (Carruth)
Brown, Francis C. (Nabors)
Brown, Harriet E. (Evetts)
Brown, Lucy (Garner)
Brown, Martha J. (Wray)
Brown, Rosaline (Hagler)
Brown, Sarah (Cox)
Bryant, Florina (Lamar)
Bugg, Sarah (Stocton)
Burk, Martha C. (Boothe)
Burk, Nancy (Thompson)
Burnell, Emily A. (Davis)
Burnes, Mary E. (Smith)
Buse, Mary C. (Wells)

Cain, Martha Ann (White)
Caldwell, Emily J. (Mounce)
Caldwell, Mary (Neil)
Calhoun, Elizabeth (Jones)
Calloway, C.C. (Owen)
Camp, Elizabeth (Shaw)
Camp, Elizabeth (Moore)
Camp, Hyburnia (Hunter)
Camp, Nancy M. (Stovall)
Campbell, Mary Ann (Boothe)
Campbell, Nancy (Cobb)
Cannon, Unity B. (Ray)
Caraker, Martha (Coe)
Card, Francis (Gassaway)
Carlisle, Eliza M. (Caldwell)
Carr, Mary A. (Bell)
Carter, Elizabeth (Pool)
Carter, Lucinda F. (Bowen)
Carter, Nancy A.E. (Corey)
Casey, Delpha (Brown)
Casteel, Louisa (Wells)
Caststull, Narcissa (Short)
Ceplinger, M.J. (Ramsey)
Chamberlin, Mary (Brown)
Chambliss, Matilda B.D. (Julian)
Chanceller, Georgianna (Shepherd)
Chancellor, Margarett W. (Bell)
Chaney, Sarah G. (Staggs)
Childers, Lucinda (Phillips)
Chisholm, Martha Jane (Neely)
Churchill, Tabitha (Kendrick)
Churchwell, Susanah (Hale)
Cheek, Elizabeth (Payne)
Clardy, Jane B. (Baily)
Clements, Martha Ann (Terry)
Coker, Elizabeth (Lackey)
Coker, Jane (Knight)
Coker, Milley E. (Wesson)

Cole, Cynthia (Hulsey)
Cole, Martha (Bramlette)
Cole, Martha C. (Bost)
Cole, Mary Ann (Lambert)
Cole, Nancy E. (Duncan)
Cole, Priscilla (Barber)
Coleman, E.R. (Pannell)
Coleman, Susan P. (Sloan)
Collin, Mary (Payne)
Collins, Elizabeth C. (Kerr)
Collins, Martha E. (McBride)
Collins, Mary (Shelton)
Collins, Nancy (Collins)
Colvin, Susan A.J. (Snipes)
Combs, Sarah A. (Simmons)
Conley, Christianna (Malan)
Conn, Jane (Jacobs)
Conn, Sarah A. (Jacobs)
Connelly, Martha Ann (Aycock)
Cook, Anna (Tackett)
Cook, Sarah Ann (Whitten)
Cooper, Frances (Wood)
Cornelius, Mary (Harris)
Cornell, Mary (Burton)
Cornell (Connell?), Rebecca (Stanford)
Cosby, Martha (Harder)
Cotton, Delany A. (Nelson)
Cotton, Susanna (Williams)
Coursey, Sarah Ann (Lile)
Courson, Sarah A. (McWhirter)
Courson, Mary M. (Joiner)
Cox, Lavina (Spencer)
Cox, Salina (Grizzard)
Cox, Sarah A. (Montgomery)
Crane, Louisa (Baker)
Crippen, Mary (Cox)
Criswell, Francis H. (Wood)
Crocker, Margarett S. (Ware)
Cromeans, Sarah (Bailey)
Crum, Maturn A. (Smith)
Cruse, Julia C. (Montgomery)
Cruse, Mary A.E. (Sossman)
Cruse, Susanna C. (Turner)
Cullins, Martha S. (Williamson)
Cunningham, Jane (Johnson)
Curray, Catharine (Night)
Cypert, Sarah A.E. (Young)

Dale, Sarah Ann (Robertson)
Dansby, E.C. (Allman)
Dansby, Jane C. (Bond)
Davidson, Harriet (Stone)
Davis, Celia (McGreger)
Davis, Cynthia E. (Adams)

Davis, E.W. (Handley)
Davis, Elizabeth (Jackson)
Davis, Eveline (Stovall)
Davis, Lettie (McBride)
Davis, Margaret E. (Teddy or Terry?)
Davis, Mary E. (Barmon)
Deason, Caroline (Hawkins)
Deel, Mary J.E. (Fulton)
Desmakis, Victoria J. (Long)
Dickson, A.M. (Parish)
Dillard, Letha (Harden)
Dillard, Martha E. (Patterson)
Dison, Jane (Martin)
Donaldson, Lucinda (Grissel)
Donaldson, Mary E. (Richey)
Donavan, Mary (Brady)
Dorsey, Amanda (Wood)
Dorsey, Martha C. (Harris)
Douglass, Mary Matilda (Hellums)
Downing, Martha (Burten)
Downs, Malinda (Lindsey)
Doxey, Ann W. (Mitchell)
Doxey, Pariley C. (Waters)
Drake, S.R. (Carr)
Drake, Signor (Haynes)
Duff, Mary A. (Hawes)
Duff, Nancy Belzora (McWhorter)
Duke, Jane (Franklin)
Duke, Mary A. (Deason)
Duke, Mary (Morrison)
Duke, Sarah A. (Hancock)
Duncan, Georgia Ann (Hampton)
Duncan, Mahala (Riggins)
Dunn, Mary Ann (Hester)
Dye, Elizabeth (Pannell)
Dyer, Nancy (Campbell)
Dysen, Carolin M. (Wray)
Dyson, Mary (Jones)

Easterwood, Sarah E. (Holt)
Ecton, Eveline (Rankin)
Edrington, Charity C. (Knowles)
Edwards, Ann (Pearson)
Edwards, Mahala (Flarity)
Elder, Paney (Sledge)
Ellis, Martha (Ruth)
Eubanks, Margarett M. (Morrow)
Eubanks, Julia E. (Morrow)
Evans, Mary (Huckabee)
Evans, Mary Ann (Bridges)
Evetts, Sarah Ann (McDodd)

Falkner, Martha (McFall)
Faught, Sarah Ann (Massey)
Fears, Elizabeth F. (Burton)

Feemster, Elizabeth (Miller)
Ferrell, Margaret J. (Nibblett)
Fincher, Elizabeth (Snider)
Fisher, Elizabeth (Bolding)
Flanekin, Nancy H. (Patton)
Fletcher, Clara M. (Parchall)
Forbes, Margaret A. (Witcher)
Forbes, Mary M. (Brandon)
Forbes, Sarah Ann (Brandon)
Fortune, Harriet (Braden)
Foster, Agnes V. (Sanders)
Foster, Martha (Robertson)
Franklin, Mary F. (Campbell)
Frazier, Frances J. (Coker)
Frazier, Margaret C. (Bridges)
Frazier, Martha J. (Bennett)
Free, Mournin C. (Carter)
Free, Nancy C. (Malone)
Free, Susanna (Malone)
Freeman, Julia A.B. (Reasons)
Freeman, Julyann (Mahon)
Freeman, Salina (Furguson)
Frost, Mary J. (Massey)
Fuller, Malinda (Rea)
Fuqua, Sarah (Jimeson)
Furguson, Nancy M. (Roe)

Gaily, Nancy G. (Mathews)
Galaspie, Margaret (Quinlan)
Galaspie, Sarah L. (Grissell)
Gale, Eliza (Mallett)
Galy, Rebecca (Sheppard)
Gamble, Jane (Arnold)
Gambrell, Martha (Medlock)
Gambrell, Martha S. (Johnson)
Gambrell, Sarah (Allbritton)
Gambrell, Susan M.E. (Smith)
Gammel, CAroline (Wilhoit)
Gammell, Mary Ann (Horton)
Garland, Nancy Ann (Neblett)
Garrett, Mary Ann (Rodgers)
Garrison, Louisa A. (Thompson)
Gary, Susan E. (Ragan)
Gholson, Matilda (Graddy)
Gill, Hannah C. (Layton)
Gill, Susan J. (Filgo)
Gilliam, Kesiah E. (Pearsall)
Gilliam, Martha A. (Furgeson)
Gilmer, Sarah A. (White)
Gilmore, Edy (Bailey)
Gladwell, Mary Ann (Martin)
Glass, Esther (Heard)
Glidwell, Martha (Burlasen)
Gocher, Margaret (Griffith)
Godfrey, Ann L. (Davis)

Goggins, Hannah (Reeder)
Goggins, Nancy (Caldwell)
Goggins, Rebecca (McCoy)
Golding, Jane (Souter)
Golding, Louisa (Alexander)
Good, Araminta (Calloway)
Goode, Sarah E. (Reed)
Goode, Sophia A. (Zinn)
Graddy, Catharine (Hughes)
Gragg, Elizabeth (Burns?)
Gray, Drucilla M. (McLelland)
Gray, Mary J. (Payne)
Gray, Nancy (Payne)
Green, Francis (Walton)
Greene, Mary A. (Parker)
Gregory, Martha C. (Davis)
Griffin, Amanda (Hubbard)
Griffin, Manerva A. (Regan)
Griffin, Martha H. (Griffin)
Griffin, Mary (Sikes)
Griffin, Mary (Stegall)
Griffin, Nancy E.E. (Wright)
Griffin, Sophia G. (Lauderdale)
Grizzard, Mary F. (Stegall)
Guess, Catharine (Vaughan)
Guess, Dosia (Gaines)
Guess, Elizabeth (Crumpton)
Guthery, Sarah A. (Greene)
Gwin, Elizabeth J. (Elder)

Haddon, Elizabeth (Freeman)
Haddox, Nelly (Huckaby)
Hadley, Nancy (McGill)
Hale, Louisa (Payton)
Hale, Mary J. (Johnson)
Hall, Sarah (Johnson)
Hambrick, Martha A. (Onley)
Hamelton, Eveline E. (Ellis)
Hamilton, Elizabeth (Bennett)
Hamlin, Nancy L. (Harkey)
Hammer, Sarah W. (Fortner)
Hampton, Elizabeth Ann (Harrison)
Handly, Grizelle A. (Rootes)
Hardwick, Cynthia (Munn)
Hardy, Emily A. (Loftis)
Hardy, Mary E. (Davis)
Haren, Adaline (Collins)
Harget, Louisa (Pitts)
Harper, Mary J. (McNeely)
Harris, Charlotte (Wilkins)
Harris, Cynthia (Swindoll)
Harris, Elizabeth (Wray)
Harris, M.E. (Jones)
Harris, Mary H.A. (Jones)

Harris, Narcissa (Vaughn)
Harris, Sarah E. (Philpot)
Harden, Samantha (Browning)
Hattox, Martha A. (Hill)
Hattox, Mary (Hunt)
Hattox, Nancy (Wiley)
Hawkins, Catharine (Deason)
Hawthorn, Emily (Murphy)
Haws(?), Pheby H. (Gibbs)
Hayes, Caroline (Morrison)
Haynes, G.M. (Hudaburg)
Haynes, Margaret C. (Williams)
Hays, Eliser (Hudaburg)
Head, Elizabeth (Wells)
Headly, Catharin (Gideon)
Heard, Jane (Manahan)
Hearston, Nancy E. (Betts)
Hellums, Mary E. (Jones)
Helms, Elizabeth Jane (Guttry)
  [One ministers return the name
   is Elizabeth Jane Williams]

Henry, Elizabeth J. (Sherrod)
Henry, Eliza L. (Sanders)
Henry, Martha O. (Hill)
Henry, Sarah M. (Hooper)
Henry, Unich (Tally)
Hensley, Emaline (Whitehurst)
Herdon, Mary (Herron)
Herring, Mary M. (Gamble)
Herron, Jane C. (Williams)
Herron, Mary A. (Wisinger)
Herron, Rhoda M. (George)
Hickman, Lucy (Allen)
Higginbottoms, Mary (White)
Hiler, Eliza Jane (Hiler)
Hiler, Nancy E. (Hopkins)
Hill, Hannah C. (Reynolds)
Hill, Sarah W. (Ball)
Hodges, Mary E. (Barr)
Holditch, Emma E. (Pruitt)
Holditch, L.F. (Wilkins)
Holiday, Martha (McCraw)
Honnell, Margaritte J. (Smith)
Hopkins, Elizabeth (Kellum)
Holly, Mary J. (Gentry)
Horen, Elizabeth N. (Wilson)
Hosford, Frances E. (Holmes)
Houlditch, Margaret E. (Sloan)
Houston, Mary E. (Duff)
Houston, S.E.T. (Pass)
Howard, Mary (Burks)
Howard, N.J. (Black)
Howard, nancy H. (Austin)
Hubbard, Elizabeth (Montgomery)

Huckeby, Charlotte (Wilson)
Hudeburg, Ann G. (Mayberry)
Hudson, Louisa F. (Hampton)
Hudson, Mary F. (Glenn)
Huffstickler, Mary A. (Lankford)
Hughes, Nancy (Fuller)
Hunt, Manerva A. (Scott)
Hunt, Nancy (Jones)
Hunter, Mary F. (Hays)
Hunter, Sarah A.E. (Hattox)
Hurley, Eliza J. (Holmes)
Hurley, Martha C. (Frazier)
Hurley, Szllar(Syllar?), A. (McFarland)
Huston, L.N. (McWhorter)

Irby, Sophia M. (Garrett)
Ivey, Mary J. (Wood)
Ivy, Mary J. (Puckett)

Jackson, Elizabeth (Baker)
Jamison, Clarisa (Dyson)
Jamison, Elizabeth (Orear)
Jarrett, Abigail (Moody)
Jenkins, Sarah J. (Fuqua)
Jennings, Mary J. (Neil)
Johnson, Della (Bevill)
Johnson, Elizabeth J. (Grisham)
Johnson, M.J. (Banks)
Johnson, Margaret J. (Farmer)
Johnson, Martha (Mitchell)
Johnson, Martha (Carter)
Johnson, Mary Ann (Fuqua)
Johnson, Mary C. (Rhodes)
Johnson, Mary E. (Shelton)
Johnson, Minney (Burch)
Johnson, Sarah (Rhyne)
Johnston, Christianna (Robinson)
Johnston, Emeline (Martin)
Johnston, Mariah C. (Butler)
Johnston, Sarah E. (Humphreys)
Jones, Agnes (Souter)
Jones, Anne (Pannell)
Jones, Eliza (Walker)
Jones, Elizabeth (Clary)
Jones, Elizabeth S. (Wilder)
Jones, Emaline (Pool)
Jones, Louisa Carolina (Epperson)
Jones, Margarett R. (Campbell)
Jones, Martha (Bolt)
Jones, Martha (Morgan)
Jones, Mary (Brock)
Jones, Melissa (Reid)
Jordan, Martha Ann (Wright)
Jourdan, Sarah (Cariker)
Justice, Eliza W. (Byrd)

Keel, Etha L.M. (Burke)
Kelly, Martha E. (Jones)
Kelly, Mary F. (Coon)
Kelly, Mary F. (Richey)
Kennady, Mary (Walker)
Kennedy, Louisa (Hubbard)
Keys, Martha Ann L. (Harris)
Keys, Mary S. (Moody)
Kidd, Nancy (Cox)
Kidd, Susan (Walker)
King, Hulda (Roy)
Kirkwood, Rebecca H. (Rankin)
Knight, Elizabeth (Cooper)
Knowles, Malinda (Ratliff)
Knowls, Mary (Kelly)
Knox, Newanna (Byers)
Kough, Sarah Ann (Cooper)

Lamb, Martha Ann (Lauderdale)
Langley, Laura Ann (Brewer)
Langum, Verlinda (Johnston)
Lankford, E.M. (White)
Lankford, Sarah C. (Jamison)
Lansdale, Parthena P. (Fincher)
Lauderdale, Mary J. (Stanford)
Lee, Martha (Jeffcoat)
Level, Sarah F. (Pitts)
Levell, Rebecca (Souter)
Leverett, Amanda C. (Baily)
Lisle, Elizabeth Ann (Jackson)
Liles, Martha (Payne)
Lockard, M.L. (Betts)
Long, Charity (Black)
Long, Julia (Donavan)
Long, Martha June (Holditch)
Long, Mary S. (Meek)
Long, Sarah E. (Abernathy)
Loving, Mary M. (Tardy)
Lyen, Matilda L. (Terry)
Lyon, Martha F. (Hill)
Lyon, V.F. (Lyon)

McAlister, Claricy C. (Hill)
McCarley, Rebecca (Sigman)
McCarter, Nancy (Wood)
McCarty, Hannah B. (Wilson)
McCarver, Margaret D. (Sword)
McClary, Ellen (Wester)
McClelland, Sarah (Gray)
McClintock, Rachael P. (Griffith)
McCord, Martha (Patton)
McCord, May L.A. (Herron)
McCraw, Emaline (Pannell)
McCraw, Lucretia (Bridges)
McCraw, Susanna C. (Daves)

McDaniel, E.M. (Waldo)
McDaniel, Mary E. (Williams)
McDonald, Sarah L. (Paschall)
McFall, Elizabeth D. (hancock)
McFarland, Elizabeth M. (Rains)
McFarland, Sarah (Phillips)
McGregor, E.J. (Cruse)
McKeown, Ellen (Swaim)
McKinney, Mary Jane (Major)
McKinney, Mildred T. (Ashby)
McKinney, Rebecca (Simmons)
McKnight, Louisa J. (Waite)
McKinyon, Isabella (Goodrich)
McLendon, Mary Jane (Looney)
McNutt, Louisa C. (Sullivan)
McPherson, Martha A. (Gill)
McRary, Rachael (Wisdom)
McReynolds, Drucilla (Huffstickler)
McRory, Mary J. (Pratt)
McWilliams, Mary (Baker)

Mabry, Frances E. (Franklin)
Maddox, Elizabeth (Hardy)
Maddox, Leah (Johnson)
Maddox, Manerva (Whatley)
Maddox, Nancy (Leathers)
Magee, A.E. (Byers)
Mahan, Nancy B. (Green)
Mahon, Mary M. (Bigham)
Mallett, Sarah J. (Jackson)
Mallory, Ann H.J. (Weatherall)
Mallory, Martha F. (Kilpatrick)
Malone, Julia (Allen)
Malone, Susan C. (Fortune)
Mann, Elizabeth (Mann)
Mann, Nancy O. (Jordan)
Markley, Eliza J. (Grisham)
Marrs, Frances A. (Westmoreland)
Martin, Rosanna (Warren)
Martin, Vina M. (Cole)
Martindale, Mary (McDonald)
Massey, Julia Ann (Davis)
Maston, Mary (Duncan)
Mauldin, Jane (Allen)
Mauldin, Mary J. (Orr)
Mauldin, Mary J. (Hudson)
May, Dianna (Harris)
May, Zelphia (Cooper)
Mayfield, Sarah J. (Morgan)
Mayo, Sarah (Sims)
Mays, Caroline E. (Houlditch)
Mays, Sarah B. (Tardy)
Meador, Ally Ann (Jarvis)
Meador, Jane (Bardin)

Merrett, Martha A. (Mallett)
Miears, Matilda (Williams)
Miers, Martha M. (Skinner)
Milam, Elizabeth (Milam)
Milam, Jane (Cannon)
Milam, Mary A. (Vaughn)
Miller, Cytha A.E. (Christman)
Miller, Elizabeth C. (Davis)
Miller, Jane (Real)
Miller, Nancy P. (Miller)
Miller, R. Raney (Jones)
Miller, Sarah I. (Morrow)
Mitchell, Dorothy H. (Golding)
Mitchell, Lucy C. (Baker)
Mitchell, Martha (Sanders)
Mitchell, Mary Anne (Rogers)
Mitchell, S.B. (Price)
Mitchell, Sarah Ann (Walker)
Mobley, L.E. (Stone)
Mobley, Sarah Ann (Pannell)
Mobly, Mary F. (Mead)
** Maffett, Margaret L. (Brown)
Monk, Jane (Evans)
Montgomery, Jane (Cox)
Moore, Eliza (Grady)
Moore, Elizabeth (Walker)
Moore, Martha Ann (Bass)
Moore, Mary J. (Horton)
Moore, Sarah Ann (Holcomb)
Moore, Susanna (Gates)
Morgan, Carmilla R. (Byrd)
Morgan, Jane (Mayfield)
Morgan, Julia Ann (Pannell)
Morgan, Mary (Huff)
Morgan, Nancy (Furgison)
Morgan, Sarah (Brassfield)
Morgan, Sounda (Gray)
Morris, Angeline (Pratt)
Morris, Ellin (Pearson)
Morris, Epsey (Edens)
Morris, H.A. (Moore)
Morris, Isabella H. (Potts)
Morris, Susan (Guthrie)
Morrison, Emeline (Herron)
Morrow, Mary (King)
Moseley, Julia F. (Ferrell)
Mosley, Margaret (Hunter)
Mounts, Sarah R. (Caldwell)
Muffett, Rosannah B. (Garrett)
Murphy, Mary (Tye)
Murphy, Winny (Bryant)
Myers, Mary Ann (Wilson)
Myers, Mary H. (Wilkins)
Myres, Brittania (Grisham)

**Out of Order

Nabors, Susan C. (Melton)
Nally, Martha (Warrington)
Neely, Eleanor (Pound)
Neely, Margaret J. (Weatherall)
Nelson, Lucinda J. (Williams)
Nelson, Margarett (Robbins)
Nelson, Mary (Owens)
Nelson, Nancy Bell (Butler)
Newby, Nancy F. (Owens)
Newell, Harriet J. (Jernagan)
Newell, Mary E. (Patterson)
Nichol, Jane C. (Mitchell)
Nix, Artha E. (Bandy)
Nix, Edy (Pate)
Nix, Mary J. (Putt)
Norris, Sarah A. (Adams)
Norvell, Sarah E. (Prather)
Norvill, Mary F. (Palmer)
Norwood, Elizabeth J. (Kelly)
Norwood, Mary (Malone)
Norwood, Sarah R.E. (Hattox)
Nowlan, Caroline (Elder)
Nowland, Jane (Dillard)

O'Briant, Sarah (Shultz)
Oliver, Mrs. C.E. (Brookshire)
Oneil, Elizabeth Ann (Maxey)
Orne, Anne F. (Orne)
Orr, Clarinda (Cornel)
Orr, Elizabeth (Ragland)
Orr, Emaline (Stone)
Orr, Harriet E. (Anderson)
Orr, Mary Jane (Gathright)
Owen, Narcissa (Glenn)

Paine, Birchett (Gent)
Pannell, Elizabeth (Pannell)
Pannell, Elizabeth (Pannell
Pannell, Malinda (Fullerton)
Pannell, Rosanna (Bell)
Pannell, Savilla (Pool)
Parks, M.S.J. (Wilson)
Parton, Malinda (Cook)
Paschall, Jane A. (Purvis)
Payne, Canzada (Phillips)
Payne, Eliza (Hoyl)
Payne, Jane (Ray)
Payne, Ladusky (Payne)
Payne, Margaret (Gray)
Payne, Margaret (Phillips)
Payne, Maria (Payne)
Payne, Martha (Orr)
Payne, Mary E. (Dickson)
Payne, Mary M. (Suggs)

Payne, Nancy E. (Cox)
Payne, Sarah M. (Patterson)
Pearsall, Susan A. (Trulove)
Pearson, Cynthia E.V. (White)
Perry, Nancy D. (Tombalin)
Perry, Rhody F. (Larue)
Perry, Rosalie (Allbaugh)
Petty, Rebecca (Hale)
Phillips, Catharine (Tate)
Phillips, Charlotte (Barden)
Phillips, Elander Ann (Collins)
Phillips, Sarah A. (Hammer)
Pilcher, Adeline A.A. (Pilcher)
Pilcher, Elizabeth L. (Morgan)
Pinson, Theodocia O. (Wilson)
Pippin, Sarah E. (Sneed)
Pippin, Selina (Hardwick)
Pippins, M.A. (Pool)
Pippins, Martha (Sneed)
Pitts, Lucinda J. (Reeves)
Pitts, Margaret C. (Smith)
Pitts, Rachael (Nabors)
Plant, Sarah M. (Lackey)
Pogue, Lucinda M. (Potts)
Pollard, Nancy (Jordain)
Pollard, Sarah (Wolf)
Pollock, Irena (Burns)
Pollock, Jane C. (Maulden)
Pollock, Minerva J. (Shelton)
Porter, Amanda W. (Turner)
Porter, Emaline (Abernathy)
Porter, Martha D. (Payne)
Potter, Nancy E. (Mitchell)
Potter, E.A. (Coleman)
Potts, Mary A. (Morris)
Pounds, Sarah (Milam)
Price, Caroline S. (Crim)
Price, Elizabeth C. (Gallaway)
Price, Martha (Richey)
Price, Martha Jane (Helms)
Price, Rebecca Jane (Whitton)
Pruitt, Elizabeth A. (Kennedy)
Pruitt, Margaret (Armstrong)
Pruitt, Rhoda (Bond)
Procter, Jane (Simpson)
Procter, Josephine (Beaver)
Province, Mary E. (Lower)
Prude, Martha B. (Givhan)
Purdon, Abegail (Reidling)
Purvine, Deborah (Robertson)

Rabey, Elizabeth (Wright)
Raby, Judy Ann (Dozier)
Raby, Mary (Sexton)

Raby, Sarah F. (Wallis)
Ragsdale, Martha P. (Gandy)
Raley, Martha A. (Wilson)
Ramage, Cynthia E. (Cunningham)
Ramsey, Martha J. (Durham)
Randle, Amanda (Hill)
Rawley, Jemima (Kennedy)
Read, Hulda (Owen)
Read, Mary (Owen)
Reader, Mary Ann (McCoy)
Reader, Mary Frances (Stephen)
Real, Margaret (Austin)
Redus, M.C. (Sanders)
Reed, Cynthia (Caldwell)
Reed, Nancy (Dickson)
Reed, Nancy (Crague)
Reid, Elizabeth E. (Stephenson)
Reid, Martha J. (Skinner)
Reid, Mary J.C. (Nabors)
Reid, Nancy G. (Bridges)
Reid, Susan C. (Fuller)
Rebell, Lucy E. (Howell)
Richardson, Elizabeth F. (Wilson)
Ritchey, Clemantine C. (Findley)
Rivers, Jane F. (Taylor)
Rivers, Nancy Ann (King)
Robbins, Rebecca (Nolen)
Robbins, Rhoda Catharine (Brummit)
Roberts, Emily F. (Howerton)
Robertson, Emeline (Christian)
Robertson, Nancy C. (Wallis)
Robison, S.H. (Moore)
Rodgers, Matilda C. (Pitts)
Rodgers, Nancy (Pearson)
Rogers, Elsamena (Buchanan)
Rogers, Elizabeth (Bolt)
Rogers, Frances C. (Brown)
Ross, Nancy (Brogden)
Rowe, Elender A. (Benson)
Rowland, Hannah S. (McCord)
Rowland, Narcissa E. (Collins)
Rowland, Sarah F. (Cunningham)
Rucker, Martha (Ward)
Rucker, Susan (Masterson)
Ruder, Eliza J. (Hooper)
Russell, Dorcus (Hamner)
Russell, Elender (Hamner)
Russell, Elizabeth (Foster)
Russell, Elizabeth (Kelly)
Russett, Mary Ann (Wilder)
Rutherford, Mary Ann (Hodges)

Sadler, Jane F.A. (Ball
Sadler, Mary (Glazener)

Salmon, Zembly (Crosby)
Sanders, A.C. (Hannell)
Sanders, C.C. (Cunningham)
Sanders, Elizabeth (Price)
Sanders, Martha (Summers)
Sauceman, Cynthia (Goldman)
Saunders, Elizabeth B. (Crockett)
Saunders, T. (King)
Saunders, Lidia C. (Stanford)
Scales, Rosemond S. (Wear)
Scott, Ellen (Grisham)
Scott, Mary (McDowell)
Scott, Permelia (Frazier)
Scott, S.A. (Shelton)
Scott, Sarah E. (Meadow)
Scott, Sarah E. (Vernon)
Seals, Martha J. (Pitts)
Sears, Margaret I. (Busby)
Self, Elizabeth (Jordan)
Seymore, Rhoda C. (Bugg)
Shaw, Jennette J. (Gill)
Shears, Lena (Archy)
Shelton, Adaline (Hall)
Shelton, Elmira (Frazier)
Shelton, Helen (Malone)
Shelton, Irena C. (Baker)
Shelton, Naoma M. (Blackburn)
Shelton, Rebecca Jane (Wade)
Shepherd, Isabella (Bailey)
Shepherd, Mary P. (Bevill)
Sheppard, Ann V. (Greene)
Shubert, Mary J. (Reed)
Shurbert, R.A.T. (Thorn)
Shuttles, Nancy (Allen)
Shuttleworth, Mary (Buchanan)
Simpson, Catherine J. (McLarty)
Simpson, Elizabeth (Whiteside)
Simpson, Margaret C. (Whiteside)
Singleton, Nancy E. (Alsup)
Singleton, S.F. (Rush)
Sledge, Elizabeth (Hill)
Sledge, Sarah (Terry)
Smith, Ellen (Smith)
Smith, Elmira G. (Hagler)
Smith, F.E. (Holditch)
Smith, Clarinda S. (Foster)
Smith, Frances (Autrey)
Smith, L.J. (Griffin)
Smith, Louisa (Brown)
Smith, Mahala (Smith)
Smith, Malissa (Wardlaw)
Smith, Mary E. (Mounce)
Smith, Mary R. (Potter)
Smith, Nancy J. (Spence)

Smith, R.E. (Stephens)
Smith, Rosanna (Staggs)
Smith, Sarah (Vaughan)
Smith, Sarah J. (Tucker)
Smith, Susan E. (Raby)
Smith, Susan J. (Harden)
Snider, Barbary T. (Bennett)
Snider, Mary H. (Newman)
South, Sarah (Alexander)
Speck, Nancy C. (Hall)
Spence, Martha Jane (Duke)
Stack, Elizabeth (Windem)
Staggs, Elizabeth (Cary)
Staggs, Rosanna (Pilcher)
Stanford, Abigail (McGill)
Stanford, Elzira (McGill)
Staples, Ruth M. (Norwood)
Staten, Lucinda (Bagwell)
Steed, Eliza (White)
Stegall, Elizabeth A. (Abernathy)
Stephens, Elvira S. (Bouland)
Stephens, M.C. (Smith)
Stephens, Penelope J. (Berry)
Stephenson, Jane C. (Caldwell)
Stewart, Susan (Taylor)
Stocker, Rachel (Sadler)
Stokes, Elizabeth J. (Bell)
Stone, Amelia (Cornelious)
Stone, Clairissa (Newby)
Stone, Elizabeth (Dickson)
Stone, Sophrona A.C. (Rowan)
Strait, Margaret S. (Shelton)
Strong, Nancy M. (Calloway)
Stroube, Margaret (Sledge)
Strowd, Lucinda Dianna (Measles)
Strowd, Mary C. (Jordan)
Strowd, Rosanna (Dodson)
Summers, Nancy (Orr)
Sullivan, Mary (Guinn)
Swafford, Nancy J. (McNeely)
Swafford, Sarah A. (Barkley)
Sweeten, Jane E. (Bolen)
Swenney, Elizabeth (Petty)
Swindoll, Eliza M. (West)
Swindoll, Jane (Gray)

Tallant, Eliza S. (Tallant)
Tally, Lucy Ann (Henry)
Taylor, Elizabeth (Coker)
Taylor, Lucretia (Gafford)
Taylor, Martha (Hulsey)
Thomas, Mary S. (Ledbetter)
Thomas, Louisa E. (Manning)
Thomas, Sarah E. (Stanford)

Thompson, Sarah E. (Carpenter)
Threldkell, Virginia (Weatherall)
Tiner, Mary (Williams)
Tippah, Almeda (Berry)
Todd, Charlotte (Smith)
Todd, Polly (Pilcher)
Tomblen, Nancy E. (Robison)
Trewett, Matilda C. (Adams)
Truit, Mary J. (Gillian)
Tucker, Mary A. (Blackburn)
Turner, Eliza (Bramblett)
Turner, Malinda (Cox)
Tuter, Martha (Mitchell)
Tyer, Susan E. (Gafford)

Ussory, Margaret J. (Baugh)

Vance, Elizabeth H. (Falkner)
Vasser, Caroline R. (Miller)
Vaughan, Ann E. (Benson)
Vaughan, Caroline (Foster)
Vaughan, Elizabeth (Fulton)
Vaughan, Frances (Nelson)
Vaughan, Jennetta (Wheatley)
Vaughn, Amanda C. (Jobe)
Vaughn, Malvina (Vaughn)
Vaulter, Elizabeth R. (Humphries)
Vernon, Cintha (Maze)
Vincent, Matilda (Cotten)
Vincent, Rebecca (Davis)
Vineyard, Mary Ann (Calvin)
Vinyard, Margarett M. (Coley)
Vinyard, Nancy (Coley)

Wade, Elizabeth A. (Ocallahan)
Wade, L.J. (Phillip)
Wages, Susan (Laney)
Wait, Virginia (Scott)
Waite, Elizabeth (Bass)
Waldrop, Mary A. (Pitts)
Waldrop, Nancy A. (Bradley)
Waldrop, Rebecca E. (Donaldson)
Walker, Celia (Sitton)
Walker, Cordelia (Mark)
Walker, Elizabeth (Griffin)
Walker, Emily (Brown)
Walker, Emily (Stone)
Walker, Nancy P. (Miller)
Wallis, Mary E. (McGregor)
Walton, Mary Ann (Green)
Walpool, Arvagine (Harrison)
Ward, Amanda A. (Rucker)
Ward, Elizabeth (Medford)
Ward, Martha A. (Beckham)

Ward, Martha Ann (Weatherington)
Ward, Sarah E. (Cobb)
Ward, Susannah J. (Dandridge)
Wardlaw, Nancy V. (Alexander)
Ware, I. (J.?) P. (Proctor)
Ware, M.A.H. (Weatherall)
Ware, Martha M. (Beavers)
Warren, Christian (Berry)
Warren, Martha (Bassham)
Warren, Mary (Smith)
Warren, Mary (Huckabee)
Watley, Mary (Stephens)
Weatherall, Emma (Grisham)
Weatherall, Jane (Liggon)
Weatherall, Mary E. (Orr)
Weir, Priscilla C. (Smith)
Weldon, Modena (Tompkins)
Wells, Eliza P. (McWhorter)
Wells, Martha (Coleman)
Wells, Sarah (White)
Wells, Sarah I. (Duff)
Wesson, Frances (Stringfellow)
West, Mary (Cornelius)
West, Emily (Bice)
Wester, Missouri C. (Knowles)
Westmoreland, Frncis (Sample)
White, Ally (Ivey)
White, Julia A. (Wilson)
White, M.E. (Murray)
White, Mary (Bridges)
White, Matilda C. (Sheppard)
White, Polly A. (Johnson)
White, Rebecca (Boatman)
Whitehurst, Amanda M. (Chapman)
Whitesides, Clementine (Wilder)
Whitesides, Elizabeth (Tindall)
Whitesides, Martha G. (Wilder)
Whitten, Harriet Rebecca (Sanders)
Whitten, E.C.C. (McMahan)
Wiley, Ellen M. (Kimmons)
Wiley, M.F. (Williamson)
Wiley, Margaret A. (Frazier)
Wiley, Martha J. (Duncan)
Wiley, Mary H. (Walker)
Wilkison, Jane T. (Caldwell)
Wilks, Amanda (Hudeburgh)
Willard, Jane (Babb)
Williams, Mary A. (Price)
Williams, Mary Ann (Draper)
Williams, Mary E. (Hill)
Williams, Sarah (Burk)
Williamson, Elizabeth F. (Hitt)
Williamson, Mary E. (Hathcock)

Wilson, Adaline E. (Barton)
Wilson, Amanda (Vincent)
Wilson, Eliza (McNutt)
Wilson, Margaret M. (Lindsey)
Wilson, Martha (Abernathy)
Wilson, Martha Ann (Wilson)
Wilson, Mary Jane (Edrington)
Winbush, Sarah F. (Smith)
Winston, Nancy (Black)
Wood, Emaline (Kimball)
Wood, Martha A. (Bowen)
Wood, Martha J. (Ritchey)
Wood, Mary F. (Collins)
Wood, Sarah M. (Wood)
Woodward, Martha (Hambrick)
Worsham, Mary A. (Harwood)
Worthington, Sophia (Gideon)
Wray, Dianna (Wilie)
Wray, Sarah (Dyson)
Wright, Permina (Gilder)

Young, Adaline (Robbins)
Young, Elizabeth (Pool)
Young, Martha K. (Brewer)
Young, Nancey (PIckens)
Young, Susan (Dye)

PONTOTOC COUNTY, MISSISSIPPI

MARRIAGE BOOK 1856 - 1867

(INCLUDES MAY - DECEMBER 1856)

INDEXED BY: HAZLE BOSS NEET
            207 N. MAIN
            PONTOTOC, MISSISSIPPI 38863

PAGE	GROOM	BRIDE	DATE	
333	Abbot, James L.	Sadler, Mary E.	16 Oct	1860
281	Abernathy, Miles	Abernathy, Mary	3 Jan	1860
778	Adair, G.W.	Hardy, Lucinda	9 Jan	1867
183	Adams, Jasper	Harvey, Louise	9 Nov	1856
731	Adams, John	Lewellen, Josephine M.	16 Oct	1866
328	Aglin, David	Guin, Margaret	16 Sept	1860
327	Aldman, John S.	Edington, Harriet A.	7 Sept	1860
398	Alexander, F.G.	Cobb, N.A.	16 July	1861
684	Alexander, S.B.	Adams, L.D.	27 Feb	1866
359	Alexander, James A.	Sherman, Sarah E.	29 Dec	1860
126	Alexander, T.C.	Montgomery, Precilla	18 Feb	1858
447	Allbritten, J.A.	Cochran, Emily E.	23 Oct	1862
280	Allen, C.J.	Fortune, C.V.	1 Jan	1860
578	Allen, George W.	McPherson, Martha	10 May	1865
690	Allen, Joel	Godfrey, A.S.	1 Apr	1866
239	Allen, John A.	Gray, Mary J.	22 Aug	1859
139	Allen, J.C.	Allen, Susan P.	14 Apr	1858
394	Anderson, Charles W.	Dozier, Mary R.	12 June	1861
111	Anderson, J.P.	Hooker, Margaret J.	7 Jan	1858
9	Anderson, Robert	Johnson, Sarah E.	6 July	1856
605	Andrews, M.W.	Cobb, Martha J.	19 Sept	1865
62	Armstrong, J.B.	Porter, Sarah	25 Feb	1857
227	Armstrong, J.D.	Morgan, Mary A.	10 June	1859
423	Armstrong, J.W.	Wade, N.A.	21 Jan	1862
771	Armstead, J.W.	Wells, Annie	29 Dec	1866
279	Arnett, W.W.	McNeil, Mary A.	27 Dec	1859
509	Astin, Robert A.	Hull, M.J.	24 Mar	1864
85	Astin, Samuel	Crow, Elizabeth	8 Sept	1857
402	Atkins, Thomas R.	Elzy, Caroline	22 Aug	1861
562	Atkinson, T.C.	Nicholson, Texas	11 Feb	1865
252	Ausborn, R.T.	Savins, Elizabeth	11 Oct	1859
229	Aycock, A.B.	Trulove, Catharin	28 May	1859
586	Babb, Thos J.	Overby, Mrs. Caroline F.	17 Aug	1865
65	Bacon, Woddy A.	Harper, Harriet T.A.	9 Apr	1857
71	Bailey, Franklin	Bevill, Thorzay	31 May	1857
224	Bailey, G.W.	Coleman, M.A.	12 May	1859
667	Bailey, J.M.	Bailey, S.C.	19 Jan	1866
371	Bailey, J.W.	Neal, Nancy	24 Jan	1861
290	Bailey, Robt M.	Redus, Isabella M.	1 Feb	1860
46	Bailey, W.J.	Bailey, Malissa	1 Jan	1857
580	Bailey, William	Coleman, Emma	6 June	1865
790	Bailey, Austin (free man)	Weatherall, Emily (free)	9 Dec	1865
700	Baily, John F.	Baker, Mollie E.	6 July	1866
179	Baker, Enoch S.	Dillard, Missouri	28 Oct	1858
652	Baker, E.	Griffin, Mrs. Catherine	17 Dec	1865
554	Baker, Nathaniel	Simmon, Samantha	26 Jan	1865
787	Ball, Charles (free man)	Cannon, Susan (free)	28 Dec	1865
752	Ball, G.W.	Weatherall, Mary M.	8 Dec	1866
509	Ball, Lewis	Sudduth, Ann E.	21 Apr	1864

PAGE	GROOM	BRIDE	DATE	
780	Ball, Mitchel	Stephen, Hamet	9 Feb	1866
435	Bangle, John	Buchanan, Mary Leanna	26 Apr	1862
19	Banyan, Thomas F.	Hardy, Mary	10 Sept	1856
403	Barkley, Robert A.	Hooker, Mary	22 Aug	1861
143	Barnett, C.E.	Flanagan, Martha	13 May	1858
387	Barringer, Paul	Herron, Kate C.	10 Apr	1861
688	Barton, J.F.	Harris, Mrs. E.R.	21 Mar	1866
590	Baxter, G.L.	Sory, Precilla E.	26 July	1865
156	Bealer, A.H.	More, C.N.J.	27 July	1858
738	Beard, Green E.	Farmer, An Eliza	5 Nov	1866
206	Beard, John	Robertson, Harriett	3 Feb	1859
591	Beard, W.A.	Jackson, Mrs. Jane	6 Aug	1865
524	Beard, W.C.	Stock, Ellendar	31 Aug	1864
273	Beasley, Andrew	Pannell, Mary Ann E.	9 Dec	1859
459	Beasley, John J.	Snipes, Jane	10 Feb	1863
553	Beasly, James L.	Darling, Moriah Frances	26 Jan	1865
570	Beauchamp, L.J.	Ramsey, Levina R.	14 Mar	1865
87	Beauchamp, Palestine	Wells, Sarah E.	17 Sept	1857
151	Beckham, B.F.	Morris, Elizabeth	4 July	1858
464	Beckham, John C.	Ward, Susan	23 May	1863
788	Beckly, Jacob (free man)	Floy, Samantha (free)	27 Dec	1865
518	Beek, J.P.	Morris, L.N.	2 July	1864
676	Beeks, D.A.	Wade, P.R.D.	6 Feb	1866
292	Beeks, Terrell	Hill, A.J.	8 Feb	1860
368	Been, J.M.	Been, P.E.	17 Jan	1861
324	Beene, Joseph C.	Smith, Hilvah	15 Aug	1860
243	Beene, R.O.	Phillips, Mary M.	22 Sept	1859
326	Bell, John W.	Henry, Martha J.	24 Aug	1860
568	Bell, Marcus M.	Parrish, Nancy	7 Mar	1865
350	Bell, William	Cumly, Mary E.	12 Dec	1860
376	Benjamin, Henry	Carwile, Mary Ann	6 Feb	1861
217	Benson, N. Jasper	Benson, Frances M.	22 Mar	1859
13	Berry, James F.	Hall, Loney Ann	23 July	1856
358	Berry, J.C.	Bradley, Malinda C.	23 Dec	1860
461	Berry, Stephen W.	Bailey, Lou E.	26 Mar	1863
369	Bevill, A.D.	Davis, Darcus	20 Jan	1861
455	Bigham, F.M.	Baker, Sinia Catharine	14 Jan	1863
106	Bigham, leondas L.	Wallis, Annie	23 Dec	1857
318	Billingsley, D.A.	Shirley, L.A.	22 July	1860
328	Billingsley, W.P.	Beene, Mary J.	2 Sept	1960
161	Billingsley, J.B.	Shurley, Mary Ann	19 Aug	1858
25	Billingsly, John C.	Hughs, Mary Jane	30 Nov	1856
270	Birge, James W.	Gambrell, Emily	4 Dec	1859
244	Black, Charles S.	Howell, Elizabeth A.	15 Sept	1859
215	Black, B.F.	Carson, Emeline	19 Mar	1859
361	Black, Ephraim	Payton, Elizabeth	28 Dec	1860
421	Black, F.H.	Connell, A.	31 Dec	1861
99	Black, T.M.	Simpson, Mary	4 Dec	1857
26	Blackwell, G.W.	Mays, Sarah E.	7 Oct	1856
254	Blackwell, M.J.	Chisohm, Carolin	11 Oct	1859

PAGE	GROOM	BRIDE	DATE	
81	Blake, C.A.	Raney, Rebecca R.	6 Sept	1857
5	Blake, Cain A.	Brown, Sarah A.R.	6 June	1856
454	Blake, Jeremiah	Cobb, Mary Ann	13 Jan	1863
255	Blansit, J.N.	Adams, Sarah A.E.	16 Oct	1859
382	Blanten, Josiah	Martindell, Mary E.	10 Mar	1861
410	Blaylock, J.M.	Houpt, Margaret C.	31 Oct	1861
686	Blocker, J.R.	Jordan, F.E.	6 Mar	1866
382	Boatman, David C.	Vaughan, Mary J.	12 Mar	1861
227	Boatman, William	Reed, Martha	9 June	1859
467	Boatman, William	Guin, Dosha	8 June	1863
154	Boatman, William M.	Kelly, Frances E.	10 July	1858
86	Boatner, J.W.	Foster, S.C.	10 Sept	1857
144	Bogue, John	Goode, Marinda	18 May	1858
601	Bolding, C.P.	Myers, E.J.V.	14 Sept	1865
744	Bolding, Marian J.	Knight, Mary J.	21 Nov	1866
662	Bolen, J.R.	Hicks, M.E.	10 Jan	1866
75	Bolen, John A.	Payne, Mary J.	12 July	1857
344	Bolen, Lafayette	Phillips, Perlina Jane	22 Nov	1860
576	Bolen, W.W.	Price, S.A.	22 Apr	1865
11	Bolin, Willaby	Bolin, Margaret	10 July	1856
146	Bolton, Edwin C.	Root, Margaret L.	20 May	1858
494	Bonds, W.H.H.	Hill, E.A.	2 Jan	1863
746	Boswell, L.J.	Middleton, Mary M.	26 Nov	1866
58	Bowen, H.H.	Dillard, Harriett	3 Feb	1857
411	Bowen, William	Raley, Mary	31 Oct	1861
222	Bowen, William E.	Read, Harriet A.	1 May	1859
790	Bowles, Ruben (free man)	Swindoll, Mrs. Jane (free)	20 Dec	1865
627	Box, G.C.	Jennings, Nancy	5 Nov	1865
572	Boyd, E.C.	Wynn, M.A.	30 Mar	1865
26	Boyd, John A.	Ross, Mary A.	8 Oct	1856
243	Boyd, Wm	Head, Matilda	7 Sept	1859
686	Boyd, W.D.	Motley, Lucy F.	9 Mar	1866
779	Bradford, Peter	Walker, Sylvia	21 Feb	1858
124	Brailey, Wm H.	Lankford, Martha M.	16 Feb	1858
150	Bramble, W.R.	Kirkland, Pamelia J.	16 June	1858
398	Bramblett, H.A.	Long, Josephine E.	14 July	1861
277	Branden, James T.	Hubbard, Mary Ann	25 Dec	1859
486	Brandon, Christopher	Yokum, Mrs. Matilda	13 Nov	1863
277	Brandon, James J.	Hubbard, Louisa E.	21 Dec	1859
653	Brandon, P.F.	Caldwell, E.R.	21 Dec	1865
596	Brandon, Richard	Fleming, Elizabeth	27 Aug	1865
561	Brandon, W.F.	Knight, Martha	12 Feb	1865
538	Brandon, W.W.	Duke, C.A.	23 Nov	1864
469	Bratton, Thomas G.	Christopher, Emily D.	5 Aug	1863
71	Braugher, C.A.	Earle, L.M.	25 May	1857
639	Brazier, James T.	League, Mary C.	7 Dec	1865
395	Breckinridge, John W.	Johnson, Mary Jane	23 June	1861
417	Briant, John J.	Dillard, Sarah F.	7 Dec	1861
161	Bridges, M.M.	Swan, Mary Ann	15 Aug	1858

PAGE	GROOM	BRIDE	DATE	
8	Brock, Jeremiah	Hayes, Sarah N.	24 June	1856
515	Brooks, John	Clifton, Hettie	13 May	1864
113	Brooks, Robert H.	Prude, Mary	19 Jan	1858
250	Brooks, W.J.	Jolly, Eartha	28 Sept	1859
483	Brown, B.D.	McPhail, Mary M.	8 Nov	1863
19	Brown, David M.	Hudiburgh, G. Minerva	20 Sept	1856
200	Brown, George A.	Davis, Margaret L.	2 Jan	1859
519	Brown, James W.	Walker, Lou M.	5 July	1864
305	Brown, John H.	Harrison, Mary	9 May	1860
60	Brown, Miller	Clark, S.A.	17 Feb	1857
600	Brown, R.B.	Robertson, S.P.	14 Sept	1865
133	Brown, R.H.	Oliver, Jane	16 Mar	1858
311	Brown, Rufus J.	Hutcheson, S.E.	27 June	1860
455	Brown, William	Wilson, Mary A.	22 Jan	1863
243	Browning, E.G.	Hale, Elizabeth	7 Sept	1859
201	Browning, J.D.	Smith, Cary J.	20 Jan	1859
80	Browning, James	Smith, Susanna	9 Sept	1857
726	Bruce, W.R.	Rowan, S.L.	6 Oct	1866
490	Brunes (?), Luther R.	Ball, J. Anna	22 Dec	1863
763	Bryan, Thos F.	Black, Mrs. Albertine	20 Dec	1866
222	Bryant, A.	Gilmer, Nancy J.	28 Apr	1859
20	Bryant, John J.	Coon, Martha M.E.	9 Sept	1856
665	Bryant, J.W.	Johnson, Elizabeth	14 Jan	1866
625	Bryant, Wm M.	Cobb, Mary A.E.	25 Oct	1865
340	Brysen, H.M.	Heard, A.M.	1 Nov	1860
54	Bryson, John	Scott, L.	22 Jan	1857
381	Bryson, Porter	Boyd, Sallie	7 Mar	1861
714	Bryson, W.D.	Bruton, Mrs. Mariah H.	27 Aug	1866
164	Buchanan, C.E.	Hill, T.C.	30 Aug	1858
466	Buchanan, J.M.	Hanks, Nannie B.	2 June	1863
739	Buchanan, J.W.	Nolan, Mary A.	3 Nov	1866
205	Buchanan, John F.	Holcomb, Harriett	27 Jan	1859
645	Buchanan, W.H.	Carr, Jane E.	11 Dec	1865
30	Bugg, Ira	Matthews, Nancy Ann	14 Nov	1856
355	Burk, Martin	Mayfield, Eliza E.	17 Dec	1860
484	Burks, A.J.	Reid, Martha	17 Dec	1863
342	Burks, Henry	Perry, Sarah Jane	12 Nov	1860
656	Burks, J.P.	Richardson, Frances	25 Dec	1865
294	Burton, M.T.	Barham, Mary F.	15 Feb	1860
177	Bruton, Phillip M.	Gambrell, Mariah H.	21 Oct	1858
90	Busby, J.M.L.	Hancock, M.E.	18 Oct	1857
57	Busby, L.P.	Portwood, Elizabeth Ann	5 Feb	1857
148	Butler, Charles	Jones, Nancy Caroline	9 June	1858
620	Butler, E.F.	Johnson, Sarah A.	15 Oct	1865
724	Butler, T.P.	Hill, Mary E.	29 Sept	1866

PAGE	GROOM	BRIDE	DATE	
306	Cain, Dr. J.S.	Worsham, M.C.	10 May	1860
556	Calder, John Henderson	Carter, Frances Texann	31 Jan	1865
651	Caldwell, C.M.	Caldwell, R.	20 Dec	1865
259	Caldwell, James	Hudson, Lucinda	23 Oct	1859
655	Caldwell, James A.	Fletcher, Isabelah	25 Dec	1865
667	Caldwell, J.C.	Gory, S.A.	18 Jan	1866
321	Caldwell, J.W.	Johnson, M.C.	2 July	1860
605	Caldwell, M.Y.	Cobb, Julia A.	20 Sept	1865
320	Caldwell, R.D.	Coleman, M.E.	31 July	1860
474	Caldwell, W.P.	Pritchard, Louiza	8 Sept	1863
676	Caldwell, William	West, Mary C.	6 Feb	1866
232	Calloway, J.G.	Wallsworth, K.J.	24 July	1859
209	Calmese, Felang (?)	Bouland, Jane	1 Mar	1859
678	Campbell, A.R.	Bridges, Sarah W.	28 Feb	1866
179	Campbell, B.R.	Cochran, Sarah Jne	4 Nov	1858
675	Campbell, S.A.	Beeks, A.J.	4 Feb	1860
84	Campbell, Thomas	Cochran, Mary E.	5 Sept	1857
486	Campbell, Wm Franklin	Orr, Synthia A.	10 Dec	1863
432	Cannady, John L.	Mark, Sarah L.	27 Mar	1862
73	Cannon, Francis M.	Davis, Nancy	23 June	1857
38	Carder, J.B.	Walker, Emily A.	11 Dec	1856
631	Cargill, Z.J.	Wood, J.A.	16 Nov	1865
463	Carpenter, A.W.A.B.	McGreger, Nettie	13 Apr	1863
339	Carpenter, B.A.	McGregor, Jemima	30 Oct	1860
219	Carpenter, Hoyl	Gammel, Manerva	8 Apr	1850
577	Carpenter, J.W.	Sinclair, Hester	27 Apr	1865
600	Carpenter, W.H.	Porter, Virginia	13 Sept	1865
235	Carr, J.W.	Wester, Mary	2 Aug	1859
485	Carson, Henry	Province, A.C.	5 Nov	1863
765	Carson, T.J.	White, Emeline	22 Dec	1866
541	Carson, W.J.	Ward, Mary E.	22 Dec	1864
724	Carson, Warren T.	Bishop, Mary Ann	29 Sept	1861
372	Carter, Ambrose	Brown, Frances	29 Jan	1861
432	Carter, Amze	Pannell, Mary Ann	26 Mar	1862
118	Carter, B.N.	Dixon, Mary C.	23 Jan	1858
332	Carter, J.B.	Taylor, P.E.	11 Oct	1860
491	Carter, James F.	Haynes, Martha J.	23 Dec	1863
78	Carter, Jesse	Tally, Elinor	27 July	1857
531	Carter, Lee	Grizzard, Adaline V.	17 Oct	1864
720	Carter, Lee	McCraw, Sallie	18 Sept	1866
525	Carter, W.H.	DeJurmott, Mary E.	31 Aug	1864
137	Caruth, Leander	Frierson, Susan	31 Mar	1858
371	Carwile, Samuel J.	Graham, Celia A.J.	23 Jan	1861
583	Cary, B.Q.	McGill, Susan R.	14 June	1865
166	Casterner, Wm	Massey, Selenia	6 Sept	1858
424	Castleberry, Wm	Coleman, Ann R.	27 Jan	1862
96	Catin, James C.	Massey, Malissa F.	22 Nov	1857
323	Cauthren, DAniel	Bolton, E.J.	8 Aug	1860
226	Cayce, James M.	Bates, E.A.	31 May	1859
265	Chambliss, Joseph R.	Freeman, Frances P.	11 Dec	1859

PAGE	GROOM	BRIDE	DATE	
190	Chaney, P.W.M.	Holleman, Nancy	27 Nov	1858
595	Chapman, John (Man of Color)	Dandridge, Catherine (Woman of Color)	20 Aug	1865
2	Cherry, Gwin R.	Bouland, Mary E.	21 May	1856
36	Christian, James	Benson, Elizabeth Ann	3 Dec	1856
195	Christian, James A.	Harvey, Frances A.	20 Dec	1858
29	Clark, Allen A.	Hancock, Permelia	30 Oct	1856
766	Clark, W.C.	Herndon, M.F.	19 Dec	1866
211	Clarke, R.R.	Harres, Mary A.	15 Mar	1859
426	Clayton, George W.	Deel, Mary Nancy A.	12 Feb	1862
184	Clayton, James	Greene, Susan C.	15 Nov	1858
345	Clayton, L.W.	Bell, M.A.	23 Nov	1860
236	Clemmans, E.D.	Scott, Susan A.	1 Aug	1859
403	Clements, W.A.	Crumpton, L.E.	29 Aug	1861
216	Cobb, Alexander	Phillips, Elizabeth	22 Mar	1859
267	Cobb, Daniel D.	Anarsan, Eliza A.	30 Nov	1859
487	Cobb, J.W.	Bradly, S.C.	10 Dec	1863
448	Cobb, W.W.	Campbell, Mary M.	13 Nov	1862
768	Coble, T.A.	Ramsy, Mrs. M.M.	26 Dec	1866
671	Cochran, L.J.	Proctor, Sallie	24 Jan	1866
72	Cochran, R.F.	Hellums, Nancy	31 May	1857
697	Cochran, W.G.	Miller, Sidney Ann	30 June	1866
504	Coggins, Jerrymiah M.	Dixen, Mary M.	11 Mar	1858
136	Coker, B.L.	Pitts, Amanda	25 Mar	1858
145	Cobb, J.J.	Anderson, Nira	20 May	1858
6	Cole, John G.	Nicholson, Albermale	19 June	1856
557	Cole, John T.	Howell, Nancy	5 Feb	1865
195	Coleman, John F.	Givens, Nancy E.	21 Dec	1858
637	Coleman, Wash (free man)	Jenkins, Millie (free)	24 Nov	1865
298	Coley, J.M.	Grubbs, Mary Ann	27 Mar	1860
295	Collins, H.E.	Cornelius, Mary E.	21 Feb	1860
777	Collins, Henry	Morgan, Amanda	1 Dec	1866
629	Collins, J.L.	Pegues, Amanda E.	14 Nov	1865
119	Colvin, A.J.	Pannell, Winna J.	25 Jan	1858
186	Colvin, C.B.	Pannell, Irena	18 Nov	1858
228	Colvin, J.F.	Vineyard, Taletha	13 June	1859
484	Colvin, William	Pannell, Emily	14 Nov	1863
565	Combs, J.W.	Simmons, Susan C.	23 Feb	1865
763	Combs, Wm M.	Neely, Ella	21 Dec	1866
563	Combs, William	Johnson, Mary C.	14 Feb	1865
297	Conaway, J.B.	Knight, R.A.J.	23 Feb	1860
98	Conley, James	Henry, Amanda	25 Nov	1857
748	Conner, Thomas	Donavan, Mary A.	4 Dec	1866
232	Corder, Eleazer	Reaves, Tempy J.	18 July	1859
152	Coon, David C.	Edington, Emily	11 July	1858
253	Cooper, A.J.	Smith, E.C.	6 Oct	1859
4	Cooper, Benjamin N.	Sartin, Eliza Ann	3 June	1856
168	Cooper, T.H.	Pass, Mary A.	13 Sept	1858
668	Cooper, W.H.	Jolly, Mary M.	18 Jan	1866
16	Cooper, William J.	Astin, Mary J.	7 Aug	1856

PAGE	GROOM	BRIDE	DATE	
64	Copeland, John W.	Buchanan, Mary A.	27 Mar	1857
272	Cornelius, C.R.	Williams, M.A.	8 Dec	1859
730	Cornelius, Jereno	Beard, Dovey A.	9 Oct	1866
56	Cornwell, Larkin	Price, Lusetta	22 Jan	1857
367	Cottrell, Thomas	Clements, Louisa	16 Jan	1861
513	Coats, F.D.	Johnson, O.E.	16 May	1864
484	Coward, Floid	Mayhew, Eliza J.	22 Nov	1863
776	Cox, Henry	Holland, N.J.	7 Jan	1867
275	Cox, J.H.J.	Payne, Frances A.	18 Dec	1859
506	Cox, John	Dnny(?), Mrs. Abbie	6 Apr	1864
11	Cox, Pleasant	Pannell, Sarah J.	10 July	1856
705	Cox, Riley	Bradford, Abigel	30 July	1866
196	Cox, Uriah N.	Brooks, Hanna	21 Dec	1858
498	Cox, William N.	Rayborn, Martha A.	3 Feb	1864
108	Crain, Crocket	Foster, Susan C.	24 Dec	1857
475	Crawford, John	Wardlaw, Sina	21 Sept	1863
457	Crawford, Thomas J.	Crawford, Susan F.	5 Feb	1863
327	Crawford, W.H.	Beckham, H.A.	1 Sept	1860
391	Crenshaw, P.H.	Matthews, M.J.	2 May	1861
340	Creseey, Thomas	Wilks, Jane	1 Nov	1860
109	Crocker, J.W.	Ware, Mary A.	29 Dec	1857
83	Cross, John B.	Woodward, Sallie	3 Sept	1857
178	Crossland, James	Breedlove, Martha	27 Oct	1858
583	Crosley, J.W.	Morrison, M.J.	19 June	1865
529	Crum, Alexander	McRunnels, Sarah	22 Sept	1864
516	Crump, Brodie S.	Edmonson, Helen L.	23 June	1864
706	Cruse, J.T.	Barlow, Lucy M.P.	2 Aug	1866
549	Cullens, Clearance	Heard, Mattie S.	16 Jan	1865
204	Cullens, F.W.	Holditch, Susanna D.	22 Jan	1859
320	Cunningham, G.H.	Mayhem, M.H.	30 July	1860
672	Cunningham, William	Redus, Catharine	29 Jan	1866
521	Cyle, G.W.	Massey, Sarah M.	2 Aug	1864
656	Dalton, J.H.	Stovall, M.E.	27 Dec	1865
317	Daniel, Alexander	Bass, Susan	12 July	1860
416	Daniel, J.M.	Ball, Mary Ann	26 Nov	1861
641	Daniel, L.F.	Tolerson, M.A.	4 Dec	1865
753	Daniel, T.A.	Clements, Martha A.	10 Dec	1866
680	Danniel, W.H.	Dunnum, Susan A.	12 Feb	1866
777	Dansby, JOhn C.	Dalton, Georgia A.	22 Dec	1866
422	Darlin, M.	Pannell, Elizabeth J.	17 Apr	1862
468	Darling, W.A.	(No Name), Elizabeth	25 June	1863
534	Davis, James C.	Mann, Caroline	9 Nov	1864
418	Davis, James D.	Young, Nancy C.	3 Dec	1861
136	Davis, Jasper N.	Harris, Rebecca J.	25 Mar	1858
775	Davis, John C.	Franklin, Mary A.E.	3 Jan	1867
293	Davis, Lucius H.	Moore, Amanda	16 Feb	1860
23	Davis, Peter	Ledbetter, Mary A.J.	22 Sept	1856
703	Davis, R.K.	McCraw, Mary J.	29 July	1866
490	Davis, Silas P.	Brandon, Mrs. Mary A.	22 Dec	1863

PAGE	GROOM	BRIDE	DATE	
	Davis, Sydney	Holms, Martha	15 Feb	1866
388	Davis, Thos B.	Hubbard, Malvina	11 Apr	1861
751	Davis, W.H.	Walker, Mett	8 Dec	1866
23	Davis, William	Reid, Martha Ann	25 Sept	1856
390	Dearing, W.A.	Dandridge, M.L.	29 Apr	1861
396	Decanter, M.F.	Green, M.E.	28 June	1861
439	Depass, Samuel C.	Twitchell, Emma E.	23 June	1862
585	Dickson, Joseph	Bridges, Mary L.	6 July	1865
194	Dickson, Joseph R.	Bacon, Harriet P.	15 Dec	1858
627	Dillard, J.T.	Meadows, Nancy A.	30 Oct	1865
352	Dillard, James	Bowen, Elizah	16 Dec	1860
730	Dillard, James M.	Laughbridge, Margaret V.	15 Oct	1866
223	Dillard, James W.	South, Mary A.E.	5 May	1859
712	Dillard, T.R.	South, Martha	25 Aug	1866
555	Dillard, W.M.	Green, Mary	31 Jan	1865
261	Dixon, Hamilton	Pitts, Matilda C.	5 Nov	1859
791	Dogan, Frank (free man)	Martin, Alice (free woman)	2 Dec	1865
85	Donaldson, J.A.	McGregor, Sarah E.	10 Sept	1857
148	Donavon, James	Long, Mary	2 May	1858
316	Dorsey, G.W.	Duncan, Mary H.	15 July	1860
363	Douglas, B.F.	Hellams, Letty J.	1 Jan	1861
727	Douglas, John W.	Sinclair, Joaner	6 Oct	1866
322	Douglas, T.B.	Tutor, Ann	4 Aug	1860
25	Dowdy, William R.	Johnson, Margaret J.	3 Oct	1856
250	Dowdy, W.W.	Hattox, Susan	2 Oct	1859
356	Drake, James W.	Doxey, Martha D.	20 Dec	1860
577	Dreher, Amos V.	Garrett, Sarah Catharine	3 May	1865
785	Duff, Ebenezer	Bell, Amanda (free woman)	1 Jan	1866
342	Duff, M.P.	Williams, Fannie	9 Nov	1860
615	Duff, W.A.	Haynes, Indiana	8 Oct	1865
660	Duke, James M.	Teeter (Tutor?), Lucinda	7 Jan	1866
112	Duke, John	Brassfield, Lucy Ann	15 Jan	1858
457	Duke, Thomas L.	Stone, Henrietta V.	9 Feb	1863
593	Duke, William	McCuchon, Jane	18 Aug	1865
131	Dulaney, James	Dulaney, Rachall	16 Mar	1858
573	Dulaney, Wm D.	Langley, Lucy Ann	10 Apr	1865
140	Dunaway, Joseph	Wells, Sarah J.	23 Apr	1868
370	Duncan, John F.	Souter, Caroline	20 Jan	1861
669	Duncan, Joseph	Thornton, Mary C.	23 Jan	1866
649	Duncan, R.H.	Huckabee, E.M.	14 Dec	1865
707	Duncan, Samuel	Wells, Kizie	4 Aug	1866
383	Duncan, W.H.	Parker, Malinda	14 Mar	1861
311	Duncan, Wm C.	Short, Malvina	24 June	1860
32	Dunlap, Leander	Dye, Lavina	20 Nov	1856
690	Dunlap, W.R.	Dunlap, L.	31 Mar	1866
555	Dunn, Henry	Thomas, Mrs. Mary J.	30 Jan	1865
725	Dunn, M.F.	Clark, Jane E.	1 Oct	1866

PAGE	GROOM	BRIDE	DATE	
358	Eagl, Samuel	Wood, Isabella	21 Dec	1860
208	Eanugton (Edrington?), George R.	Pannell, Nancy A.R.	20 Feb	1859
619	Earle, C.W.	Walker, Mary F.	12 Oct	1866
511	Easterwood, Newton	Elzey, Jennie	18 May	1865
70	Eave, R.S.	Johnston, C.E.	21 May	1857
466	Eaves, A.L.	Conlee, Tabitha	16 May	1863
606	Eaves, J.G.	Forrester, Mary A.	21 Sept	1865
604	Eaves, Jno E.	Forrester, M.A.	18 Sept	1865
285	Eaves, W.P.	Forrester, Virginia	15 Jan	1860
94	Echols, W.E.	Buchanan, M.J.	8 Nov	1857
324	Eckles, Wm F.	Gentry, Mary J.	13 Aug	1860
134	Edington, John	Goodwin, Nancy	1 Apr	1858
739	Edington, R.S.	Edwards, Elizabeth Ann	5 Nov	1866
774	Edwards, A.A.	Johnson, N.C.	2 Jan	1867
685	Edwards, J.M.	Johnson, M.L.	24 Feb	1866
679	Edwards, James	Williams, R.W.	19 Apr	1866
510	Edwards, W.A.	Sewell, M.M.	1 May	1864
276	Edwards, Wm	Wood, Gilly Ann	22 Dec	1859
433	Ellis, Benjamin	Duncan, Rachel	13 Apr	1862
239	Ellison, Jesse	Godfrey, Eliza J.	28 Aug	1859
405	Enoch, M.E.	Thomas, Sarah C.	14 Sept	1861
378	Epps, Joseph	Boyd, Frances E.	13 Feb	1861
692	Ervin, F.H.	Anderson, Mary E.	19 Nov	1866
369	Eubanks, Robert M.	Abernathy, Caroline	20 Jan	1861
233	Evans, J.B.	Baker, M.E.	27 July	1859
260	Evans, John L.	Welburn, Martha A.	26 Oct	1859
633	Evans, J.P.	Pittman, Mary E.	21 Nov	1865
171	Evans, W.J.	Huckaby, Missouri Ann	30 Sept	1858
445	Evens, Robert	Handly, Catharine	20 Sept	1862
317	Evetts, Henry	Pain, M.A.	10 July	1860
742	Evetts, L.	Ragan, M.E.	19 Nov	1866
133	Ewing, Charles	McClennan, Elizabeth	16 Mar	1858
101	Ewing, John	Simpson, Mary	7 Dec	1857
193	Ewing, John M.	Fear, N.A.	16 Dec	1858
617	Ewing, Silas (free man)	Hams, Amanda (free woman)	9 Oct	1865
530	Fagins, T.J.	Isom, Mary C.	4 Oct	1864
578	Falkner, S.F.	Adams, Emily	9 May	1865
689	Farmer, J.D.	Robinson, Sarah J.	27 Mar	1866
754	Farrar, Josiah	Thornton, Mary E.	11 Dec	1866
52	Farrer, W.C.	Harvey, Elizabeth R.	11 Jan	1857
784	Farror, Geo (free man)	Tate, Jane (free woman)	4 Jan	1866
39	Fear, Wm A.	Burten, Miss A.P.	17 Dec	1856
673	Fears, John C.	Holmes, Louisa	6 Feb	1866
202	Feemster, S.K.	Redus, A.C.	18 Jan	1859
497	Feilds, Jefferson	Mitchell, Virginia	1 Feb	1864
60	Femster, Andrew	Parish, Eliza	15 Feb	1857

PAGE	GROOM	BRIDE	DATE	
188	Ferrell, Benjamin	Fulton, Maria Jane E.	23 Nov	1858
413	Ferrell, Berkley D.	Nix, Mary A.	14 Nov	1861
677	Fields, A.F.	Taylor, Mary H.	8 Feb	1866
396	Fields, W.H.	Kelly, Emphema	30 June	1861
335	Findley, W.C.	Berry, Marisa J.	21 Oct	1860
553	Fisk, J.T.	McGill, Mary	26 Jan	1865
681	Fitzgerald, M.A.	Burris, Elizabeth	14 Feb	1865
592	Fizgerald, N.M.	Williams, J.A.	13 Aug	1865
761	Fitzgerald, J.T.	Bramblett, Bettie E.	18 Dec	1866
158	Flannagan, P.F.	Manning, Sarah Ann	5 Aug	1858
76	Flarherty, Colomon G.	King, Martha Ann	21 July	1857
264	Flarherty, Wm M.	Pearsall, Sarah E.	24 Nov	1859
253	Fleming, H.H.	Strain, Louisa V.	10 Oct	1859
178	Fleming, John R.	Robertson, Sarah Ann	24 Oct	1858
781	Forbes, William	Scales, Maryetta	(No Date ca 9 Feb 1867)	
174	Forbes, Marion	Wood, D.J. (D.J. Hood on bond and license)	20 Oct	1858
379	Ford, R.D.	Tyre, Mildred E.	3 Mar	1861
348	Fortune, A.L.	King, N.A.	3 Dec	1860
241	Fortune, G.W.L.	Pitts, Mary J.	4 Sept	1859
520	Foster, R.H.	Godfrey, E.F.	26 July	1864
229	Foster, W.J.	Dunn, Nancy E.	21 June	1859
385	Fowler, Allin P.	Gibbs, Sarah Ann	4 Apr	1861
562	Fowler, H.G.	Steelman, Elizabeth	10 Feb	1865
496	Fowler, Robert F.	Hutson, Mrs. Guertha C.	21 Jan	1861
458	Fradier, J.A.	Robbins, Matilda	10 Feb	1863
45	Funk, A.W.	Golding, M.E.	14 Jan	1857
187	Frank, Lemuel B.	Fullington, Melinda	18 Nov	1857
606	Franklin, J.W.	Stone, R.E.	19 Sept	1865
467	Frazier, Aaron	Botts, Delitia	25 June	1863
622	Frazier, Aran	Young, Lucinda	19 Oct	1865
337	Frazier, J.H.	Blocker, Harriet E.	25 Oct	1860
223	Frazier, John	Hays, Jane	8 May	1859
256	Frazier, J.R.	Wiley, Mary L.	18 Oct	1859
266	Free, David	Knight, Mary A.F.	1 Dec	1859
192	Free, Solomon	Pannell, F.E.	13 Dec	1858
616	Freeman, G.W.	Wilkins, S.S.I.	11 Oct	1865
192	Freeman, Wm	Campbell, Nancy G.	16 Dec	1858
624	Fretwell, Wm L.	Wells, E.F.	25 Oct	1865
87	Friarson, Daniel	Ward, Harriet E.	15 Sept	1857
409	Friarson, Sidney	Martin, Nannie O.	22 Oct	1861
120	Frieman, John W.	White, Martha L.	28 Jan	1858
712	Fuller, A.	Gatewood, Sallie	21 Aug	1866
17	Fuller, James C.	Horn, Sarah M.	14 Aug	1856
37	Fuller, M.R.	White, T.J.	16 Dec	1856
236	Fulton, J.O.	Freeman, Mrs. Martha S.	9 Aug	1859
14	Fulton, Josiah O.	Frieson, Elvina	26 July	1856
354	Fuqua, Benjamin J.	Whitlow, Elizabeth R.	20 Dec	1860
173	Fuqua, Wm M.	Milam, Elizabeth	4 Oct	1858

PAGE	GROOM	BRIDE	DATE	
609	Furr, Allison	Waddell, Elizabeth	28 Sept	1865
275	Furr, J.S.	Bigger, Sarah E.	22 Dec	1859
527	Gafford, M.	Paine, N.A.	12 Sept	1864
450	Gain, Marshall H.	Smith, Mrs. Charlotte	18 Dec	1859
213	Gaines, Thos C.	Strait, Salina A.	17 Mar	1859
447	Gambrell, J.D.	Ball, C.E.	9 Nov	1862
304	Gambrel, Saml D.D.	Boyd, Catharine J.	10 May	1860
63	Gambrell, W.C.	Neely, Elizabeth	17 Mar	1857
123	Garmon, John S.	Mathis, Martha A.	17 Feb	1858
631	Garmon, Marshall M.	Camfield, E.F.	17 Nov	1865
117	Garner, A.T.	Andrews, Louisa	17 Jan	1858
585	Garner, James P.	McCoy, Rebecca	6 July	1865
638	Garrett, James G.	Brumett (?), Martha C.	30 Nov	1865
207	Garrett, Joseph	Pannell, Catharine	6 Feb	1859

(Sarah C. Pannell on license)

PAGE	GROOM	BRIDE	DATE	
581	Garrison, A.J.	Thompson, Mary A.	7 June	1865
234	Gary, R.W.	Jolley, Mary F.	2 Aug	1859
695	Gary, J.W.	Henley, M.A.	4 June	1866
354	Gayle, A.J.	Hoyl, C.L.	20 Dec	1860
296	Gearan, Wm W.	Hunter, Martha G.	26 Feb	1860
90	Gentry, John	Screws, Mary	14 Oct	1857
702	Gentry, John T.	Winfield, Rose Ann	15 July	1866
514	Gentry, Wm J.	Freeman, M.E.	13 Apr	1865
491	Geter, William	Bolen, A.C.	22 Dec	1863
729	Gibbons, N.B.	Wells, Mary	12 Oct	1866
648	Gibson, W.G.	Rogers, Jane C.	18 Dec	1865
723	Gilder, P.N.	Mitchell, Louiza	28 Sept	1866
167	Gill, John W.	Milam, Mary	7 Sept	1858
544	Gill, M.	Miller, Martha J.	31 Dec	1864
746	Gill, S.C.	Poole, Emma B.	26 Nov	1866
237	Gilliam, J.F.	Higginbottom, Sarena A.	10 Aug	1859

(Serena A. Wiggins on minister's return)

PAGE	GROOM	BRIDE	DATE	
740	Gilmer, James E.	Mulikin, Mollie C.	12 Nov	1866
63	Gilmer, William	McCaw, Jennie Ann	24 Feb	1857
572	Gilmon, P.E.	Walker, Louisa A.B.	30 Mar	1865
501	Gilum, Littleberry	Dennis, Mrs. Mary A.	17 Mar	1864
206	Givens, James D.	Stone, Mary R.	2 Feb	1859
153	Givens, Samuel A.	Fuqua, Docia C.	8 July	1858
588	Glasgow, F.N.	Barnett, E.A.	23 July	1865
462	Glenn, J.J.	Bridges, Jane	2 Apr	1863
293	Glover, Wm B.	Porter, Geneva	12 Feb	1860
326	Godfrey, T.P.N.	Rodgers, R.O.F.	26 Aug	1860
435	Goggan, Gabriel T.	Dillard, Celia	1 May	1862
247	Goggins, Thomas G.	Dillard, Sally	21 Sept	1859
265	Golding, Richard	Wesson, M.M.H.E.	28 Nov	1859
103	Golding, W.C.	Allen, Nancy J.	22 Dec	1857
683	Goode, Frederick	Montgomery, Bernetta	21 Feb	1866

PAGE	GROOM	BRIDE	DATE	
380	Goode, Joseph G.	Johnson, Sarah	5 Mar	1863
247	Goodman, N.D.	Miller, L.J.	21 Sept	1859
22	Goodman, W.W.	Reeder, Sarah W.	17 Sept	1856
637	Googer, J.M.	Montgomery, Elizabeth	23 Nov	1865
118	Gordon, Leroy P.	Alexander, Dorcas	21 Jan	1858
	(Bond reads Golding)			
484	L.P.	Sansing, P.E.	30 Nov	1863
240	Gould, N.G.	Wells, Sarah E.	1 Sept	1859
138	Grady, W.W.	Wood, Mary	11 Apr	1858
181	Graham, J.J.	Warren, Sarah B.	4 Nov	1858
492	Graham, James	Caswell, Susan	11 Dec	1863
428	Graham, John W.	Gafford, Martha A.	26 Feb	1862
357	Graham, Saml J.	Carwile, Rebecca	23 Dec	1860
218	Grant, Abner	Wilson, Teletha E.	3 Apr	1859
654	Grant, B.L.	Duff, M.F.	24 Dec	1865
279	Grant, T.J.	Bell, Mary Jane	27 Dec	1859
514	Graves, T.L.	Long, R.M.	11 Apr	1865
508	Gray, Benjamin	Bradon, Ann	18 Apr	1864
764	Gray, J.B.	Hall, D.A.	21 Dec	1866
704	Gray, H.A.	Mitchell, Selena	27 July	1866
548	Green, H.N.	Stovall, M.A.	12 Jan	1865
221	Green, James C.	Thompson, Sally	28 Apr	1859
453	Green, John F.	Green, Nancy B.	5 Jan	1863
274	Green, Samuel R.	McDaniel, Nancy J.	15 Dec	1859
399	Green, T.M.	Long, Mary S.	28 July	1861
664	Green, W.S.	Powell, Matilda M.	11 Jan	1866
	(M.M. Pannell on minister's return)			
98	Greene, Phillip A.	Williams, J.A.	26 Nov	1857
112	Griffen, James B.	McGill, W.E.	5 Jan	1858
70	Griffen, Morgan	Oliver, Louiza	7 May	1857
400	Griffen, Simon	Kelly, Catharin	1 Aug	1861
238	Griffin, Eli	Stone, Susannah	18 Aug	1859
569	Griffin, J.D.	Redding, Mrs. Julia M.	11 Mar	1865
786	Grisham, Dogan (free man)	Elison, Amanda (free woman)	30 Dec	1865
319	Grisham, John W.	Cochran, Eliza A.	26 July	1860
332	Grisham, P.P.	Newby, M.A.	5 Oct	1860
370	Grisham, R.A.	Duff, E.C.	20 Jan	1861
234	Grisham, Laban	Beasley, Emeline	31 July	1859
460	Grisham, T.J.	Moore, Jacca Ann	22 Feb	1863
475	Grubb, W.H.	Roberts, C.M.	16 Sept	1863
463	Guinn, Thomas P.	Powell, Nancy J.	19 Apr	1863
214	Haddox, G.H.	Dowdy, A.A.	20 Mar	1859
733	Hadley, Joseph	Wheeler, Jane	25 Oct	1866
552	Hadley, T.J.	Garrigus, M.A.	20 Jan	1865
476	Hail, Joel	Caple, Eliza J.	17 Sept	1863
220	Hailey, Wm	Hood, Martha M.	14 Apr	1859
408	Hair, David F.	Addison, J.S.	17 Oct	1861
395	Halcom, James M.	Buchanan, Lucinda	22 June	1861

PAGE	GROOM	BRIDE	DATE	
646	Hale, A.D.	Baggett, M.A.	20 Dec	1865
643	Hale, C.M.	Dillard, Mary J.	7 Dec	1865
147	Hale, E.	Petty, Mary D.	1 June	1858
674	Hale, J.H.	Grace, Eliza	4 Feb	1866
134	Hale, James C.	Parr, Caroline	18 Mar	1858
95	Hale, Jermiah	Russell, Nancy	19 Dec	1857
360	Hale, Joel	Conner, T.A.E.	27 Dec	1860
410	Hale, Joel, Sr.	Wheatley, Mrs. Nancy	29 Oct	1861
632	Hale, W.T.	Fulks, F.E.	7 Nov	1865
362	Hall, A.H.	Goggin, Hannah E.J.	30 Dec	1860
521	Hall, George	Alexander, Margaret W.	2 Aug	1864
42	Hall, John	Gray, Jane	23 Dec	1856
437	Hall, John B.	Richman, Sarah L.	4 June	1862
495	Hall, John C.	McWhorter, M.E.	20 Jan	1864
231	Hall, William Colvin	Reaves, Sarah A.F.	21 July	1859
433	Hamaker, Joshua	Williams, Martha Jane	1 Apr	1862
510	Hamilton, Thomas M.	Connell, Elvira H.	2 Apr	1864
412	Hamilton, W.W.	Bigham, Margaret Ann Eliza	4 Nov	1861
125	Hampten, B.F.	McKinney, Mary C.	18 Feb	1858
143	Hampton, John W.	Wells, Adaline Martha	9 May	1858
94	Hampton, William	Jordon, Mary	22 Nov	1857
404	Hanah, W.B.	Knight, E.J.	2 Sept	1861
341	Hancock, John T.	Wood, Cynthia A.	7 Nov	1860
298	Haney, Wm H.	Smith, Elizabeth	23 Feb	1860
699	Haney, W.M.	Moore, M.J.	3 July	1866
41	Hanna, William J.	Shaw, Susanna	19 Dec	1856
445	Harden, Robert B.	Fields, Martha A.	28 Sept	1862
584	Hardin, James H.	Cobb, Margaret	20 June	1865
217	Hargroves, C.C.	Johnson, Catharine	3 Feb	1859
101	Hargroves, V.C.	McCurley, Sarah	18 Dec	1857
558	Harmon, M.V.	McCraw, Malinda	8 Feb	1865
352	Harris, E.M.	Johnson, Harriet	19 Dec	1860
3	Harris, P.R.	Harper, Laurinda	19 June	1856
391	Harris, P.R.	Swindoll, M.C.	7 May	1861
664	Harris, T.J.	Cannon, Mollie	10 Jan	1866
649	Harrison, J.S.	Hattox, Sarah J.	10 Dec	1866
598	Harrison, C.F.	Gillespie, nancy B.	14 Sept	1865
512	Harrison, Wm L.	Ward, Sarah	28 Feb	1864
749	Harvey, J.D.	Ross, S.A.	5 Dec	1866
7	Harvey, Thomas	Buzby, M.A.	22 June	1856
364	Hathcock, James L.	Smith, Abigal S.	4 Jan	1861
519	Hattox, J.C.	Kelly, E.F.	8 July	1864
742	Hay, N.M.	Scales, S.J.	17 Nov	1866
536	Haynie, Henry M.	Thomas, S.W.	16 Nov	1864
658	Haynie, J.R.	Caldwell, Rebecca F.	4 Jan	1866
380	Haze, William	Wicker, Lucinda	3 Mar	1861
5	Head, Elijah	Noles, Mary	11 June	1856
349	Head, James M.	Noles, Nancy	6 Dec	1860

PAGE	GROOM	BRIDE	DATE	
83	Heard, Elijah	Knowles, Mary	6 Sept	1857
27	Heard, Stephen A.	Holditch, Eliza C.	30 Oct	1856
141	Hearn, Joel A.	Allman, Ellen C.	2 May	1858
355	Hearnsan, James M.	Sullivan, Eliza E.	23 Dec	1860
709	Heidelberg, J.C.	Porter, A.R.	8 Aug	1866
21	Hellum, James A.	Weatherall, Harriet	17 Sept	1856
66	Hellum, R.C.	Kelly, D.A.	14 May	1857
630	Helms, J.W.	McNiel, V.A.	16 Nov	1865
312	Helms, John	Smith, Isabella	25 June	1860
547	Henderson, J.L.	Johnson, Josephine	11 Jan	1865
713	Henderson, Silas T.	Garrett, Amanda L.	27 Aug	1866
539	Henry, A.L.	McCord, Ele C.	27 Nov	1864
189	Henry, James B.	Reed, Nancy	28 Nov	1858
100	Henry, J.F.	Wells, Susan A.	8 Dec	1857
775	Henry, J.R.	Phillips, Sarah E.	4 Jan	1867
514	Henry, John	Stanley, Polly	1 Dec	1863
353	Hensan, James A.	Cooper, Ellen	18 Dec	1860
231	Hensley, John H.	Bowles, Sarah A.	11 July	1859
567	Hensley, R.W.	Pannell, Martha J.	6 Mar	1865
549	Herndon, J.L.	Bell, Isabella	12 Jan	1865
737	Herndon, Meryman	Hellums, Jemima	1 Oct	1866
619	Herndon, Warren	Douglass, Nancy	12 Oct	1865
323	Herring, Stephen G.	Fuller, Elizabeth R.	12 Aug	1860
691	Herring, S.G.	Hill, Paralee	14 Apr	1866
750	Herron, Thos F.	Benson, S.A.	5 Dec	1866
599	Hester, Joseph	Foster, N.E.	14 Sept	1865
205	Hicks, M.A.	Newell, S.E.	25 Jan	1859
309	Hickman, James A.	Pruitt, Amanda A.	22 May	1860
449	Hickman, Wm F.	Kee, Mary	24 Nov	1862
581	Higgenbothum, W.R.	White, S.A.	9 June	1865
470	Higgins, Wm W.	Rogers, M.E.	26 Aug	1863
499	Higgs, L.R.	Ray, Annie	1 Feb	1864
365	High, R.H.	Browning, M.A.	13 Jan	1861
163	Hightower, W.J.	Whitely, Pamelia	26 Aug	1858
482	Hightower, W.J.	Stuart, Ellen(?)	6 Nov	1863
313	Hiler, Henry	Neighbors, Jane	20 July	1860
695	Hill, J.H.	Wise, Sarah E.	31 May	1866
551	Hill, James	Russell, Mary E.	18 Jan	1865
713	Hill, James H.	Anderson, Harriet E.	25 Aug	1866
238	Hill, John R.	Jones, Permelia J.	17 Aug	1859
732	Hill, Jno R.	Bigham, America E.	24 Oct	1866
184	Hill, Levi N.	Pinson, Lucinda	9 Nov	1858
257	Hill, William	White, Sarah	19 Oct	1859
487	Hitt, Peter C.	Bryant, Mrs. Parthenia	14 Dec	1863
48	Hitt, William	Montgomery, Sarah	7 Jan	1857
693	Hitt, William	Cox, Hannah	23 Apr	1866
47	Hodges, E.	Cypert, Eliza J.	6 Jan	1857
419	Hodges, John J.	Reed, Mary	15 Dec	1861
246	Hodges, J.T.	Head, Sarah A.	20 Sept	1859

PAGE	GROOM	BRIDE	DATE	
614	Hodges, R.S.	Wood, N.E.	5 Oct	1865
784	Hodges, Simon (free man)	Laney, Sally (free woman)	4 Jan	1866
538	Hodges, Wm	Stewart, Harriet A.	27 Nov	1864
147	Hogge, E.D.	Wiley, C.C.	26 May	1858
642	Holden, G.W.	Camfield, A.B.	3 Jan	1866
722	Holleman, James W.	McNile, Martha	26 Sept	1866
181	Holmes, J.B.W.	Billingsly, M.	3 Nov	1858
186	Holmes, T.J.	Heard, R.J. (I?)	20 Nov	1858
150	Holmes, T.M.	Mallory, Eliza Jane	22 June	1858
494	Holmes, William G.	Carruth, Mary E.	20 Jan	1864
768	Holt, P.A.	Pitts, Lodusky	25 Dec	1866
734	Hooper, Isaac	Carter, Martha	27 Oct	1866
231	Hooper, Jackson	Brown, Narcissa	19 July	1859
55	Horn, E.	McClenon, H.A.	20 Jan	1857
657	Horton, D.A.	Renolds, H.C.	31 Dec	1866
559	Horton, J.C.	Jenkins, S.C.	7 Feb	1865
58	Horton, John L.	Prince, Elizabeth	10 Feb	1857
782	Horton, Madison	Wiley, Nely Ann	27 Jan	1866
670	Horton, Rufus	Morrison, Lucinda	24 Jan	1866
286	Houpt, L.D.	Copeland, Sarah A.	18 Jan	1860
662	Houpt, T.J.	Phillips, S.F.A.	1 Feb	1866
765	Howard, F.M.	Bullock, Ann M.	21 Dec	1866
288	Howard, J.L.	Seals, Nancy F.	18 Jan	1860
296	Howell, G.W.	Harrison, Lou A.	21 Feb	1860
170	Howell, J.S.	Ivey, E.A.	19 Sept	1858
79	Hoyl, J.M.	Johnson, A.C.	18 Aug	1857
393	Hoyl, John W.	Gayle, Martha A.	15 Nay	1861
505	Hubbard, James M.	Hutcherson, M.A.	2 Apr	1864
97	Hubbard, John G.	Alexander, Mary E.	24 Nov	1857
757	Hubbard, T.L.	Bright, M.A.E.	17 Dec	1866
282	Hubbard, W.M.	Bright, Susan A.	4 Jan	1860
34	Hubbard, William M.	Hudiburgh, Nancy Jane	30 Nov	1856
614	Huckabee, Calvin	Shaw, Mary A.	4 Oct	1865
565	Huckabee, William	Vaughan, Nancy	29 Feb	1865
372	Huckbee, Exekiel	Shaw, Sarah C.	26 Jan	1861
322	Huckbee, William	Holbert, Martha	8 Aug	1860
787	Huckeby, Alee (free man)	Mayhue, Sarah (free woman)	27 Dec	1865
44	Hudiburgh, James S.	Mooney, Mary J.	29 Dec	1856
67	Hudson, E.G.	Warren, Permelia	3 May	1857
34	Hudson, James E.	Freeman, Mary E.	27 Nov	1856
3	Hudson, John E.	Sanders, Sarah J.	29 May	1856
762	Huffstickler, C.G.	Ball, Jemima J.	19 Dec	1866
408	Huffstickler, S.C.	Golson, Malissa	17 Oct	1861
106	Hughes, E.M.	Billingsly, Courtney P.	23 Dec	1857
443	Humphrey, David	Camfield, Mary F.	3 Sept	1862
590	Hunley, A.J.	Garey, M.A.	31 July	1865
591	Hunt, James	Wynn, Louisa J.	2 Aug	1865
12	Hunt, Thomas	Williams, Louisa	17 July	1856
633	Hunt, Talton	McNiel, Susan	23 Nov	1865
636	Hunt, Talton (free man)	McNiel, Susan (free woman	22 Nov	1865

PAGE	GROOM	BRIDE	DATE	
495	Hurley, A.J.	Pannell, L.J.	20 Jan	1864
159	Hurley, F.M.	James, Martha J.	12 Aug	1858
686	Hurley, F.M.	Richardson, M.J.	8 Mar	1866
95	Husten, W.J.	Coleman, L.T.	17 Nov	1857
654	Hutchison, W.B.	Maxey, M.A.	26 Dec	1865
278	Hutcherson, J.H.	Andrews, Sarah J.	27 Dec	1859
779	Ingates, Andy	Fields, Elin	15 Feb	1866
233	Ivey, James M.	Pettygrew, Hannah A.	28 July	1859
523	Ivey, F. Marion	Thompson, N.E.	14 Aug	1864
745	Ivins, Benjamin	Bradley, Bettie F.	23 Nov	1864
645	Ivy, J.A.	Snow, E.	11 Dec	1865
51	Ivy, Lovinski	Abernathy, Martha E.	8 Jan	1857
100	Ivy, Pulaski	Stanford, S.A.	6 Dec	1857
414	Ivy, Wm H.	Pope, Isabella	17 Nov	1861
505	Jackson, F.D.	Ivy, P.A.	1 Mar	1864
397	Jackson, J.H.	Thomason, M.E.	3 July	1861
552	Jackson, James M.	Moore, Elizabeth	25 Jan	1865
779	Jackson, James T.	Glover, Margaret	9 Jan	1867
47	Jackson, W.H.	Clark, Matilda A.	14 Jan	1857
152	Jackson, W.H.	Fuqua, Mary E.	8 July	1858
220	Jacco, John J.	Burk, Mellissa J.	9 Apr	1859
262	James, Isaac	Shelton, Mary M.	14 Nov	1859
532	James, John C.	Ware, Margarett S.	2 Nov	1864
566	James, Phillip	Winn, Elizabeth P.	5 Feb	1866
659	James, W.M.	Thomas, M.J.	11 Jan	1866
309	Jarvis, Francis L.	Hurley, Nancy	27 May	1860
575	Jennings, Saml	Higgin, Mrs. Sallie	18 Apr	1865
687	Jernigan, G.W.	Newell, Francis Ann	8 Mar	1866
442	Jernigan, Harris	Brown, Sarah	6 Aug	1862
149	Jeter, Cornelius	Adams, Rachail L.	14 June	1858
197	Jeter, James W.	Jordan, Caroline	25 Dec	1858
359	Johnson, Alexander	Harris, Mary	26 Dec	1860
190	Johnson, A.J.M.	Donaldson, Anna L.	30 Nov	1858
684	Johnson, B.F.	Smith, Martha	15 Feb	1866
286	Johnson, James M.	Lowery, Elizabeth	16 Jan	1859
488	Johnson, James T.	Alexander, Mrs. M.W.	17 Dec	1863
719	Johnson, John W.	Jolly, Savena	18 Sept	1866
153	Johnson, Joab	Brown, Mary U.	8 July	1858
187	Johnson, Joseph	Pritchard, Lettice B.	19 Nov	1858
51	Johnson, N.P.	Ward, D.C.	8 Jan	1857
650	Johnson, T.S.	Abernathy, M.E.	19 Dec	1865
362	Johnson, Thomas	Manes, Margarett	30 Dec	1860
500	Johnson, William	Deane, S.J.	11 Feb	1864
131	Johnson, William W.	Lowry, Sarah A.	14 Mar	1858
426	Johnson, Wilson	Wait, Virginia	12 May	1862
728	Johnston, J.C.	Pritchard, S.F.	11 Oct	1866
460	Johnston, R.R.	Dunken, Telethia	25 Feb	1863

PAGE	GROOM	BRIDE	DATE	
167	Joiner, C.F.	Fulton, Sarah R.	6 Sept	1858
309	Joiner, F.L.	Hurley, Nancy	27 May	1860
351	Jolly, Thomas J.	McPhearson, Caroline	13 Dec	1860
225	Jones, A.J.	King, Mary D.	30 May	1859
102	Jones, H.W.	Rivers, Susan	20 Dec	1857
508	Jones, Holt	Eubanks, Amanda	19 Apr	1864
464	Jones, Jacob J.	Harper, Martha Ann	26 Apr	1863
248	Jones, T.W.	Duncan, Martha J.	22 Sept	1859
774	Jones, Robert	Reeder, Eugenia (?)	3 Jan	1867
430	Jones, Russell T.	Cooper, Margaret Ann	6 Mar	1862
404	Jones, Silas L.	Bradley, Martha G.	8 Sept	1861
628	Jones, T.W.	Eubanks, E.C.A.	8 Dec	1865
389	Jones, W.P.	Nash, Martha	19 Apr	1861
169	Jones, W.H.	Campbell, Parthena	24 Sept	1858
92	Jones, W.L.	Wells, Martha A.	29 Oct	1857
1	Jones, William S.	Hunter, Hannah	13 May	1856
607	Jones, Wm J.	Black, Ann	23 Sept	1865
741	Jordan, John	Thompson, A.R.	15 Nov	1866
68	Jumper, B.S.	Hunter, F.C.	10 May	1857
607	Jumper, W.G.	Hattox, Sarah A.E.	21 Sept	1865
142	Kelly, B.	Holcomb, Nancy	5 May	1858
732	Kelly, Dallas	Hellums, Thena	23 Oct	1866
580	Kelly, Isom	Holcomb, Sarah	29 May	1865
276	Kelly, Jeramiah	Long, Emma C.	21 Dec	1859
472	Kelly, M.M.	Hauckum, Nancy	31 Aug	1863
82	Kelly, Newton	Chapman, Sarah	30 Aug	1857
731	Kelly, R.S.	Bruce, Martha P.	17 Oct	1866
175	Kelly, Thomas D.	Dillard, Lucy	19 Oct	1858
198	Kelly, Thomas	Milam, Rebecca	29 Dec	1858
200	Kelly, Thos S.	Chapman, Rebecca	5 Jan	1859
596	Kelly, W.M.	Johnson, M.J.	31 Aug	1865
274	Kennady, Thomas J.	Johnson, Josephine L.	13 Dec	1859
299	Kerr, L.S.	Ewing, martha E.	29 Feb	1860
592	Kerr, Z.M.	Ewing, R.C.	6 Aug	1865
114	Kimball, W.J.	Simmon, Adaline	12 Jan	1858
528	King, Samuel T.	Saterwhite, J.	18 Sept	1864
163	King, Thomas	Reed, Clarisa	28 Aug	1858
18	King, Wright	Eubanks, Amanda E.	26 Aug	1856
623	Knight, J.M.	Pitts, Annie	21 Oct	1865
379	Knight, T.B.	Moore, Mary Joan	23 Feb	1861
708	Kyle, W.P.	Davis, Mrs. M.E.	6 Aug	1866
496	Lamar, J.H.	Morris, Lusina	23 Jan	1864
633	Lambreth, J.W.	Morrow, Sarah F.	18 Nov	1865
561	Langley, R.L.	Dunham, M.A.	9 Feb	1865
48	Langley, Thomas	Pannell, Orena	15 Jan	1857
423	lankford, Frank	Casteel, S.V.	23 Jan	1862
65	Lankford, Minor C.	Moore, Sarah J.	2 Apr	1857

PAGE	GROOM	BRIDE	DATE	
550	Lantrip, Francis M.	Harris, Lucinda	18 Jan	1865
73	Leatherburg, George S.	Gresham, Jane B.	3 June	1857
235	Leathers, C.M.	Spence, M.A.	11 Aug	1859
618	Leathers, J.S.	Beauchamp, M.P.	12 Oct	1865
717	Leathers, James N.	Mathews, Margaret S.	10 Sept	1866
559	Lesley, Robt W.	Stegall, Mary Jane	8 Feb	1865
626	Leslie, J.H.	Pritchard, S.J.	1 Nov	1865
717	Lewellen, J.W.	McWhorter, Nancy J.	10 Sept	1866
701	Lewis, Chis	Floyed, Perlena	9 July	1866
303	Lewis, E.H.	Dandrage, Zelia P.	18 May	1860
232	Liddell, C.G.	Huston, Selitia F.	21 July	1859
681	Ligon, C.P.	Raymond, Emily H.	16 Feb	1866
91	Lilly, J.L.	Dale, Elizabeth	27 Oct	1857
470	Lilly, R.G.	Wylie, M.H.	26 Aug	1863
503	Lindsey, Nuton	Halcombe, Sarah Ann	27 Mar	1864
663	Lindsey, Saml H.	McDole, Sarah	12 jan	1866
349	Listenbee, W.T.	Hellums, Martha A.	11 Dec	1860
500	Little, J.W.	Owens, Leanna	12 Feb	1864
4	Livingston, R.J.	Sadlin, Caroline	8 June	1856
290	Lockhart, G.W.	King, Leonora M.	31 Jan	1860
485	Loftis, James M.	Loftis, Mary	30 Nov	1863
	(Mary Nolen on bond, Mary Loftis on license, no minister's return)			
560	Long, W.P.	Turner, Fannie	7 Feb	1865
339	Long, William	Edwards, Mary C.	28 Oct	1860
169	Looney, David	Fowler, Mary Ann	16 Sept	1858
546	Looney, Wm J.	Irvin, Nancy A.	8 Jan	1865
37	Loot, W.E.	Buchanan, Nancy J.	4 Dec	1856
69	Love, Henry O.N.	Harrison, Mary C.	12 May	1857
50	Lovejoy, F.J.	Warner, Mary A.	6 Jan	1857
92	Lovings, W.W.	Malone, Sarah	29 Oct	1857
540	Lore, W.A.	Real, Tabitha	18 Dec	1864
677	Lower, J.M.	Stanton, A.R.	7 Feb	1866
130	Lowery, W.P.	Johnsen, Nancy Ann	7 Mar	1858
347	Lowry, A.C.	Calloway, Araminta	2 Dec	1860
655	Lowry, W.P.	Johnson, Mary Jane	24 Dec	1865
522	Ludiwick, Nicklass	Cox, Ellender	6 Aug	1864
104	Luke, James G.	Bailey, Sarah F.	24 Dec	1857
366	Luke, R.L.	Bailey, Adeline R.	17 Jan	1861
69	Luke, Wm A.	Bailey, Elizabeth	17 May	1857
330	Luker, M.M.	Roberts, M.J.	20 Sept	1860
199	Lynch, H.F.	Price, Mary M.	3 Jan	1859
550	Lyon, W.H.	Neely, E.F.	15 Jan	1865
613	Lyon, T.J.	Rodgers, Martha J.	1 Oct	1865
115	McAlister, W.A.	Faulkner, Sosanna	19 Jan	1858
24	McCall, Martin L.	Meador, Sarah E.	23 Sept	1856
764	McCanless, Wm Alex	Elliott, Jennie Albula	21 Dec	1866
270	McCarter, G.A.	Barksdale, J.E.	6 Dec	1859
193	McCarter, James H.	Strain, Susan T.	16 Dec	1858

PAGE	GROOM	BRIDE	DATE	
641	McCarver, H.S.	Stephens, M.F.	4 Dec	1865
579	McClellan, Wade H.	Pollard, Cordelia D.	11 May	1865
135	McClelland, William	McCoy, Polly Ann	18 May	1858
594	McClure, J.K.	White, M.C.	18 Aug	1865
425	McCollough, John	Wade, S.R.	12 Feb	1862
760	McCord, J.N.	Edwards, L.J.	18 Dec	1866
334	McCord, John M.	Johnston, Martha A.	16 Oct	1860
678	McCord, L.P.	Wood, Mary A.	11 Feb	1866
392	McCord, William A.	Henry, Edna E.	19 May	1863
302	McCoy, John T.	Reeder, Catharin	5 Apr	1860
414	McCraw, A.J.	Wells, Martha Jane	20 Nov	1861
385	McCraw, J.B.	Beauchamp, Selina	3 Aug	1861
203	McCraw, Gustavus L.	Moore, Sarah J.L.	18 Jan	1859
74	McCraw, Jesse M.	Beasley, Mary Jane	2 May	1857
112	McCraw, L.N.	Holliday, Mary A.	17 Jan	1858
122	McCraw, P.G.	Johnson, Susanna	8 Feb	1858
215	McCraw, S.G.	Roberts, Sarah E.	19 Mar	1859
617	McCullough, James R.	Buchanan, Nancy J.	9 Oct	1865
442	McCullough, Samuel D.	Duke, Sarah	23 Aug	1862
268	McCutchen, James A.	Short, Mary A.	30 Nov	1859
601	McDaniel, Elihu	Bolen, Lucinda	12 Sept	1865
752	McDaniel, J.C.	Jones, Amanda	10 Dec	1866
273	McDaniel, John F.	Watley, Amanda	8 Dec	1859
434	McDaniel, John K.	Allen, Martha P.	22 Apr	1862
718	McDaniel, S.A.	McDaniel, Mrs. M.P.	12 Sept	1866
28	McDonald, James	Blake, C.A.	20 Oct	1856
646	McDonald, James W.	Riggan, Sarah E.	19 Dec	1865
473	McDonald, W.W.	Dobbins, J.B.	3 Sept	1863
145	McEarchern, Samuel L.	Dale, Margarett M.	14 Feb	1858
123	McEasthern, Jas W.	Hooker, Margarett M.	14 Feb	1858
446	McEwen, John B.	Handley, Sarah S.	7 Oct	1862
237	McGill, John	Stanford, Elsira	11 Aug	1859
634	McGreger, G.	Tutor, Lucy A.	21 Nov	1865
166	McKeon, Tresvean	Pool, Elizabeth	5 Sept	1858
659	McKinsey, Newton	Carr, Martha	11 jan	1866
39	McKnight, L.J.	McWhirter, S.J.	14 Dec	1856
471	McLarty, Thomas P.	Griffen, Martha J.	31 July	1863
673	McNeely, J.P.	Payton, Nancy Ann	4 Feb	1866
786	McNeil, Feelix (free man)	Weatherall, Sarah (free)	28 Dec	1865
93	McNutt, Wm P.	Forrister, Elizabeth	30 Oct	1857
755	McPherson, L.A.	Blansit, S.E.	11 Dec	1866
197	McPherson, Wm K.	McDonald, Miss L.	22 Dec	1858
41	McWhirter, B.F.	Fisher, Ellin	25 Dec	1856
545	McWhirter, G.W.	Hampton, Mrs. A.M.	31 Dec	1864
392	McWhorter, H.H.	Gould, N.J.	3 May	1861
480	McWhorter, John P.	Gill, Rebecca C.	11 Jan	1860
287	McWhorter, Matt D.	Gould, Sarah H.	28 Oct	1863

PAGE	GROOM	BRIDE	DATE	
182	Malone, A.W.	Coon, Frances C.	5 Nov	1858
520	Malone, C.C.	Johnson, Malinda	26 July	1864
657	Malone, C.H.	Ward, Martha	28 Dec	1865
428	Malone, John D.	Price, Mahala	24 Feb	1862
185	Malone, Sampson	Trice, Elizabeth	18 Nov	1858
291	Mann, C.D.	Letford, C.T.	5 Feb	1860
587	Mann, David	Holmes, Martha Ann	15 July	1865
121	Mann, JOhn J.	Warren, Emily E.	31 Jan	1858
539	Mann, Lemuel	Isom, Luraine	2 Dec	1864
336	Manning, John R.	Hensley, Artamintre	23 Oct	1860
526	Manning, Wm H., Jr.	Hightower, T.E.	6 Sept	1864
469	Marable, H.	Miller, E.P.	4 Aug	1863
295	Marion, R.B.	Kirkpatrick, Martha M.	18 Feb	1860
616	Marks, E.M.C.	Thornton, M.J.	10 Oct	1865
304	Marks, James	Evans, Caroline	6 May	1860
199	Marlin, H.	Barr, Sarah E.	3 Jan	1859
582	Marrs, J.	Westmoreland, M.A.	14 June	1865
759	Marshall, Harbert	Bullock, Mary A.J.E.	18 Dec	1866
125	Marshall, John H.	Gibson, Frances G.	23 Feb	1858
431	Marshall, John	Sanders, Ellen J.	6 Mar	1862
789	Martheny, Henry (free man)	Dandridge, Mariah (free)	16 Dec	1865
75	Martin, James H.	Wilie, Jane	24 July	1857
77	Martin, Murdock	Miller, Margarett	23 July	1857
540	Mathews, N.P.	Mauldin, Narcissa T.	7 Dec	1864
171	Mathewson, G.P.	Bridges, Martha J.	4 Oct	1858
103	Mattox, Martin	Calfee, Amanda C.	21 Dec	1857
	(Bond reads Amanda C. Coffee)			
714	Mauldin, Charles N.	Betts, Margaret L.	31 Aug	1866
680	Mauldin, H.M.	West, A.E.	14 Feb	1866
377	Mauldin, Joseph H.	Worsham, Margaret C.	7 Feb	1861
748	Maxey, Edward V.	Hanan, Elizia A.	4 Dec	1866
151	May, John	Taylor, C.J.	23 June	1858
89	May, Moses	Cooper, Susan A.	1 Oct	1857
330	Mayben, James O.	Barr, F.C.	26 Sept	1860
254	Mayberry, Henry L.	Baker, Sarah A.	11 Oct	1859
735	Mayhew, A.A.	Wison, Sarah E.	29 Oct	1866
611	Mayhew, J.G.	Johnson, Jane H.	27 Sept	1865
210	Meador, John J.	Sexton, Nancy A.	6 Mar	1859
504	Mears, A.J.	Hanks, L.	2 Mar	1864
610	Milam, H.P.	Nixon, M.A.	25 Sept	1865
49	Milam, Joseph A.	Lamar, Susan C.	7 Dec	1857
758	Milam, W.A.	Nixon, Mollie C.	17 Dec	1866
608	Milam, W.F.	Jackson, Mary E.	24 Sept	1865
49	Miller, A.G.	Billingsly, A.E.	8 Jan	1857
115	Miller, J.E.M.	Rye, Mary E.	12 Jan	1858
413	Miller, J.F.C.	Kennedy, Marissa	17 NOv	1861
527	Miller, J.L.	Head, Martha J.	12 Sept	1864
52	Miller, J.M.	Milam, Mary F.	8 Jan	1857
62	Miller, I.T.	Taylor, Louisa .	19 Feb	1857

PAGE	GROOM	BRIDE	DATE	
347	Miller, R.	Zinn, Harriet F.	6 Dec	1860
110	Miller, John W.	Neely, Mary E.	29 Dec	1857
769	Miller, Mark	Reynolds, Mrs. Martha	27 Dec	1866
516	Miller, Henry	Malone, Mrs. M.E.	30 May	1864
711	Miller, Prior L.	Allbritton, Emily	18 Aug	1866
481	Miller, Thomas J.	Province Sabina A.	31 Oct	1863
597	Mitchell, C.B.	Dennis, V.E.	31 Aug	1865
751	Mitchell, Carpender	Bennett, Mary M.	8 Dec	1866
53	Mitchell, Charley G.	Foreman, Sarah F.	15 Jan	1857
481	Mitchell, James R.	Seal, Sarah	4 Nov	1863
602	Mitchell, John S.	Maddox, Leah A.E.	18 Sept	1865
522	Mitchell, T.B.	Drake, Julia D.	5 Aug	1864
701	Mitchell, T.B.	Dennis, Mary N.	11 July	1866
518	Mitchell, Thomas B.	Kennedy, Ella	2 July	1864

(The above was scratched out)

PAGE	GROOM	BRIDE	DATE	
444	Monahan, W.A.W.	Redus, Elizabeth A.	16 Sept	1862
24	Montgomery, Alexander	Perry, Rebecca	26 Sept	1856
207	Montgomery C.L.	McDonald, Mary A.	3 Feb	1859
35	Montgomery, George	Gernigan, Harriet Ann	2 Dec	1856
649	Montgomery, James R.	Braden, Mrs. E.A.	19 Dec	1865
635	Montgomery, R.E.	Jones, Matilda A.	28 Nov	1865
128	Montgomery, Robert	Caldwell, Martha L.	24 Feb	1858
389	Montgomery, Robert	Hatfield, Elizabeth	17 Apr	1861
405	Montgomery, Samuel C.	Henry, N.F.	12 Sept	1861
336	Moore, Elijah	Lacy, Mary	23 Oct	1860
124	Moore, J.A.	Beckham, Elizabeth H.	16 Feb	1858
182	Moore, James W.	Gaines, Frances C.	7 Nov	1858
280	Moore, L.C.	Savely, Mary E.	29 Dec	1859
694	Moore, M.J.M.	Smith, A.D.	16 May	1866
770	Moore, M.P.	Jordan, F.M.	28 Dec	1866
699	Moreland, W.P.	Russell, M.E.	3 July	1866
387	Morgan, Edward	Pannell, Catharin	11 Apr	1861
28	Morgan, John	Brassfield, Caroline	24 Oct	1856
66	Morgan, Joseph F.	Sherman, Martha C.	18 Apr	1857
214	Morgan, Thomas	Ferguson, Susan J.	17 Mar	1859
365	Morris, A.J.	Pope, Cela T.	10 Jan	1861
542	Morris, james	Russell, Eliza M.	29 Dec	1864
284	Morris, Jesse	Payne, J.S.	8 Jan	1860
489	Morris, William E.	Dillard, Martha J.	20 Dec	1863
373	Morris, Wm H.	Satterwhite, Mary E.	31 Jan	1861
532	Morrison, A.P.	Horton, Susan	17 Oct	1864
651	Morrow, E.G.	Eubanks, M.C.	19 Dec	1866
760	Morrow, E.M.	Hampton, Mary E.	18 Dec	1866
176	Morrow, James	Huckaby, Sarah	20 Oct	1858
31	Morrow, J.S.	Furr, Mary A.	18 Nov	1856
394	Morton, Charles	Kohlhim, Alma	10 June	1861
671	Motley, John W.	Picket, Eliza	29 June	1861
563,	Mullekin, Dr. J.J.	Ragland, C.M.	16 Feb	1865
363	Mullins, David	Nabours, Mary Frances	1 Jan	1861
612	Mullins, J.W.	Knox, M.L.	15 Oct	1865

PAGE	GROOM	BRIDE	DATE	
507	Murphrey, Felix J.	Lovins, E.A.	18 Apr	1864
648	Murphrey, Rufus J.	Golden, Mary E.	19 Dec	1865
287	Murphy, Wm H.	Wilks, L.E.	17 Jan	1860
230	Musick, G.W.	Stuart, Malissa C.	3 July	1859
718	Musey, Francis	Gray, L.L.	15 Sept	1866
528	Nabors, L.A.	Blue, Mrs. R.L.	20 Sept	1864
194	Nabors, R.C.	Sadler, S.J.	21 Dec	1858
202	Nabors, W.D.	Wiley, Amanda	14 Jan	1859
59	Nason, Richard J.	Miller, Margaret A.	10 Feb	1857
666	Neal, Wiley	Luke, R.A.	17 Jan	1866
459	Neblett, Robert A.	Barbee, Adora E.	14 Feb	1863
321	Neely, Clayton	Rodgers, Narcissa	2 Aug	1860
315	Neely, S.L.	Pickens, Sarah A.	30 July	1860
56	Neil, Samuel J.	Wright, Martha A.	20 Jan	1857
736	Nelson, Robert	Vinson, N.E.	29 Oct	1866
230	Nelson, Z.G.	Pearson, Martha C.C.	10 July	1859
271	Nesbit, William A.	Dunn, Charity A.	7 Dec	1859
216	Newell, S.S.	Mooney, M.J.	24 Mar	1859
783	Newell, William	Grady, Ligg	8 Jan	1866
108	Newman, W.M.	Ward, H.T.	24 Dec	1857
431	Newsom, William H.	Wiley, Emma A.	20 Mar	1862
615	Newton, John (free man)	Malissa, Susan (free)	8 Oct	1865
679	Nix, A.	Calder, Margaret	16 Feb	1860
625	Nixson, W.J.	Vaughn, D.E.	26 Oct	1865
551	Noland, Thomas J.	Holcomb, Lucinda	18 Jan	1865
109	Norwood, George W.	Pollach, Viola J.	6 Jan	1858
	(Viola on bond, Violin on license and ministers return)			
40	Norwood, Liberty W.	Keys, Jane N.	18 Dec	1857
6	Norwood, W.P.L.	Farrer, Mary	22 June	1856
613	Nowlin, W.C.	Robbins, Martha	2 Oct	1865
96	Nowlin, William M.	Young, Martha E.	2 Dec	1857
514	Odle, Noah	Johnson, Mary	24 Dec	1863
569	Oglesby, James P.	Garmon, L.J.	12 Mar	1865
568	Oglesby, James P.	Garman, L.J.	11 Mar	1865
426	Orne, William P.	Dandridge, Elizabeth B.	13 Feb	1862
571	Ornsby, G.W.	Paschall, S.L.	18 Mar	1865
705	Orr, H.C.	Leavell, L.J.	28 July	1866
779	Orr, Samuel	Camfula, Sigga	17 Feb	1866
36	Osborn, James W.B.	Walker, Tabitha Z.	29 Dec	1858
198	Osburn, William	Kelly, Thomas S.	29 Dec	1858
409	Oshields, Alford	Pitts, Catharine	29 Oct	1861
582	Osier, Joseph	Trice, Virginia A.	27 June	1865
126	Overby, N.W.	Grant, Carrie F.	23 Feb	1858
141	Owen, Joseph	Ball, E.E.C.W.	2 May	1858
663	Owens, C.R.	Robins, M.C.	11 Jan	1866
757	Owens, G.A.	Davis, Malvina	17 Dec	1866
292	Owens, Gabriel	McKay, Elizabeth	5 Feb	1860

PAGE	GROOM	BRIDE	DATE
138	Owens, Jno S.	Box, Lucinda	15 Apr 1858
427	Owens, William G.	Hale, Mary J.	20 Feb 1862
	(Mary J. Hale on bond and minister's return. Mary J. Hall on license)		
456	Paine, C.F.	Webster, L.C.	4 Feb 1863
241	Palmer, Joshua	Duggen, Catharine	1 Sept 1859
711	Pannell, B.P.	Armstrong, N.C.	17 Aug 1866
397	Pannell, E.J.	Hensley, Lucinda	5 July 1861
196	Pannell, John R.	Sadler, Martha Jane	22 Dec 1858
401	Pannell, M.R.W.	Hensley, Rosanah	7 Aug 1863
45	Pannell, T.G.	Young, Elizabeth	31 Dec 1856
412	Pannell, W.E.	Dye, Elizabeth	25 Dec 1861
20	Pannell, William J.	Wages, Catharine	4 Sept 1856
199	Pannell, Wm R.	Strickland, Elizabeth	3 Jan 1859
501	Parker, A. Marion	Shorter, Nancy E.	23 Mar 1864
367	Parker, A.	Coker, D.J.	17 Jan 1861
406	Parker, E.	Farrer, E.A.	29 Sept 1861
225	Parker, J.M.	Wesson, Rebecca A.	12 May 1859
157	Parker, W.S.	Coker, Susan	28 July 1858
788	Parks, Henry (free man)	Dawda, Mary (free woman)	27 Dec 1865
754	Parks, James S.	McCullough, Sarah B.	10 Dec 1866
33	Parks, W.J.	Wilson, Elizabeth	25 Nov 1856
666	Parks, William T.	Williams, Martha	16 Jan 1866
525	Parks, W.B.	Hudson, Clester V.	4 Sept 1864
736	Parr, M.T.	Deaton, C.	29 Oct 1866
300	Parr, w.M.	Warren, Sarah Ann	11 Mar 1860
104	Pass, J.H.	Burke, Mary	24 Dec 1857
81	Pate, Richard	Putt, Mary J.	27 Aug 1857
726	Patterson, M.A.	Rogers, Mary A.	4 Oct 1866
643	Paulett, J.A.	Rutledge, Susan E.	28 Dec 1865
140	Payne, Bayan	Ward, Ann	29 Apr 1858
388	Payne, F.M.	Billingsly, Mary C.	18 Apr 1861
478	Payne, J.C.	Smith, A.E.	22 Aug 1863
526	Payne, Phillip	Sandford, Mary	5 Sept 1864
72	Payne, William	Cobb, Sarah A.	3 June 1857
738	Payne, William W.	Potteete, Phoebe A.	3 Oct 1866
137	Pearsall, Jeth	Porter, Frances T.	6 Apr 1858
107	Pearson, B.T.	Calloway, Elvira E.	22 Dec 1857
632	Pegues, M.T.	Stephens, N.A.	18 Nov 1865
255	Pegues, Saml B.	McNiel, Permelia J.	11 Oct 1859
91	Perkins, James S.	Newsom, Mary C.	15 Oct 1857
245	Perkins, John	Buchanan, Josephine	13 Sept 1859
761	Perry, John M.	Middleton, E.M.S.	18 Dec 1866
476	Phillips, A.M.	Caruth, C.E.	17 Sept 1863
386	Phillips, E.S.	Wilkinson, Elizabeth	11 Apr 1861
439	Phillips, Isaac B.	Hubbard, Sarah J.	17 June 1862
338	Phillips, J.F.	Moore, Frances E.	25 Oct 1860
105	Phillips, John H.	McGee, Jane	23 Dec 1857
725	Phillips, L.W.	Raburn, Susan	3 Oct 1866
483	Phillips, Redick	Phillips, Sallie	12 Nov 1863

PAGE	GROOM	BRIDE	DATE	
772	Phillips, S.T.	Reed, Venecia	31 Dec	1866
121	Phillips, William	McGee, Fanny H.	3 Feb	1858
155	Pilcher, Jackson D.	Smith, Delila J.	21 July	1858
170	Pilcher, Marion	Nelson, Jane	28 Sept	1858
507	Pinson, R.A.	Duke, Sinia E.	12 Apr	1864
68	Pipkins, Samuel	Long, Nancy	4 May	1857
117	Pitts, Felbert	Flannagen, Sarah E.	14 Jan	1858
262	Pitts, Ira	Webb, Susan, J.	14 Nov	1858
465	Pitts, Joshua	Pitts, Parmelia	24 May	1863
473	Pitts, Robert	Pegues, Mattie	5 Sept	1863
283	Pitts, S.H.	Jenkins, Martha	4 Jan	1860
289	Pitts, Sanford	Boswell, S.E.	26 Jan	1860
767	Pitts, W.C.	Mounce, Narcissa	25 Dec	1866
312	Pitts, Wm	Reeder, Selina F.	30 June	1860
741	Pittman, James M.	Thornton, L.V.	14 Nov	1866
191	Plant, James M.	Mitchell, Hulet	21 Dec	1858
111	Pogue, R.H.	Abernathy, M.J.	10 Jan	1858
177	Polk, Wm C.	Stanford, Mary E.	19 Oct	1858
172	Pollard, J.M.	Isom, Cordilla	5 Oct	1858
30	Ponders, C.E.	Stegall, Sarah B.	12 Nov	1856
307	Poore, GEorge W.	Franks, Mary E.	12 May	1860
	[George W. Poore on bond and license. Porter on minister's return]			
430	Pope, A.J.	Morgan, Timanda	18 Mar	1862
438	Pope, James A.	Jones, Martha Ann	15 June	1862
122	Potter, H.H.	Davis, Martha C.	2 Feb	1858
226	Porter, Jesse D.	Whitesides, Martha E.	29 May	1859
479	Posey, J.D.	Belk, Emily M.	25 Oct	1863
97	Potter, C.O.	Hill, Margaret E.	20 Nov	1857
149	Potter, James T.	Gasaway, Leoma	14 June	1858
8	Potter, Thomas	Staggs, Sarah	23 June	1856
32	Potts, George	Strong, Virginia C.	20 Nov	1856
497	Potts, Isaac N.	Stuart, G.R.	24 Oct	1863
661	Potts, J.S.	Coats, N.	9 Jan	1866
454	Potts, W.H.	Potts, Elizabeth	11 Jan	1863
674	Powell, H.W.	Lovins, Nannie J.	3 Feb	1866
644	Prewitt, J.T.	Cypert, F.J.	12 Dec	1865
683	Price, George W.	Freeman, Fannie O.	23 Feb	1866
721	Price, John	Screws, Fany	25 Sept	1866
769	Price, Joseph	Wilson, Mary E.	26 Dec	1866
132	Price, Rufus M.	Cooper, Zuleika	16 Mar	1858
219	Price, Thos J.	McCuskey, O.A.C.	3 Apr	1859
331	Pritchard, G.C.	Russell, Sarah J.	27 Sept	1860
259	Pritchard, J.W.	Brown, Margaret A.	3 Nov	1859
443	Pritchard, R.E.	Russell, Linea	3 Sept	1862
291	Proctor, C.P.	Howell, E.A.	1 Feb	1860
629	Prude, Jesse W.	Turner, Fannie A.	15 Nov	1865
626	Prude, Joseph	Lesly, A.J.	1 Nov	1865
13	Purden, Alexander C.	Phillips, Susan A.	24 July	1856
721	Purdon, Thomas I.	Hutchinson, Sarah E.	21 Sept	1866

PAGE	GROOM	BRIDE	DATE
162	Purvine, D.S.	Hicks, M.J.	25 Aug 1858
160	Purvis, Isaac C.	Shelton, Alvina Jane	31 Aug 1858
79	Putt, A.J.	Pate, Mary Frances	29 May 1857
105	Putt, John	Dunaway, Letha Ann	23 Dec 1857
650	Putt, John F.	Thomas, Mary F.	16 Dec 1863
306	Putt, Washington	Dunaway, Sarah E.	10 May 1860
564	Puttman, John F.	Phillips, Nancy Jane	22 Feb 1865
271	Ragan, Charles C.	Combs, Mary E.	7 Oct 1859
297	Ragland, John L.	Good, A. Alicia	22 Feb 1860
59	Rainey, John C.	Payne, S.M.	12 Feb 1857
463	Rains, J.L.	Matthews, Ann	15 Apr 1863
305	Rowsey, Thomas	Rivers, Tabitha H.	6 May 1860
418	Randolph, Tolbert F.	Gidden, Elizabeth	5 Dec 1861
302	Rasberry, B.F.	Kirkpatrick, Jane	25 Apr 1860
437	Ray, James M.	Alton, Carrie L.	20 June 1862
338	Ray, Joseph G.	Phillips, Rachel J.	24 Oct 1860
682	Rayborn, N.M.	Gregory, Sarah A.	21 Feb 1866
335	Rayner, Wm	Bolen, Datia A.	25 Oct 1860
164	Rea, John	Hall, Martha	1 Sept 1858
282	Reaves, J.B.	Jarvis, M.E.	25 Jan 1860
289	Reaves, W.D.	Speck, Mary Ann	21 Jan 1860
165	Reed, John B.	Grant, Sarah Jane	1 Sept 1858
318	Reed, R.J.	McNeil, Anna	14 July 1860
610	Reeder, Joseph	Milam, Sue J.	25 Sept 1865
157	Reeves, H.G.	Reaves, Virginia	28 July 1858
42	Regan, Abner J.	McCraw, Matilda	24 Dec 1856
703	Regan, John T.	Griffin, L.A.	23 July 1866
657	Reid, J.F.	Davis, Julyan	28 Dec 1865
173	Reid, R.G.	Fuller, Sarah W.	12 Oct 1858
782	Renneau, Washington [A man of color]	Clark, Mary (Free woman)	11 Jan 1866
743	Rhodes, L.J.	Andrew, M.J.	19 Nov 1866
337	Rhyne, J.W.	Hill, Martha	1 Nov 1860
696	Rice, James M.	Heard, A.L.	4 June 1866
272	Richardson, P.L.	Hale, Margaret E.	11 Dec 1859
224	Richman, Berry	Harvey, Mary A.	8 May 1859
771	Riggan, B.J.	Whiteside, Paralee J.	29 Dec 1866
156	Ritchie, John	Wood, Martha D.	27 July 1858
368	Rivers, E.F.	Alexander, Susan E.	22 Jan 1861
374	Rivers, Joel L.	Ford, Mary E.	31 Jan 1861
231	Roach, Henry O.	Teague, Susan C.	14 July 1859
351	Roach, James H.	Deel, P.A. Florence	20 Dec 1860
333	Roach, W.E.	Hamelton, Charity	20 Oct 1860
624	Robbins, E.J.	Wells, E.S.	24 Oct 1865
400	Robbins, G.B.	Friday, Margaret Jane	3 Aug 1861
773	Robbins, G.J.	Thomas, Martha A.A.A.E.	31 Dec 1866
727	Robbins, J.H.	Hale, Rachel E.	8 Oct 1866
353	Robbins, James W.	Dyson, Polly C.	19 Dec 1860
740	Robbins, W.J.	Jarvis, Margaret E.	6 Nov 1866

PAGE	GROOM	BRIDE	DATE
248	Roberson, H.S.	Billingsly, Lucy M.	22 Sept 1859
249	Roberson, John P.	McWhorter, Ruth C.	28 Sept 1859
767	Roberts, A.	Roberts, Jane	22 Dec 1866
644	Roberts, David J.	Moore, A.S.	9 Dec 1865
308	Roberts, Dixon	Saven, Jane	16 May 1860
489	Roberts, John	Caldwell, Nancy E.	18 Dec 1863
477	Roberts, Killis M.	Ward, Barbara A.	3 Sept 1863
753	Roberts, R.D.	Ried, Martha A.	10 Dec 1866
135	Roberts, John L.	Jolly, L.S.C.	20 Mar 1858
114	Robertson, Saml H.	Pitts, Emily F.	12 Jan 1858
608	Robinson, James D.	Robinson, Martha J.	25 Sept 1865
38	Robinson, T.W.	Pitts, Lucinda S.	9 Dec 1856
251	Robinson, Wm K.	Foster, Mrs. Pricilla	31 Sept 1859
734	Rodgers, D.S.	Roberts, Louisa C.	27 Oct 1866
257	Rodgers, David	Coon, Nancy	20 Oct 1859
544	Rodgers, H.F.	Bradley, D.B.	31 Dec 1864
488	Rodgers, John	Bradly, Nancy	14 Dec 1863
240	Rodgers, Joseph	Hardin, Elizabeth	26 Aug 1859

[Josiah Rodgers on bond and license - Joseph Rodgers signature]

PAGE	GROOM	BRIDE	DATE
381	Rodgers, Samuel H.	Goggins, R.J.F.	7 Mar 1861
308	Root, T.J.	Bolton, Matilda M.	17 May 1860
46	Rootes, P.G.	Robbinson, Elizabeth	1 Jan 1857
315	Rosenan, Newton	Dickson, Margaret	8 July 1860
744	Ross, C.L.	Hall, M.E.	21 Nov 1866
548	Ross, John	Moore, Mary C.	12 Jan 1865
61	Ross, S.H.	Cunningham, Elizabeth V.	17 Feb 1857
669	Ross, T.A.	Morrow, Sarah A.	18 Jan 1866
77	Ross, Thomas A.	Farrer, Milly B.	21 July 1857
477	Rouch, William	Coker, Mary A.	6 Oct 1863
43	Rouzer, William H.	Earle, Mary	24 Dec 1856
14	Rowan, Daniel	Boatman, Lydia A.	23 July 1856
710	Rowan, G.M.	Reid, Mary L.	12 Aug 1866
35	Rowan, James	Bacon, E.J.	4 Dec 1856
384	Rowan, W.P.	Chamblis, Susan	2 Apr 1863
301	Rowe, W.T.	Ware, Mary	30 Mar 1860
534	Rowsey, T.G.	Hudson, S.J.	9 Nov 1864
305	Rowsey, Thomas	Rivers, Tabitha H.	6 May 1860
547	Russell, James	Windham, E.F.	12 Jan 1865
446	Russell, James F.	Whitesides, Margaret E.	29 Sept 1862
598	Russell, John A.	Russell, Margaret C.	7 Sept 1865
288	Russell, John G., Jr.	Warren, Mary S.	18 Jan 1860
642	Russell, L.N.	Mayhen, M.E.	5 Dec 1865
533	Russell, Mathew M.	Dean, Ann	8 Nov 1864
747	Russell, Thos. L.	Grisham, Sarah A.	4 Dec 1866
537	Russell, W.H.H.	Nubee, Mildred	17 Nov 1864
533	Rutledge, Jackson	Lindsey, Martha E.	6 Nov 1864
263	Rutledge, James H.	Edwards, Mary A.	20 Nov 1859
720	Rutledge, John	Warren, M.J.	20 Sept 1866
536	Rutledge, Wm	Hammons, Mary L.	16 Nov 1864
142	Ryan, Thomas	Lyons, Margarett	6 May 1858
639	Rye, Thomas J.	Mallory, S.A.	29 Nov 1865

PAGE	GROOM	BRIDE	DATE
655	Sadler, H.P.	Simms, E.C.	11 Jan 1866
716	Sage, Jefferson C.	Harrison, Susan L.	4 Sept 1866
15	Sanders, B.F.	Feemster, M.A.	29 July 1856
10	Sanders, Charles W.	Hudson, Sarah M.	17 July 1856
172	Sanders, Elisha	Sanders, Aminda S.	5 Oct 1858
218	Sanders, H.C.	Jones, Mary E.	3 Apr 1859
411	Sanders, Hardiman H.	Deaton, Julia	31 Oct 1861
492	Sanders, Henry	Green, M.E.	14 Jan 1864
307	Sanders, Joseph H.	Motley, Clara T.	15 May 1860
168	Sanders, M.S.	Gray, Martha A.	8 Sept 1858
692	Sanders, R.G.	McDonal, M.P.	16 Apr 1866
86	Sanders, R.J.	Motley, Martha W.	10 Apr 1857
541	Sanders, Thomas	Harrison, Candis	20 Dec 1864
638	Sanders, Wesley	Russell, Elizabeth J.	28 Nov 1865
127	Sanders, Wm H.	Shingleton, Charlotte R.	23 Feb 1858
251	Sanford, James	Strain, L.J.	2 Oct 1859
694	Sappington, R.D.	Suddeth, Manerva	12 May 1866
630	Satawhite, W.H.	Lamar, M.A.	15 Nov 1865
175	Satterwhite, Soloman	Morris, Elizabeth	11 Oct 1858
44	Saul, William	Millsaps, Nancy E.	30 Dec 1856
27	Sausaman, J.A.	Bright, Ann	19 Oct 1856
269	Savins, Jackson	Fortune, Cynthia	1 Dec 1859
781	Scales, Elijah	Williams, Mariot	(No Dates ca 9 Jan 1866)
653	Schrews, J.M.	Coker, Nancy	21 Dec 1865
759	Scott, A.M.	Cox, Martha A.	18 Dec 1866
120	Scott, J.F.	Wesson, Letty	28 Jan 1858
88	Scott, J.W.	Bridges, E.A.	23 Sept 1857
499	Scott, Jno	Russell, Mary F.	17 Feb 1864
310	Scott, W.A.	Saul, N.E.	21 June 1860
111	Scott, W.T.H.	Coleman, Laura	31 Dec 1857
672	Screw, Simon	Terrell, Mary	5 Feb 1866
303	Screws, James	Pool, Elizabeth	10 Apr 1860
331	Screws, Obediah	Oglesbee, Tilda A.	28 Sept 1860
373	Seal, A.J.	Ware, Mary Addie	5 Feb 1861
116	Seal, George	Friffin, Elizabeth	14 Jan 1858
189	See, A.J.	Camp, Leona J.	25 Nov 1858
658	Setzler, G.A.	High, Mary	1 Jan 1866
213	Setzler, J.B.	Haran, Elizabeth	15 Mar 1859
770	Sexton, J.H.	Thomas, Mary E.	27 Dec 1866
393	Sexton, J.W.	Williamson, Sarah	9 June 1861
130	Shaw, Archibald A.	Proctor, Epsey	7 Mar 1858
697	Shaw, N.A.	McCraw, Millie	27 June 1866
82	Shaw, W.A.	Shanon, Mary Kate	1 Sept 1857
360	Shaw, W.W.	Farra, Susan	27 Dec 1860
586	Shawver, J.B.	Frierson, Harriet E.	11 July 1865
440	Shelton, David	Hall, Nancy	24 July 1862
18	Shelton, John W.	Russell, Sarah E.	24 Aug 1856

PAGE	GROOM	BRIDE	DATE	
498	Shelton, John W.	Early, Mrs. Eliza	20 Jan	1864
269	Shelton, Patrick	Braden, Nancy E.	30 Nov	1859
426	Shelton, S.W.	Freeman, E.C.	15 Feb	1862
16	Shelton, William H.	Ferrell, Sarah E.	6 Aug	1856
80	Sheppard, R.J.	Neely, S.H.	27 Aug	1857
176	Sherman, James J.	Crain, Martha	21 Oct	1858
110	Shettles, J.E.	Buchanan, Rebecca J.	28 Dec	1857
451	Shive, Clinton T.	Furr, Jane A.	12 Dec	1862

[Clinton T. Shire on minister's return]

112	Shurley, O.P.	Perry, T.R.C.	9 Jan	1858
61	Simmons, Edward	Hooper, A.E.	19 Feb	1857
766	Simmons, Thos M.	NO BRIDES NAME	22 Dec	1866

[Bond only without brides name]

129	Simpson, John W.	Black, Eliza	2 Mar	1858
22	Simpson, Thompson M.	Simpson, Elizabeth A.	16 Sept	1856
756	Sims, R.H.	Solomon, T.E.	18 Dec	1866
513	Singleton, W.P.H.	Duncan, Emeline	19 May	1864
209	Skinner, R.L.	Williams, Sarah C.	2 Mar	1859
479	Skinner, W.R.	Shelton, Mary J.	12 Oct	1863
789	Sloan, Ned (free man)	Wilkins, patsy (free)	29 Dec	1865
609	Sloan, T.B.	Henry, Mary L.	28 Sept	1865
603	Smith, B.F.	Epting, Mary J.	18 Sept	1865
556	Smith, D.J.	Pitts, Kessiah	2 Feb	1865
776	Smith, David L.	Browning, Susan J.	4 Jan	1867
55	Smith, F.C.C.	Johnson, Rebecca	21 Jan	1857
621	Smith, J.L.	Pilcher, Mary	16 Oct	1865
652	Smith, J.H.	Gardiner, Nancy R.	19 Dec	1866
695	Smith, F.M.	Robertson, M.A.	20 June	1866
416	Smith, J.W.	Arnold, Margaret	1 Dec	1861
440	Smith, James	McFarland, Mary	29 July	1862
200	Smith, James	Clements, Mary N.	4 Jan	1859
461	Smith, John F.	Gidden, Martha J.	19 Mar	1863
511	Smith, John W.	Skinner, Easter C.	3 May	1864
421	Smith, Leroy, H.	Hardy, Martha Ann	29 Dec	1861
573	Smith, Nip	Barrow, Malvina	10 Apr	1865
597	Smith, T.S.	Miller, M.A.	15 Aug	1865
450	Smith, Thomas J.	Nabor, Matilda C.	12 Dec	1862
377	Smith, William	Wheatley, Elizabeth	6 Feb	1861
723	Smith, Wm B.	Lawrence, Eliza J.	26 Sept	1866
709	Smyth, M.M.	Stone, Mattie M.	7 Aug	1866
378	Sneed, A.D.	Hooker, M.F.	8 Feb	1861
201	Sneed, A.L.	Sullivan, Susan	6 Jan	1859
402	Sneed, M.D.	McGehee, Charlit Josephine	18 Aug	1861
685	Snider, A.B.	Camel, Martha J.	4 Mar	1866
772	Snider, B.F.	Mobley, J.T.	30 Dec	1866
429	Snider, G.W.	Henry, Elizabeth Ann	2 Mar	1862
281	Snider, S.	Duff, M.E.	17 Jan	1860

[L. Snider on license and minister's return. S. Snider on bond]

PAGE	GROOM	BRIDE	DATE
456	Snipes, J.T.	Wells, Mannerva	30 Jan 1863
319	Snipes, L.T.	Ried, Margaret R.	24 July 1860
10	Snipes, Sion	Stone, Caroline	9 July 1856
263	Soutere, Henry B.	Mounce, Emily F.	15 Nov 1859
361	South, Wm D.	Dillard, Mary	27 Dec 1860
407	Sparks, Soloman	Buchanan, Martha M.	1 Oct 1861
384	Spears, M.E.	Long, Nancy C.	18 Mar 1861
228	Speck, George	Reeves, Melissa	20 June 1859
31	Speck, James W.	Langley, Martha E.	20 Nov 1856
356	Speck, W.S.	Speck, Mary M.	21 Dec 1860
88	Spencer, S.B.	Fletcher, L.C.	24 Sept 1857
506	Spencer, Samuel B.	Smith, Jane	11 Apr 1864
436	Stamp, James	Only, Rachel	7 May 1862
756	Stanford, Henry C.	Brown, Sarah E.	14 Dec 1866
706	Stanford, M.H.	Redus, M.A.	3 Aug 1866
162	Stack, P.B.	Young, Mary Ann	18 Aug 1858
21	Staggs, James M.	Jamison, Clarentine	13 Sept 1856
1	Staggs, John M.	Berry, Sirena	7 May 1856
537	Starks, T.T.	Goodman, Sallie A.	20 Nov 1864
750	Staten, M.F.	Pannell, Polina L.	5 Dec 1866
517	Staten, R.B.	Gillispie, Sallie E.	20 June 1864
261	Steelman, W.H.	Hudson, Elizabeth	2 Nov 1859
278	Stegall, Jeremiah G., Jr.	Jenkins, Elizabeth	27 Dec 1859
524	Stegall, Wm H.	Lantrip, N.E.	12 Mar 1864
636	Stegall, Wm H.	McMahen, E.C.	22 Nov 1865
53	Stephen, John A.	Ball, Sarah H.	13 Jan 1857
158	Stephen, E.P.	Hightower, Harriett A.	29 July 1858
647	Stewart, B.W.	Rutledge, Mrs. M.L.	13 Dec 1865
745	Stewart, J.B.	Roach, Charity	21 Nov 1866
747	Stewart, J.F.	Crim, Mrs. S.C.	30 Nov 1866
451	Stoats, Joseph	Todd, Mary Jane	28 Dec 1862
415	Stone, E.	Henderson, Mary Ann	21 Nov 1861
185	Stone, John S.T.	Bell, Julia Ann	18 Nov 1858
556	Story, William	Knight, Mrs. Sarah J.	31 Jan 1865
584	Stovall, A.R.	Thomason, Rebecca A.	27 June 1865
702	Stovall, W.P.	Green, Mary E.	11 July 1866
670	Strain, Brice B.	Cochran, Paralee	25 Jan 1866
93	Strait, C.L.	Mastison, Rhoda M.	8 Nov 1857
478	Stringfellow, William	Moore, S.F.	16 Oct 1863
689	Stroud, T.M.	Dunum, M.A.	22 Mar 1866
17	Suferman, Samuel S.	Donavan, Julia C.	12 Aug 1856
301	Suggett, J.E.	Sissan, Elizabeth	18 Mar 1860
325	Suggs, Brantley	Raner, Elizabeth	24 Aug 1860
313	Sullivan, G.C.	Carr, Eliza A.	30 June 1860
452	Sullivan, J.E.	Barnes, Polly Ann	1 Jan 1863
448	Sullivan, J.P.	Stark, Matilda	18 Nov 1862
688	Sullivan, William H.	Maxey, Mary E.	16 Mar 1866
589	Sullivan, Wm S.	Hemp, Luzia E.E.	22 July 1865

PAGE	GROOM	BRIDE	DATE	
116	Swarford, John	Portwood, Mariam	13 Jan	1858
594	Swearinger, W.H.	Brown, Mrs. Susan A.	17 Aug	1865
449	Swindoll, Wm C.	Plant, Susan C.	14 Dec	1862
188	Swinson, James H.	Youngblood, Lucinda J.	24 Nov	1858
119	Sword, William	Howard, Milly M.	22 Jan	1858
545	Tankersley, George	Rucker, Susan	28 Dec	1864
256	Tankersley, J.F.	Calhoun, Cornelia	17 Oct	1859
212	Tapley, G.W.	Dye, Sarah A.	10 mar	1859
599	Tate, H.B.	Johnson, Sarah F.	10 Sept	1865
132	Tate, John W.	Hampton, Caroline	19 Mar	1859
376	Taylor, John	Pitts, Frances	7 Feb	1861
211	Taylor, John L.	Hudson, Margaret A.	8 Mar	1859
260	Taylor, P.J.	James, M.A.	26 Oct	1859
698	Taylor, J.W.	Mann, Margaret	3 July	1866
102	Taylor, Uriah	Thompson, Epsey C.	30 Dec	1857
64	Tedder, F.	Meek, Elizabeth	26 Mar	1857
57	Teeter, Joseph L.	Smith, Lucinda	22 Jan	1857
576	Temple, C.R.	Duncan, E.M.	23 Apr	1865
344	Templeton, J.W.	Kennedy, Martha Jane	25 Nov	1860
558	Terrell, J.M.	Bass, Frances	4 Feb	1865
199	Terry, William D.	Miller, Mary M.	29 Dec	1858
623	Thomas, P.R.	Duff, A.V.	21 Oct	1865
640	Thomas, T.A.	Burnett, Mrs. R.C.	2 Dec	1865
622	Thomason, G.C.	Fears, A.P. [Mrs. Agatha Fears]	20 Oct	1865
512	Thomason, James B.	Dandridge, Esther F.	12 Apr	1864
407	Thomason, Turner	Wilch, Mary E.	8 Oct	1861
76	Thomason, W.A.	Root, Calie	20 July	1857
535	Thompson, Isaac	Rucker, Amanda A.	10 Nov	1864
517	Thompson, James A.	Satterwhite, M.A.	31 July	1864
210	Thompson, Nathan	Morris, Nancy	5 Mar	1859
493	Thompson, Wm	Jones, Lucy	14 Jan	1864
564	Tidwell, F.J.	Barnett, M.J.	26 Feb	1865
204	Tollison, John	Roberts, Mary A.	20 Jan	1859
675	Trailer, James	Nolen, Mary	4 Feb	1866
434	Tucker, S.J.	Kelly, Ellen O.	23 Apr	1862
325	Tucker, S.J.	Reid, Caroline	14 Aug	1860
612	Tucker, Samuel	Flanagan, Mary	29 Sept	1865
139	Turner, Moses	Berry, Manerva T.	2 May	1858
502	Tutor, Allen H.	Johnson, Mary F.	24 Mar	1864
458	Tutor, H.D.	Foster, Jane	11 Feb	1863
698	Tutor, H.L.	Johnson, Julyan	3 July	1866
708	Tutor, Jefferson	Herndon, Frances	7 Aug	1866
755	Tutor, John A.	Connell, Nancy	13 Dec	1866
575	Tutor, Richard	Tutor, A.H.	13 Apr	1865
579	Tutor, S.J.	Beard, R.M.	23 May	1865
285	Tutor, W. Henry	Herndon, Aley	15 Jan	1860
299	Tynes, H.C.	Mobley, M.C.	4 Mar	1860

PAGE	GROOM	BRIDE	DATE	
593	Vance, J.B.	Ward, L.E.	10 Aug	1865
9	Vance, P.A.	Bumgardner, Narcissa M.	3 July	1856
174	Varner, e.T.	Merrett, Caroline	20 Oct	1858
155	Vaughan, E.H.	Bell, P.A.	18 July	1858
595	Vaughan, J.C.	McCoy, P.F.	19 Aug	1865
345	Vaughan, W.P.	Reeder, D.E.	19 Nov	1860
111	Vaughn, J.W.	Graham, Elvira J.	30 Dec	1857
704	Vaughn, John W.	Berks, Sarah D.	27 July	1866
127	Vicke, jasper	Steel, Mary	23 Feb	1858
252	Viles, Alfred	Burks, Mary A.	2 Oct	1859
128	Vincent, Thomas	Bice, Martha	25 Feb	1858
668	Vinson, George W.	Buchanan, Sarah	17 Jan	1866
471	Vinyard, B.R.	Canon, Martha J.	28 Aug	1863
542	Wade, B.H.	Andrews, Rebecca Latitia	25 Dec	1864
657	Wade, R.H.	Andrews, N.J.	28 Dec	1865
419	Waggener, W.H.	Moore, Mary E.	18 Dec	1861
733	Wait, M.L.	Vinson, Amanda	28 Oct	1866
661	Waldo, J.M.	Hughey, Mary J.	7 Jan	1866
221	Waldrop, John	Petty, S.J.	18 Apr	1859
543	Waldrop, John	Anderson, Mrs. A.	28 Dec	1864
249	Waldrop, John H.	Hutcheson, Nancy J.	25 Sept	1859
620	Waldrop, W.F.	Donaldson, Sarah E.	12 Oct	1865
375	Waldrop, William C.	Barry, Kate R.	30 Jan	1861
78	Walker, John C.	Stone, Mary	9 Aug	1857
287	Walker, John W.	Watts, Elizabeth	19 Jan	1860
12	Walker, Levi W.	Porter, Martha L.	13 July	1856
15	Walker, L.V.	Moses, Jane	5 Aug	1856
165	Walker, Stephen A.	Stephens, Mary	2 Sept	1858
762	Wall, W.A.J.	Hopt, C.C.	19 Dec	1866
2	Wallace, Brison	McNeely, Sarah	24 May	1856
515	Wallace, James P.	Burrow, Ann M.	5 Mar	1864
420	Ward, B.S.	Ware, Sarah R.	24 Dec	1861
258	Ware, Demba	Caldwell, Nancy A.	20 Oct	1859
502	Ward, E.J.	Phillips, Martha J.	19 Mar	1864
543	Ward, L.M.	Province, J.	25 Dec	1864
67	Ward, Thomas	Winder, Harriet L.	2 May	1857
417	Ward, Ugenin	Cobb, J.A.	1 Dec	1861
660	Ward, Wm R.	Brown, Mary A.	10 Jan	1866
453	Wardlaw, J.M.	Busby, Mary H.	4 Jan	1863
406	Ware, Elam	Collins, Canzider	3 Oct	1861
682	Ware, W.T.	Gregory, M.H.C.	15 Feb	1866
567	Warren, A.	McNeely, Ruth	9 Mar	1865
350	Warren, Ezekell	McNeely, Nancy	10 Dec	1860
294	Warren, Frederick	McNeely, Hamet M.	18 Feb	1860
334	Warren, William	Wallis, Rachiel	21 Oct	1860
268	Washington, John C.	Lewellen, M.A.	4 Dec	1859
267	Watts, T.J.	Potts, Martha K.	30 Nov	1859

PAGE	GROOM	BRIDE	DATE	
310	Weatherall, Allen S.	Rodgers, Mary A.	14 June	1860
300	Weatherall, J.H.	Smith, S.A.	14 Mar	1860
212	Weatherall, R.A.	Coleman, Emma F.	8 Mar	1859
208	Weatherall, William S.	Tucker, Jane	17 Feb	1859
33	Welborn, John S.	Hutcheson, M.A.	27 Nov	1856
628	Welch, J.C.	Hill, Frances	14 Nov	1865
180	Welch, Thomas	Churchill, Martha	3 Nov	1858
773	Wells, J.P.	Grisham, M.C.	31 Dec	1866
415	Wells, James A.	Calder, Rebecca	18 Nov	1861
154	Wells, John B.	Brandon, Mary	18 July	1858
785	Wells, Joseph (free man)	Weatherall, Rachel (free)	3 Jan	1866
728	Wells, M.M.	Grisham, Sarah J.	10 Oct	1866
707	Wells, W.J.	Ball, Martha	6 Aug	1866
343	Wells, W.W.	Morris, Martha C.	22 Nov	1860
328	West, William R.	Carlisle, Martha	13 Sept	1860
399	Wester, A.T.	Nowlin, Ann	21 July	1861
84	Wester, James M.	Godfrey, Nancy C.	8 Sept	1857
382	Wester, W.R.	Wester, Eliza	11 Mar	1861
523	Weatherford, C.C.	Duke, Ann	13 Aug	1864
246	Wheatley, R.P.	Kidd, Margaret	22 July	1859
691	Wheeler, F.M.	Simpson, A.M.P.	6 Apr	1866
341	White, J.S.	Middleton, M.J.	7 Nov	1860
198	White, James S.	Henry, Marianne	28 Dec	1858
266	White, Colomon J.	Carter, Martha M.	30 Nov	1859
422	White, W.R.	Wilkerson, Mary	14 May	1862
373	White, Wm H.	Satterwhite, Mary E.	31 Jan	1861
401	White, William	Wester, Frances A.	12 Aug	1861
554	Whitlow, W.D.	Robinson, M.A.	28 Jan	1865
357	Whitlow, P.W.	Smith, Sarah	21 Dec	1860
	[Returned - Not completed]			
386	Whitlow, P.W.	Sappington, Mary M.	7 Apr	1861
40	Whitesides, Hugh	Wilder, Amy P.	23 Dec	1856
54	Whitesides, Wm H.	Harper, Jane M.	15 Jan	1857
571	Whitten, C.W.	Ellis, Mary L.	22 Mar	1865
529	Whitten, J.N.	Marr, J.P.	29 Sept	1864
429	Whitten, John H.L.	Carter, Nancy E.	1 Mar	1862
43	Wicker, D.B.R.	Richmond, Mary Ann	30 Dec	1856
716	Widenor, Samuel	Harrison, Jennie	1 Sept	1866
438	Wilburn, Dority	Reader, Eliza	8 June	1862
159	Wiley, Martin L.	Camp, Margarett	5 Aug	1858
375	Wiley, W.L.	Caldwell, Sarah A.	30 Jan	1861
621	Wiley, Wm J.	Switzer, Mary E.	17 Oct	1866
264	Wilks, M.J.	Johnson, M.M.	24 Nov	1859
200	Williams, Charley	Dorsey, Tabitha C.	30 Dec	1858
144	Williams, D.C.	McGowen, Nancy A.	18 May	1858
183	Williams, G.W.	Willard, Mareah	9 Nov	1858
531	Williams, J.J.	Goodwin, Mary	13 Oct	1864
29	Williams, Thomas H.	Crawford, Elizabeth J.	4 Nov	1856
743	Williams, Thos J.	Freeman, C.M.	19 Nov	1866
232	Williams, William	Perry, Ruth	21 July	1859
729	Williams, William	Martin, Deborah	12 Oct	1866

PAGE	GROOM	BRIDE	DATE	
50	Williamson, James H.	Foster, Sarah E.	6 June	1857
480	Williamson, L.C.	Mathews, Rhody	27 Oct	1863
444	Wilmoth, Mack	Leach, Martha Ann Frances	9 Sept	1865
566	Wilson, Benjamin	Swafford, L.M.	27 Feb	1865
374	Wilson, James K.	Little, Mary E.	3 Feb	1861
316	Wilson, James R.	Owens, Sarah A.	10 July	1860
346	Wilson, John A.	White, Jane	2 Dec	1860
749	Wilson, Marion C.	Huckbee, C.A.	5 Dec	1866
735	Wilson, w.J.	Mayhew, Emeline	27 Oct	1866
474	Winders, H.H.	Souter, Emily F.	12 Sept	1863
283	Windham, Peyton H.	Coker, Mary M.	16 Jan	1860
343	Windham, S.S.	Coker, M.H.B.	15 Nov	1860
604	Wingo, J.A.	Shelton, N.E.	25 Sept	1865
570	Winn, F.M.	Caldwell, Margaret	16 Oct	1865
611	Winn, G.W.	Vinyard, E.J.	28 Sept	1865
530	Witcher, James F.	Brandon, Sarah A.	27 Oct	1864
715	Witcher, William	Lankford, Mary	1 Sept	1866
346	Witt, W.A.	Phillips, Naomi	30 Nov	1860
89	Wolf, J.H.	Pollard, Julia Ann	29 Sept	1857
7	Wolf, Joseph	Walker, Rebecca	22 June	1856
107	Wood, F.M.	Simmon, Mary E.	24 Dec	1857
146	Wood, J.B.	Brooksher, Sarah	25 May	1858
710	Wood, James P.	Hodges, Sarah E.	11 Aug	1866
589	Wood, James W.	Funk, Mary H.	26 July	1856
99	Wood, Moses	Abernathy, Sarah M.	3 Dec	1857
424	Wood, P.W.	Singleton, Sinia D.	29 Jan	1861
160	Wood, Thomas J.	Baker, Martha E.	12 Aug	1858
180	Wood, Wm J.	Jarnigan, Sarah E.	1 Nov	1858
700	Woodard, J.T.	Carothers, Caty	7 July	1866
693	Woods, Geo D.	Wood, Mary E.	5 May	1866
366	Woodward, A.G.	Dickson, Sarah P.	14 Jan	1861
244	Workman, Wm C.	Jones, Elizabeth M.	14 Sept	1859
129	Worley, Elijah E.	Martin, Augusta	2 Mar	1858
722	Wray, John F.	Wiley, Sue	27 Sept	1866
468	Wylie, James M.	Carter, Mary C.	5 July	1863
462	Wynn, T.L.	Swafford, C.A.	28 June	1863
420	Yager, Adam	Walker, Nancy W.	26 Dec	1861
348	Yancy, James C.	Echols, Martha D.	3 Dec	1860
618	Yocum, John W.	Brandon, Margaret E.	10 Oct	1865
634	Young, Thomas N.	Mobley, Kisy	23 Nov	1865
364	Young, S.P.	McKeowan, Sarah	8 Jan	1861
503	Young, W.G.	Collins, S.C.	7 Jan	1864
425	Young, W.J.	Ritear, Margaret C.	16 Feb	1862
635	Youngblood, A.W.	Johnson, M.E.	21 Nov	1865
640	Youngblood, C.J.	Morrison, S.E.	30 Nov	1865
74	Youngblood, John G.	Pearsall, Charlotte	16 July	1857
452	Younger, Wm	Shelton, Martha Ann	28 Dec	1862
203	Zinn, A.J.	Steele, Cynthia C.	20 Jan	1859
737	Zinn, Henry P.	Blaylock, Mrs. M.C.	1 Nov	1866
191	Zinn, J.C.	Cooper, Charlotte	7 Dec	1858

BRIDE INDEX
GROOM SURNAME IN BRACKETS

Abernathy, Caroline (Eubanks)
Abernathy, M.E. (Johnson
Abernathy, Martha E. (Ivy
Abernathy, Mary (Abernathy)
Abernathy, M.J. (Pogue)
Abernathy, Sarah M. (Wood)
Adams, Emily (Falkner)
Adams, Miss L.D. (Alexander)
Adams, Rachail L. (Jeter)
Adams, Sarah A.E. (Blansit)
Addison, J.S. (Hair)
Alexander, Dorcas (Gordon)
Alexander, Margaret R. (Hall)
Alexander, Mary E. (Hubbard)
Alexander, Mrs. M.W. (Johnson)
Alexander, Susan E. (Rivers)
Allen, Martha P. (McDaniel)
Allen, Nancy (Golding)
Allen, Susan P. (Allen)
Allman, Ellen C. (Hearn)
Alton, Carrie L. (Ray)
Anarsan, Eliza A. (Cobb)
Anderson, Mrs. A. (Waldrop)
Anderson, Mary E. (Ervin)
Anderson, Harriet E. (Hill)
Anderson, Nira (Cobb)
Andrew, M.J. (Rhodes)
Andrews, Louisa (Garner)
Andrews, N.J. (Wade)
Andrews, Rebecca (Wade)
Andrews, Sarah J. (Hutcherson)
Albritton, M.A. (Gory)
Allbritton, Emily (Miller)
Armstrong, M.C. (Pannell)
Arnold, Margaret (Smith
Astin, Mary J. (Cooper)

Bacon, E.J. (Rowan)
Bacon, Harriet P. (Dickson)
Baggett, M.A. (Hale)
Bailey, Adaline R. (Luke)
Bailey, Elizabeth (Luke)
Bailey, Lou E. (Berry)
Bailey, Malissa (Bailey)
BAiley, S.C. (Bailey)
Bailey, Sarah F. (Luke)
Baker, Martha E. (Wood)
Baker, M.E. (Evans)

Baker, Mollie E. (Bailey)
Baker, Sinia (Bigham)
Baker, Sarah A. (Mayberry)
Ball, C.E. (Gambrell)
Ball, E.E.C.W. (Owen)
Ball, J. Anna (Brunes?)
Ball, Jemmie (Huffstickler)
Ball, Martha (Wells)
Ball, Mary Ann (Daniel)
Ball, Mary Jane (Grant)
Ball, Sarah (Stephen)
Barbee, Adora (Neblett)
Barham, mary (Burton)
Barksdale, J.E. (McCarter)
Barlow, Lucy M.P. (Cruse)
Barnes, Polly (Sullivan)
Barnett, E.A. (Glasgow)
Barnett, M.J. (Tidwell)
Barr, F.C. (Mayben)
Barr, Sarah E. (Marlin)
Barrow, Malvina (Smith)
Barry, Katc R. (Waldrop)
Bass, Francis (Terrell)
Bass, Susan (Daniel)
Bates, E.A. (Cayce)
Beard, Dovey (Cornelius)
Beard, R.M. (Tutor)
Beasley, Emeline (Grisham)
Beasley, Mary J. (McCraw)
Beauchamp, M.P. (Leathers)
Beauchamp, Selina (McCraw)
Beckham, Elizabeth H. (Moore)
Beckham, H.A. (Crawford)
Beeks, A.J. (Campbell)
Been, P.E. (Been)
Beene, Mary (Billingsley)
Belk, Emily M. (Posey)
Bell, Amanda (Duff)
Bell, Isabella (Herndon)
Bell, Julia A. (Stone)
Bell, M.A. (Clayton)
Bell, P.A. (Vaughan)
Bennett, Mary (Mitchell)
Benson, Elizabeth Ann (Christian)
Benson, Francis M. (Benson)
Benson, S.A. (Herron)
Berks, Sarah (Vaughn)
Berry, Manerva (Turner)

Berry, Marisa (Findly)
Berry, Sirena (Staggs)
Betts, Margaret (Mauldin)
Bevill, Thorzay (Bailey)
Bice, Martha (Vincent)
Bigger, Sarah E. (Furr)
Bigham, America (Hill)
Bigham, Margaret Ann E.
Bigham, Margaret Ann E. (Hamilton)
Billingsly, A.E. (Miller)
Billingsly, Courtney P. (Hughes)
Billingsly, Lucy M. (Roberson)
Billingsly, Mary C. (Payne)
Bishop, Hazy Ann (Carson)
Black, Mrs. Albertine (Bryan)
Black, Ann (Jones)
Black, Eliza (Simpson)
Blake, C.A. (McDonald)
Blansit, S.E. (McPherson)
Blaylock, Mrs. M.C. (Zinn)
Blocker, Harriet E. (Frazier)
Blue, Mrs. R.L. (Nabors)
Boatsman, Lydia A. (Rowan)
Bolen, Datia A. (Rayner)
Bolen, Lucinda (McDaniel)
Bolen, Mary A.C. (Geter)
Bolin, Margaret (Bolin)
Bolton, E.J. (Cauthern)
Bolton, Matilda M. (Root)
Boswell, S.E. (Pitts)
Botts, Delitia (Frazier)
Bouland, Jane (Calmes)
Bouland, Mary E. (Cherry)
Bowen, Elizah (Dillard)
Bowles, Sarah A. (Hensley)
Box, Lucinda (Owens)
Boyd, Catharine J. (Gambrell)
Boyd, Francis E. (Epps)
Boyd, Sallie (Bryson)
Braden, Mrs. E.A. (Montgomery)
Braden, Nancy E. (Shelton)
Bradford, Abigal (Cox)
Bradley, Bettie F. (Ivins)
Bradley, D.B. (Rodgers)
Bradley, Malinda C. (Berry)
Bradley, Martha G. (JOnes)
Bradly, Nancy (Rodgers)
Bradly, S.C. (Cobb)
Bradon, Ann (Gray)

Bramblett, Bettie E. (Fitzpatrick)
Branden, Mary (Wells)
Brandon, Margaret E. (Yocum)
Brandon, Mrs. Mary A. (Davis)
Brandon, Sarah A. (Witcher)
Brassfield, Caroline (Morgan)
Brassfield, Lucy Ann (Duke)
Breedlove, Martha (Crossland)
Bridges, E.A. (Scott)
Bridges, Jane (Glenn)
Bridges, Martha J. (Mathewson)
Bridges, Mary L. (Dickson)
Bridges, Sarah W. (Campbell)
Bright, Ann (Sausaman)
Bright, M.A.E. (Hubbard)
Bright, Susan A. (Hubbard)
Brooks, Hanna (Cox)
Brooksher, Sarah (Wood)
Brown, Frances (Carter)
Brown, Margaret A. (Pritchard)
Brown, Mary A. (Ward)
Brown, Mary U. (Johnson)
Brown, Narcissa (Hooper)
Brown, Sarah (Jernigan)
Brown, Sarah A.R. (Blake)
Brown, Sarah E. (Stanford)
Brown, Mrs. Susan A. (Swearinger)
Browning, M.A. (High)
Browning, Susan J. (Smith)
Bruce, Martha P. (Kelly)
Brumett (?), Martha C. (Garrett)
Bruton, Mrs. Mariah H. (Bryson)
Bryant, Mrs. Parthenia (Hitt)
Buchanan, Josephine (Perkins)
Buchanan, Mary A. (Copeland)
Buchanan, M.J. (Echols)
Buchanan, Mary Leanna (Bangle)
Buchanan, Nancy J. (McCullough)
Buchanan, Nancy J. (Loot)
Buchanan, Martha A. (Sparks)
Buchanan, Rebecca J. (Shettles)
Buchanan, Sarah (Vinson)
Buchanan, Lucinda (Halcom)
Bullock, Ann M. (Howard)
Bullock, Mary A.J.E. (Marshall)
Bumgardner, Narcissa M. (Vance)
Burk, Mellissa J. (Jaco)
Burke, Mary (Pass)
Burke, Mary A. (Viles)

Burnett, Mrs. R.C. (Thomas
Burrow, Ann M. (Wallace)
Burris, Elizabeth (Fitzgerald)
Burten, A.P. (Fear)
Busby, Mary H. (Wardlaw)
Buzby, M.A. (Harvey)

Calder, Margaret (Nix)
Calder, Rebecca (Wells)
Caldwell, E.R. (Brandon)
Caldwell, Margaret (Winn)
Caldwell, Martha L. (Montgomery)
Caldwell, Nancy A. (Ward)
Caldwell, Nancy E. (Roberts)
Caldwell, R. (Caldwell)
Caldwell, Rebecca F. (Haynie)
Caldwell, Sarah A. (Wiley)
Calfee, Amanda C. (Mattox)
Calhoun, Cornelia (Tankersly)
Calloway, Aramita (Lowry)
Calloway, Elvira E. (Pearson)
Camel, Martha J. (Snider)
Camfield, A.B. (Holden)
Camfield, E.F. (Garmon)
Camfield, Mary F. (Humphrey)
Camfula, Sigga (Orr)
Camp, Leona J. (See)
Camp, Margaret (Wiley)
Campbell, Mary M. (Cobb)
Campbell, Nancy G. (Freeman)
Campbell, Parthena (Jones)
Cannon, Mollie (Harris)
Cannon, Susan (Ball)
Canon, Martha J. (Vinyard)
Caple, Eliza J. (Hail)
Carlisle, Martha (West)
Carothers, Caty (Woodard)
Carr, Eliza A. (Sullivan)
Carr, Jane E. (Buchanan)
Carr, Martha (McKinzey)
Carruth, Mary E. (Holmes)
Carson, Emeline (Black)
Carter, Frances Texann (Calder)
Carter, Martha (Hooper)
Carter, Martha M. (White)
Carter, Mary C. (Wylie)
Carter, Nancy E. (Whitten)
Caruth, C.E. (Phillips)
Carwile, Mary Ann (Benjamin)
Carwile, Rebecca (Graham)

Casteel, S.V. (Lankford)
Caswell, Susan (Graham)
Chambliss, Susan (Rowan)
Chapman, Rebecca (Kelly)
Chapman, Sarah (Kelly)
Chisohm, Carolin (Blackwell)
Christopher, Emily D. (Bratten)
Churchill, Martha (Welch)
Clark, Jane E. (Dunn)
Clark, Matilda A. (Jackson)
Clark, Mary (Renneau)
Clark, S.A. (Brown)
Clements, Louisa (Cottrell)
Clements, Martha Ann (Daniel)
Clements, Mary N. (Smith)
Clifton, Hettie (Brooks)
Coats, N. (Potts)
Cobb, J.A. (Ward)
Cobb, Julia A. (Caldwell)
Cobb, Margaret D. (Hardin)
Cobb, Martha J. (Andrews)
Cobb, Mary Ann (Blake)
Cobb, Mary A.E. (Bryant)
Cobb, N.A. (Alexander)
Cobb, Sarah (Payne)
Cochran, Eliza A. (Grisham)
Cochran, Emily E. (Allbritten)
Cochran, Mary E. (Campbell)
Cochran, Paralee (Strain)
Cochran, Sarah Jane (Campbell)
Coker, D.J. (Parker)
Coker, M.H.B. (Windham)
Coker, Mary A. (Rouch)
Coker, Mary M. (Windham)
Coker, Nancy (Schrews)
Coker, Susan (Parker)
Coleman, Ann R. (Castleberry)
Coleman, Emma (Bailey)
Coleman, Emma J. (Weatherall)
Coleman, M.A. (Bailey)
Coleman, M.E. (Caldwell)
Coleman, Laura (Scott)
Coleman, L.T. (Husten)
Collins, Canzider (Ware)
Collins, S.C. (Young)
Combs, Mary E. (Ragan)
Conlee, Tabitha (Eaves)
Connell, A. (Black)
Connell, Elvira (Hamilton)
Connell, Nancy (Tutor)

Conner, T.A.E. (Hale)
Coon, Frances C. (Malone)
Coon, Martha M.E. (BRyant)
Coon, Nancy (Rodgers)
Cooper, Charlotte (Zinn)
Cooper, Margaret Ann (Jones)
Cooper, Susan A. (May)
Cooper, Zuleika (Price)
Copeland, Sarah (Houpt)
Cornelius, Mary E. (Collins)
Cox, Ellender (Luidwick)
Cox, Hannah (HItt)
Cox, Martha A. (Scott)
Crain, Martha (Sherman)
Crawford, Elizabeth J. (Williams)
Crawford, Susan F. (Crawford)
Crim, Mrs. S.C. (Stewart)
Crow, Elizabeth (Astin)
Crumpton, L.E. (Clements)
Cumly, Mary E. (Bell)
Cunningham, Elizabeth V. (Ross)
Cypert, Eliza J. (Hodges)
Cypert, F.J. (Prewitt)

Dale, Elizabeth (Lilly)
Dale, Margaret (McEarchern)
Dalton, Georgia A. (Dansby)
Dandrage, Zelia P. (Lewis)
Dandridge, Catherine (Chapman)
Dandridge, Elizabeth B. (Orne)
Dandridge, Ester F. (Thomason)
Dandridge, M.L. (Darling)
Dandridge, Mariah (Martheny)
Darling, Moriah Frances (Beasley)
Davis, Darcus (Bevill)
Davis, Julyan (Reid)
Davis, Mrs. M.E. (Kyle)
Davis, Malvina (Owens)
Davis, Margaret L. (Brown)
DAvis, Martha C. (Porter)
Davis, Nancy (Cannon)
Dawda, Mary (Parks)
Dean, Ann (Russell)
Deane, S.J. (Johnson)
Deaton, C. (Parr)
Deaton, Julia (Sanders)
Deel, Nancy A. (Clayton)
Deel, P.A. Florence (Roach)
Dejurmott, Mary E. (Carter)

Dennis, Mrs. Mary A. (Gillum)
Dennis, Mary N. (Mitchell)
Dennis, V.E. (Mitchell)
Dickson, Margaret (Roseman)
Dickson, Sarah F. (Woodward)
Dillard, Celia (Goggans)
Dillard, Harriett (Bowen)
Dillard, Lucy (Kelly)
Dillard, Martha J. (Morris)
Dillard, Mary (South)
Dillard, Mary J. (Hale)
Dillard, Missouri (Baker)
Dillard, Sally (Goggins)
Dillard, Sarah F. (Briant)
Dixen, Mary M. (Coggins)
Dixon, Mary C. (Carter)
Dnny (?), Mrs. Abbie (Cox)
Dobbins, J.B. (McDonald)
Donaldson, Ann L. (Johnson)
Donaldson, Sarah E. (Waldrop)
Donavan, Julia C. (Suferman)
Donavan, Mary A. (Cannon)
Dorsey, Tabithia C. (Williams)
Douglass, Nancy (Herndon)
Dowdy, A.A. (Haddox)
Doxy, Martha (Drake)
Dozier, Mary R. (Anderson)
Drake, Julia D. (Mitchell)
Duff, A.V. (Thomas)
Duff, E.C. (Grisham)
Duff, M.E. (Snider)
Duff, M.F. (Grant)
Duggen, Catharine (Palmer)
Duke, Ann (Wetherford)
Duke, C.A. (Brandon)
Duke, Sarah (McCullough)
Duke, Sinia E. (Pinson)
Dulaney, Rachell (Dulaney)
Dunaway, Letha Ann (Putt)
Dunaway, Sarah E. (Putt)
Duncan, E.M. (Temple)
Duncan, Emeline (Singleton)
Duncan, Martha J. (Jones)
Duncan, Mary H. (Dorsey)
Duncan, Rachel (Ellis)
Dunham, M.A. (Langley)
Dunken, Telithia (Johnston)
Dunlap, L. (Dunlap)
Dunn, Charity A. (Nesbit)
Dunn, Nancy E. (Foster)

Dunnum, Susan A. (Danniel)
Dunum, M.A. (Stroud)
Dye, Elizabeth (Pannell)
Dye, Lavina (Dunlap)
Dye, Sarah A. (Tapley)
Dyson, Polly C. (Robbins)

Earle, L.M. (Braugher)
Earle, Mary (Rouzer)
Early, Mrs. Eliza (Shelton)
Echols, Martha D. (Yancy)
Edington, Emily (Coon)
Edington, Harriet (Alderman)
Edmondson, Helen (Crump)
Edwards, Mary A. (Rutledge)
Edwards, Elizabeth Ann (Edington)
Edwards, Mary C. (Long)
Edwards, L.J. (McCord)
Elison, Amanda (Grisham)
Elliott, Jennie Albula (McCanless)
Ellis, Mary L. (Whitten)
Elzey, Jennie (Easterwood)
Elzy, Caroline (Atkins)
Epting, Mary (Smith)
Eubanks, Amanda (Jones)
Eubanks, Amanda E. (King)
Eubanks, E.C.A. (Jones)
Eubanks, M.C. (Morrow)
Evans, Caroline (Marks)
Ewing, Martha E. (Kerr)
Ewing, R.C. (Kerr)

Farmer, An Eliza (Beard)
Farra, Susan (Shaw)
Farrer, E.A. (Parker)
Farrer, Mary (Norwood)
Farrer, Milly B. (Ross)
Faulkner, Sosanna (McAlister)
Fear, N.A. (Ewing)
Fears, A.P. (Thomason)
Feemster, M.A. (Sanders)
Ferguson, Susan J. (Morgan)
Ferrell, Sarah E. (Shelton)
Fields, Elin (Ingates)
Fields, Martha A. (Harden)
Fisher, Ellin (McWhirter)
Flanagan, Martha (Barnett)
Flanagan, Mary (Tucker)
Flannagin, Sarah E. (Pitts)
Fleming, Elizabeth (Brandon)
Fletcher, Isabelah (Caldwell)

Ford, Mary E. (Rivers)
Foreman, Sarah F. (Mitchell)
Forrester, M.A. (Eaves)
Forrester, Mary A. (Eaves)
Forrester, Virginia (Eaves)
Forrester, Elizabeth (McNutt)
Fortune, C.V. (Allen)
Fortune, Cynthia (Savins)
Foster, Jane (Tutor)
Foster, N.E. (Hester)
Foster, Mrs. Pricilla (Robinson)
Foster, Sarah E. (Williamson)
Foster, S.C. (Boatner)
Foster, Susan C. (Crain)
Fowler, Mary Ann (Looney)
Franks, Mary E. (Poore)
Franklin, Mary A.E. (Davis)
Freeman, C.M. (Williams)
Freeman, E.C. (Shelton)
Freeman, Fannie O. (Price)
Freeman, Frances P. (Chambliss)
Freeman, Mrs. Martha S. (Fulton)
Freeman, M.E. (Gentry)
Freeman, Mary E. (Hudson)
Friday, Margaret Jane (Robbins)
Frierson, Elvina (Fulton)
Frierson, Harriet E. (Shawver)
Frierson, Susan (Caruth)
Fulks, F.E. (Hale)
Fuller, Elizabeth R. (Herring)
Fuller, Sarah W. (Reid)
Fullington, Melinda (Frank)
Fulton, Maria Jane E. (Ferrell)
Fulton, Sarah R. (Joiner)
Funk, Mary H. (Wood)
Fuqua, Docia C. (Givens)
Fuqua, Mary E. (Jackson)
Furr, Jane A. (Shive)
Furr, Mary A. (Morrow)

Gafford, Martha A. (Graham)
Gaines, Frances G. (Moore)
Gambrell, Emily (Birge)
Gambrell, Mariah H. (Bruten)
Gammel, Manerva (Carpenter)
Gardiner, Nancy R. (Smith)
Gorey, M.A. (Hunley)
Garman, L.J. (Oglesby)
Garmon, L.J. (Oglesby)
Garrett, Amanda L. (Henderson)
Garrett, Sarah Catharine (Dreher)

Fletcher, L.C. (Spencer)
Floy, Samatha (Beckly)
Floyed, Perlena (Lewis)

Gatewood, Sallie (Fuller)
Gayle, Martha A. (Hoyl)
Gedden, Mary E. (Murphy)
Gentry, Mary J. (Eckles)
Gernigan, Harriet Ann (Montgomery)
Gibbs, Sarah Ann (Fowler)
Gibson, Frances G. (Marshall)
Gidden, Elizabeth (Randolph)
Gidden, Martha J. (Smith)
Gill, Rebecca C. (McWhorter)
Gillespie, Nancy B. (Harrison)
Gillispie, Sallie E. (Staten)
Gilmer, Nancy J. (Bryant)
Givens, Nancy E. (Coleman)
Glover, Margaret (Jackson)
Godfrey, E.F. (Foster)
Godfrey, Eliza J. (Ellison)
Godfrey, Nancy C. (Wester)
Godfrey, S.A. (Allen)
Goggin, Hannah E.J. (Hall)
Goggins, R.J.F. (Rodgers)
Golding, M.E. (Funk)
Golson, Malissa (Huffstickler)
Good, A. Alicia (Ragland)
Goode, Marinda (Bogan)
Goodman, Sallie A. (Starks)
Goodwin, Mary (Williams)
Goodwin, Nancy (Edington)
Gould, N.J. (McWhorter)
Gould, Sarah H. (McWhorter)
Grace, Eliza (Hale)
Grady, Ligg (Newel)
Graham, Celia J. (Carwile)
Graham, Elvira J. (Vaughn)
Grant, Carrie F. (Overby)
Grant, Sarah Jane (Reed)
Gray, Jane (Hall)
Gray, L.L. (Musey)
Gray, Martha A. (Sanders)
Gray, Mary J. (Allen)
Green, Mary (Dillard)
Green, M.E. (Decanter)
Green, Mary E. (Stovall)
Green, M.E. (Sanders)
Green, Nancy B. (Green)
Greene, Susan C. (Clayton)
Gregory, M.H.C. (Ware)
Gregory, S.A. (Rayborn)
Gresham, Jane B. (Leatherburg)

Garrigus, M.A. (Hadley)
Gory, S.A. (CAldwell)
Gassaway, Leoma (Potter)
Griffin, L.A. (Regan)
Griffen, Martha J. (McLarty)
Griffin, Mrs. Catherine (Baker)
Griffin, Elizabeth (Seal)
Grisham, M.C. (Wells)
Grisham, Sarah A. (Russell)
Grisham, Sarah J. (Wells)
Grizzard, Adaline V. (Carter)
Grubbs, Mary Ann (Coley)
Guin, Dosha (Boatman)
Guin, Margaret (Aglin)

Halcomb, Nancy (Kelly)
Halcombe, Sarah Ann (LIndsey)
Hale, Elizabeth (Browning)
Hale, Margaret E. (Richardson)
Hale, Mary J. (Owens)
Hale, Rachel E. (Robbins)
Hall, D.A. (Gray)
Hall, Elizabeth J. (Shelton)
Hall, Loney Ann (Berry)
Hall, M.E. (Ross)
Hall, Martha (Rea)
Hall, M.E. (Ross)
Hall, Nancy (Shelton)
Hamelton, Charity (Roach)
Hammons, Mary (Rutledge)
Hampton, Mrs. A.M. (McWhirter)
Hampton, Caroline (Tate)
Hampton, Mary E. (Morrow)
Hams, Amanda (Ewing)
Hanan, Elizia A. (Maxey)
Hancock, M.E. (Bushy)
Hancock, Permilia (Clark)
Handley, Sarah S. (McEwen)
Hanks, L. (Mears)
Hanks, Nannie B. (Buchanan)
Hopt, C.C. (Wall)
Haran, Elizabeth (Setzler)
Hardin, Elizabeth (Rodgers)
Hardy, Lucinda (Adair)
Hardy, Martha Ann (Smith)
Hardy, Mary (Banyan)
Harper, Harriet T.A. (Bacon)
Harper, Jane M. (Whitesides)
Harper, Laurinda (Harris)
Harper, Martha Ann (Jones)
Harres, Mary A. (Clark)
Harris, Mrs. E.R. (Barton)
Harris, Lucinda (Lantrip)

Harris, Mary (Johnson)
Harris, Rebecca J. (Davis)
Harrison, Candie (Sanders)
Harrison, Jennie (Widenor)
Harrison, Lou A. (Howell)
Harrison, Mary (Brown)
Harrison, Mary C. (Love)
Harrison, Susan L. (Sage)
Harvey, Elizabeth R. (Farrer)
Harvey, Frances A. (Christian)
Harvey, Louisa (Adams)
Harvey, Mary A. (Richman)
Hatfield, Elizabeth (Montgomery)
Hattox, Sarah A.E. (Jumper)
Hattox, Sarah J. (Harrison)
Hattox, Susan (Dowdy)
Hauckum, Nancy (Kelly)
Hayes, Sarah N. (Brock)
Haynes, Indiana (Duff)
Haynes, Martha J. (Carter)
Hays, Jane (Frazier)
Haynes, Indiana (Duff)
Haynes, Martha J. (Carter)
Hays, Jane (Frazier)
head, Martha (Miller)
Head, Matilda (Boyd)
Head, Susan A. (Hodges)
Heard, A.M. (Bryson)
Heard, A.L. (Rice)
Heard, Martha S. (Cullens)
Heard, R.J. (Holmes)
Hellums, Letty J. (Douglas)
Hellems, Martha A. (Listenbee)
Hellums, Jemima (Herndon)
Hellums, Nancy (Cochran)
Hellums, Thena (Kelly)
Hemp, Luzia (Sullivan)
Henderson, Mary Ann (Stone)
Henley, M.A. (Gary)
Henry, Amanda (Conley)
Henry, Edna E. (McCord)
Henry, Elizabeth Ann (Snider)
Henry, Marianne (White)
Henry, Mary L. (Sloan)
Henry, Martha J. (Bell)
Henry, N.F. (Montgomery)
Hensley, Artamintre (Manning)
Hensley, Lucinda (Pannell)
Hensley, Rosanah (Pannell)

Herndon, Aley (Tucker)
Herndon, Frances (Tutor)
Herndon, M.F. (Clark)
Herron, Kate C. (Barringer)
Hicks, M.E. (Bolen)
Hicks, M.J. (Purvine)
Higgin, Mrs. Sallie (Jennings)
Higginbottom, Serena Adaline (Gillum)

High, Mary (Setzler)
Hightower, Harriett A. (Stephens)
Hightower, T.E. (Manning)
Hill, A.J. (Beeks)
Hill, E.A. (Bonds)
Hill, Frances (Welch)
Hill, Margaret E. (Potter)
Hill, Martha (Thyne)
Hill, Mary E. (Butler)
Hill, Paralee (Herring)
Hill, T.C. (Buchanan)
Hodges, Sarah E. (Wood)
Holbert, Martha (Huckbee)
Holcomb, Harriett (Buchanan)
Holcomb, Lucinda (Noland)
Holcomb, Sarah (Kelly)
Holditch, Eliza C. (Heard)
Holditch, Susanna D. (Cullens)
Holland, N.J. (Cox)
Holleman, Nancy (Chaney)
Holliday, Mary A. (McCraw)
Holmes, Louisa (Fears)
Holmes, Martha Ann (Mann)
Holms, Martha (Davis)
Hood, Martha M. (Hailey)
Hooker, Mary (Barkley)
Hooker, M.F. (Sneed)
Hooker, Margaret M. (McEasthern)
Hooker, Margaret J. (Anderson)
Hooper, A.E. (Simmons)
Hopt, C.C. (Wall)
Horn, Sarah M. (Fuller)
Horton, Susan (Morrison)
Houpt, Margaret C. (Blaylock)
Howard, Milly M. (Sword)
Howell, E.A. (Proctor)
Howell, Elizabeth A. (Black)
Howell, Nancy C. (Cole)
Hoyl, C.L. (Gayle)

Hubbard, Louisa E. (Brandon)
Hubbard, Malvina (Davis)
Hubbard, Mary Ann (Brandon)
Hubbard, Sarah J. (Phillips)
Huckaby, Missouri Ann (Evans)
Huckaby, Sarah (Morrow)
Huckbee, C.A. (Wilson)
Huckbee, E.M. (Duncan)
Hudiburgh, G. Minerva (Brown)
Hudiburgh, Nancy Jane (Hubbard)
Hudson, Clester V. (Parks)
Hudson, Elizabeth (Steelman)
Hudson, Lucinda (Caldwell)
Hudson, Margaret A. (Taylor)
Hudson, S.J. (Rowsey)
Hudson, Sarah M. (Sanders)
Hughey, Mary J. (Waldo)
Hughs, Mary Jane (Billingsly)
Hull, M.J. (Astin)
Hundly, Catharine (Evens)
Hunter, F.C. (Jumper)
Hunter, Hannah W. (Jones)
Hunter, Martha G. (Gearan)
Hurley, Nancy (Joiner)
Huston, Selitia F. (Liddell)
Hutcheson, M.A. (Hubbard)
Hutcheson, M.A. (Welborn)
Hutcheson, Nancy J. (Waldrop)
Hutcheson, S.E. (Brown)
Hutchison, Sarah D. (Purdon)
Hutson, Mrs. Guertha C. (Fowler)

Irvin, Nancy A. (Looney)
Isom, Cordilla (Pollard)
Isom, Luraine (Mann)
Isom, Mary C. (Fagins)
Ivey, E.A. (Howell)
Ivy, P.A. (Jackson)

Jackson, Mrs. Jane (Beard)
Jackson, Mary E. (Milam)
James, M.A. (Taylor)
James, Martha J. (Hurley)
Jamison, Clarentine (Staggs)
Jarnigan, Sarah E. (Wood)
Jarvis, M.E. (Reaves)
Jarvis, Margaret E. (Robbins)
Jenkins, Elizabeth (Stegall)
Jenkins, Martha (PItts)
Jenkins, Mollie (Coleman)
Jenkins, S.C. (Horton)

Jennings, Nancy (Box)
Johnsen, Nancy Ann (Lowery)
Johnson, A.C. (Hoyl)
Johnson, Cathrine (Hargroves)
Johnson, Elizabeth (Bryant)
Johnson, Harriet (Harris)
Johnson, Jane H. (Mayhew)
Johnson, Josaphine (Henderson)
Johnson, Josaphine L. (Kennedy)
Johnson, Julyan (Tutor)
Johnson, M.L. (Edwards)
Johnson, Malinda (Malone)
Johnson, Margaret J. (Dowdy)
Johnson, Mary (Odle)
Johnson, Mary C. (Combs)
Johnson, Mary F. (Tutor)
Johnson, Mary Jane (Breckingridge)
Johnson, M.C. (Caldwell)
Johnson, M.E. (Youngblood)
Johnson, M.J. (Kelly)
Johnson, Mary Jane (Lowry)
Johnson, M.M. (Wilks)
Johnson, N.C. (Edwards)
Johnson, O.F. (Coats)
Johnson, Rebecca (Smith)
Johnson, Sarah A. (Butler)
Johnson, Sarah C. (Goode)
Johnson, Sarah E. (Anderson)
Johnson, Sarah F. (Tate)
Johnson, Susanna (McCraw)
Johnston, C.E. (Eave)
Johnston, Martha A. (McCord)
Jolley, Mary F. (Gary)
Jolly, Eartha (Brooks)
Jolly, L.S.C. (Roberts)
Jolly, Mary M. (Cooper)
Jolly, Savena (Johnson)
Jones, Amanda (McDaniel)
Jones, Elizabeth M. (Workman)
Jones, Lucy (Thompson)
Jones, Martha Ann (Pope)
Jones, Mary E. (Sanders)
Jones, Matilda A. (Montgomery)
Jones, Nancy Caroline (Butler)
Jones, Permelia J. (Hill)
Jordan, Caroline (Jeter)
Jordan, F.E. (Blocker)
Jordan, F.M. (Moore)
Jordan, Mary (Hampton)

Kee, Mary (Hickman)

Kelly, Catharine (Griffen)
Kelly, D.A. Hellum)
Kelly, E.F. (Hattox)
Kelly, Ellen O. (Tucker)
Kelly, Emphema (Fields)
Kelly, Frances E. (Boatman)
Kelly, Thomas S. (Osburn)
Kenedy, Ella (Mitchell)
Kennedy, Marissa (Miller)
Kennedy, Martha Jane (Templeton)
Keys, Jane H. (Norwood)
Kidd, Margaret (Wheatley)
King, Leonora M. (Lockhart)
King, Martha Ann (Flarherty)
King, Mary D. (Jones)
King, N.A. (Fortune)
Kirkland, Pamelia J. (Bramble)
Kirkpatrick, Jane (Rasberry)
Kirkpatrick, Martha M. (Marion)
Knight, E.J. (Hanah)
Knight, Martha (Brandon)
Knight, Mary A.F. (Free)
Knight, Mary J. (Bolding)
Knight, R.A.J. (Conaway)
Knight, Mrs. Sarah J. (Story)
Knowles, Mary (Heard)
Knox, M.L. (Mullins)
Kohlhim, Alma (Morton)

Lacy, Mary (Moore)
Lamar, M.A. (Satawhite)
Lamar, Susan G. (Milam)
Laney, Sally (Rodgers)
Langley, Lucy Ann (Dulaney)
Langley, Martha E. (Speck)
Lankford, Martha M. (Brailey)
Lankford, Mary (Witcher)
Lantrip, N.E. (Stegall)
Laughridge, Margaret V. (Dillard)
Lawrence, Eliza J. (Smith)
League, Mary C. (Brazier)
Leach, Martha Ann Frances (Wilmoth)
Leavell, L.J. (Orr)
Ledbetter, Mary A.J. (Davis)
Lesley, A.J. (Prude)
Letford, C.T. (Mann)
Lewellen, Josephine M. (Adams)
Lewellen, M.A. (Washington)

LIndsey, Martha E. (Rutledge)
Little, Mary D. (Wilson)
Loftis, Mary (Loftis)
Long, Emma C. (Kelly)
Long, Josephine E. (Bramblett)
Long, Mary (Donavan)
Long, Mary S. (Green)
Long, Nancy (Pipkins)
Long, Nancy D. (Spears)
Long, R.M. (Graves)
Lovins, E.A. (Murphy)
Lovins, Nannie J. (Powell)
Lowery, Elizabeth (Johnson)
Lowry, Sarah A. (Johnson)
Luke, R.A. (Neal)
Lyons, Margaret (Ryan)

McCaw, Jennie Ann (Gilmer)
McClennan, Elizabeth (Ewing)
McClenon, H.A. (Horn)
McCord, Ele C. (Henry)
McCowan, Nancy (Williams)
McCoy, P.F. (Vaughan)
McCoy, Polly Ann (McClelland)
McCoy, Rebecca (Garner)
McCraw, Malinda (Harmon)
McCraw, Matilda (Regan)
McCraw, Mary J. (Davis)
McCraw, MIllie (Shaw)
McCraw, Sallie (Carter)
McCuchon, Jane (Duke)
McCullough, Sarah B. (Parks)
McCurley, Sarah (Hargroves)
McCuskey, O.A.C. (Price)
McDaniel, Mrs. M.P. (McDaniel)
McDaniel, Nancy J. (Green)
McDole, Sarah (Lindsey)
McDonel, M.P. (Sanders)
McDonald, Mary A. (Montgomery)
McDonald, L. (McPherson)
McFarland, Mary (Smith)
McGee, Jane (Phillips)
McGee, Fannie H. (Phillips)
McGehee, Charlit Josephine (Sneed)
McGill, Mary (Fish)
McGill, Susan R. (Cary)
McGill, W.E. (Griffen)
McGreger, Nettie (Carpenter)

McGregor, Jemima (Carpenter)
McGregor, Sarah E. (Donaldson)
McKay, Elizabeth (Owens)
McKeowen, Sarah (Young)
McKinney, Mary C. (Hampton)
McMahen, E.C. (Stegall)
McNeely, Hamet (Warren)
McNeely, Nancy (Warren)
McNeely, Ruth (Warren)
McNeely, Sarah (Wallace)
McNeil, Anna (Reed)
McNeil, Mary A. (Arnett)
McNiel, Permelia J. (Pegues)
McNiel, Susan (Hunt)
McNiel, Susan (Hunt)
McNiel, V.A. (Helms)
McNile, Martha (Holleman)
McPhail, Mary M. (Brown)
McPhearson, Caroline (Jolly)
McPhearson, Martha (Allen)
McRunnels, Sarah (Crum)
McWhirter, S.J. (McKnight)
McWhorter, M.E. (Hall)
McWhorter, Nancy J. (Lewellen)
McWhorter, Ruth C. (Robertson)
McWhorter, Ruth C. (Robertson)

Maddox, Leah A.E. (Mitchell)
Malissa, Susan (Newton)
Mallory, Eliza Jane (Holmes)
Mallory, S.A. (Rye)
Malone, Mrs. M.E. (Miller)
Malone, Sarah (Lovings)
Manes, Margarett (Johnson)
Mann, Caroline (Davis)
Mann, Margaret (Taylor)
Manning, Sarah Ann (Flannagan)
Mark, Sarah L. (Cannady)
Marr, J.P. (Whitten)
Martin, Alice (Dugan)
Martin, Augusta (Worley)
Martin, Deborah (Williams)
Martin, Nannie O. (Friarson)
Martindale, Mary E. (Blanten)
Massey, Malissa (Catin)
Massey, Sarah M. (Cyle)
Massey, Selinia (Casterner)
Mastison, Rhoda M. (Strait)
Mathews, Margaret S. (Leathers)
Mathews, Rhody (Williamson)

Mathis, Martha A. (Garmon)
Matthews, Ann (Rains)
Matthews, M.J. (Crenshaw)
Matthews, Nancy Ann (Bugg)
Mauldin, Narcissa T. (Mathews)
Maxey, M.A. (Hutchison)
Maxey, Mary E. (Sullivan)
Mayfield, Eliza E. (Burk)
Mayhem, M.H. (Cunningham)
Mayhen, M.E. (Russell)
Mayhew, Eliza J. (Coward)
Mayhew, Emeline (Wilson)
Mayhue, Sarah (Huckeby)
Mays, Sarah E. (Blackwell)
Meador, Sarah E. (McCall)
Meadows, Nancy A. (Dillard)
Meek, Elizabeth (Tedder)
Merrett, Caroline (Varner)
Middleton, E.M.S. (Perry)
Middleton, M.J. (White)
Middleton, Mary M. (Boswell)
Milam, Elizabeth (Fuqua)
Milam, Mary (Gill)
Milam, Mary F. (Miller)
Milam, Rebecca (Kelly)
Milam, Rebecca (Kelly)
Milam, Sue J. (Reeder)
Miller, E.P. (Marable)
Miller, L.J. (Goodman)
Miller, M.A. (Smith)
Miller, Margaret A. (Nason)
Miller, Margaret (Martin)
Miller, Martha J. (Gill)
Miller, Mary M. (Terry)
Miller, Sidney Ann (Cochran)
Millsaps, Nancy E. (Saul)
Mitchell, Hulet (Plant)
Mitchell, Louiza (Gilder)
Mitchell, Selena (Gray)
Mitchell, Virginia (Fields)
Mobley, J.T. (Snider)
Mobley, Kisy (Young)
Mobley, M.C. (Tynes)
Montgomery, Elizabeth (Googer)
Montgomery, Pricilla (Alexander)
Montgomery, Sarah (Hitt)
Mooney, Mary J. (Hudiburgh)
Mooney, M.J. (Newell)
More, C.N.J. (Bealer)
Moore, Amanda (Davis)
Montgomery, Bernetta (Goode)

Moore, A.S. (Roberts)
Noore, Elizabeth (Jackson)
Moore, Mary Joan (Knight)
Noore, S.F. (Stringfellow)
Moore, Sarah J. (Lankford)
Moore, Sarah J.L. (McCraw)
Morgan, Amanda (Collins)
Morgan, Mary A. (Armstrong)
Morgan, Timanda (Pope)
Morris, Elizabeth (Satterwhite)
Morris, Elizabeth (Beckham)
Morris, Lusina (Lamar)
Morris, Martha C. (Wells)
Morris, Nancy E. (Thompson)
Morris, L.N. (Beek)
Morrison, Lucinda (Horton)
Morrison, M.J. (Crosley)
Morrison, S.E. (Youngblood)
Morrow, S.A. (Ross)
Morrow, Sarah F. (Lambreth)
Moses, Jane (Walker)
Motley, Clara (Sanders)
Motley, Lucy F. (Boyd)
Motley, Martha W. (Sanders)
Mounce, Emily F. (Soutere)
Mounce, Narcissa (Pitts)
Myers, E.J.V. (Bolding)
Myers, Martha G. (Mulligan)
Mulikin, Molie C. (Gilmer)

nabor, Matilda C. (Smith
Nabours, Mary Frances (Mullins)
Nash, Martha (Jones)
Neal, Nancy (Bailey)
Neely, E.F. (Lyon)
Neely, Elizabeth (Gambrell)
Neely, Ella (Combs)
Neely, Mary E. (Miller)
Neely, S.H. (Sheppard)
Neighbors, Jane (Hiller)
Nelson, Jane (Pilcher)
Newby, M.A. (Grisham)
Newell, Frances Ann (Jernigan)
Newell, S.E. (Hicks)
Newsom, Mary C. (Perkins)
Nicholson, Albermale (Cole)
Nicholson, Texas (Atkinson)
Nix, Mary A. (Ferrell)
Nixon, M.A. (Milam)
Nixon, Mollie C. (Milam)

Nolan, Mary A. (Buchanan)
Nolen, Mary (Trailer)
Nolen, Mary (Loftis)
Noles, Mary (Head)
NOles, Nancy (Head)
Nowlin, Ann (Wester)
Nubee, Mildred (Russell)

Oglebee, Tilda A. (Screws)
Oliver, Jane (Brown)
Oliver, Louisa (Griffen)
Only, Rachel (Stamp)
Orr, Synthia (Campbell)
Overby, Mrs. Caroline F. (Babb)
Owens, Leana (LIttle)
Owens, Sarah A. (Wilson)

Pain, M.A. (Evetts)
Paine, N.A. (Gafford)
Pannell, Catherin (Morgan)
Pannell, Catharine C. (Garret)
Pannell, Elizabeth J. (Darlin)
Pannell, Emily (Colvin)
Pannell, F.E. (Free)
Pannell, Irene (Colvin)
Pannell, L.P. (Hurley)
Pannell, Martha J. (Hensley)
Pannell, Matilda M. (Green)
Pannell, Mary Ann (Carter)
Pannell, Mary Ann E. (Beasley)
Pannell, Nancy A.R. (Eanugton?)
Pannell, Orens (Langley)
Pannell, Polina (Staten)
Pannell, Sarah J. (Cox)
Pannell, Winna J. (Colvin)
Parker, Malinda (Duncan)
Parish, Eliza (Femster)
Parr, Caroline (Hale)
Parrish, Nancy (Bell)
Paschall, S.L. (Ornsby)
Pass, Mary A. (Cooper)
Pate, Mary Frances (Putt)
Payne, Frances A. (Cox)
Payne, J.S. (Morris)
Payne, Mary J. (Sloan)
Payne, S.M. (Rainey)
Payton, Elizabeth (Black)
Payton, Nancy Ann (McNeely)
Pearsall, Charlotte (Youngblood)
Pearsall, Elizabeth (Flarherty)

BRIDE

Pearsall, Sarah E. (Flarherty)
Pearsen, Martha C.C. (Nelson)
Pegues, Amanda E. (Collins)
Pegues, Mattie E. (Pitts)
Perry, Rebecca (Montgomery)
Perry, Ruth (Williams)
Perry, Sarah Jane (Burks)
Perry, T.R.C. (Shurley)
Petty, Mary D. (Hale)
Petty, S.J. (Waldrop)
Pettygrew, Hannah A. (Ivey)
Phillips, Elizabeth (Cobb)
Phillips, Martha J. (Ward)
Phillips, Mary M. (Beene)
Phillips, Nancy Jane (Puttman)
Phillips, Naomi (Witt)
Phillips, Perlina (Bolen)
Phillips, Rachel J. (Ray)
Phillips, S.F.A. (Houpt)
Phillips, Sallie (Phillips)
Phillips, Susan A. (Purdon)
Phillips, Sarah E. (Henry)
Picket, Eliza (Motley)
Pickens, Sarah A. (Neely)
Pilcher, Mary (Smith)
Pinson, Lucinda (Hill)
Pitts, Amanda (Coker)
Pitts, Annie (Knight)
Pitts, Catharine (Oshields)
Pitts, Emily F. (Robertson)
Pitts, Frances (Taylor)
Pitts, Kessiah (Smith)
Pitts, Loduskey (Holt)
Pitts, Lucinda S. (Robinson)
Pitts, Mary J. (Fortune)
Pitts, Matilda C. (Dixon)
Pitts, Parmelia (Pitts)
Pittman, Mary E. (Evans)
Plant, Susan C. (Swindoll)
Pollach, Violin J. (Norwood)
Pollard, Cordelia D. (McClellan)
Pollard, Julia Ann (Wolf)
Pool, Elizabeth (McKeown)
Pool, Elizabeth (Screws)
Poole, Emma B. (Gill)
Pope, Cela T. (Morris)
Pope, Isabella (Ivy)
Porter, A.R. (Heidelberg)
Porter, Frances T. (Pearsall)
Porter, Geneva (Glover)

BRIDE

Porter, Martha L. (Walker)
Porter, Sarah (Armstrong)
Porter, Virginia (Carpenter)
Portwood, Elizabeth Ann (Busby)
Portwood, Mariam (Swarford)
Potteete, Phoebe A. (Payne)
Potts, Elizabeth (Potts)
Potts, Martha K. (Watts)
Powell, Matilda M. (Green)
Powell, Nancy J. (Guinn)
Price, Lusetta (Cornwell)
Price, Mahalia (Malone)
Price, Mary M. (Lynch)
Price, S.A. (Bolen)
Prince, Elizabeth (Horton)
Pritchard, Lettice B. (Johnson)
Pritchard, Louiza (Caldwell)
Pritchard, S.F. (Johnston)
Pritchard, S.J. (Leslie)
Proctor, Epsey (Shaw)
Proctor, Sallie (Cochran)
Province, A.C. (Carson)
Province, J. (Ward)
Province, Sabina A. (Miller)
Prude, Mary (Brooks)
Pruitt, Amanda A. (Hickman)
Putt, Mary J. (Pate)

Raburn, Susan (Phillips)
Ragan, M.E. (Evetts)
Ragland, C.M. (Mullekin)
Raley, Mary (Bowen)
Ramsey, Levina R. (Beauchamp)
Ramsy, Mrs. M.M. (Coble)
Raner, Elizabeth (Suggs)
Raney, Rebecca R. (Blake)
Ray, Annie (Higgs)
Rayborn, Martha A. (Cox)
Raymond, Emily H. (Ligon)
Read, Harriet A. (Bowen)
Reader, Eliza (Wilburn)
Real, Tabitha (Lore)
Reaves, Sarah, A.F. (Hall)
Reaves, Tempy J. (Corder)
Reaves, Virginia (Reeves)
Redding, Mrs. Julia M. (Griffin)
Redus, A.C. (Feemster)
Redus, Catharine (Cunningham)
Redus, Elizabeth A. (Monahan)
Redus, Isabella M. (Bailey)

Redus, M.A. (Stanford)
Reed, Clarisa (King)
Reed, Martha (Boatman)
Reed, Mary (Hodges)
Reed, Nancy (Henry)
Reed, Venecia (Phillips)
Reeder, Catharin (McCoy)
Reeder, D.E. (Vaughan)
Reeder, Eugenia(?) (Jones)
Reeder, Salina F. (PItts)
Reeder, Sarah W. (Goodman)
Reeves, Malissa A. (Speck)
Reid, Caroline (Tucker)
Reid, Martha Ann (Davis)
Reid, Martha (Burks)
Reid, Mary L. (Rowan)
Rennolds, H.C. (Barton)
Reynolds, Mrs. Martha (Miller)
Richardson, Frances (Burks)
Richardson, M.J. (Hurley)
Richman, Sarah L. (Hall)
Richmond, Mary Ann (Wicker)
Ried, Martha A. (Roberts)
Ried, Margaret R. (Snipes)
Riggan, Sarah E. (McDonald)
Ritear, Margaret C. (Young)
Rivers, Susan (Jones)
Rivers, Tabitha H. (Rowsey)
Roach, Charity (Stewart)
Robbins, Martha (Nowlin)
Robbins, Matilda (Fradier)
Robbinson, Elizabeth (Rootes)
Roberts, C.M. (Grubbs)
Roberts, Jane (Roberts)
Roberts, Louisa C. (Rodgers)
Roberts, Mary A. (Tollison)
Roberts, M.J. (Luker)
Roberts, Sarah E. (McCraw)
Robertson, Harriett (Beard)
Robertson, M.A. (Smith)
Robertson, S.P. (Brown)
Robertson, Sarah Ann (Flemming)
Robins, M.C. (Owen)
Robinson, M.A. (Whitlow)
Robinson, Martha J. (Robinson)
Robinson, Sarah J. (Farmer)
Rodgers, Martha J. (Lyons)
Rodgers, Mary A. (Weatherall)
Rodgers, Mary A. (Patterson)
Rodgers, Narcissa (Neely)

Rodgers, R.O.F. (Godfrey)
Rogers, Jane C. (Gibson)
Rogers, M.E. (Higgins)
Root, Calie (Thomason)
Root, Margaret L. (Bolton)
Ross, Mary A. (Boyd)
Ross, S.A. (Harvey)
Rowan, S.L. (Bruce)
Rucker, Amanda. (Thompson)
Rucker, Susanna (TAnkersley)
Russell, Eliza M. (Morris)
Russell, Elizabeth J. (Sanders)
Russell, Linea (Pritchard)
Russell, M.E. (Moreland)
Russell, Margaret C. (Russell)
Russell, Mary E. (Hill)
Russell, Mary F. (Scott)
Russell, Nancy (Hale)
Russell, Sarah E. (Shelton)
Russell, Sarah J. (Pritchard)
Rutledge, Mrs. M.L. (Stewart)
Rutledge, Susan E. (Paulett)
Rye, Mary E. (Miller)

Sadler, Martha Jane (Pannell)
Sadler, Mary E. (Abbott)
Sadler, S.J. (Nabors)
Sadlin, Caroline (Livingston)
Sanders, Aminda S. (Sanders)
Sanders, Ellen J. (Marshall)
Sanders, Sarah J. (Hudson)
Sandford, Mary (Payne)
Sansing, P.E. (Gordon)
Sappington, Mary (Whitlow)
Sartin, Eliza Ann (Cooper)
Saterwhite, Eliza J. (King)
Satterwhite, M.A. (Thompson)
Satterwhite, Mary E. (White)
Saul, N.E. (Scott)
Saven, Jane (Roberts)
Savely, Mary E. (Moore)
Savins, Elizabeth (Ausborn)
Scales, Maryetta (Forbes)
Scales, S.J. (Hay)
Scott, L. (Bryson)
Scott, Susan A. (Clemmans)
Screws, Fany (Price)
Screws, Mary (Gentry)
Seal, Sarah (Mitchell)
Seals, Nancy F. (Howard)

Sewell, M.M. (Edwards
Sexton, Nancy A. (Meador)
Shanon, Mary Kate (Shaw)
Shaw, Mary A. (Huckabee)
Shaw, Sarah C. (Huckbee)
Shaw, Susanna (Hanna)
Shelton, Alvina Jane (Purvis)
Shelton, Martha Ann (Younger)
Shelton, Mary J. (Skinner)
Shelton, Mary M. (James)
Shelton, N.E. (Wingo)
Sherman, Martha C. (Morgan)
Sherman, Sarah E. (Alexander)
Shingleton, Charlotte R. (Sanders)
Shirley, L.A. (Billingsly)
Short, Mary A. (McCutchen)
Shorter, Nancy E. (Parker)
Shurley, Mary Ann (Billingsly)
Simmon, Adaline (Kimball)
Simmon, Mary E. (Wood)
Simmon, Samantha (Baker)
Simmons, Susan C. (Combs)
Simms, E.C. (Sadler)
Simpson, A.M.P. (Wheeler)
Simpson, Elizabeth A. (Simpson)
Simpson, Mary (Black)
Simpson, Mary (Ewing)
Sinclair, Hester (Carpenter)
Sinclair, Joaner (Douglas)
Singleton, Sinia D. (Wood)
Sissan, Elizabeth (Sugget)
Skinner, Easter C. (Smith)
Smith, A.D. (Moore)
Smith, Abigal S. (Hathcock)
Smith, A.E. (Payne)
Smith, Cary J. (Browning)
Smith, Mrs. Charlotte (Gain)
Smith, Delila J. (PIlcher)
Smith, E.C. (Cooper)
Smith, Elizabeth (Haney)
Smith, Hilvah (Beene)
Smith, Isabella (Helms)
Smith, Jane (Spencer)
Smith, Lucinda (Teeter)
Smith, Martha (Johnson)
Smith, S.A. (Weatherall)
Smith, Sarah (Whitlow)
Smith, Susanna (Browning)
Snipes, Jane (Beasley)

Snow, E. (Ivy)
Soloman, T.E. (Sims)
Sory, Pricilla E. (Baxter)
Souter, Caroline (Duncan)
Souter, Emily F. (Winder)
South, Martha (Dillard)
South, Mary A.E. (Dillard)
Speck, Mary Ann (Reaves)
Speck, Mary M. (Speck)
Spence, M.A. (Leathers)
Staggs, Sarah (Potter)
Stanford, Elsira (McGill)
Stanford, Mary E. (Polk)
Stanford, S.A. (Ivy)
Stanley, Polly (Henry)
Stanton, A.R. (Lower)
Stark, Matilda (Sullivan)
Steel, Mary (Vicke)
Steele, Cynthia C. (Zinn)
Steelman, Elizabeth (Fowler)
Stegall, Mary Jane (Lesley)
Stegall, Sarah B. (Ponders)
Stephen, Hamet (Ball)
Stephens, M.F. (McCarver)
Stephens, Mary (Walker)
Stephens, N.A. (Pegues)
Stewart, Harriet A. (Hodges)
Stock, Ellendar (Beard)
Stone, Caroline (Snipes)
Stone, Henrietta V. (Duke)
Stone, Mary (Walker)
Stone, Mary R. (Givens)
Stone, Mattie M. (Smyth)
Stone, R.E. (Franklin)
Stone, Susannah (Griffin)
Stovall, M.A. (Green)
Stovall, M.E. (Dalton)
Strain, L.J. (Stanford)
Strain, Louisa V. (Fleming)
Strain, Susan T. (McCarter)
Strait, Salina A. (Gaines)
Strickland, Elizabeth (Pannell)
Strong, Virginia C. (Potts)
Stuart, Ellen (Hightower)
Stuart, Malissa C. (Museck)
Stuart, O.R. (Potts)
Sudduth, Ann E. (Ball)
Sudduth, Manerva (Sappington)
Sullivan, Eliza E. (Hearnsan)
Sullivan, Susan (Sneed)

Swafford, C.A. (Wynn)
SWafford, L.M. (Wilson)
Swan, Mary Ann (Bridges)
Swindoll, Mrs. Jane (Bowles)
Swindoll, M.C. (Harris)
Switzer, Mary E. (Wiley)

Tally, Elinor (Carter)
Tate, Jane (Farrow)
Taylor, C.J. (May)
Taylor, Louisa (Miller)
Taylor, Mary H. (Fields)
Taylor, P.E. (Carter)
Teague, Susan C. (Roach)
Teeter, Lucinda (Duke
Terrell, Mary (Screw)
Thomas, M.J. (James)
Thomas, Martha A.A.E. (Robbins)
Thomas, Mary E. (Sexton)
Thomas, Mary F. (Putt)
Thomas, Mrs. Mary J. Dunn)
Thomas, Sarah C. (Enoch)
Thomas, S.W. (Haynie)
Thomason, M.E. (Jackson)
Thomason, Rebecca A. (Stovall)
Thompson, A.R. (Jordan)
Thompson, Epsey C. (Taylor)
Thompson, Mary A. (Garrison)
Thompson, N.E. (Ivy)
Thompson, Sally (Green)
Thornton, L.V. (Pittman)
Thornton, M.J. (Marks)
Thornton, Mary C. (Duncan)
Thornton, Mary E. (Farrar)
Todd, Mary Jane (Stoats)
Tolerson, M.A. (Daniel)
Trice, Elizabeth (Malone)
Trice, Virginia A. (Osier)
Trulove, Catharin (Aycock)
Tucker, Jane (Weatherford)
Turner, Fannie (Long)
Turner, Fannie A. (Prude)
Tutor, A.H. (Tutor)
Tutor, Ann (Douglass)
Tutor, Lucy A. (McGreger)
Twitchell, Emma E. (Depass)
Tyre, Mildred E. (Ford)

Vaughan, Mary J. (Boatman)
Vaughan, Nancy (Huckabee)
Vaughn, D.E. (Nixon)
Vineyard, Taletha (Colvin)
Vinson, Amanda (Wait)
Vinson, N.E. (Nelson)
Vinyard, E.J. (Winn)

Wade, N.A. (Armstrong)
Wade, P.R.D. (Beeks)
Wade, S.R. (McCullough)
Waddell, Elizabeth (Furr)
Wages, Catharine (Pannell)
Wait, Virginia (Johnson)
Walker, Emily A. (Carder)
Walker, L.E. (Vance)
Walker, Lou M. (Brown)
Walker, Louisa A.B. (Gilmon)
Walker, Mary F. (Earle)
Walker, Mett (Davis)
Walker, Nancy W. (Yager)
Walker, Rebecca (Wolf)
Walker, Sylvia (Bradford)
Walker, Tabitha Z. (Osborn)
Wallis, Annie (Bigham)
Wallis, Rachiel (Warren)
Wallsworth, K.J. (Calloway)
Ward, Ann (Payne)
Ward, Barbara (Roberts)
Ward, D.C. (Johnson)
Ward, Harriet E. (Friarson)
Ward, H.T. (Newman)
Ward, L.E. (Vance)
Ward, Martha (Malone)
Ward, Mary E. (Carson)
Ward, Sarah (Harrison)
Ward, Sarah (Beckham)
Wardlaw, Sina (Crawford)
Ware, Margarett S. (James)
Ware, Mary (Rowe)
Ware, Mary Addie (Seal)
Ware, Mary A. (Crocker)
Ware, Sarah R. (Ward)
Warner, Mary A. (Lovejoy)
Warren, Emily E. (Mann)
Warren, Mary S. (Russell)

Warren, M.J. (Rutledge)
Warren, Permelia (Hudson)
Warren, Sarah Ann (Parr)
Warren, Sarah B. (Graham)
Watley, Amanda (McDaniel)
Watts, Elizabeth (Walker)
Weatherall, Emily (Baily)
Weatherall, Harriet (Hellum)
Weatherall, Mary M. (Ball)
Weatherall, Sarah (McNeil)
Webb, Susan J. (Pitts)
Webster, L.C. (Paine)
Welburn, Martha A. (Evans)
Wells, Adaline Martha (Hampton)
Wells, Annie (Armstead)
Wells, E.F. (Fretwell)
Wells, E.S. (Robbins)
Wells, Kizie (Duncan)
Wells, Mannerva (Snipes)
Wells, Martha A. (Jones)
Wells, Martha Jane (McCraw)
Wells, Mary (Gibbons)
Wells, Sarah E. (Beauchamp)
Wells, Sarah E. (Gould)
Wells, Sarah J. (Dunaway)
Wesson, Letty (Scott)
Wesson, M.M.H.E. (Golding)
Wesson, Rebecca A. (Parker)
West, A.E. (Mauldin)
West, Mary C. (Caldwell)
Wester, Eliza (Wester)
Wester, Frances A. (White)
Wester, Mary (Carr)
Westmoreland, M.A. (Marrs)
Wetherall, Rachel (Wells)
Wheatley, Elizabeth (Smith)
Wheatley, Mrs. Nancy (Hale)
Wheeler, Jane (Hadley)
White, Emeline (Carson)
White, jane (Wilson)
White, M.C. (McClure)
White, Martha L. (Frieman)
White, S.A. (Higgenbothum)
White, Sarah (Hill)
White, T.J. (Fuller)
Whitely, Pamelia (Hightower)
Whitesides, Margaret E. (Russell)
Whitesides, Martha E. (Porter)

Whitesides, Paralee J. (Riggin)
Whitlow, Elizabeth R. (Fuqua)
Wicker, Lucinda (Haze)
Wiggins, Serena (Gilliam)
Wilch, Mary E. (Thomason)
Wilder, Amy P. (Whitesides)
Wiley, Amanda (Nabors)
Wiley, C.C. (Hogge)
Wiley, Emma A. (Newsom)
Wiley, Mary L. (Frazier)
Wiley, Mely Ann (Horton)
Wiley, Sue (Wray)
Wilie, Jane A. (Martin)
Wilkerson, Mary (White)
Wilkins, Patsy (Sloan)
Wilkins, S.S.I. (Freeman)
Wilkinson, Elizabeth (Phillips)
Wilks, Jane (Creseey)
Wilks, L.E. (Murphy)
Willard, Mareah (Williams)
Williams, Fannie (Duff)
Williams, J.A. (Greene)
Williams, J.A. (Fitzgerald)
Williams, Louisa (Hunt)
Williams, M.A. (Cornelius)
Williams, Martha (Parks)
Williams, Martha Jane (Hamaker)
Williams, R.W. (Edwards)
Williams, Sarah C. (Skinner)
Williamson, Sarah (Sexton)
Wilson, Elizabeth (Parks)
Wilson, Mary A. (Brown)
Wilson, Mary E. (Price)
Wilson, Sarah E. (Mayhew)
Wilson, Teletha E. (Grant)
Winder, Harriet L. (Ward)
Windham, E.F. (Russell)
Winfield, Rose Ann (Gentry)
Winn, Elizabeth P. (James)
Wise, Sarah E. (Hill)
Wood, Cintha A. (Hancock)
Wood, D.J. (Forbes)
Wood, Gilly Ann (Edwards)
Wood, Isabella (Eagl)
Wood, J.A. (Cargill)
Wood, Martha D. (Ritchie)
Wood, Mary (Grady)
Wood, Mary A. (McCord)

Wood, Mary E. (Woods)
Wood, N.E. (Hodges)
Woodward, Sallie (Cross)
Worsham, M.C. (Cain)
Worsham, Margaret C. (Mauldin)
Wright, Martha A. (Neil)
Wylie, Jane (Martin)
Wylie, M.H. (Lilly)
Wynn, Louisa J. (Hunt)
Wynn, M.A. (Boyd)

Yokum, Mrs. Matilda (Brandon)
Young, Elizabeth (Pannell)
Young, Lucinda (FRazier)
Young, Martha E. (Nowlin)
Young, Mary Ann (Stack)
Young, Nancy C. (Davis)
Youngblood, Lucinda J. (Swinson)

Zinn, Harriet F. (Miller)

PONTOTOC COUNTY, MISSISSIPPI

"MISSING MARRIAGES" 1867 – 1880

THESE MARRIAGES CANNOT BE FOUND IN THE CIRCUIT CLERK'S OFFICE BECAUSE THEY WERE DESTROYED BY STORM IN 1936 – HOWEVER – BEFORE THE STORM D.W. FRANKS, THE CIRCUIT CLERK, REPORTED THESE MARRIAGES TO THE MISSISSIPPI STATE BOARD OF HEALTH AND ARE NOW ON MICRO-FILM.

INDEXED BY: HAZLE BOSS NEET
             207 NORTH MAIN
             PONTOTOC, MISSISSIPPI 38863

PONTOTOC COUNTY, MISSISSIPPI MARRIAGES 1867 - 1880

THE PONTOTOC COUNTY MARRIAGES BOOK/BOOKS CONTAINING PART OF 1867, ALL OF 1868, 1869, ALL OF THE 1870'S AND PART OF 1880 ARE MISSING. THESE CANNOT BE FOUND IN THE COURTHOUSE, BUT ARE ON MICRO-FILM AT THE PONTOTOC COUNTY, MISSISSIPPI LIBRARY. SOME ARE VERY DIFFICULT TO READ. SO BESURE TO CHECK ALL POSSIBLE SPELLINGS. SOME OF THE HANDWRITING WAS NOT EASY TO READ, SOME WERE TOO DIM AND SOME WERE TOO DARK ON MICRO-FILM. WHERE THERE WAS A DOUBT OF THE SPELLING THERE IS A QUESTION MARK THAT FOLLOWS.

PAGE	GROOM	BRIDE	DATE	
707	Aaron, John	Thompson, Anna	30 Oct	1879
297	Abernathy, J.R.	Walden, Callie	9 Mar	1871
349	Abernathy, R.B.	Rutledge, Eliza	30 Jan	1872
88	Abernathy, W.J.	Stewart, M.C.	13 Feb	1868
89	Albritton, W.W.	Turner, M.T.	10 Feb	1868
240	Aldridge, P.A.	Moore, Ruth	30 July	1870
168	Aldridge, W.R.	Moore, A.H.	7 Sept	1869
653	Aldridge, R.P.	Hale, M.E.	15 Sept	1878
318	Alexander, Newton	Kelley, Sarah	14 Sept	1871
121	Alexander, J.D.	Johnson, E.A.	15 Nov	1868
398	Alexander, W.H.	Brown, S.D.	23 Jan	1873
549	Allan, Wm	Reid, Dorah	27 Sept	1876
287	Allen, J.C.	Kimbrough, M.E.	26 Jan	1871
485	Allen, R.D.	Gregory, M.A.	23 Dec	1874
287	Allen, W.D.	Kimbrough, M.J.C.	26 Jan	1871
435	Allen, W.T.	Fowler, A.P.	11 Dec	1873
88	Allsup, S.A.	Stevenson, A.G.	6 Feb	1868
601	Alsup, E.	McNeeley, Barbara	2 Dec	1877
265	Alsup, R.T.	Ruod(?), M.E.	22 Nov	1870
691	Alsup, W.B.	McAbie, Fannie	3 July	1879
634	Anderson, B.D.	Miller, A.H.	28 Feb	1878
92	Anderson, J.Q.	Bramlett, Nancy	12 Mar	1868
233	Anderson, M.H.	Prints (?), Malissa	28 Apr	1870
365	Anderson, P.M.	Tallie, Sallie	24 July	1872
423	Ange, J.E.	Walls, Rebecca	30 Oct	1873
375	Archer, David L.	Turner, Nancy	3 Oct	1872
83	Armisted (?), S.(?) J.	Morrow, N.M.	28 Jan	1868
640	Armstrong, Dr. F.M.	Johnson, Mattie J.	18 Apr	1879
224	Ashton, J.K.	Hyler, Martha	6 Mar	1870
269	Atkins, G.H.	Horton, Martha O.	1 Dec	1870
51	Austin, J.A.	Bass, Mary Ann	20 Sept	1870
41	Austin, J.O.	Real, Charlotte	3 Nov	1867
177	Austin, J.R.	Austin, Sarah A.	10 Oct	1869
597	Austin, S.H. (?)	Blount, Lou	11 Mar	1877
661	Avent, A. (?) D.	Sneed, Mattie	4 Dec	1878
353	Aycock, T.P.	Parker, Emma	10 Feb	1872

PAGE	GROOM	BRIDE	DATE	
521	B---, T.(?) C.	Hardin, Elizer	26 Dec	1875
326	Bailey, P.N.	Fooshee, Frances	1 Nov	1871
482	Bailey, W.W.	Hester, Elizabeth	9 Dec	1874
319	Baker, A.D.	Calcote, Lucy	1 Oct	1871
377	Baker, J.C.	West, Fannie	9 Oct	1872
298	Baker, Lafayette	Wetherford, Jane	9 Mar	1871
477	Baker, W.G.	Shettles, Sallie	18 Nov	1874
129	Baker, W.H.	Smith, M.R.	24 Dec	1868
610	Barefield, A.J.	Bickers, Manerva	17 Dec	1877
746	Baldwin, Savannah	Maddy (?), Margaret	18 Apr	1880
593	Barksdale, J.S.	Wells, Millie	21 Jan	1877
731	Barksdale, J.S.	Harris, Eva	15 Jan	1880
635	Barlow, W.B.	Gilmer, A.C.	28 Feb	1878
392	Baroen, J.D.	Atkins, L.A.	19 Dec	1873
705	Barton, W.P.K.	Perry, Mollie	9 Oct	1879
682	Bass, John T.	Crunup, Mary	29 Jan	1879
209	Bauchamp, P.	Harmon, Malinda	11 Jan	1870
384	Baxter, A.J.	Mauldin, C.B.	28 Nov	1872
22	Baxter, William	Golding, Margaret E.	7 Apr	1867
4	Beard, J.C.	Harain, C.A.	16 Jan	1867
725	Beard, W.J.	Beard, J.L.	30 Dec	1879
105	Beasley (or Busby?), J.C.	Pruitt, Pauline	3 July	1868
570	Beasly, H. (?) S.	Beasley, Caraling	13 Jan	1877
465	Beazly, C.C.	Luther, Mrs. E.	12 July	1874
6	Beauchamp, Zilaby(?)	Ramsey, Sarah A.	29 Jan	1867
688	Beavers, J.M.	Carter, Nancy	1 Apr	1879
194	Butts, J.E.	Hanley, Caroline	16 Dec	1869
626	Belk, H.C.	Gaines, Eliza Ann	27 Jan	1878
362	Bell, Alsey	Rogers, Gillie	16 May	1872
472	Bell, Isaac	Pinson, Sallie	15 Oct	1874
545	Bell, J.W.	Flournay, M.L.	30 Oct	1876
541	Bell, R.M.	Neely, Addie B.	1 June	1876
410	Bennett, W.S.	Smith, Elizabeth K.	10 July	1873
714	Benjamin(?), W.D.	Burton, Mariah H.	27 Aug	1866
663	Benson, J.L.	McPherson, B.C.	19 Dec	1878
135	Benson, W.C.	Cox, Mrs. M.A.	26 Jan	1869
124	Benson, W.E.	Daggett, Jennie H.	3 Dec	1868
334	Bennett, Joseph	Reed, Mary F.	23 Nov	1871
25	Berry, J.T.B.	Bamba(?), Jessie J.	14 Sept	1884
581	Bevell, F.N.	Wood, Fannie D.	11 May	1877
348	Bevel, J.R.D.	Mayhew, Martha	23 Jan	1872
191	Bevil, H.P.	Mayhew, Sallie	10 Dec	1869
609	Bevil, Samuell	Wells, Mary	18 May	1877
716	Bevill, A.(?) B.	Swaim, B.J.	14 Dec	1879
684	Bevill, F.W.	Wood, Annie G.	13 Feb	1879
599	Bevill, Fontaine	Berry, Lizzie	8 Nov	1877
456	Bevill, H.P.	Grisham, Harriett	1 Mar	1874
362	Bigha(?), Henry	Washington, Ella	19 June	1877
259	Bishop, W.T.	Williamson, Mary	6 Apr	1872
47	Black, B.M.	Johnson, R.L.	28 Oct	1867
87	Black, T.H.	Terry, Mrs. Martha	6 Feb	1868

PAGE	GROOM	BRIDE	DATE	
248	Blackstock, T.A.	Sledge, Julia	9 Sept	1870
350	Blagg, A.R.	Jernigan, Elizabeth	30 Jan	1872
288	Blair, W.B.	Price, N.J.	26 Jan	1871
460	Blakesly, S.L.	Davis, Matilda	17 May	1874
397	Bolding, B.D.	Miers, S.(?) L.	16 Jan	1873
744	Bolen, C.J.	Gregory, M.C.	5 Apr	1880
530	Bolen, H.P.	Little, Elizabeth	3 Feb	1876
408	Bolton, Greenbury	Warner, Elizabeth	17 May	1873
405	Bolton, J.C.	Hoy, M.J.	8 Apr	1873
585	Bost, Sidney(?)	Hardin, Elizar	7 Dec	1877
151	Bowen, J.D.	Walker, Catherine	4 Mar	1869
76	Bowen, J.W.	Walker, J.M.	19 Jan	1868
737	Bower (or Brewer?), J.C.	Gooch, L.S.	18 Feb	1880
483	Boyd, William	Kelly, Eliza	18 Dec	1874
533	Bradon, J.W.	Greenwood, Mississippi	27 Feb	1876
473	Bradon, W.F.	Shields, Joshie	24 Oct	1874
5	Bramlett, J.G.	Malone, Mollie	9 Aug	1877
495	Bramlett, T.A.	Miller, Annie E.	23 Feb	1875
245	Bramlett, Thomas	Shannon, Harriet	5 Aug	1870
632	Bramlitt, J.F.	Roberson, Agnes	18 Feb	1878
681	Bramlitt, L.M.	Conlee, E.A.	28 Jan	1878
747	Bramlitt, L.M.	Conlee, P.C.	9 Sept	1880
354	Branan, C.C.	Bowen, Julia M.	15 Feb	1872
646	Branan, G.W.	Robinson, S.A.	1 Aug	1878
513	Brandon, T.D.	Conway, E.N.	2 Dec	1875(?)
502	Bratton, J.L.	Withers, N.A.	30 June	1875
13	Bratton, L.P.	Jones, Callie	6 Jan	1882
529	Brazell, J.W.	Hendrix, Sarah	27 Jan	1876
394	Breye(?), Franklin	Thornton, Malissa	2 Jan	1873
174	Bridges, T.G.	Wedden, C.A.	29 Sept	1869
64	Brinkley, E.C.	Alsap, Frances	22 Dec	1867
649	Britt, F.M.	Reeder(?), Lizzie	23 Aug	1878
172	Brooks, L.R.	Wilks, M.A.	9 Nov	1869
114	Brooks, W.J.	Swindle, Mallasie	7 July	1868
490	Broom, Robert	Reed, Julia	17 Jan	1875
615	Broome, R.F.	McDonald, Sallie	20 Dec	1871
138	Brown, A.B.	Neely, M.J.	26 Jan	1869
690	Brown, A.F.	Bell, E.P.	29 May	1869
169	Brown, A.J.	Grubbs, Martha C.	6 Sept	1869
70	Brown, A.J.	McNeil, Lizzie A.	30 Dec	1867
718	Brown, J.M.	Gay, Sallie	18 Dec	1879
96	Brown, J.O.	Smith, Sarah J.	5 Apr	1868
252	Brown, Joseph	Roland, Narcissa	20 Oct	1870
487	Brown, R.R.	Pegues, Carrie F.	22 Dec	1874
467	Brown, William	Dunarett, Emma	3 Sept	1874
115	Browning, J.R.	High, Rebecca J.	11 Oct	1868
138	Browning, W.H.	Hattox, Ann	27 Jan	1869
721	Browning, W.H.	Burks, Mrs. Mary	18 Dec	1879
123	Brumett, William	Stamphill, Elizabeth	26 Nov	1868
371	Brummet, L.M.	Heard, G.A.	5 Sept	1872
662	Bryant, T.R.	Swain, Mrs. M.C.	11 Dec	1878

PAGE	GROOM	BRIDE	DATE	
99	Buchanan, A.J.	Porter, O.B.	3 May	1868
110	Buchanan, A.T.	Carr, Mary E.	6 Sept	1868
327	Buchanan, Jackson	Kelley, Elmira	2 Nov	1871
452	Buchannan, W.M.	Buchannan, Mrs. D.B.	21 July	1878
55	Bugg, A.G.	Conld(?), M.A.	5 Dec	1867
107	Bullard, J.W.	Bullard, E.J.	22 July	1868
376	Burlison, J.R.	Betts, H.A.	14 Oct	1872
637	Burrow, John T.	Harlow, Louisa	7 Nov	1878
105	Busby, J.H.	Pruitt, Pauline	5 July	1868
423	Butler, E.F.	Buse, R.S.	27 Oct	1873
35	Buttram, L.D.	Evans, C.V.	1 Sept	1867
539	Bynum, T.C.	Vaughn, S.F.	20 May	1876
595	Caffee, M.R.	Horton, Judson(?)	15 Oct	1877
365	Caldwell, B.W.	Greenwood, E.F.	23 July	1872
414	Caldwell, Dickson	Medlock, Lenie	24 Aug	1873
45	Caldwell, E.B.	Boswell, Nancy C.	23 Oct	1867
490	Caldwell, J.C.	Foster, Harriet	20 July	1875
515	Caldwell, J.D.	Weaver, Caroline	10 Dec	1875
289	Caldwell, J.H.	Berry, L.A.	26 Jan	1871
412	Caldwell, M.L.(S?)	Haron, Laura F.	2 Aug	1873
703	Caldwell, Pinkney	Dillard, Paralee	9 Oct	1879
26	Caldwell, S.P.	Cobb, T.N.	23 May	1867
345	Caldwell, T.L.	Greenwood, H.J.	11 Jan	1872
180	Caldwell, W.D.	Sims, Mollie C.	20 Oct	1869
575	Caldwell, W.M.	Campbell, Nannie E.	22 Feb	1877
527	Callaway, C.E.	Weatherall, E.V.	29 Jan	1878
601	Callaway, J.J.	Hightower, Malinda	15 Nov	1877
422	Cap, A.A.	Bauldwin, Sallie	13 Oct	1877
690	Card, J.N.	Guttery, Rebecca	12 June	1879
692	Carlisle, W.H.	Ward, Frances	17 July	1879
150	Carnes, T.R.	Hall, M.T.	6 Jan	1869
608	Carson, T.J.	Stegall, Sarepta	9 Dec	1877
23	Carson, William	Pitts, Cornelia	7 May	1867
358	Carter, B.D.	Hulet, Becca	5 Mar	1872
492	Carter, L.H.	Lee, R.A.	31 Jan	1875
192	Carter, J.M.	Dagett, Hattie H.	7 Dec	1867
383	Carter, J.M.	Christian, Mary A.	7 Nov	1872
503	Carter, J.M.	McKinney, M.J.	11 Aug	1875
181	Carter, Lee	McDonald, Louisa	26 Oct	1869
34	Carter, Samuel	Overcalh(?), Mary	29 Aug	1867
409	Case, W.H.	Powel, N.P.	18 May	1873
449	Castleberry, S.A.	Lee, S.A.	1 Feb	1874
658	Campbell, A.C.	White, A.E.	7 Nov	1878
274	Campbell, R.A.	Gafford, M.E.	20 Dec	1870
128	Cannon, N.E.	Price, Martha J.	22 Dec	1868
210	Cannon, Nathan	Wilkins (or Williams?), Jennie	13 Jan	1870
467	Cannon, Q.C.	McKnight, Mary	15 Aug	1874
139	Cannon, T.B.	McKnight, S.J.	31 Jan	1869

PAGE	GROOM	BRIDE	DATE	
199	Carpenter, J.W.	Anderson, M.E.	22 Dec	1869
435	Carpenter, J.W.	Hardin, Misty	11 Dec	1873
405	Carr, O.C.	Miller, C.A.	8 Apr	1873
75	Carr, O.J.	Carpenter, Mary E.	9 Jan	1868
13	Chapman, John	Reed, Mollie O.	12 Feb	1867
2	Childers, A.	Calaway, Mattie A.	13 Jan	1867
501	Clark, F.M.	Stewart G. (or S?)	21 June	1875
219	Clark, J.D.	Todd, Mary	17 Jan	1879
696	Clark, J.P.	Price, Sarah	17 Aug	1879
428	Clark, William	Lambert, N.A.	19 Nov	1873
704	Clay, John	Abernathy, E.J.	7 Oct	1879
604	Clayton, J.J.	Hardin, G.A.	29 Nov	1877
488	Clayton, Jacob	Potter, M.J.	1 Jan	1875
630	Clayton, R.(?)	Weaver, Susan	7 Feb	1878
427	Clayton, Ransom	Daniel, Lueann	13 Nov	1873
32	Clayton, W.J.	McKnight, C.H.	8 Aug	1867
634	Clayton, William	Dillard, Margarett	28 Feb	1878
621	Clements, D.F.	Skinner, L.F.	9 Jan	1878
648	Clements, J.H.	Skinner, L.E.	14 Aug	1878
153	Coats, A.A.	Skinner, Martha E.M.F.	18 Apr	1869
586	Coats, F.M.	Cannon, M.J.	2 Aug	1877
433	Coats, J.G.	Miears, Anna	4 Dec	1873
583	Cobb, D.H.	Tapley, Ellen R.	9 June	1877
594	Cobb, J.A.	Rodgers, Josephine	11 Oct	1877
182	Coffin, R.L.	Martin, Mollie D.	27 Oct	1869
562	Coker, Easley	Walls, Martha J.	23 Aug	1877
661	Coker, G.W.	Starkey, Catharine	3 Dec	1878
56	Cole, J.M.	Kimbrough, Elizabeth	4 Aug	1868
187	Collins, Carter	Langston, Emily	27 Nov	1867
321	Collins, J.H.	Fleming, Martha D.	27 Sept	1871
178	Collins, Riley	Doxey, Rachel	10 Oct	1869
456	Collier, W.M.	Stegall, Elina	15 Feb	1874
715	Collins, W.R.	Bell, L.C.	24 Dec	1879
367	Combs, J.W.	Ray, R.J.	6 Aug	1872
229	Conlee, C.W.	Helms, M.A.	31 Mar	1870
52	Conley, Wm	Duncan, E.J.	20 Nov	1867
51	Conn, W.T.	Williams, M.E.	20 Nov	1867
702	Cook, James R.	Owens, J.D.	9 Oct	1879
154	Cooper, J.B.	Crittenden, Mrs. Mary	21 Apr	1869
212	Cowert, J.W.	Miller, Thursey E.	16 Jan	1870
363	Cox, A.P.	Pritchard, M.R.	30 June	1872
389	Cox, Joseph Y.	Pitts, Luisa	5 Dec	1872
333	Crow, C.C.	Jinkins, Dollie	19 Nov	1871
303	Crow, Jefferson	Jenkins, Alice	23 Apr	1871
342	Crawford, A.M.	Bramlett, L.C.	24 Dec	1871
446	Crawford, J.H.	McJunken, J.A.	13 Jan	1874
459	Crawford, William	Wood, Mrs. S.E.	27 May	1874
404	Creed, P.C.	Brown, Mary	2 Aug	1873
399	Crenshaw, A.B.	Cobb, S.A.	6 Feb	1873
695	Crenshaw, W.M.	Roye, M.M.	3 Aug	1879
381	Crittenden, J.W.	Henry, S.F.	27 Oct	1872
205	Crocker, Stephen	Crawford, Ellen	6 Jan	1870

PAGE	GROOM	BRIDE	DATE	
270	Cromwell, W.N.	Azlin, Frances M.	13 Dec	1870
201	Crosley, A.H.	Bramlett, Martha	9 Jan	1870
269	Crosley, G.W.	Hightower, M.E.	6 Dec	1870
216	Crosley, U.V. (or V.V.)	Johnston, J.A.	2 Feb	1870
133	Crum, J.C.	Bigham, Susan	21 Jan	1869
701	Cruse, J.M.	Jackles(?), M.M.	9 Sept	1879
400	Cruse, H.A.	Wilder, N.R.	8 Feb	1873
655	Cruse, H.A.	Griffin, Colen	29 Oct	1878
355	Cummings, J.M.	Edington, Martha A.	28 Feb	1872
207	Daggett, George	Wardlaw, Rachel	6 Jan	1870
86	Daniel, W.B.	Davis, T.E.	23 Jan	1868
140	Daniel, Wilson	Terrell, Mrs. M.M.	30 Jan	1869
228	Davis, A.J.	Allen, M.E.	20 Mar	1870
510	Davis, G.	Salmon, Mary	2 Nov	1875
190	Davis, G.W.	Hooper, Mary E.	5 Dec	1869
251	Davis, Henry	Pugh, Nancy	25 Sept	1870
695	Davis, S.P.	Bramlitt, R.A.	7 Aug	1879
82	Deale, J.W.	Caldwell, Mary F.	4 Feb	1868
102	Deaton, J.S.	Turner, C.E.	14 Nov	1867
347	Deen, A.J.	Wyn, Frances	18 June	1872
583	Dejournett, R.E.	Hudson, Susan E.	26 July	1877
24	Dees, J.A.	Murrey, Martha Ann	9 May	1867
452	Deford, H.D.	Card, A.C.	1 Feb	1874
281	Dickson, H.F.	Thornton, E.A.	9 Jan	1871
34	Dickson, J.A.	Morgan, Mary E.	18 Aug	1867
673	Dickson, J.M.	McNeil, F.E.	7 Jan	1879
438	Dillard, George	Clayton, D.A.B.	17 Dec	1873
524	Dillard, H.B.	Hale, S.C.	11 jan	1876
360	Dillard, J.C.	Vaughn, Nancy Ann	16 Apr	1872
80	Dillard, J.P.	Dyson, E.E.	25 Jan	1868
147	Dillard, J.T.	Richie, L.C.	21 Feb	1869
572	Dillard, J.T.	Jordan, S.E.	24 Jan	1877
366	Dillard, jack	Grisle, Mrs. Sarah	8 Aug	1872
448	Dillard, K.D.	Green, Margaret	3 Mar	1867
324	Dillard, Lafayette	Todd, Mary E.	12 Oct	1871
438	Dillard, P.A.	Clayton, N.E.	17 Dec	1873
509	Dillard, P.A.	Vaughn, Adaline	14 Oct	1875
617	Dillard, R.D.	Swindle, Rebecca	27 Dec	1877
462	Dillard, Slack	Booth, Bettie	25 May	1876
129	Dixon, C.C.	Boyd, Malisia	24 Dec	1868
408	Dodd, John	Leach, M.J.	11 May	1873
107	Dorsey, A.F.	Jones, Mollie E.	19 July	1868
440	Douglas, J.W.	Hardin, Frances	25 Dec	1873
548	Douglass, J.A.	Stewart, S.A.	21 Sept	1876
424	Douglass, J.E.	Stewart, R.V.	29 Oct	1873
542	Douglass, J.W.	Hardin, Sinderilla	20 July	1876
94	Douglass, S.J.	Steward, F.D.	12 Mar	1868
537	Douglass, S.W.	Philips, S.	18 Dec	1873
479	Dover, J.M.	Brayer, Elizabeth	23 July	1874
650	Dowdy, E.	Pilcher, R.M.E.	25 Aug	1878
130	Dowdy, John	McNeely, Ann	6 Jan	1869
36	Dowdy, W.W.	Warren, R.F.	5 Sept	1867

PAGE	GROOM	BRIDE	DATE	
146	Downs, S.J.	Bowen, Martha J.	16 Feb	1869
578	Donaldson, J.C.	Bell, T.E.	14 Mar	1877
514	Donaldson, R.A.	Miller, M.H.	1 Dec	1875
527	Donaldson, T.A.	Stegall, M.L.	19 Jan	1876
10	Donaldson, W.E.	Wagner, Alice	30 Jan	1867
285	Donaldson, W.H.	Callaway, N.J.	19 Jan	1871
274	Dozier, J.S. (or L.?)	Miller, Corrie F.	20 Dec	1870
654	Dozier, Oliver	Gage, Nancy E.	6 Oct	1878
656	Drake, J.B.	Carr, H.D.	30 Oct	1878
183	Drennen, Simon	Berry, Fannie	27 Oct	1869
130	Duff, D.A.	Chambliss, Martha D.	19 Nov	1868
705	Duke, J.D.	McCord, Susan M.	12 Oct	1879
599	Duncan, M.L. (or S.?)	McKelvy, L.C.	3 Nov	1877
735	Duncan, T.B.	Cox, R.C.	28 Jan	1880
311	Duncan, W.C.	Short, Melvina	24 June	1880
698	Durham, T.G.	Rayburn, L.A.	27 Aug	1879
213	Durham, W.B.	Allen, Sarah F.	18 Jan	1870
640	Durham, W.B.	Aycock, Buelah	2 May	1878
63	Dyer, J.C.	Snipes, M.R.	19 Dec	1867
279	Dyson, J.S.	Todd, Mary E.	28 Dec	1870
607	Easley, J.T.	Hampton, M.T.	9 Dec	1877
83	Easterwood, GEorge	McCraw, Martha S.	22 Jan	1868
282	Easterwood, Jas W.	Aycock, Virginia C.	8 Jan	1871
699	Echols, J.F.	Powell, E.G.	29 Dec	1878
318	Edington, B.F.	Powell, Arabella	17 Sept	1871
175	Edwards, Wm	Robertson, Jane	2 Oct	1869
425	Ellett, Joseph	Youngblood, R.E.	4 Nov	1873
254	Ellis, William	Johnston, S.H.	5 Oct	1870
204	Ellison, John	Weatherall, Margaret	28 Dec	1869
344	Ellzy, P.S.	Matthews, M.A.	3 Jan	1872
264	Eubanks, G.D.	Elzey, Sallie	17 Nov	1870
198	Evans, C.C.	Huckabee, Sarah	23 Dec	1869
158	Ezell, J.R.	White, Elizabeth	30 May	1869
518	Fair, W.F.	Montgomery, Dena	20 Dec	1875
429	Falkner, E.	Fowler, Savannah	27 Nov	1873
672	Falkner, George	Haney, Lucinda	2 Jan	1879
378	Faulkner, J.T.	Jones, F.A.	17 Oct	1872
302	Faughn, W.H.	Youngblood, H.E.	12 Apr	1871
143	Farmer, J.T.	Beard, C.V.	28 Jan	1869
145	Farror, James	Saint, Margaret	13 Dec	1868
280	Fields, J.A.	Perry, Frances	5 Jan	1871
111	Fields, J.M.	Jenkins, Mary	20 Sept	1868
441	Fields, S.S.	Taylor, Caty	23 Dec	1873
1	Fisher, W.B.	Coleman, Margaret	17 Jan	1867
142	Fitzgerald, S.J.	Funk, Nancy M.	17 Feb	1869
671	Flaherty, F.S.	Landing, Eliza	31 Dec	1878
147	Flaharty, W.M.	Pearsall, Nancy E.	18 Feb	1868
328	Fleming, M.A.	Wood, S.E.	2 Nov	1871
535	Fleming, W.C.	Nowlan, H.M.	20 Mar	1876
556	Fleming, W.J.	Shelton, M.C.	7 Nov	1876

PAGE	GROOM	BRIDE	DATE	
425	Floyd, Dayly	Hartley, Elizabeth	30 Oct	1873
444	Floyd, Samuel	Ragan, M.A.	1 Jan	1874
486	Floyd, Thomas	Alexander, Kate	23 Dec	1874
510	Fontaine, B.B.	Cary, A.B.	11 Nov	1875
675	Fooshee, Bryan	Douglass, S.J.	9 Jan	1879
627	Fooshee, E.M.	Tallant, Clarentine	3 Feb	1878
397	Fooshee, J.B.	Tutor, Rebecca H.	29 Jan	1873
446	Fooshee, John	Tallant, Dalia	15 jan	1874
368	Ford, J.W.	Alexander, Sarah	22 Aug	1872
336	Fortune, R.A.	Simpson, M.C.	3 Dec	1871
579	Foster, George	Helms, lavenia	2 Apr	1877
167	Foster, J.R.	Langley, M.A.	25 Aug	1869
4	Fowler, G.J.	Harrison, Mary	13 Jan	1867
447	Fowler, J.A.	Moore, H.C.	15 Jan	1874
370	Fowler, M.W.	Williams, Mrs. E.J.	10 Sept	1872
417	Franklin, B.E.	Turner, Sarah	9 Sept	1873
501	Franklin, J.B.	Gilespie, A.G.	1 June	1875
716	Franklin, J.C.	Kizer, N.M.	21 Dec	1879
606	Franklin, J.W.	Greenwood, M.C.	9 Dec	1877
508	Franklin, S.P.	Franklin, S.A.	5 Oct	1875
536	Franklin, W.M.	Nicks, M.J.	28 Mar	1876
233	Franklin, Wesley	Sibley, Serina	7 May	1870
137	Frazier, C.A.	Bradshaw, Mrs. E.R.	26 Jan	1869
239	Frazier, W.H.	Gafford, Lucinda	11 July	1870
300	Freeman, Richard	Rush, Maude	6 Apr	1871
484	Freeman, Thomas	Rush, Mollie	17 Dec	1874
376	Fretwell, W.F.	Madox, Zennelin L.	8 Oct	1872
532	Fuller, H.W.	Britt, Margaret Ann	16 Feb	1876
540	Furgerson, B.F.	Hill, N.A.	4 June	1876
681	Furgerson, William	Ornsby, Ella	26 Jan	1869
70	Furr, Alison	Carpenter, Mrs. Catherine	1 Jan	1868
262	Furr, J.J.	Gilmore, Sarah C.	13 Nov	1870
101	Fuqua, A.A.	Robinson, N.L.	31 May	1868
652	Fuqua, William	Horton, M.J.	5 Sept	1878
498	Gafford, W.R.	Wood, M.L.	18 Apr	1875
27	Gain, J.W.	Bell, Rosana	6 June	1867
440	Gaines, R.W.	Medlock, Emily	21 Dec	1873
644	Gaines, T.C.	Williams, Jane	23 June	1878
624	Gaines, Thomas	Medlock, M.A.	17 Jan	1878
132	Gaines, Z.T.	Stamphill, Lugany	14 Jan	1869
646	Galloway, J.W.	Wood, C.V.	28 July	1878
141	Gammel, W.R.	Carr, Mary Ann	4 Oct	1868
259	Garman, David	Greene(?), Julia	23 Oct	1870
93	Garmon, J.P.	Anderson, Elizabeth	5 mar	1868
455	Garner, William	McCoy, D.A.E.	12 Feb	1874
651	Garrett, John A.	Simmons, Emma	29 Aug	1878
286	Garrett, M.T. (or M.F.?)	Jones, Frances V.	23 Jan	1871
228	Garrison, Alexander	Horton, Mary E.	21 Mar	1870
154	Garrison, T.B.	Kidd, L.C.	22 Apr	1869
190	Gates, J.W.	Herring, Mollie	4 Dec	1869
335	Gatewood, A.J.	Busbee, Narcissa	27 Mar	1870
565	Gay, R.(?) C.	Real, Jane	2 Jan	1877
623	Gay, W.D.	Morgan, Mary A.	17 Jan	1878

PAGE	GROOM	BRIDE	DATE	
518	Gentry, D.P.	Reed, N.C.	23 Dec	1875
546	George, J.W.	Bolen, Ola	10 Sept	1876
172	Geter, Thomas	Sulivan, Sarah	19 Aug	1869
395	Gideon, S.A. (or G.A.?)	Carr, E.C.	23 Jan	1873
475	Gill, S.C.	Brown, Adie L.	8 Nov	1874
574	Gill, T.S.	Gammitt, Francis	12 Feb	1877
589	Gillespie, G.W.	Fuller, L.F.	27 Aug	1877
670	Gillespie, H.N.	Dillard, Carrie B.	30 Dec	1878
298	Gillespie, T.J.	Furgerson, Addie	9 Mar	1871
64	Gilliam, J.L.	Baker, Sabrina	31 Dec	1867
230	Gilsman, S.F.	Walker, Percilla	10 Apr	1870
459	Gilmore, Jessy	Miller, Elizabeth	26 Mar	1874
225	Gilmore, John	Bell, Elizabeth	10 Mar	1870
218	Gilstrap, C.J.	Bullard, L.A.	10 Feb	1870
348	Glenn, J.M.	Evens, Mrs. Martha	21 Jan	1872
293	Glover, J.S.	Crewe, B.T.	8 Feb	1871
52	Godfrey, B.W.	Moore, Louiza	21 Nov	1867
66	Godfrey, T.P.	Bullard, Isabellah	26 Dec	1867
31	Goggans, J.J.	Wilber, E.J.	28 July	1867
273	Golding, Goforth	Phifer, Mary	24 Dec	1870
184	Golding, Harry	Stephens, Hannah	13 Dec	1869
385	Gooch, C.	Poyner, S.A.	28 Nov	1872
305	Goode, T.W.	Waite, Rebecca	1 May	1871
598	Goodlett, G.A.	Lilly, Bettie	30 Oct	1877
732	Goodman, Willis	Shipman, Cora	15 Jan	1880
220	Goodwin, J.C.	Rodgers, C.M.	11 Feb	1870
171	Gordon, J.T.	Knox, Sarah	21 Sept	1869
612	Gordon, Robt	Easley, Thrase	18 Dec	1877
198	Gordon, W.D.	Gafford, H.M.	18 Dec	1872
605	Goulding, Geo	Phifer, Verona	2 Dec	1877
649	Graddy, John	Grant, Fannie	15 Aug	1878
22	Graham, S.J.	McClelland, C.	11 Apr	1867
208	Grant, G.A.	Carter, George Ann	7 Jan	1870
422	Grant, Jesse	Knighton, Elizabeth	9 Dec	1873
476	Grant, William	Sudduth, Cate	12 Nov	1874
16	Gray, J.W.	Potter, D.E.	14 Feb	1867
698	Gray, James	Purdon, Washey	29 Aug	1879
290	Gray, John	Pope, Mrs. Martha	2 Feb	1871
697	Gray, John A.	Whitworth, Mary	19 Aug	1879
351	Gray, W.W.	Hollaman, Lizzie	5 Feb	1872
476	Green, A.B.	Philips, M.C.	17 Nov	1874
177	Green, C.M.	Bolton, Matilday	7 Oct	1869
363	Green, Callaway	David, Mrs. Selma C.	30 June	1872
283	Greene, D.F.	Powell, Mary E.	12 Jan	1871
626	Greene, Smith	Clayton, Adeline	27 Jan	1878
620	Gregory, J.B.	Rea, S.E.S.	3 Jan	1878
602	Gregory, J.E.	Mauldin, G.L.	15 Nov	1877
127	Gregory, S.J.	Bright, Sarah J.	17 Dec	1868
296	Griffin, A.W.	Pearson, Louisiann	24 Feb	1871
259	Griffin, B.F.	Rodgers, Sarah J.	27 Oct	1870
156	Griffin, E.M.	Youngblood, Sarah	28 Apr	1867
188	Griffin, Eli	Reel, Susan	1 Dec	1869

PAGE	GROOM	BRIDE	DATE	
98	Griffin, G.J.	Thompkins, Nancy A.	25 Apr	1868
552	Griffin, G.J.	Brummitt, Nannie	12 Oct	1876
418	Griffin, James	Smith, Harriet	11 Sept	1873
291	Griffin, John	Walker, Eliza	8 Feb	1871
519	GRiffin, John	Wages, Sallie	27 Dec	1875
525	Griffin, Morgan	Collums, Sarah	13 Jan	1876
215	Griffin, W.F.	Dixon, D.A.	26 Jan	1870
344	Grisham, G.S.	Hall, G.A.	4 Jan	1872
670	Grisham, J.J.	White, Jodie	2 Jan	1879
167	Grisham, J.W.	Hattox, L.A.	24 Aug	1869
434	Grysell, T.L.	Dillard, Martha F.	5 Dec	1873
369	Guthrie, J.W.	Long, P.C.	25 Aug	1872
21	Hackett, J.H.	Hollis, Mrs. Rebecca E.	27 Mar	1867
327	Hackett, J.H.	Carter, Jane	26 May	1871
641	Hale, B.F.	Kiplinger, S.A.M.	4 May	1878
596	Hale, C.M.	Williams, M.A.	23 Oct	1877
592	Hale, J.W.	Jones, Laura A.	27 Sept	1877
41	Hale, Nathaniel	Tribble, S.E.	29 July	1867
36	Hall, A.J.	Huntington, Vallie R.	3 Sept	1867
385	Hamilton, L.	Avant, A.A.	28 Nov	1872
18	Hamilton, W.D.	Broom, A.J.	20 Feb	1867
483	Hampton, J.A.	Todd, S.F.	17 Dec	1876
15	Hampton, Robert	Riddle, I.E.	14 Feb	1867
712	Hampton, William	Martin, Louisa	25 Nov	1879
175	Hancock, Belford	Hancock, Renna	29 Sept	1869
299	Handy, J.J.	Gill, Margaret	14 Mar	1871
522	Haney, H.J.	Rodgers, Martha T.	2 Jan	1876
2	Haney, J.B.	Barlow, O.C.	10 Jan	1867
72	Hanie, E.C.H.	Carlisle, Mary E.	9 June	1868
574	Haney, S.M.	Weatherall, Mollie R.	3 Feb	1877
454	Haney, Samuel	Smith, E.V.	8 Feb	1874
133	Hanley, W.C.	Pegues, Sarah A.	17 Jan	1869
450	Hapaway, E.	Young, E.M.	28 Feb	1874
631	Hardin, D.N.	Burton, S.J.	16 Aug	1878
563	Hardin, E.A.	Sullivan, M.E.	28 Dec	1876
49	Hardin, J.H.	McKnight, S.H.	3 Nov	1867
144	Hardin, J.J.	Vance, Hester E.	16 Feb	1869
455	Hardin, J.W.	Echles, Caroline	18 Feb	1874
427	Hardin, Jonathan	Eelistoe(?), Mary E.	12 Nov	1873
159	Hardin, Orange	Jones, Caroline	4 July	1869
313	Hardin, Reuben	Campbell, Nancy E.	11 Aug	1871
365	Hardin, S.D.	Blanton, P.F.	28 July	1872
351	Hardy, Joseph	Vinson, Martha S.	4 Feb	1872
723	Harmon, Joseph	Edington, M.C.	24 Dec	1879
407	Harmon, William	Nolen, Ida	13 May	1873
525	Harris, B.F.	Fuller, Mary	11 Jan	1876
159	Harris, D.M.	Youngblood, Sallie	30 June	1869
693	Harris, E.J.	Butt, A.E.	19 July	1879
305	Harris, H.H.	Berry, Corinna	4 May	1871
322	Harris, J.T.	Kenedy, Elizabeth	11 Oct	1871
291	Harris, J.W.	Harris, Margaret	5 Feb	1871
170	Harris, Ned	Payne, Amanda	7 Sept	1869

PAGE	GROOM	BRIDE	DATE	
684	Harris, S.D.	Smith, Mrs. M.	20 Feb	1879
375	Harris, William	Thomas, Eliza	3 Oct	1872
59	Harrison, J.E.	Elward, Annie	17 Dec	1867
283	Harrison, Thomas	Johnson, Nancy E.	15 Jan	1871
652	Hartley, J.Y.	Jackson, Mrs. Margaret	4 Sept	1878
226	Hartley, Y.T.	Jones, M.C.	17 Mar	1870
674	Harwood, A.W.	Moor, G.A.	9 Jan	1879
246	Hatcher, George	Witherspoon, Ella	1 Sept	1870
356	Hatley, William	Aaron, Sopha	29 Feb	1872
325	Hattox, J.B.	Smith, N.J.	25 Oct	1871
715	Hattox, James	Browning, Mary J.	11 Dec	1879
118	Hattox, P.H.	Thornton, Frances E.	5 Nov	1868
206	Head, Dack	Scott, Caledonia	5 Jan	1870
73	Heard, G.F.	Plant, Fannie E.	27 Nov	1867
357	Heard, J.C.	Cown, M.E.	29 Feb	1872
219	Heard, Madison	Goulden, Sallie M.	15 Feb	1870
536	Hearn, J.C.	Graham, Mary J.	6 Aug	1877
303	Hearn, S.L.	Wave, Hattie	15 Apr	1871
148	Heatlp(?), R.P.	Staggs, Amanda	25 Feb	1869
454	Helms, David	Montgomery, Mary	1 Feb	1876
221	Helms, J.A.	Callahan, Nancy E.	21 Feb	1870
189	Helms, L.N.	Chilcoat, Temple	5 Dec	1869
313	Helms, R.A.	Grist, Jane	14 Aug	1871
522	Helms, S.W.	Jones, Ann	2 Jan	1876
222	Henderson, D.W.	Robinson, Martha E.	26 Feb	1870
430	Henderson, Eugene	Abernathy, Callie	24 Nov	1873
155	Henderson, Geo	Horton, Martha	27 June	1869
354	Henderson, J.L.	Longest, Mollie	8 Oct	1878
514	Hendrix, D.J.	Sanders, C.	5 Dec	1875
537	Henry, H.L.	McCord(?)NOT READABLE	--------------	
572	Henry, Rufus L.	Gordon, Emma	25 Jan	1877
642	Hensley, J.M.	Harris, Sallie	16 May	1878
722	Herring, J.W.	Tutor, N.J.	24 Dec	1879
377	Hester, H.C.	Hendrix, E.J.	11 Oct	1872
453	Hester, Joseph	Harris, M.F.	5 Feb	1874
719	Hewlett, W.R.	Martin, S.R.	15 Dec	1879
205	Hide, Dallas	Bolton, Ellen	28 Dec	1869
323	Hignite, D.N.	Suggs, Jane C.	11 Oct	1871
255	Hignite, J.W.	McNair, Callie	6 Oct	1870
403	Hill, Augustus	Gains, C.E.	13 Mar	1873
81	Hill, E.T.	Carr, Lettie J.	29 Jan	1868
334	Hill, Isaac	Randle, Syntry	27 Nov	1871
112	Hill, J.A.	Smith, T.B.	27 Nov	1879
197	Hill, R.M.	Prewitt, Emma T.	20 Dec	1869
77	Hipp, Alfred	Harrington, Mary F.	15 Jan	1868
495	Hitchcock, S.M.	Stewart, Mary	25 Feb	1875
213	Hitt, William	Duff, Mary F.	17 Jan	1870
241	Hobson, J.B.	Beasley, Mary F.	4 Aug	1870
386	Hodges, Benjamin	Wardlaw, Florence	3 Dec	1872
511	Hodges, G.W.	Wardlaw, E.	17 Nov	1875
279	Hoke, J.E.	Widener, Mary Jane	29 Dec	1870

PAGE	GROOM	BRIDE	DATE	
262	Hollcum, J.R.	Moore, M.C.	8 Nov	1870
689	Holleman, Alfred	Johnson, Sarah J.	1 May	1879
693	Homan, A.P.	Maddox, R.B.	4 Oct	1877
346	Homan, Jack	Thompson, Sallie	17 Jan	1872
110	Homan, John	Bryant, Sarah F.	11 Aug	1868
368	Hood, Captain, C.B.	Wiley, Martha L.	20 Aug	1872
527	Hood, Richard	Wallace, Josephine	23 Jan	1876
600	Hood, W.R.	Tunnell, Mary C.	14 Nov	1877
346	Hooks, Julious	Helms, Mary Will	10 Jan	1872
227	Hopper, Ruben	Hopper, Mrs. Melvina	20 Mar	1870
324	Horan, F.F.	McCord, Ellen B.	12 Oct	1871
647	Horton, F.	Lawson, Mrs. Margaret	30 July	1878
680	Horton, J.T.	Potts, Willette	21 Jan	1879
14	Horton, T.D.	Eubanks, Emma T.	6 Feb	1867
330	Horton, T.M.	Ivy, Nannie	15 Nov	1871
214	Horton, W.M.	Bolding, J.A.	23 Jan	1870
281	Horton, William	Roberts, Mary V.	6 Jan	1871
91	Howard, J.O.	Andrew, P.E.	27 Feb	1868
539	Howell, T.B.	Archer, Ella	27 Apr	1876
665	Hoyle, Ben	Strain, M.E.	24 Dec	1878
409	Hoyle, John	Campbell, Alice	23 May	1873
215	Hoyle, Levi	Hoyle, Mrs. Eliza E.	23 Jan	1870
236	Hudson, Lewis	Walker, Emily	19 June	1870
61	Hudson, R.G.	Black, C.L.	12 Dec	1867
707	Hudson, R.G.	Holleman, N.A.	21 Oct	1879
264	Huffstickler, Lewis	Goodman, Sallie N.	14 Nov	1870
625	Huey, James M.	Faulkner, M.E.	24 Jan	1878
481	Huey, John	Brown, Una	10 Dec	1874
42	Huey, T.B.	Fuqua, E.R.	8 Oct	1867
339	Huglett, R.M.	Smith, Sarah A.E.	20 Dec	1871
687	Hughey, W.H.	Wilder, A.E.	9 Mar	1879
526	Hulsey, T.G.	Gillion, M.A.	16 Jan	1876
195	Hunt, W.A.	Hutchinson, Josie	14 Dec	1869
174	Hunter, H.W.	Jones, E.U.	12 Oct	1869
273	Huntsman, George	Weatherall, J.W.	20 Dec	1870
35	Hutchens, S.A.	Lesley, L.C.	9 Sept	1867
149	Hutchenson, W.P.	Crosley, Mary A.	4 Mar	1869
90	Hutcherson, W.M.	Tallant, Josephine	27 Feb	1868
502	Hutchinson, G.W.	Tutor, M.A.	4 July	1875
416	Hutchinson, J.M.	Tutor, Louisa	31 Aug	1873
560	Hutchinson, M.L.	Hardin, Mary E.	7 Dec	1876
90	Inman, W.D.	Gordon, Mary M.	27 Feb	1868
137	Isom, W.F.	Jumper, S.E.	26 Jan	1867
11	Ivey, J.P.	McDaniel, M.A.	3 Feb	1867
463	Jackson, Frank	Malone, Louisa	7 June	1874
42	Jackson, ? . C.	Simmons, J.A.	10 Oct	1867
254	Jackson, J.H.	Pearsall, Lucy J.	6 Oct	1870
470	Jackson, J.L.	Lee, Permela	19 Sept	1874
91	Jackson, J.R.	Allsey, A.E.	27 Feb	1868
480	Jackson, J.R.	Smith, D.R.	6 Dec	1874

-97-

PAGE	GROOM	BRIDE	DATE	
1	Jackson, J.T.	Glover, Margaret	10 Jan	1867
196	Jackson, Jeff	Coleb, Lizzie	16 Dec	1869
706	Jackson, W.F.	Alsop, Nannie	16 Oct	1879
77	James, W.L.	McDonald, M.F.	15 Jan	1868
8	Jenkins, E.P.	Simmons, M.C.	27 Jan	1867
358	Jenkins, J.A.	Jolly, C.F.	4 Mar	1872
8	Jenkins, W.K.	Stegall, Margaret C.M.	23 Jan	1867
330	Jernigan, J.H.	George, D.A.	12 Nov	1871
458	Jernigan, Wiley	George, Altha	8 Mar	1874
411	Jeter, Charles	Sullivan, H.I.	31 July	1873
88	Johnson, A.M.	Coats, A.L.	28 Dec	1867
662	Johnson, F.E.	Sudduth, F.C.	12 Dec	1878
12	Johnson, G.A.	Andrews, M.E.	3 Feb	1867
497	Johnson, G.W.	Melaway, H.	2 May	1875
746	Johnson, Henry	Adams, Mattie	2 May	1880
685	Johnson, Henry N.	Alinder, Adelis	21 Feb	1879
521	Johnson, J.L.	Steel, Lizzie	29 Dec	1875
73	Johnson, J.P.	Simmons, E.L.	7 Jan	1868
317	Johnson, J.R.	Russell, Nancy A.	13 Sept	1871
629	Johnson, J.R.	Almon, Mrs. Amanda	9 Feb	1878
741	Johnson, J.T.	Jones, Fannie C.	2 Mar	1880
123	Johnson, Josiah	Abernathy, Harriet	26 Nov	1868
9	Johnson, L.S.	Hampton, R.A.	27 Jan	1867
402	Johnson, Levy	Armstrong, Lizzie	27 Feb	1873
464	Johnson, W.A.	Ellis, Sallie	18 June	1874
62	Johnson, W.H.	West, E.C.	22 Dec	1867
69	Johnson, W.L.	Evans, E.F.	1 Jan	1868
534	Johnson, W.L.	Fields, M.J.	2 Mar	1876
184	Johnson, W.S.	Easterwood, Lizzie M.	11 Nov	1869
266	Johnson, W.S.	Lowrey, Sarah E.	24 Nov	1870
569	Johnston, C.A.	McCharen, G.G.	8 Jan	1877
257	Johnston, J.L.	White, Catie	20 Oct	1870
739	Johnston, T.J.	Pilcher, Rebecca	12 Feb	1880
118	Jones, A.C.	Mitchell, M.A.	1 Nov	1868
337	Jones, A.J.	Hubbard, M.A.	7 Dec	1871
407	Jones, D.D.	Rodgers, Mary	4 May	1873
101,	Jones, E.A.	Province, A.E.	14 May	1868
464	Jones, E.H.	Eastling, May	20 June	1874
238	Jones, George	Young, Rebecca	30 June	1870
356	Jones, J.L.	Russell, M.F.	29 Feb	1872
10	Jones, J.W.	Bigham, M.F.	30 Jan	1867
420	Jones, John W.	Miller, Mrs. M.E.	27 Sept	1873
412	Jones, Sandy	Herron, Liddy	18 July	1873
396	Jones, Taylor	Rodgers, J.L.	15 Jan	1873
557	Jones, W.F.	Tedford, M.J.	5 Dec	1876
629	Jordan, A.J.	Harrison, L.C.	5 Feb	1878
17	Jordan, James	Hunt, M.E.	15 Feb	1867
354	Jordan, W.D.	Bradshaw, R.A.P.	19 Feb	1872
355	Jumper, T.A.	Mann, Susan C.	21 Feb	1872
341	Jumper, J.G.	Jordan, Nancy A.	24 Dec	1871

PAGE	GROOM	BRIDE	DATE	
393	Kelley, George	Venson, Tempa	21 Dec	1872
417	Kelley, I.D.	Kimbrough, M.E.	7 Sept	1873
294	Kelley, J.B.	Hitt, Sarah	11 Feb	1871
106	Kelley, Nathaniel	Caldwell, Nancy J.	14 July	1868
548	Kelley, S.A.	Spence, Sarah	21 Sept	1876
404	Kelley, T.D.	Leathers, M.A.	19 Mar	1873
109	Kenady, Robert	Coon, E.B.	5 Aug	1868
240	Kennedy, J.P.	McCluskey, Mary Susan	26 July	1870
444	Keplinger, Samuel	Dillard, Malissa	1 Jan	1877
268	Kidd, George	Cruse, Elmore F.	1 Dec	1870
441	Kimbrough, W.B.	Mildway, S.M.	25 Dec	1873
622	King, G.D.	Miears, M.F.	15 Jan	1878
317	King, G.M.	Tyer, M.H.	11 Sept	1871
499	King, J.B.	Holley, A.L.	14 Apr	1875
397	King, J.D.	Pickens, M.S.	19 Dec	1872
528	King, R.A.	Shelton, Frances	27 Jan	1876
374	King, R.F.	Russell, R.A.	20 Dec	1872
116	King, W.H.	Buchanan, Sarah Ann	9 Nov	1868
168	Kingman, J.N.	Harrington, L.C.	26 Aug	1869
667	Kirkpatrick, William	Moore, Alice	25 Dec	1878
709	Knighton, J.W.	Howell, Fannie	16 Nov	1879
619	Knox, J.A.	Rodgers, Eloise B.	1 Jan	1878
195	Kyle, A.	Williams, Masury	14 Dec	1869
532	[Blacked Out]	____mon, Sarah A.E.	16 Feb	1876
134	Lamar, T.S.	Frazier, H.E.	21 Jan	1869
162	Lambert, J.W.	Combs, Emily S.	8 Aug	1869
445	Lambert, J.T.	Lucas, Mrs. S.C.	4 Jan	1874
720	Lansing, G.D.	Flaherty, E.P.	18 Dec	1879
714	Laprade, A.M.	Clayton, Susan C.	4 Dec	1879
333	Laprade, J.F.	Camel, Frances J.	19 Nov	1871
559	Laprade, W.B.	Vaughn, M.J.	9 Dec	1876
720	Lauderdale, W.B.	Green, Fannie	18 Dec	1879
450	Lawrence, St Clair	Eaves, Lizzie	25 Jan	1874
603	League, Hunter	Poole, Julia	28 Nov	1877
361	Leavell, George	Berry, Corra	14 May	1872
547	Ledbetter, J.R.	Leland, Lena A.	20 Sept	1876
419	Lee, A.L.	Crinn, U.E.	17 Sept	1873
103	Lee, J.C.	Davis, N.C.M.	8 Jan	1868
419	Lee, J.C.	Pursell, Nancy E.	17 Aug	1873
531	Lee, R.B.	Combs, N.E.	3 Feb	1876
79	Leland, T.B.	Wilson, Bettie	23 Feb	1868
421	Lench, James M.S.	Knighton, Katie	9 Oct	1873
710	Lesley, R.W.	Godfrey, M.E.	16 Nov	1879
15	Lesley, W.S.	Bearnett, N.E.	16 Feb	1867
622	Lewis, T.A.	Warren, Permila	3 Jan	1878
132	Levell, J.A.	Edwards, T.J.	13 Jan	1869
139	Leverett, J.F.	Copeland, Nancy P.	2 Feb	1869
113	Lewellen, G.W.	Salmon, C.L.	15 Oct	1868

PAGE	GROOM	BRIDE	DATE	
738	Lewelling, Samuel	Gregory, Sally	12 Feb	1880
157	Lile, W.M.	Farmer, A.T.	15 May	1869
744	Lilly, Lawrence	Hendrix, M.P.	8 Apr	1880
689	Linsey, A.J.	Stephens, Elizabeth	1 May	1871
727	Little, A.W.	Neel, S.E.	4 Jan	1880
400	Little, C.	Brown, F.	10 Feb	1873
682	Little, C.	Bowen, Harriet	4 Feb	1879
126	Livingston, R.H.	Milam, S.G.C.	10 Dec	1868
71	Lockhart, J.E.	King, F.S.	1 Jan	1868
675	Looney, Calvin	Owen, Ellen	9 Jan	1879
709	Loveless, W.H.	Lovins, S.C.	9 Nov	1879
383	Lowery, A.C.	Mosley, M.J.	7 Nov	1872
487	Lowry, J.L.	Looney, Caty	30 Dec	1874
633	Lowry, John	Kendrick, Mary M.	24 Feb	1878
526	Lowry, M.W.M.	Carter, E.J.	13 Jan	1876
79	Lyon, N.J.	Neely, Narcissa	22 Jan	1868
403	Luke, J.G.	Robards, E.J.	13 Mar	1873
315	Luke, M.L.	Coleman, L.E.	2 Sept	1871
241	Lyon, Samuel	Miller, Kiziah	25 Aug	1870
58	Lyon, W.H.	Atkins, H.T.	8 Dec	1867
360	McAnally, Manchester	Bishop, Eliza	5 Mar	1872
384	McBride, S.G.	Surratt, Minny	24 Nov	1872
668	McCamey, R.N.	Bray, T.E.	25 Dec	1878
43	McCarver, J.R.	Smith, Mary C.	16 Oct	1867
597	McCarver, M.A.	Andrews, Millie	23 Oct	1877
482	McClarty, A.M.	Dickerson, E.B.	10 Dec	1874
489	McClarty, W.W.	Martin, M.O.	6 Jan	1875
292	McCluskey, J.P.	Lower, I.H.	5 Feb	1871
272	McClusky, B.J.	Ellis, M.C.	14 Dec	1870
535	McClusky, D.(?) J.	Hamilton, A.P.	26 May	1876
567	McCord, J.A.	Hubbard, C.M.	3 Jan	1877
667	McCord, J.N.	Pritchard, Nancy	21 Dec	1878
611	McCoy, G.W.	Goodman, Susan W.	18 Dec	1877
500	McCoy, J.S.	Stokes, H.	30 May	1875
436	McCoy, S.L.	Vaughn, M.L.	15 Dec	1873
436	McCoy, S.S.	Garner, M.F.	15 Dec	1873
520	McCullough, W.W.	Fuller, Q.(?)	29 Dec	1875
618	McDaniel, C.E.	Grisham, M.J.	8 Jan	1878
379	McDaniel, E.C.	Bolen, M.C.	7 Oct	1872
112	McDaniel, J.E.	Aldridge, M.E.	15 Sept	1868
203	McDonald, J.A.	Wardlaw, Mary L.	27 Dec	1869
604	McDonald, W.A.	Montgomery, M.A.	29 Nov	1877
82	McDonald, Walter	Laprade, M.A.F.	29 Jan	1868
434	McDowell, F.M.	Baldwin, S.M.	7 Dec	1873
7	McDowell, W.A.	Roberts, Barthena	24 Jan	1867
58	McGary, J.W.	Rodgers, Sallie A.	5 Dec	1867
200	McGlover, Hardy	Lynch, Mrs. Mary	23 Dec	1869

PAGE	GROOM	BRIDE	DATE	
260	McGregor, Ezekiel	Tutor, Mary	3 Nov	1870
221	McGregor, J.J.	Tutor, Mary	1 Mar	1870
108	McGregor, Wiley	Swaim, Sarah E.	4 Aug	1868
638	McHuff, J.W.	Wait, Mary F.	24 Mar	1878
504	McKinney, W.P.	Whitley, M.J.	15 Aug	1875
46	McKnight, D.W.	Cooper, Mary	29 Oct	1867
117	McKnight, R.H.	Bachman, Nancy C.	9 Nov	1868
245	McKnight, S.B.	Price, Sarah A.	24 Aug	1870
299	McLadery, H.C.	Cook, Fannie C.	12 Mar	1871
145	McLure, J.K.	White, N.J.	24 Dec	1868
541	McMillan, J.S.	Kelley, Janie	10 Sept	1877
554	McMullen, J.A.	McKiney, Martha A.	19 Nov	1876
453	McNeel, J.W.	Discon, M.A.	5 Feb	1874
210	McNeel, Ruban	Babb, Margaret	12 Jan	1870
253	McNeely, Jessie	Boyd, Mrs. Sarah	8 Oct	1870
437	McNeil, A.E.	Vaughn, Frances	15 Dec	1873
104	McNeil, John	Strube, Mary S.	24 June	1868
301	McNeil, W.H.	Attwood, L.A.	6 Dec	1877
371	McNight, J.J.	Bachman, Lucinda F.	18 Sept	1872
602	McNutt, J.J.	Sullivan, Ann	22 Nov	1877
641	McPherson, J.J.	Brown, Callie	5 May	1878
84	McReynolds, P.R.	Pitts, M.R.	4 Feb	1868
271	McWhirter, John	Johnson, Isabella H.	15 Dec	1870
112	McWhirter, W.H.	Johnson, Nancy A.	15 Sept	1868
524	McWhorter, E.F.	Broom, M.V.	10 Jan	1876
258	M........	Brown, Nancy F.	22 Oct	1870

[Grooms name too dark on micro-film to read. Could be Miller or Mauldin surname]

PAGE	GROOM	BRIDE	DATE	
148	Maffett, S.L.	Perry, Mary	21 Feb	1868
732	Mahan, A.J.	Guinn, F.J.	15 Jan	1880
41	Major, J.M.	Tyer, C.A.	10 Oct	1867
203	Major, W.A.	Gilliam, Martha M.	29 Dec	1869
103	Mallory, King	Sanders, Nancy	28 Jan	1868
48	Marlow, George	Henry, Elizabeth	1 Nov	1867
49	Martin, Andrew	Gibson, Martha P.	28 Apr	1868
61	Martin, C.R.	Major, N.L.	13 Dec	1867
273	Martin, E.L.	Hale, Mary L.	16 Dec	1870
122	Martin, Edison	Greene, Elizabeth	22 Nov	1868
402	Martin, G.W.	Philips, Matilda	11 Mar	1873
111	Martin, H.L.	Johnson, Arthana	13 Sept	1868
143	Martin, J.R.	Duvall, M.J.	11 Feb	1869
163	Martin, J.W.	Johnson, Martha J.	15 Aug	1869
505	Martin, P.J.	Martin, M.C.	7 Sept	1875
267	Martin, Samuel	Dillard, Mary	30 Nov	1870
576	Mask, S.S.	Austin, L.A.	11 Mar	1877
451	Mathis, E.P.	Holleman, Jane	29 Jan	1876
98	Mathis, Johnson	Jack, Mariah F.	26 Apr	1868

PAGE	GROOM	BRIDE	DATE	
327	Matthews, W.H.	Roy, Harriet A.	1 Nov	1871
692	Mattox, L.T.	Brandon, M.L.T.G.	14 July	1879
185	Mauldin, J.H.	Duke, Martha C.	15 Nov	1869
75	Mauldin, John	Butts, Susan	7 Dec	1867
124	Mauldin, W.H.	Svett (or Scott?), E.H.	1 Dec	1868
30	Mayers, W.J.	Tigert, Sarah D.	23 July	1867
588	Mayhew, a.J.	Coward, S.E.	19 Aug	1877
263	Mayo, J.R.	Ellis, S.C.	13 Nov	1870
575	Mayo, J.S.	Longest, Anna	26 Feb	1877
105	Mears, E.J.	Moses, Elizabeth	5 July	1868
398	Medford, H.C.	Weatherall, Emma	28 Jan	1873
504	Medlock, W.G.	Brandon, Sarah	15 Aug	1875
536	Miears, J.P.	King, E.E.	23 Mar	1871
302	Miears, J.P.	Whitten, M.A.	16 Apr	1871
691	Miears, John P.	Page Ann	15 June	1879
18	Milam, L.C.	Schoggens, Jaffie	24 Feb	1867
546	Milam, L.C.	Russell, Martha	3 Sept	1876
706	Milam, Willis A.	Hardy, M.A.	4 Dec	1879
739	Miller, J.A.	Kizer, M.J.	22 Feb	1880
96	Miller, J.A.T.	Pannell, M.A.R.	13 Feb	1868
636	Miller, James	McClennard, Eliza	3 Mar	1878
566	Miller, John	Laverett, Sarah S.	3 Jan	1878
23	Miller, Robert	Wages, Martha J.	20 Apr	1867
517	Miller, S.	Daggett, Ida	16 Dec	1875
508	Miller, T.	Kendrick, Virginia	15 Oct	1875
740	Miller, Thomas	Suggs, Sara	19 Feb	1880
63	Miller, Wm	Bice, Sarah C.	18 Dec	1867
336	Mills, Abraham	Witherspoon, Millie	7 Dec	1877
582	Mills, C.H.	Gaines, Joanna A.	26 May	1877
393	Mim, James	Cobb, M.W.	22 Dec	1872
234	Mitchell, Andrew	Warren, Martha	24 May	1870
100	Mitchell, B.F.	Coleman, Nettie	4 May	1868
7	Mitchell, C.G.	Duncan, Mary T.P.B.	17 Jan	1867
19	Mitchell, T.B.	Dennis, Mary N.	1 Mar	1867
578	Montgomery, James	Rayburn, Ann	14 Mar	1877
736	Montgomery, John	Thomas, P.A.	5 Feb	1880
52	Montgomery, R.H.	Tuter, S.E.H.	5 Dec	1876
541	Montgomery, S.C.	Hardin, M.E.	21 June	1876
443	Montgomery, T.E.	McClesky, Fannie	1 Jan	1874
62	Montgomery, W.B.	Hall, Callie	26 Dec	1867
674	Moor, J.H.	Eddington, M.E.	9 Jan	1879
235	Moore, Allen	Hamilton, Elizabeth	9 June	1870
85	Moore, C.C.	Collins, Mary Ann	3 Dec	1867
192	Moore, George	Fitzpatrick, Alsey	17 Dec	1869
432	Moore, W.D.	Street, M.A.	4 Dec	1873
49	Moore, W.H.	Clayton, Matilda	3 Nov	1867
406	Moore, W.H.	Edwards, Louisa	30 Apr	1873
531	Morgan, R.M.	Swindle, Dorris	9 Feb	1876
9	Morgan, R.C.	Furguson, Nancy M.	31 Jan	1867

PAGE	GROOM	BRIDE	DATE	
335	Morris, J.W.	King, Susan F.	27 Nov	1871
276	Morris, T.J.	Ribers, A.L.	25 Dec	1870
223	Morrison, R.H.	Wilie, Jeannette	2 Mar	1870
439	Morrison, Henry	Vance, Hester	21 Dec	1873
216	Morrison, J.R.	Helms, Emily	6 Feb	1870
496	Morrow, B(?). M.	Huckabee, Eva	27 Mar	1875
697	Moseley, G.B.	Abernathy, Eletha	24 Aug	1879
474	Moseley, Wm	Grant, M.M.	3 Nov	1874
120	Mounce, M.L.	Hitt, Lucy	12 Nov	1868
653	Murphy, Marshall	Wosten, M.C.	30 Sept	1878
516	Murphy, W.L.	Washington, Lucy	15 Dec	1875
520	Murrah, J.M.	Arnold, P.E.	6 Jan	1875
178	Myears, Tilman	Givhan, Silva	10 Oct	1869
623	Myrostie, D.N.	Kellams, Lou	15 Jan	1878
30	Nabors, W.D.	Wallace, Sallie (Saddie?)	13 July	1867
486	Nance, N.G.	Wardlaw, F.P.	22 Dec	1874
20	Neal, Ranam	Baily, A.J.	9 Mar	1867
31	Neal, William	Plant, Susan J.	1 Aug	1867
724	Neel, J.D.	Little, C.A.	25 Dec	1879
205	Neel, Westly	Starks, George Ann	30 Dec	1869
294	Neely, J.M.	Montgomery, P.W.	12 Feb	1871
76	Neely, S.L.	Hagood, T.E.	7 Jan	1868
708	Nelson, F.P.	Archer, M.F.	5 Nov	1879
722	Nelson, J.B.	Archer, A.L.	21 Dec	1879
85	Nelson, Joshua	Winn, C.A.	6 Feb	1868
146	Nelson, Sam	Collins, Martha	4 Feb	1869
136	Nelson, W.A.	Swafford, L.M.	28 Feb	1869
493	Newell, S.L.	Mooney, Bettie	23 Feb	1875
92	Newell, W.J.	Furr, Sarah	2 Mar	1868
308	Newman, P.A.	Dixon, Mary C.	21 July	1871
92	Nichols, J.J.	Grizell, Mary	4 Mar	1868
733	Nichols, J.W.	Tindall, N.A.	25 Jan	1880
643	Nix, Chesley	Carroll, Francis E.	2 June	1878
679	Nisbet, J.M.	Bell, Annie	22 Jan	1879
67	Nisbet, W.A.	Gates, Mary C.	24 Dec	1867
583	Nixon, E.B.	Vaughn, C.M.	20 June	1877
543	Nixon, J.H.	Jones, A.C.	30 July	1876
247	Nixon, H.D.	Stegall, M.H.	6 Sept	1870
451	Nobles, T. O.	Owens, M.J.	1 Feb	1874
631	Noe, J.R.	Holly, Alice K.	17 Feb	1878
509	Norton, J.J.	Bolding, N.J.	26 Oct	1875
673	Oakes, A.B.	Stegall, M.C.	6 Jan	1879
332	Odell, John	Dillard, Sarah	18 Nov	1871
592	Odell, John	Screws, Josephine	20 Dec	1877
592	Oliver, S.M.	Johnson, Mollie	9 Oct	1877
29	Only, Lewis	Miller, Mary A.	8 July	1867
499	Oriley, M.	Taylor, M.F.	10 May	1875
231	Orr, D.B.	Seales, Mary	10 Apr	1870

PAGE	GROOM	BRIDE	DATE	
642	Osborn, R.H.	Pilcher, Sarah M.	16 June	1878
266	Osbourne, J.M.	Garrett, Darcas	30 Nov	1870
507	Owen, B.B.	Taylor, M.	17 Sept	1875
364	Owen, E.J.B.	McKiney, E.J.	24 July	1872
430	Owen, J.T.	Jones, Elizabeth A.	27 Nov	1873
103	Owen, S.S.	Russell, Kansas	27 Feb	1867
559	Owens, A.R.	Gambel, Nannie	13 Dec	1876
247	Owens, ?	Sewell, Adeline	7 Sept	1870

[Grooms name too dark on micro-film to read]

PAGE	GROOM	BRIDE	DATE	
471	Owens, D.D.	Smith, S.C.	8 Oct	1874
196	Owens, J.P.	Bright, J.A.	14 Dec	1869
381	Owens, J.T.	Gorey, Martha	29 Oct	1872
639	Otha, James	Smith, Mary J.	30 Mar	1878
170	P_____	Bolen, P.C.	9 SEpt	1869

[Grooms name too dark on micro-film to read]

| 388 | P_____ | Sappington, Nelly | 3 Dec | 1872 |

[Grooms name too dark on micro-film to read]

PAGE	GROOM	BRIDE	DATE	
468	Page, J.E.	Garner, Louisa	6 Sept	1874
496	Palmer, R.T.	Porter, Mary	23 Mar	1875
439	Pannell, S.M.	Whitley, M.C.	23 Dec	1873
179	Pannell, Soleman	Hooper, Laura	16 Oct	1869
665	Parks, B.C.	Lewelling, M.L.	23 Dec	1878
421	Parish, C.C.	Gody, Mary A.	1 Oct	1873
6	Parker, Ambrose	Wells, Mary	22 Jan	1867
378	Parrish, J.C.	Duke, Mary	17 Oct	1872
141	Parrish, J.N.	Butts, Catherine	4 Feb	1869
415	Parrish, V.P.	Young, Mary	25 Aug	1873
431	Patterson, J.A.	George, Sallie	30 Nov	1873
74	Patterson, J.R.	Hooker, M.R.	13 Jan	1868
191	Patterson, J.W.	Loe, Mrs. N.C.M.	7 Dec	1869
544	Patterson, T.P.	Thornton, N.A.	10 Aug	1876
220	Patterson, M.L.	Douglass, Mrs. A.	16 Feb	1870
3	Payne, E.F.	Lawson, Elizabeth	13 Jan	1867
339	Payne, G.W.	McCoy, Nannie A.	19 Dec	1871
199	Payne, Huston	Gibson, Ann	22 Dec	1869
669	Payne, James I.	Brown, Sallie E.	28 Dec	1878
481	Payne, W.K.	Cox, Sallie	10 Dec	1874
666	Pearsell, J.D.	Waddell, A.K.	16 Jan	1878
386	Pearson, J.H.	Griffin, M.E.	28 Nov	1872
184	Peden, A.A.	Junkin, Catherine	11 Nov	1869
577	Pegues, John K.	McCoy, Emma	10 Mar	1877

PAGE	GROOM	BRIDE	DATE		
568	Pernell, M.S.	Rayburn, Mollie	8	Jan	1877
11	Perry, A.M.	Bumgarner, Lucy C.C.	31	jan	1867
315	Perry, J.M.	Stack, Martha E.J.	1	Sept	1871
218	Peters, George	Simpson, Emeline	10	Feb	1870
352	Phifer, J.B.	Souter, Sallie	3	Feb	1872
234	Phillips, F.M.	Dickerson, M.A.	24	May	1870
234	Phillips, G.W.	Witt, A.A.	27	Feb	1876
249	Phillips, J.A.	Sansing, E.H.	12	Sept	1870
505	Phillips, J.W.	Salmon, Bettie	5	Sept	1875
457	Phillips, W.H.	Williams, Julia	4	Mar	1874
614	Phillips, W.M.	Galloway, Susan	6	Aug	1879
201	Phillips, W.W.	Price, Nancy C.	28	Dec	1869
78	Phillips, Z.	Williams, Mrs. E.	23	Jan	1868
84	Pickens, Elias M.	Ball, Emma	4	Feb	1868
465	Pickens, J.V.	Peples, P.I.	25	June	1874
474	Pickens, W.A.	Alexander, Jane	15	Nov	1874
469	Pickering, Nathan	Griffin, Hope	9	Sept	1874
255	Pinson, Daniel	Nisbet, Emeline	23	Oct	1870
211	Pinson, Louis	Sanders, Sarah	3	Jan	1870
527	Pitts, _____ [Name unreadable]	McCoy, N.M.	17	Aug	1877
516	Pitts, A.	Silvan, N.E.	9	Dec	1875
180	Pitts, A.P.	Cottnell, Louisa	18	Oct	1869
519	Pitts, D.T.	Hill, Fanny	30	Dec	1875
55	Pitts, El.....	Smith, E.C.	1	Dec	1867
713	Pitts, F.E.	Caldwell, Carra	4	Dec	1867
319	Pitts, J.F.	Grant, E.J.	21	Sept	1871
217	Pitts, R.L.	Pegues, M.M.	8	Feb	1870
603	Pitts, S.H.	Whitten, Mrs. M.L.	24	Nov	1877
163	Pitts, Scott	Hardin, Eliza	18	Aug	1869
284	Pitts, W.H.	Pounds, S.A.	15	Jan	1871
387	Pitts, W.W.	Hunt, Louisa	3	Dec	1872
414	Pitts, William	Clayton, Sarah E.	23	Aug	1873
614	Poe, T.W.	Rodgers, E.T.	12	Dec	1877
708	Polk, W.R.	Price, Mary	2	Nov	1879
261	Pollard, J.M.	Furr, Idria (Idris?)	8	Nov	1870
268	Ponder, J.W.	Edington, E.J.	4	Dec	1870
300	Poole, J.M.	Lindsey, Isabella J.	6	Apr	1871
491	Poole, w.H.	Furam, E.S.	27	Jan	1875
270	Pope, J.F.	Pritchard, Rachel A.	11	Dec	1870
27	Pope, William	Forendland, Rebecca	27	May	1867
719	Porter, L.A.	Bullard, Bettie	18	Dec	1879
65	Porter, Russell	McCracken, Hulda	22	Dec	1867
25	Potter, A.B.	Gray, Rebecca	22	May	1867
95	Potter, Abraham	Welch, Mary J.	23	Mar	1868
573	Pound, J.W.	Garner, D.A.	30	Jan	1877
396	Pounds, D.A.	Johnson, S.J.	14	Jan	1873

PAGE	GROOM	BRIDE	DATE	
725	Powell, G.F.	Barlow, M.E.	3 Dec	1879
397	Powell, T.M.	Brown, J.A.	26 Jan	1873
696	Powell, W.H.	Rucker, M.J.	28 Aug	1879
472	Poyner, D.H.	Nance, L.F.	14 Oct	1874
343	Poyner, J.S.	Gorman, Carrie C.	28 Dec	1871
618	Poyner, N.J.	McPherson, Maggie	1 Jan	1878
295	Prewett, J.M.	Caldwell, Harriet C.	19 Feb	1871
43	Price, G.A.	Stokes, Sallie	20 Oct	1867
737	Price, J.A.N.	Parish, S.J.	5 Feb	1880
337	Price, J.N.	Eubanks, Margaret	14 Dec	1871
169	Price, J.R.	Maddox, Mrs. Lea	5 Sept	1869
331	Price, N.M.	Bolding, Mary E.	16 Nov	1871
610	Price, R.E.B.	Johnson, R.A.	25 Dec	1877
60	Price, T.J.	Armsted, Allie	12 Dec	1867
39	Price, W.H.	McDaniel, M.A.	15 Sept	1867
288	Priest, J.P.	Duke, Terrissa G.	26 Jan	1871
95	Pritchard, J.H.	Potter, Nancy E.	13 Mar	1868
13	Pritchard, R.J.	Reed, Jane C.	12 Feb	1867
686	Pritchard, Singleton	Holloway, Mattie	6 Mar	1879
391	Pritchard, William	Skinner, Mary Jane	19 Dec	1872
39	Pulliam, A.R.	Berry, M.D.	16 Sept	1867
512	Pulliam, J.W.	Hearn, C.B.	25 Nov	1875
142	Purdon, L.H.	Hutchinson, Susan C.	7 Jan	1869
651	Purnell, Henry	Sledge, G.A.	30 Aug	1878
308	Purvine, D.S.	Hicks, E.E.	8 June	1871
560	Ramey, J.R.M.	Hooker, N.E.	19 Dec	1876
537	Rasberry, Geo	Kirkpatrick, Hannah	1 Apr	1876
699	Ray, J.B.	Ponder, Mrs. R.A.	29 Aug	1879
33	Ray, J.M.	Taylor, Mary S.	15 Aug	1867
225	Ray, S.O.	Deton, Mary J.	10 Mar	1870
613	Rayburn, W.C.	Houpt, Dora	19 Dec	1877
665	Rea, J.H.	Tutor, S.C.	24 Dec	1878
28	Rea, J.M.	Fuller, Elizabeth	17 June	1867
636	Reagh, J.C.	Reagh, M.F.	4 Mar	1878
380	Real, John	Austin, S.A.M.	21 Oct	1872
686	Reeder, John C.	Reader, M.E.	6 Mar	1879
188	Reeder, W.H.	Flemming, Susan M.	23 Nov	1869
200	Reid, B.S.	Wallace, Nancy	24 Dec	1869
307	Reneau, Coreliuse	Parrish, Lutitia	15 May	1871
16	Revis, John	Dillard, Lousinder	14 Feb	1867
373	Reynolds, John	Little, Amanda L.	25 Sept	1872
297	Rice, J.W.	Beasley, M.A.	27 Feb	1871
700	Richey, J.C.	Jackson, Emma	4 Sept	1879
747	Ridling, T.J.	Hutchinson, J.A.	23 Mar	1880
301	Riley, J.W.	Sattawhite, Matilda	16 Apr	1871
648	Roach, Anderson	Jones, Alice V.	15 Aug	1878
395	Roalin, Samuel	Spence, Jane A.	9 Jan	1873

PAGE	GROOM	BRIDE	DATE
155	Roberson, Geo	Wilson, Narcissia	2 Apr 1869
582	Roberson, J.J.	Phifer, Laura A.	19 May 1877
401	Roberson, J.W.	Vassaur, Emma	18 Feb 1873
229	Roberson, Young	Pitts, Lear	19 Apr 1870
267	Roberts, H.T.	Long, Clementine	30 Nov 1870
3	Roberts, J.C.	Burton, E.C.	17 Jan 1867
87	Roberts, M.Y.	Caldwell, M.J.	17 Feb 1868
475	Robertson, G.A.	Hicks, Sallie	5 Nov 1874
253	Robertson, R.H.	Phillips, Eliza D.	2 Oct 1870
553	Robins, G.W.	Owens, M.J.	5 Nov 1876
731	Robins, J.A.	Wells, Malinda	15 Jan 1880
275	Robbins, Buck (or Boot?)	Robbins, E.J.	23 Dec 1870
488	Robbins, G.A.	Browning, Bettie	7 Jan 1875
50	Robbins, J.C.	Young, Sarah	31 Oct 1867
121	Robbins, William	Norwood, S.A.E.	26 Nov 1868
3	Robinson, J.H.	Hale, Adeline M.	15 Jan 1867
222	Robinson, J.W.	Henderson, Amanda S.	27 Feb 1870
567	Robinson, M.A.	Vinson, N.E.	5 Jan 1877
237	Rodgers, J.C.	Jackson, E.C.	26 June 1870
672	Rodgers, J.D.	Thornton, S.C.	5 Jan 1879
166	Rodgers, J.W.	Golding, Sallie	27 Aug 1869
539	Rodgers, John	Waldo, Aria	28 Mar 1877
24	Rodgers, T.J.	Cox, Martha A.	16 May 1867
489	Rodgers, T.N.	Thornton, F.E.	7 Jan 1875
512	Rodgers, William	Harrison, Adeline	24 Nov 1875
241	Roland, Henry	Clark, Mary	4 Aug 1870
256	Rosamond, Joseph	Hitt, Mary	13 Oct 1870
323	Ross, J.S.	Harvey, Sarah	10 Oct 1871
316	Ross, M.M.	Thornton, Martha	7 Sept 1871
543	Ross, T.A.	Hattox, Nancy	25 May 1876
244	Rowan, W.C.	Reed, J.S.	30 Aug 1870
66	Rowzee, J.H.	Webster, B.F.	24 Dec 1867
367	Roye, H.C.	Nobles, C.E.	15 Aug 1872
97	Rucker, R.T.	Gordon, Mary A.	14 Apr 1868
545	Rush, D.G.	Boyd, Malissa	20 Aug 1876
718	Russell, A.J.	Givhan, Annie F.	17 Dec 1879
289	Russell, E.T.	Sneed, S.L.	26 Jan 1871
117	Russell, G.R.	Sneed, Mary	3 Nov 1868
551	Russell, I.F.N.	Jones, America	7 Oct 1876
272	Russell, J.G.	Wilder, Jane	15 Dec 1870
366	Russell, J.H.	Emison, G.H.	9 aug 1872
338	Russell, J.M.	Wilson, Martha M.	19 Dec 1871
236	Russell, Ja....	Jones, Rachael C.	16 June 1870

[Micro-film too dark to read given name of Russell]

PAGE	GROOM	BRIDE	DATE
426	Russell, Jerry	Dowdy, E.D.	4 Nov 1873
165	Rutledge, Daniel	Martin, Isabella	22 Aug 1869
571	Rutledge, S.H.	Holeman, C.J.	13 Jan 1877

PAGE	GROOM	BRIDE	DATE	
237	S....., George	Geeter, Mrs. Sallie	25 June	1870
	[Micro-film too dark to read surname of George]			
521	Sage, J.C.	Pritchard, Mrs. N.E.	29 Dec	1875
593	Salman, S.A.	Rea, M.A.E.	5 Oct	1877
186	Salman, W.H.	Golding, Rachel M.	19 Dec	1869
306	Sanders, H.R.	Bishop, Emma	11 May	1871
568	Sanders, R.P.	Lee, M.M.	8 Jan	1877
16	Sanders, W.A.	Harrison, Lucy	8 Aug	1869
535	Sanders, Wm	Beasley, D.B.	16 Apr	1876
258	Sappington, Richard	Clements, Elizabeth	30 Oct	1870
362	Sappington, William	Fields, Fannie	13 June	1872
379	Sartain, J.P.	Cannon, L.E.	20 Oct	1872
309	Screws, Enoch	Griffin, Martha	23 July	1871
62	Screws, Wm	Clements, M.A.	12 Dec	1867
78	Seale, A.H.	Seale, Mary	16 Jan	1868
359	Seale, J.C.	Jackson, M.A.	7 Mar	1872
204	Seale, W.H.	Pitts, H.T.	27 Dec	1869
149	Segler, W.R.	Guthrie, Mary R.	4 Mar	1868
558	Sewell, W.D.	Grissard, C.A.	9 Dec	1876
265	Sexton, S.T.	Johnson, E.D.	23 Nov	1870
120	Seymore, John	Sanders, Eliza A.	12 Nov	1868
262	Shaddox, T.D.	Atkins, Sarah C.	25 Dec	1869
59	Shan, J.M.	Farrare, Martha	7 Dec	1867
740	Shannon, R.L.	Holman, Etta (Ella?)	9 Feb	1880
134	Shelton, D.G.	Pegues, Mrs. P.J.	21 Jan	1869
676	Shelton, T.A.	Wood, R.A.	9 Jan	1879
224	Shelton, T.P.	Harris, Mrs. Sarillie	7 Mar	1870
563	Shelton, T.P.	McGill, Eliza	25 Dec	1876
311	Shelton, W.T.	Pickens, Emily	3 Aug	1871
106	Sherly, G.B.	Pool, Ellen	16 July	1868
278	Shettles, G.W.	Black, Mary	27 Dec	1870
443	Shettles, G.W.	Black, Nannie	30 Dec	1873
53	Shettles, J.P.	Andrews, M.F.	22 Nov	1867
530	Shields, G.B.	Kent, Martha	1 Feb	1876
701	Shields, James	Young, Alice	6 Sept	1879
734	Shields, S.B. (G.B.?)	Flarherty, M.A.M.	28 Jan	1880
320	Sibley, G.W.	Perry, Sallie A.	27 Sept	1871
542	Silvey, J.G.	Rook, Thursey	23 July	1876
498	Simmons, A.W.	Bramlett, Sallie	2 Apr	1875
724	Simmons, C.C.	Rowan, N.J.	25 Dec	1874
538	Simmons, J.B.	Miears, Martha J.	14 Dec	1871
619	Simmons, J.D.	Garrett, Ellen H.	3 Jan	1878
28	Simmons, W.R.	Jenkins, Mary A.	30 June	1867
155	Simmons, Willis	Simmons, Becky	25 Apr	1869
347	Simpson, G.W.	Pilcher, Sarah Jane	23 Jan	1872
311	Simms, A.C.	Stewart, L.E.	2 Aug	1871
401	Singleton, Wm	Reel, Elizabeth	16 Feb	1873
537	Skinner, J.T.L.	Ingram, M.A.	29 Mar	1876
650	Skinner, S.E.	Mayfield, M.E.	29 Aug	1878

PAGE	GROOM	BRIDE	DATE	
553	Slaughter, G.W.	Murphrey, Nancy A.	22 Oct	1876
335	Slaughter, James	Harvey, Josephine	29 Nov	1871
461	Slaughter, R.G.	PItman, S.J.	26 May	1874
402	Slaughter, T.J.	Johnson, L.H.	29 May	1874
517	Sledge, C.F.	Tallant, Minerva	16 Dec	1875
109	Sledge, J.W.	Gray, Mary	2 Aug	1868
314	Sledge, J.W.	Daniel, M.J.	23 Aug	1871
656	Sledge, Lewis C.	Parker, Eliza	31 Oct	1878
55	Sledge, Samuel	Herring, Florida	14 Dec	1867
44	Sledge, T.F.	Montgomery, Jane (Ione?)	20 Oct	1867
250	Smith, B.B.	York, T.E.	18 Sept	1870
301	Smith, D.C.	King, Nancy C.	13 Apr	1871
182	Smith, D.W.	Ferguson, Melvina	28 Oct	1869
321	Smith, F.C.	Glover, Martha E.	27 Sept	1871
683	Smith, F.M.	Lovins, L.J.	13 Feb	1879
214	Smith, G.W.	Mitchell, Mary J.	26 Jan	1870
426	Smith, H.E.	Lowery, Lucy A.	7 Nov	1873
45	Smith, I.E. (J.E.?)	Higginbotham, M.C.	22 Oct	1867
555	Smith, J.D.	PIttman, Rebecca	29 Oct	1878
100	Smith, J.L.	Carr, A.G.V.	22 Apr	1868
372	Smith, J.L.	Willard, Sarah	15 Sept	1872
184	Smith, J.M.	Pitts, Keron	31 Oct	1869
468	Smith, J.S.	Jones, M.E.	2 Aug	1874
304	Smith, J.T.	Grubbs, Nancy T.	26 Apr	1871
187	Smith, N.O.	Smith, Aelesia	25 Oct	1869
647	Smith, Neely M.	Flaherty, M.A.	7 Aug	1878
704	Smith, R.P.	McElvany, N.M.	9 Oct	1879
131	Smith, Ruffin	Shawver, Harriet	24 Dec	1868
581	Smith, S.M.	Dozier, Mrs. Mary C.	7 May	1877
468	Smith, S.P.	Seats, Fanny	4 Sept	1874
509	Smith, T.P.	McKnight, Sarah	4 Sept	1877
144	Smith, W.J.	Teeter, Sarah M.	10 Feb	1869
372	Smith, W.W.	Seats, Mattie	11 Sept	1872
552	Smith, W.W.	Miller, Catherine	16 Oct	1876
616	Smith, W.W.	Young, Martha E.	27 Dec	1877
720	Sneed, J.M.	Willard, Alice	7 Jan	1880
127	Snipes, Joel M.	Martin, Nancy E.	5 Jan	1869
230	Snow, C.O.	Rayburn, E.C.	14 Apr	1870
283	Snow, P.C.	Card, Julyan	12 Jan	1871
151	Snyder, W.E.B.	Cox, Rebecca	29 Dec	1868
122	Souter, G.W.	Rodgers, S.A.	22 Nov	1868
617	Spain, W.B.	Browning, C.E.	29 Dec	1877
721	Sparks, J.M.	Morgan, Martha A.	18 Dec	1879
620	Spence, M.F.	Bowen, Callie	31 Jan	1878
155	Spencer, A.H.	White, M.J.	18 Mar	1869
717	Spencer, J.J.	Ivy, Katie	17 Dec	1879
4	Spencer, W.W.	Gorey, P.L.	3 Feb	1867
286	Southern, J.T.	Pearson, Leona	22 Jan	1871
119	Staggs, Pinckny	Stewart, Deliah	8 Nov	1868
218	Starkey, J.J.	Foster, C.A.	27 Dec	1870

PAGE	GROOM	BRIDE	DATE	
509	Staten, L.M.	Aycock, Elizabeth E.	26 Dec	1876
723	Staten, W.A.	Neely, S.S.	23 Dec	1879
528	Stegall, M.B.	Miller, M.A.	22 Jan	1876
638	Stephens, E.D.	Bigham, A.F.	20 Mar	1878
242	Stephenson, Virgil	Darling, R.J.	4 Aug	1870
613	Stepp, Aaron	Suggs, Della	18 Dec	1873
295	Stepp, John	Porter, Jane	16 Feb	1871
312	Stewart, Geo	Craig, Mary	4 Aug	1871
357	Stewart, J.M.	Hardin, Missouria	29 Feb	1872
494	Stewart, J.M.	Hardin, Catherine	28 Jan	1874
416	Stewart, J.S.	Fair, Emma	6 Sept	1873
463	Stewart, James	Clements, E.A.	10 June	1874
549	Stewart, R.G.	McClusky, S.J.	28 Sept	1876
108	Stewart, R.S.	Stewart, Mary J.	28 July	1868
389	Stewart, T.J.	Jones, M.J.	11 Dec	1872
207	Stewart, W.D.	Burham, Jane	6 Jan	1870
250	St John, C.W.	Rood, Mary E.	17 Sept	1870
411	St John, James	Meadows, Amanda	17 July	1873
493	Stokes, J.F.	McCoy, Louiza	15 Feb	1875
57	Stokes, W.D.	Skinner, Love Ann	10 Nov	1867
503	Stovall, J.B.	Mitchell, M.A.	10 Aug	1875
615	Stovall, J.B.	Johnston, Angeline	20 Dec	1877
310	Strain, C.F.	Proctor, Mollie A.	27 July	1871
226	Strange, Martin	Reeder, L.E.	17 Mar	1870
113	Stricklin, E.R.	Bridges, Sarah J.	3 Oct	1868
394	Strube, Franklin	Mayhen, Elizabeth	5 Jan	1873
280	Sudduth, Captain A.D.	Miller, Hibernia F.	5 Jan	1871
614	Sudduth, John	Lowry, Janie	19 Dec	1877
457	Sudduth, W.A.	McLendon, M.P.	6 Mar	1874
606	Sullivan, R.M.	Vance, Laura	7 Dec	1877
418	Sullivan, Robert	Sartain, Mary Jane	11 Sept	1873
428	Sullivan, W.A.	McGill, Bettie A.	16 Nov	1873
136	Swafford, J.J.	Smith, M.J.	22 Feb	1869
86	Swaim, George	Vance, Margaret J.	11 Feb	1868
21	Swaim, John	Anderson, Rutha	24 Mar	1867
442	Tackett, G.W.	Burton, Nannie	28 Dec	1873
608	Tallant, B.W.	Tallant, Martha A.E.	9 Oct	1877
320	Tallant, J.W.	Sledge, Pamela	27 Sept	1871
664	Tapley, W.W.	Smith, Frances	22 Dec	1878
329	Tate, H.N.	Johnson, L.A.	16 Nov	1871
305	Tate, J.E.	Witt, M.B.	23 Dec	1869
310	Tate, Z.J.	Simmons, M.R.	3 Aug	1871
47	Taylor, George	Jeter, S.E.	2 Nov	1867
628	Taylor, J.M.	Fulks, L.A.M.	31 Jan	1878
556	Taylor, J.M.G.	Palmer, Mrs. C.C.	27 Nov	1876
38	Taylor, J.W.	Norwood, L.C.	17 Sept	1867
245	Taylor, L.A.	Lewis, Mary F.	25 Aug	1870
243	Taylor, Wyatt	Wood, Emma	17 Aug	1870

PAGE	GROOM	BRIDE	DATE	
551	Thaxton, M.C.	Farrar, M.E.	15 Oct	1876
306	Thomas, F.A.	Hardy, P.A.	14 May	1871
115	Thomas, J.W.	Hale, Nancy E.	14 Oct	1868
125	Thomas, W.C.	Dowdy, Isabella	5 Dec	1868
331	Thomason, S.H.	Jones, Rebecca	21 Nov	1871
329	Thompson, T.W.	Mattox, N.T.	8 Nov	1871
420	Thompson, T.W.	Harwood, Fannie	24 Sept	1873
119	Thompson, W.B.	Garrison, Martha A.	8 Nov	1868
328	Thornton, A.D.	Wyn, L.J.	6 Nov	1871
413	Thornton, Henry	Ross, M.E.	14 Aug	1873
260	Thornton, J.H.	Dickson, Sarah	1 Nov	1870
176	Thornton, W.C.	Pittman, M.E.	3 Oct	1868
658	Thornton, W.C.	Wiley, America	24 Nov	1878
276	Todd, C.H.	Cook, N.	2 Oct	1869
316	Todd, J.A.	Spencer, Florence M.	6 Sept	1871
244	Todd, J.T.	Dyson, M.A.	20 Aug	1870
625	Todd, S.J.	May, Elizabeth	22 Jan	1878
565	Torrence, James	Helms, Josephine	27 Dec	1876
389	Traitor, Wm	Combs, R.A.	13 July	1871
677	Tunnell, J.T.	Hood, S.C.	12 Jan	1879
676	Turner, A.J.	Bullard, Josie	11 Jan	1879
702	Turner, E.C.	Kizer, M.A.	4 Oct	1879
352	Turner, G.W.	Salman, P.A.	13 Feb	1872
471	Turner, S.H.	Bigham, E.A.	13 Oct	1874
424	Turner, S.P.	Buchanan, Ann	30 Oct	1873
65	Turner, W.S.	Wren, Sarah J.	22 Dec	1867
340	Turner, W.T.	Salman, Henrietta	24 Dec	1871
484	Tutor, D.G.	Washington, M.E.	22 Dec	1874
431	Tutor, D.H.	Tallant, S.V.	3 Dec	1873
494	Tutor, F.D.	Lyons, M.L.	20 Feb	1875
664	Tutor, G.F.	Westmoreland, B.A.	22 Dec	1878
48	Tutor, H.B.	Lewelling, Elizabeth	4 Nov	1867
135	Tutor (Teeter?), H.H.	Smith, H.E.	21 Jan	1869
126	Tutor, H.T.	Cornell, Harriet	10 Dec	1868
429	Tutor, J.H.	Swaim, Mrs. Violet	23 Nov	1873
57	Tutor, J.L.	Smith, Lucinda	22 Jan	1867
64	Tutor, J.L.	Gregory, Sis	2 Oct	1871
511	Tutor, J.W.	Swain, S.E.	21 Nov	1875
639	Tutor, Joseph W.	Jones, E.M.M.	14 Apr	1878
197	Tutor, M.F.	Pritchard, L.L.	15 Sept	1875
176	Tutor, M.W.	Bridges, H.F.	3 Oct	1869
34	Tutor, R.H.	Johnston, Joanah	31 Aug	1871
659	Tutor, W.B.	Donaldson, Rachel	17 Nov	1878
442	Tutor, W.H.	McGregory, M.A.V.	31 Dec	1873
678	Tutor, W.J.	Allen, L.M.	19 Jan	1879
257	Tutor, William	Stewart, Sara J.	25 Oct	1870

PAGE	GROOM	BRIDE	DATE	
165	Van Vleek, U.G.	Hearn, Sarah F.C.	23 Aug	1869
523	Vance, J.F.	Phillips, E.	6 Jan	1876
87	Vance, Thomas	Bushet, Nancy E.	6 Feb	1868
325	Vanlandingham, H.J.	Hearn, M.F.	24 Oct	1871
657	Vann, T.K.	Souter, Laura	4 Nov	1878
630	Vaughn, J.H.	Robinson, S.C.	2 Feb	1878
729	Vaughn, J.W.	Browzell, A.H.	7 Jan	1880
40	Vickers, W.J.	McGill, Sarah A.	26 Sept	1867
296	Wade, J.T.	Pitts, E.C.	19 Feb	1871
114	Wages, W.P.	Gray, M.C.	20 Aug	1868
730	Wagner, W.F.	Johnson, Mollie	11 Jan	1880
202	Wagoner, David	Jackson, Jennie	28 Dec	1869
252	Wait, Thomas	Box, Mrs. Sarah	25 Oct	1870
571	Waites, J.N.	McEachern, M.J.	23 Jan	1877
326	Walden, G.L.	White, O.F.	26 Oct	1871
307	Waldo, E.J.	Moody, Louisa	25 Dec	1872
714	Waldo, J.P.	Griffin, Amanda	8 Dec	1879
415	Walker, D.F.	Jenkins, Linda	27 Aug	1873
574	Walker, D.F.	Jones, Mattie	10 Oct	1877
290	Walker, J.E.	Trott, Anna B.	26 Jan	1871
157	Wall, J.W.	Hattox, M.A.	10 May	1869
734	Wall, J.W.	Arnold, Lucy	28 Jan	1880
212	Waller, Noah	Heard, Laura	20 Jan	1870
282	Wallis, H.T.	Kelley, Laura D.	12 Jan	1871
198	Wallis, Jerry	Williams, Eliza	20 Dec	1869
410	Walls, J.W.	Aycock, Susanna	17 July	1873
492	Ward, J.H.	Bigham, Mrs. S.P.	7 Feb	1875
711	Ward, J.M.	McWhorter, Sarah J.	23 Nov	1879
29	Wardlaw, J.H.	Kidd, Sarah	7 July	1867
547	Wardlaw, John	Bramlett, F.H.	10 Sept	1876
197	Wardlaw, William	Lagrane, Mary	24 Dec	1869
249	Ware, Jasper	Cameron, Ellen	15 Sept	1870
562	Ware, Robert	Ingram, Mary	22 Dec	1876
275	Ward, J.A.	Wilson, M.F.	5 Jan	1871
37	Warren, Author	Lewis, Charlotte A.	9 Sept	1867
223	Warren, J.H.	McDonald, S.A.C.	27 Feb	1870
470	Warren, J.M.	Laprade, N.C.	4 Oct	1874
687	Warren, James H.	Dillard, Francis	17 Mar	1879
271	Warren, J.R.	McCullough, M.E.	13 Dec	1870
513	Warren, J.R.	Rodgers, A.M.S.	5 Dec	1875
128	Warren, T.J.	Dillard, Elizabeth	20 Dec	1868
432	Warren, T.J.	Patterson, Nancy	3 Dec	1873
597	Warren, T.R.	Laprade, Idella	25 Oct	1877
40	Waters, H.A.	White, Sarah	2 Sept	1867
345	Watts, A.J.	Smith, Mary J.	2 Jan	1872
743	Watts, Jefferson	White, kate	1 Apr	1880
726	Watts, William	Laprade, Sallie D.	-- Dec	1879

PAGE	GROOM	BRIDE	DATE	
685	Weatherall, Geo	Pearson, Nannie	27 Feb	1879
211	Weatherall, J.W.	Caldwell, Hagary	13 Jan	1870
660	Webb, Z.T.	Warren, Mary A.	10 Dec	1878
74	Webster, J.F.	McCord, M.J.	9 Jan	1868
44	Weeks, J.W.	Malone, Frances E.	20 Oct	1867
555	Welch, S.(?) A.)?)	Harden, N.J.	20 Nov	1876
713	Wells, C.C.	Grisham, N.A.	10 Dec	1879
505	Wells, H.W.	Miller, Sallie N.	14 Sept	1875
156	Wells, J.F.	Swafford, M.E.D.	2 May	1869
603	Wells, J.S., Jr.	Word, I.P.	18 Dec	1878
703	Wells, T.W.	Phillips, Albertine	8 Oct	1879
164	Wells, W.C.	Miller, Mary E.	18 Aug	1869
219	Wells, William	Houpt, Harriet	20 Feb	1870
189	West, D.R.	Caldwell, N.F.	1 Dec	1869
748	West, J.F.	Pinkard, Mrs. Maggie	30 May	1880
595	West, Lewis F.	Jennings, N.E.	15 Oct	1877
341	West, T.F.	Hitt, Nancy	24 Dec	1871
616	Westmoreland, Alex	Tutor, Angeline	27 Dec	1877
580	Westmoreland, E.B.	Jackson, M.A.	23 Apr	1877
679	Westmoreland, George	Boatman, P.A.G.	21 Jan	1879
448	Westmoreland, J.W.	Hitchcock, S.A.	22 Jan	1874
238	Westmoreland, T.J.	McGregor, Mexico	3 July	1870
576	Wharton, Richard	McKinney, Mattie E.	7 Mar	1877
380	Wheeler, R.C.	Sawyers(?), A.E.	23 Oct	1872
600	Whisnant, Z.P.	Jakson, Lula A.E.	14 Nov	1877
688	White, B.E.	Henderson, N.E.A.	20 Mar	1879
591	White, F.M.	Bagwell, S.E.	10 Sept	1877
243	White, Henry	Dawson, Annie	15 Aug	1870
748	White, J.M.	Amsley, M.A.	23 June	1880
227	White, R.M.	Campbell, Mollie C.	17 Mar	1870
660	White, T.R.	Harrison, Emma	21 Nov	1878
587	White, T.W.	Wesainger, M.L.	7 Aug	1877
550	White, W.A.	Wilson, N.J.	28 Sept	1876
607	White, W.M.	Pickens, I.J.	9 Dec	1877
94	Whitlow, Major	Rodgers, Sarah	11 Mar	1868
632	Whitlow, P.W.	Roberson, Virginia	17 Feb	1878
37	Whitten, J.M.	Rutledge, Mary V.	5 Sept	1867
544	Wilbanks, R.	Wilder, M.J.	6 Aug	1876
38	Wilburn, George	Gafford, Elizabeth A.	15 Sept	1867
25	Wilburn, R.T.	Gafford, Mary E.	19 May	1867
370	Wilcher, H.T.	Haynes, M.J.	1 Sept	1872
555	Wilder, H.F.	Russell, F.D.	29 Nov	1876
479	Wilder, J.W.	Hagler, Nancy	30 Nov	1874
209	Wiley, William	Dillard, Laugenia	8 Jan	1870
126	Wilkerson, J.G.	McGhee, N.C.	31 Dec	1879
406	Wilkinson, Ed	Russell, Martha E.	1 May	1873
248	Wilkison, W.R.	Phillips, Sarah	7 Sept	1870

PAGE	GROOM	BRIDE	DATE	
276	Williams, A.J.	Vinson, Prudy	27 Dec	1870
747	Williams, A.J.	Munn, Fannie	7 Mar	1880
205	Williams, Charles	Dorsey, T.C.	30 Dec	1868
494	Williams, E.H.	Beckham, A.H.	23 Feb	1875
529	Williams, G.T.	Ware, Amanda	25 Jan	1876
72	Williams, J.A.	Wiley, J.J.	7 June	1868
507	Williams, J.C.	Baskin, Kate	29 Sept	1875
388	Williams, Neely	Gates, A.C.	5 Dec	1872
304	Williams, Richard	Thomas, Sarah	14 May	1871
624	Williams, Silas	Gates, Ella	24 Jan	1878
413	Williams, T.G.	Bell, M.E.	14 Aug	1873
206	Williams, Taylor	Gordon, Ella	2 Jan	1871
97	Williams, W.P.	Robertson, Lucinda J.	24 Apr	1868
17	Williams, W.W.	Potts, Mary L.	14 Feb	1867
239	Williams, Wiley	Harris, Muria	7 July	1870
71	Williamson, J.H.	Johnson, M.A.E.	2 Jan	1868
140	Williamson, R.B.	Davis, S.P.	31 Jan	1869
461	Wilson, G.B.	Gregory, Mollie	27 May	1874
232	Wilson, J.P.	Byrd, Minerva	21 Apr	1870
447	Wilson, James	Bruce, Mrs. V.G.	15 Jan	1874
263	Wilson, Robt	Brown, Mrs. Ara Ella	13 Nov	1870
361	Winders, W.H.	Mounce, Polly	5 May	1872
500	Winfield, John	Swindle, Rebecca	4 May	1875
633	Winfield, John B.	Ingram, Sarah	20 Feb	1878
598	Winfield, R.G.	Ingram, Sarah	20 Feb	1878
659	Wingo, E.J.	Park, Mrs. D.D.	18 Dec	1878
645	Wingo, H.C.	Jernigan, Mary	7 July	1878
166	Winn, J.W.	Worthy, Susanah	24 Aug	1869
261	Winston, Wm	Furr, Emma	8 Nov	1870
350	Winters, J.W.	Price, Charlotte	31 Jan	1872
711	Winters, W.A.	Powell, Mary E.	27 Nov	1879
678	Witt, A.F.	Adams, Parks	16 Jan	1879
333	Witt, C.L.	Pitts, Frances	28 Nov	1871
473	Witt, J.M.	Bowen, E.C.	25 Oct	1874
620	Witt, John M.	Jones, Georgia E.	6 Jan	1878
480	Wood, D.H.	Souter, Nannie	3 Dec	1874
160	Wood, David	Wood, Francis J.	15 July	1869
680	Wood, W.C.	George, Callie	23 Jan	1879
540	Wood, W.W.	Edwards, M.C.	20 Dec	1871
478	Wood, William	Bright, Charlie	26 Nov	1874
231	Woods, B.B.	Burns, Mrs. Julia	17 Aug	1870
232	Woods, J.M.	Harvey, S.E.	30 Apr	1870
58	Woodson, F.M.	Allan, S.E.	19 Nov	1867
161	Woodward, J.R.	Spencer, M.A.	28 July	1869
637	Wooten, T.L.	Fields, M.E.	10 Mar	1878
534	Wyett, J.B.	Hamilton, Ollie	3 Mar	1876

PAGE	GROOM	BRIDE	DATE	
566	Young, B.C.	Moore, Elizabeth	7 Jan	1877
557	Young, J.A.	Parish, Margaret	7 Dec	1876
485	Young, J.H.	Mitchell, Eliza J.	22 Dec	1874
173	Young, Jas. Jacob	Malind, Ceraller(?)	17 Oct	1870
179	Young, W.S.	Wiggington, Harriet	14 Oct	1867
374	Youngblood, E.H.	Jennings, Amanda M.	2 Oct	1872
125	Youngblood, Thomas	Bright, Caroline M.	8 Dec	1868
81	Zinn, B.A.	Hill, E.D.	30 Jan	1868

ADDITIONAL INFORMATION

Page 5 - W.M. Collier - Elina Stegall - 15 Feb 1874
       She was Alcy Emaline Stegall, called Lina

Page 7 - J.T. Faulkner - J.A. Jones - 17 Oct 1872
       He was J. Timmons Faulkner

Page 8 - William Fuqua - M.H. Horton - 5 Sept 1878
       She was Minerva Jane Horton

Page 18 - H.D. Nixon - M.H. Stegall - 6 Sept 1870
       She was Minerva Haseltine Stegall

Page 19 - W.K. Payne - Sallie Cox - 10 Dec 1874
       She was Sarah Nebraska Cox

Page 19 - James I. Payne - Sallie E. Brown - 28 Dec 1878
       He was James Isaac Payne

BRIDE INDEX
GROOM SURNAME IN BRACKETS

Aaron, Sopha (Hatley)
Abernathy, Callie (Henderson)
Abernathy, D.J. (Clay)
Abernathy, Eletha (Moseley)
Abernathy, Harriet (Johnson)
Adams, Mattie (Johnson)
Adams, Parks (Witt)
Aldridge, M.E. (McDaniel)
Alexander, Jane (PIckens)
Alexander, Kate (Floyd)
Alexander, Sarah (Ford)
Alinder, Adelis (Johnson)
Allan, S.E. (Woodson)
Allen, L.M. (Tutor)
Allen, M.E. (Davis)
Allen, Sarah F. (Durham)
Allsey, A.E. (Jackson)
Almon, Mrs. Amanda (Johnson)
Alsap, Frances (Brinkley)
Alsop, Nannie (Jackson)
Amsley, M.A. (White)
Anderson, Elizabeth (Garmon)
Anderson, M.E. (Carpenter)
Anderson, Rutha (Swaim)
Andrew, P.E. (Howard)
Andrews, M.E. (Johnson)
Andrews, M.F. (Shettles)
Andrews, Millie (McCarver)
Archer, A.L. (Nelson)
Archer, Ella (Howell)
Archer, M.F. (Nelson)
Armsted, Allie (Price)
Armstrong, Lizzie (Johnson)
Arnold, Lucy (Wall)
Arnold, P.E. (Murrah)
Atkins, H.T. (Lyon)
Atkins, L.A. (Barden)
Atkins, Sarah C. (Shaddox)
Attwood, L.A. (McNeil)
Austin, L.A. (Mask)
Austin, S.A.M. (Real)
Austin, Sarah A. (Austin)
Avant, A.A. (Hamilton)
Aycock, Buelah (Durham)
Aycock, Elizabeth E. (Staten)
Aycock, Susanna (Walls)
Aycock, Virginia C. (Easterwood)
Azlin, Frances (Cromwell)

Babb, Margaret (McNeel)
Bachman, Lucinda F. (McNight)
Bachman, Nancy C. (McKnight)
Bagwell, S.E. (White)
Baily, A.J. (Neal)
Baker, Subrina (Gilliam)
Baldwin, S.M. (McDowell)
Ball, Emma (PIckens)
Bamba(?), Jessie J. (Berry)
Barlow, M.E. (Powell)
Barlow, O.C. (Haney)
Baskin, Kate (Williams)
Bass, Mary Ann (Austin)
Bauldwin, Sallie (Cap)
Beard, C.V. (Farmer)
Beard, J.L. (Beard)
Bearnett, N.E. (Lesley)
Beasley, Caraling (Beasly)
Beasley, D.B. (Sanders)
Beasley, M.A. (Rice)
Beasley, Mary F. (Hobson)
Beckham, A.H. (Williams)
Bell, Annie (Nisbet)
Bell, E.P. (Brown)
Bell, Elizabeth (Gilmore)
Bell, L.C. (Collins)
Bell, M.E. (Williams)
Bell, Rosana (Gain)
Bell, T.E. (Donaldson)
Berry, Corinna (Harris)
Berry, Corra (Leavell)
Berry, Fannie (Drennen)
Berry, L.A. (Caldwell)
Berry, Lizzie (Bevill)
Berry, M.D. (Pulliam)
Betts, H.A. (Burlison)
Bice, Sarah C. (Miller)
Bickers, Manerva (Barefield)
Bigham, A.F. (Stephens)
Bigham, E.A. (Turner)
Bigham, M.F. (Jones)
Bigham, Mrs. S.P. (Ward)
Bigham, Susan (Crum)
Bishop, Eliza (McAnally)
Bishop, Emma (Sanders)
Black, C.L. (Hudson)
Black, Mary (Shettles)

Black, Nannie (Shettles)
Blanton, P.F. (Hardin)
Blount, Lou (Austin)
Boatman, P.A.G. (Westmoreland)
Bolding, J.A. (Horton)
Bolding, Mary E. (Price)
Bolding, N.J. (Norton)
Bolen, M.C. (Daniel)
Bolen, OLa (George)
Bolen, P.C. (P.....)
Bolton, Ellen (Hide)
Bolton, Matilday (Green)
Booth, Bettie (Dillard)
Boswell, Nancy C. (Caldwell)
Bowen, Callie (Spence)
Bowen, E.C. (Witt)
Bowen, Harriett (Little)
Bowen, Julia M. (Branan)
Bowen, Martha J. (Downs)
Box, Mrs. Sarah (Wait)
Boyd, Malisia (Dixon)
Boyd, Malissa (Rush)
Boyd, Mrs. Sarah (McNeely)
Bradshaw, Mrs. E.R. (Frazier)
Bradshaw, R.A.P. (Jordan)
Bramlett, F.H. (Wardlaw)
Bramlett, L.C. (Crawford)
Bramlett, Martha (Crosley)
Bramlett, Nancy (Anderson
Bramlett, Sallie (Simmons)
Bramlitt, R.A. (Davis
Brandon, M.L.I.G. (Mattox)
Brandon, Sarah (Medlock)
Bray, T.E. (McCamey)
Brayer, Elizabeth (Dover)
Bridges, H.F. (Tutor)
Bridges, Sarah J. (Stricklin)
Bright, Caroline M. (Youngblood)
Bright, Charlie (Wood)
Bright, J.A. (Owens)
Bright, Sarah J. (Gregory)
Britt, Margaret Ann (Fuller)
Broom, A.J. (Hamilton)
Broom, M.V. (McWhorter)
Brown, Adie L. (Gill)
Brown, Mrs. Ara Ella (Wilson)
Brown, Callie (McPherson)
Brown, F. (Little)
Brown, J.A. (Powell)

Brown, Mary (Creed)
Brown, Nancy F. (M....)
Brown, S.D. (Alexander)
Brown, Sallie E. (Payne)
Brown, Una (Huey)
Browning, Bettie (Robbins)
Browning, C.E. (Spain)
Browning, Mary J. (Hattox)
Browzell, A.H. (Vaughn)
Bruce, Mrs. V.G. (Wilson)
Brummitt, Nannie (Griffin)
Bryant, Sarah F. (Homan)
Buchanan, Ann (Turner)
Buchanan, Mrs. D.B. (Buchanan)
Buchanan, Sarah Ann (King)
Bullard, Bettie (Porter)
Bullard, E.J. (Bullard)
Bullard, Isabella (Godfrey)
Bullard, Josie (Turner)
Bullard, L.A. (Gilstrap)
Bumgarner, Lucy C.C. (Perry)
Burham, Jane (Stewart)
Burks, Mrs. Mary (Browning)
Burns, Mrs. Julia (Woods)
Burton, E.C. (Roberts)
Burton, mariah H. (Benjamin)
Burton, Nannie (Tackett)
Burton, S.J. (Hardin)
Busbee, Narcissa (Gatewood)
Ruse, R.S. (Butler)
Bushet, Nancy E. (Vance)
Butt, A.E. (Harris)
Butts, Catherine (Parrish)
Butts, Susan (Mauldin)
Byrd, Minerva (Wilson)

Calcote, Lucy (Baker)
Caldwell, Carra (Pitts)
Caldwell, Hagary (Weatherall)
Caldwell, Harriet C. (Prewett)
Caldwell, M.J. (Roberts)
Caldwell, Mary F. (Deale)
Caldwell, N.F. (West)
Caldwell, Nancy J. (Kelley)
Callaham, Nancy E. (Helms)
Callaway, N.J. (Donaldson)
Camel, Frances J. (Laprade)
Cameron, Ellen (Ware)
Campbell, Alice (Hoyl)

Campbell, Mollie C. (White)
Campbell, Nancy E. (Hardin)
Campbell, Nannie E. (Caldwell)
Cannon, L.E. (Sartain)
Cannon, M.J. (Coats)
Card, A.C. (Deford)
Card, Julyan (Snow)
Carlisle, Mary E. (Hanie)
Caprenter, Mrs. Catherine (Furr)
Carpenter, Mary E. (Carr)
Carr, A.G.V. (Smith)
Carr, E.C. (Gideon)
Carr, H.D. (Drake)
Carr, Lettie J. (Hill)
Carr, Mary Ann (Gammel)
Carr, Mary E. (Buchanan)
Carroll, Francis E. (Nix)
Carter, E.J. (Lowry)
Carter, George Ann (Grant)
Carter, Jane (Hackett)
Carter, Nancy (Beavers)
Cary, A.B. (Fontaine)
**Cox, Sallie (Payne)
Chambliss, Martha D. (Duff)
Chilcoat, Temple (Helms)
Christian, Mary A. (Carter
Clark, Mary (Roland)
Clayton, Adeline (Greene)
Clayton, D.A.B. (Dillard)
Clayton, Matilda (Moore)
Clayton, N.E. (Dillard)
Clayton, Sarah E. (Pitts)
Clayton, Susan C. (Laprade)
Clements, E.A. (Stewart)
Clements, Elizabeth (Sappington)
Clements, M.A. (Screws)
Coats, A.L. (Johnson)
Cobb, M.W. (Mim)
Cobb, S.A. (Crenshaw)
Cobb, T.N. (Caldwell)
Coleb, Lizzie (Jackson)
Coleman, L.E. (Luke)
Coleman, Margaret (Fisher)
Coleman, Nettie (Mitchell)
Collins, Martha (Nelson)
Collins, Mary Ann (Moore)
Collums, Sarah (Griffin)
Combs, Emily S. (Lambert)
Combs, N.E. (Lee)
Combs, R.A. (Traitor)

Conlee, E.A. (Bramlitt)
Conlee, P.C. (Bramlitt)
Cook, Fannie C. (McLadery)
Cook, N. (Todd)
Coon, E.B. (Kenedy)
Cooper, Mary (McKnight)
Conld, M.A. (Bugg)
Conway, E.N. (Brandon)
Copeland, Nancy P. (Leverett)
Cornell, Harriet (Tutor)
Cottnell, Louisa (Pitts)
Coward, S.E. (Mayhew)
Cown, M.E. (Heard)
Cox, Mrs. M.A. (Benson)
Cox, Martha A. (Rodgers)
Cox, Rebecca (Snyder)
Craig, Mary (Stewart)
Crawford, Ellen (Crocker)
Crewe, B.T. (Glover)
Crinn, U.E. (Lee)
Crittenden, Mrs. Mary (Cooper)
Crosley, Mary A. (Hutchenson)
Crump, Mary (Bass)
Cruse, Elmore F. (Kidd)
**Cox, R.C. (Duncan

Daggett, Ida (Miller)
Daggett, Hattie H. (Carter)
Daggett, Jennie H. (Benson)
Daniel, Lueann (Clayton)
Daniel, M.J. (Sledge)
Darling, R.J. (Stephenson)
David, Mrs. Selma C. (Green)
Davis, Matilda (Blakesly)
Davis, N.C.M. (Lee)
Davis, S.P. (Williamson)
Davis, T.E. (Daniel)
Dawson, Annie (White)
Dennis, Mary N. (Mitchell)
Deton, Mary J. (ray)
Dickerson, E.B. (McClarty)
Dickerson, M.A. (Phillips)
Dickson, Sarah (Thornton)
Dillard, Carrie B. (Collins)
Dillard, Elizabeth (Warren)
Dillard, Francis (Warren)
Dillard, Laugenia (Wiley)
Dillard, Louisinder (Revis)
Dillard, Malissa (Keplinger)
Dillard, Margaret (Clayton)

** - Out of Order

Dillard, Martha E. (Grysell)
Dillard, Mary (Martin)
Dillard, Paralee (Caldwell)
Dillard, Sarah (Odell)
Discon, M.A. (McNeel)
Dixon, D.A. (Griffin)
Dixon, Mary C. (Newman)
Donaldson, Rachel (Tutor)
Dorsey, T.C. (Williams)
Douglass, Mrs. A. (Patterson)
Douglass, S.J. (Fooshee)
Dowdy, E.D. (Russell)
Dowdy, Isabella (Thomas)
Doxey, Rachel (Collins)
Dozier, Mrs. Mary C. (Smith)
Duff, Mary F. (Hitt)
Duke, Martha C. (Mauldin)
Duke, Mary (Parrish)
Duke, Terrissa G. (Priest)
Dunarett, Emma (Brown)
Duncan, E.J. (Conley)
Duncan, Mary T.P.B. (Mitchell)
Duvall, M.J. (Martin)
Dyson, E.E. (Dillard)
Dyson, M.A. (Todd)

Easley, Thrase (Gordon)
Easterwood, Lizzie M. (Johnson)
Eastling, Mary (Jones)
Eaves, Lizzie (Lawrence)
Edington, E.J. (Ponder)
Edington, M.C. (Harmon)
Edington, Martha A. (Cummings)
Edington, M.E. (Moor)
Edwards, Louisa (Moore)
Edwards, M.C. (Wood)
Edwards, T.J. (Levell)
Echles, Caroline (Hardin)
Eelistoe, Mary E. (Hardin)
Ellis, M.C. (McClusky)
Ellis, S.C. (Mayo)
Ellis, Sallie (Johnson)
Elward, Annie (Harrison)
Elzey, Sallie (Eubanks)
Emison, G.H. (Russell)
Eubanks, Emma T. (Horton)
Eubanks, Margaret (Price)
Evans, C.V. (Buttram)
Evans, E.F. (Johnson)
Evens, Mrs. Martha (Glenn)

Fair, Emma (Stewart)
Farmer, A.T. (Lile)
Farrar, M.E. (Thaxton)
Farrare, Martha (Shan)
Faulkner, M.E. (Huey)
Ferguson, Melvina (Smith)
Fields, Fannie (Sappington)
Fields, M.E. (Wooten)
Fields, M.J. (Johnson)
Fitzpatrick, Alsey (Moore)
Flaherty, M.A. (Smith)
Flaherty, E.P. (Lansing)
Flarherty, M.A.M. (Shields)
Fleming, Martha D. (Collins)
Flemming, Susan M. (Reeder)
Flournay, M.L. (Bell)
Fooshee, Frances (Bailey)
Forendland, Rebecca (Pope)
Foster, C.A. (Starkey)
Foster, Harriet (Caldwell)
Fowler, A.P. (Allen)
Fowler, Savannah (Falkner)
Franklin, S.A. (Franklin)
Frazier, H.E. (Lamar)
Fulks, L.A.M. (Taylor)
Fuller, Elizabeth (Rea)
Fuller, L.F. (Gillespie)
Fuller, Mary (Harris)
Fuller, Q. (McCullough)
Funk, Nancy M. (Fitzgerald)
Furam, S.E. (Poole)
Furgerson, Addie (Gillespie)
Furguson, Nancy M. (Morgan)
Fuqua, E.R. (Huey)
Furr, Emma (Winston)
Furr, Idria (Pollard)
Furr, Sarah (Newell)

Gafford, Elizabeth A. (Wilburn)
Gafford, Mary S. (Wilburn)
Gafford, H.M. (Gordon)
Gafford, Lucinda (Frazier)
Gafford, M.E. (Campbell)
Gaines, Eliza Ann (Belk)
Gaines, Joanna A. (Mills)
Gains, C.E. (Hill)
Gage, Nancy E. (Dozier)
Galaway, Mattie A. (Childers)
Galloway, Susan (Phillips)
Gambel, Nannie (Owens)

Gammitt, Francis (Gill)
Garner, D.A. (Pound)
Garner, Louisa (page
Garner, M.F. (McCoy)
Garrett, Darcas (Osbourne)
Garrett, Ellen H. (Simmons)
Garrison, Martha A. (Thompson)
Gates, A.C. (Williams)
Gates, Ella (Williams
Gates, Mary C. (Nisbet)
Gay, Sallie (Brown)
Geeter, Mrs. Sallie (S....)
GEorge, Altha (Jernigan)
George, Callie (Wood)
George, D.A. (Jernigan)
George, Sallie (Patterson)
Gibson, Ann (Payne)
Gibson, Martha P. (Martin)
Gilespie, A.G. (Franklin)
Gill, Margaret (Handy)
Gilliam, Martha M. (Major)
Gillion, M.A. (Hulsey)
Gilmer, A.C. (Barlow)
Gilmore, Sarah G. (Furr)
Ginn, F.J. (Mahan)
Givhan, Annie F. (Russell)
Givhan, Silva (Myears)
Glover, Margaret (Jackson)
Glover, Martha E. (Smith)
Godfrey, M.E. (Lesley)
Gody, Mary A. (Parish)
Golding, Margaret E. (Baxter)
Golding, Rachel M. (Salman)
Golding, Sallie (Rodgers)
Gooch, L.S. (Bower)
Goodman, Sallie N. (Huffstickler)
Goodman, Susan W. (McCoy)
Gordon, Ella (Williams)
Gordon, Emma (Henry)
Gordon, Mary A. (Rucker)
Gordon, Mary M. (Inman)
Gorey, Martha (Owens)
Gorey, P.L. (Spencer)
Gorman, Carrie C. (Poyner)
Goulden, Sallie M. (Heard)
Graham, Mary J. (Hearn)
Grant, E.J. (Pitts)
Grant, Fannie (Graddy)
Grant, M.M. (Moseley)

Gray, M.C. (Wages)
Gray, Mary (Sledge)
Gray, Rebecca (Potter)
Green, Fannie (Lauderdale)
Green, Margaret (Dillard)
Greene, Elizabeth (Martin)
Greene, Julia (Garman)
Greenwood, E.F. (Caldwell)
Greenwood, H.J. (Caldwell)
Greenwood, M.C. (Franklin)
Greenwood, Mississippi (Bradon)
Gregory, M.A. (Allen)
Gregory, M.C. (Bolen)
Gregory, Mollie (Wilson)
Gregory, Sally (Lewelling)
Gregory, Sis (Tutor)
Griffin, Amanda (Waldo)
Griffin, Colen (Cruse)
Griffin, Hope (Pickering)
Griffin, M.E. (Pearson)
Griffin, Martha (Screws)
Grisham, Harriet (Bevill)
Grisham, M.J. (McDaniel)
Grisham, N.A. (Wells)
Grisle, Mrs. Sarah (Dillard)
Grissard, C.A. (Sewell)
Grist, Jane (Helms)
Grizell, Mary (Nichols)
Grubbs, Martha C. (Brown)
Grubbs, Nancy T. (Smith)
Guthrie, Mary R. (Segler)
Guttery, Rebecca (Card)

Hagler, Nancy (Wilder)
Hagood, T.E. (Neely)
Hale, Adeline M. (Robinson)
Hale, M.E. (Aldridge)
Hale, Mary L. (Martin)
Hale, Nancy E. (Thomas)
Hale, S.C. (Dillard)
Hall, Callie (Montgomery)
Hall, G.A. (Grisham)
Hall, M.T. (Carnes)
Hamilton, A.P. (McClusky)
Hamilton, Elizabeth (Moore)
Hamilton, Ollie (Wyett)
Hampton, M.T. (Easley)
Hampton, R.A. (Johnson)
Hancock, Renna (Hancock)

Haney, Lucinda (Falkner)
Hanley, Caroline (Butts)
Harain, C.A. (Beard)
Harden, N.J. (Welch)
Hardin, Catherine (Stewart)
Hardin, Elizar (Bost)
Hardin, Eliza (Pitts)
Hardin, Elizer (B......)
Hardin, Frances (Douglas)
Hardin, G.A. (Clayton)
Hardin, M.E. (Montgomery)
Hardin, Mary E. (Hutchinson)
Hardin, Missouria (Stewart)
Hardin, Misty (Carpenter)
Hardin, Sinderilla (Douglass)
Hardy, M.A. (Milam)
Hardy, P.A. (Thomas)
Harlow (?), Louisa (Burrow)
Harmon, Malinda (Bauchamp)
Haron, Laura F. (Caldwell)
Harrington, L.C. (Kingman)
Harrington, Mary F. (Hipp)
Harris, Eva (Barksdale)
Harris, M.F. (Hester)
Harris, Margaret (Harris)
Harris, Muria (Williams)
Harrison, Emma (White)
Harrison, Mary (Fowler)
Harris, Sallie (Hensley)
Harris, Sarillie (Shelton)
Harrison, Adeline (Rodgers)
Harrison, L.C. (Jordan)
Harrison, Lucy (Sanders)
Hartley, Elizabeth (Floyd)
Harvey, Josephine (Slaughter)
Harvey, S.E. (Woods, J.M.
Harvey, Sarah (Ross)
Harwood, Fannie (Thompson)
Hattox, Ann (Browning)
Hattox, L.A. (Grisham)
Hattox, M.A. (Wall)
Hattox, Nancy (Ross)
Haynes, M.J. (Wilcher)
Heard, G.A. (Brummet)
Heard, Laura (Waller)
Hearn, G.B. (Pulliam)
Hearn, M.F. (Vanlandingham)
Hearn, Sarah F.C. (Van Vleek)
Horton, Mary E. (Garrison)

Helms, Emily (Morrison)
Helms, Josephine (Torrence)
Helms, Lavenia (Foster)
Helms, M.A. (Conlee)
Helms, Mary Will (Hooks)
Henderson, Amanda S. (Robinson)
Henderson, N.E.A. (White)
Hendrix, E.J. (Hester)
Hendrix, M.P. (Lilly)
Hendrix, Sarah (Brazell)
Henry, Elizabeth (Marlow)
Henry, S.F. (Crittenden)
Herring, Florida (Sledge)
Herring, Mollie (Gates)
Herron, Liddy (Jones)
Hester, Elizabeth (Bailey)
Hicks, E.E. (PUrvine)
Hicks, Sallie (Robertson)
Higginbotham, M.C. (Smith)
High, Rebecca J. (Browning)
Hightower, M.E. (Crosley)
Hightower, Malinda (Callaway)
Hill, E.D. (Zinn)
Hill, Fanny (Pitts)
Hill, N.A. (Furgerson)
Hitchcock, S.A. (Westmoreland)
Hitt, Lucy (Mounce)
Hitt, Mary (Rosamond)
Hitt, Nancy (West)
Hitt, Sarah (Kelley)
Holeman, C.J. (Rutledge)
Hollaman, Lizzie (Gray)
Holleman, Jane (Mathis)
Holleman, N.A. (Hudson)
Holley, A.L. (King)
Hollis, Mrs. Rebecca E. (Hackett)
Holloway, Mattie (Pritchard)
Holly, Alice K. (Noe)
Holman, Etta (Shannon)
Hood, S.C. (Tunnell)
Hooker, M.R. (Patterson)
Hooker, N.E. (Ramey)
Hooper, Laura (Pannell)
Hooper, Mary E. (Davis)
Hopper, Mrs. Melvina (Hopper)
Horton, Judson (Caffee)
Horton, Martha (Henderson)
Horton, Martha O. (Atkins)
Horton, N.J. (Fuqua)

Houpt, Dora (Rayburn)
Houpt, Harriet (Wells)
Howell, Fannie (Knighton)
Hoy, M.J. (Bolton)
Hoyle, Mrs. Eliza E. (Hoyle)
Hubbard, C.M. (McCord)
Hubbard, M.A. (Jones)
Huckabee, Eva (Morrow)
Huckabee, Sarah (Evans)
Hudson, Susan E. (DeJournett)
Hulet, Becca (Carter)
Hunt, Louisa (Pitts)
Hunt, M.E. (Jordan)
Huntington, Vallie R. (Hall)
Hutchinson, J.A. (Ridling)
Hutchinson, Josie (Hunt)
Hutchenson, Susan C. (Purdon)
Hyler, Martha (Ashton)

Ingram, M.A. (Skinner)
Ingram, Mary (Ware)
Ingram, Sarah (Winfield)
Ingram, Sarah (Winfield)
Ivy, Katie (Spencer)
Ivy, Nannie (Horton)

Jack, Mariah (Mathis)
Jackles, M.M. (Cruse)
Jackson, E.C. (Rodgers)
Jackson, Emma (Richey)
Jackson, Jennie (Wagnor)
Jackson, M.A. (Westmoreland)
Jackson, M.A. (Seale)
Jackson, Mrs. Margaret (Hartley)
Jakson, Lula A.E. (Whisnant)
Jenkins, Alice (Crow)
Jenkins, Mary A. (Simmons)
Jenkins, Linda (Walker)
Jenkins, Mary (Fields)
Jennings, Amanda M. (Youngblood)
Jennings, N.E. (West)
Jernigan, Elizabeth (Blagg)
Jernigan, Mary (Wingo)
Jeter, S.E. (Taylor)
Jinkins, Dollie (Crow)
Johnson, Arthana (Martin
Johnson, E.A. (Alexander)
Johnson, E.D. (Sexton)
Johnson, L.A. (Tate)

Johnson, Isabella H. (McWhirter)
Johnson, L.H. (Slaughter)
Johnson, M.A.E. (Williamson)
Johnson, Martha J. (Martin)
Johnson, Mattie J. (Armstrong)
Johnson, Mollie (Wagner)
Johnson, Mollie (Oliver)
Johnson, Nancy A. (McWhirter)
Johnson, Nancy E. (Harrison)
Johnson, R.A. (Price)
Johnson, R.I. (Black)
Johnson, S.J. (Pounds)
Johnson, Sarah J. (Holleman)
Johnston, Angeline (Stovall)
Johnston, J.A. (Crosley)
Johnston, Joanah (Tutor)
Johnston, S.H. (Ellis)
Jolly, C.F. (Jenkins)
Jones, A.C. (Nixon)
Jones, Alice V. (Roach)
Jones, America (Russell)
Jones, Ann (Helms)
Jones, Callie (Bratton)
Jones, Caroline (Hardin)
Jones, E.M.M. (Tutor)
Jones, E.U. (Hunter)
Jones, Elizabeth A. (Owen)
Jones, F.A. (Faulkner)
Jones, Fannie C. (Johnson)
Jones, Frances V. (Garrett)
Jones, Georgia E. (Witt)
Jones, Laura A. (Hale)
Jones, M.C. (Hartley)
Jones, M.E. (Smith)
Jones, M.J. (Stewart)
Jones, Mattie (Walker)
Jones, Mollie E. (Dorsey)
Jones, Rachael C. (Russell)
Jones, Rebecca (Thompson)
Jordan, Nancy A. (Jumper)
Jordan, S.E. (Dillard)
Jumper, S.E. (Isom)
Junkin, Catherine (Peden)

Kellams, Lou (Myrostie)
Kelley, Elmira (Buchanan)
Kelley, Janie (McMillan)
Kelley, Laura D. (Wallis)
Kelly, Sarah (Alexander)
Kelly, Eliza (Boyd)

Kendrick, Mary M. (Lowry)
Kendrick, Virginia (Miller)
Kenedy, Elizabeth (Harris)
Kent, Martha (Shields)
Kidd, L.C. (Garrison)
Kidd, Sarah (Wardlaw)
Kimbrough, Elizabeth (Cole)
Kimbrough, M.E. (Kelley)
Kimbrough, M.E. (Allen)
Kimbrough, M.J.C. (Allen)
King, E.E. (Miears)
KIng, F.S. (Lockhart)
King, Nancy C. (Smith
King, Susan F. (Morris)
Kiplinger, S.A.M. (Hale)
Kirkpatrick, Hannah (Rasberry)
Kizer, M.A. (Turner)
Kizer, M.J. (Miller)
Kizer, N.M. (Franklin)
Knighton, Elizabeth (Grant)
Knighton, Katie (Lench)
Knox, Sarah (Gordon)

Lagrane, May (Wardlaw)
Lambert, N.A. (Clark)
Landing, Eliza (Flaherty)
Langley, M.A. (Foster)
Langston, Emily (Collins)
Laprade, Idella (Warren)
Laprade, M.A.F. (McDonald (McCord)
laprade, N.C. (Warren)
Laprade, Sallie D. (Watts)
Laverett, Sallie S. (Miller)
Lawson, Elizabeth (Payne)
Lawson, Mrs. Margaret (Horton)
Leach, M.J. (Dodd)
Leathers, M.A. (Kelley)
Lee, M.M. (Sanders)
Lee, Permela (Jackson)
Lee, R.A. (Carter)
Lee, S.A. (Castleberry)
Leland, Lena A. (Ledbetter)
Lesley, L.C. (Hutchens)
Lewelling, Elizabeth (Tutor)
Lewelling, M.L. (Parks)
Lewis, Charlotte A. (Warren)
Lewis, Mary F. (Taylor)
Lilly, Bettie (Goodlett)

Lindsey, Isabella J. (Poole)
Little, Amanda L. (Reynolds)
Little, C.A. (Neel)
Little, Elizabeth (Bolen)
Loe, Mrs. N.C.M. (Patterson)
Long, Clementine (Roberts)
Long, P.C. (Guthrie)
Longest, Anna (Mayo)
Longest, Mollie (Henderson)
Loony, Caty (Lowry)
Love, Ann (Stokes)
Lovins, S.C. (Loveless)
Lovins, L.J. (Smith)
Lower, I.H. (McCluskey)
Lowery, Lucy A. (Smith)
Lowrey, Sarah E. (Johnson)
Lowry, Janie (Sudduth)
Lucas, Mrs. S.C. (Lambert)
Luther, Mrs. E. (Beazly)
Lynch, Mrs. Mary (McGlover)
Lyons, M.I. (Tutor)

McAbie, Fannie (Alsup)
McCharen, G.G. (Johnston)
McClelland C. (Graham)
McClennard, Eliza (Miller)
McClesky, Fannie (Montogmery)
McCluskey, Mary Susan (Kennedy)
McClusky, S.J. (Stewart)
McCord, ... (Henry)
McCord, Ellen B. (Horan)
McCord, M.J. (Webster)
McCord, Susan M. (Duke)
McCoy, D.A.E. (Garner)
McCoy, Emma (Pegue)
McCoy, Louisa (Stokes)
McCoy, N.M. (Pitts)
McCoy, Nannie A. (Payne)
McCracken, Hulda (Porter)
McCraw, Martha S. (Easterwood)
McCullough, M.E. (Warren)
McDaniel, M.A. (Ivey)
McDaniel, M.A. (Price)
McDonald, Louisa (Carter)
McDonald, M.F. (James)
McDonald, S.A.C. (Warren)
McDonald, Sallie (Broome)
McEachern, M.J. (Waites)

McElvany, N.M. (Smith)
McGhee, N.C. (Wilkerson)
McGill, Bettie A. (Sullivan)
McGill, Eliza (Shelton)
McGill, Sarah A. (Vickers)
McGregor, M.A.V. (Tutor)
McGregor, Mexico (Westmoreland)
McJunken, J.A. (Crawford)
McKelvy, L.C. (Duncan)
McKiney, E.J. (Owen)
McKiney, Martha A. (McMullen)
McKinney, M.J. (Carter)
McKinney, Mattie E. (Wharton)
McKnight, C.H. (Clayton)
McKnight, Mary (Cannon)
McKnight, S.H. (Hardin)
McKnight, S.J. (Cannon)
McKnight, Sarah (Smith)
McLendon, M.P. (Sudduth)
McNair, Callie (Hignite)
McNeeley, Barbara (Alsup)
McNeely, Ann (Dowdy)
McNeil, F.E. (Dickson)
McNeil, Lizzie A. (Brown)
McPherson, B.C. (Benson)
McPherson, Maggie (Poyner)
McWhorter, Sarah J. (Ward)

Maddy, Margaret (Baldwin)
Maddox, Mrs. Lea (Price)
Maddox, R.B. (Homan)
Madox, Zennelin L. (Fretwell)
Major, N.L. (Martin
Malind, Ceraller (Young)
Malone, Frances E. (Weeks)
Malone, Louisa (Jackson)
Malone, Mollie (Bramlett)
Mann, Susan C. (Jumper)
Martin, Isabella (Rutledge)
Martin, Louisa (Hampton)
Martin, M.C. (Martin)
Martin, M.O. (McClarty)
Martin, Mollie D. (Coffin)
Martin, Nancy E. (Snipes)
Martin, S.R. (Hewlett)
Matthews, M.A. (Ellzy)
Mattox, N.T. (Thompson)
Mauldin, C.B. (Baxter)
Mauldin, G.L. (Gregory)

May, Elizabeth (Todd)
Mayfield, M.E. (Skinner)
Mayhen, Elizabeth (Strube)
Mayhew, Martha (Bevel)
Mayhew, Sallie (Bevil)
Meadows, Amanda (St John)
Medlock, Emily (Gaines)
Medlock, Lenie (Caldwell)
Medlock, M.A. (Gaines)
Melaway, H. (Johnson)
Miears, Anna (Coats)
Miears, M.F. (King)
Miears, Martha J. (Simmons)
Miers, S.L. (Bolding)
Milam, S.G.C. (Livingston)
Mildway, S.M. (Kimbrough)
Miller, A.H. (Anderson)
Miller, Annie E. (Bramlett)
Miller, C.A. (Carr)
Miller, Catherine (Smith)
Miller, Corrie F. (Dozier)
Miller, Elizabeth (Gilmore)
Miller, Hibernia (Sudduth)
Miller, Kiziah (Lyon)
Miller, M.A. (Stegall)
Miller, Mrs. M.E. (Jones)
Miller, M.H. (Donaldson)
Miller, Mary A. (Only)
Miller, Mary E. (Wells)
Miller, Sallie N. (Wells)
Miller, Thursey E. (Cowert)
Mitchell, Eliza J. (Young)
Mitchell, M.A. (Stovall)
Mitchell, M.A. (Jones)
Mitchell, Mary J. (Smith)
Montgomery, Dena (Fair)
Montgomery, Jane (Sledge)
Montgomery, M.A. (McDonald)
Montgomery, Mary (Helms)
Montgomery, P.W. (Neely)
Moody, Louisa (Waldo)
Mooney, Bettie (Newell)
Moor, G.A. (Harwood)
Moore, A.H. (Aldridge)
Moore, Alice (Kirkpatrick)
Moore, Elizabeth (Young)
Moore, H.C. (Fowler)
Moore, Louiza (Godfrey)
Moore, M.C. (Holcum)
Moore, Ruth (Aldridge)

Morgan, Martha A. (Sparks)
Morgan, Mary A. (Gay)
Morgan, Mary E. (Dickson)
Morrow, N.M. (Armisted)
Moses, Elizabeth (Mears)
Mosley, M.J. (Lowery)
Mounce, Polly (Winders)
Munn, Fannie (Williams)
Murphrey, Nancy A. (Slaughter)
Murrey, Martha Ann (Dees)

Nance, L.F. (Poyner)
Neel, S.E. (Little)
Neely, Addie B. (Bell)
Neely, M.J. (Brown)
Neely, Narcissa (Lyon)
Neely, S.S. (Staten)
Nicks, M.J. (Franklin)
Nisbet, Emeline (PInson)
Nobles, C.E. (Roye)
Nolen, Ida (Harmon)
Norwood, L.C. (Taylor)
Norwood, S.A.E. (Robbins)
Nowlan, H.M. (Fleming)

Ornsby, Ella (Furgerson)
Overcalh(?), Mary (Carter)
Owen, Ellen (Looney)
Owens, J.D. (Cook)
Owens, M.J. (Nobles)
Owens, M.J. (Robins)

Page, Ann (Miears)
Palmer, Mrs. C.C. (Taylor)
Pannell, M.A.R. (Miller)
Parish, Margaret (Young)
Parish, S.J. (Price)
Park, Mrs. D.D. (Wingo)
Parker, Eliza (Sledge)
Parker, Emma (Aycock)
Parrish, Lutitia (Reneau)
Parrish, Maude (Baker)
Patterson, Nancy (Warren)
Payne, Amanda (Harris)
Pearsall, Lucy J. (Jackson)
Pearsall, Nancy E. (Flaharty)
Pearson, Leona (Southern)
Pearson, Louisiann (Griffin)
Pearson, Nannie (Weatherall)

Pegues, Carrie F. (Brown)
Pegues, M.M. (Pitts)
Pegues, Mrs. P.J. (Shelton)
Pegues, Sarah A. (hanley)
Peples, P.I. (Pickens)
Perry, Frances (Fields)
Perry, Mary (Maffett)
Perry, Mollie (Barton)
Perry, Sallie A. (Sibley)
Phifer, Laura A. (Roberson)
Phifer, Mary (Golding)
Phifer, Verona (Goulding)
Philips, Matilda (Martin)
Philips, M.C. (Green)
Philips, S. (Douglass)
Phillips, Albertine (Wells)
Phillips, E. (Vance)
Phillips, Eliza D. (Robertson)
Phillips, Sarah (Wilkison)
Pickens, Emily (Shelton)
Pickens, I.J. (White)
Pickens, M.S. (King)
Pilcher, Sarah Jane (Simpson)
Pilcher, Sarah M. (Osborn)
Pilcher, R.M.E. (Dowdy)
Pilcher, Rebecca (Johnston)
Pinkard, Mrs. Maggie (West)
Pinson, Sallie (Bell)
Pitman, S.J. (Slaughter)
Pittman, M.E. (Thornton)
Pittman, Rebecca (Smith)
Pitts, Cornelia (Carson)
Pitts, E.C. (Wade)
Pitts, Frances (Witt)
Pitts, H.T. (Seale)
Pitts, Keron (Smith)
Pitts, Lear (Roberson)
Pitts, Luisa (Cox)
Pitts, M.R. (McReynolds)
Plant, Fannie E. (Heard)
Plant, Susan J. (Neal)
Ponder, Mrs. R.A. (Ray)
Pool, Ellen (Sherly)
Poole, Julia (League)
Pope, Mrs. Martha (Gray)
Porter, O.B. (Buchanan)
Porter, Jane (Stepp)
Porter, Mary (Palmer)
Potter, D.E. (Gray)

BRIDE

Potter, M.J. (Clayton)
Potter, Nancy E. (Pritchard)
Potts, Mary L. (Williams)
Potts, Willette (Horton)
Pounds, S.A. (Pitts)
Powell, Arabella (Edington)
Powell, E.G. (Echols)
Powell, Mary E. (Winters)
Powell, Mary E. (Greene)
Powel, N.P. (Case)
Poyner, S.A. (Gooch)
Prewitt, Emma T. (Hill)
Price, Charlotte (Winters)
Price, Martha J. (Cannon)
Price, Mary (Polk)
Price, N.J. (Blair)
Price, Nancy C. (Phillips)
Price, Sarah (Clark)
Price, Sarah A. (McKnight)
Prints, Malissa (Anderson)
Pritchard, L.L. (Tutor)
Pritchard, M.R. (Cox)
Pritchard, Mrs. N.E. (Sage)
Pritchard, Nancy (McCord)
Pritchard, Rachel A. (Pope)
Pruitt, Pauline (Busby)
Proctor, Mollie A. (Strain)
Province, A.E. (Jones)
Pugh, Nancy (Davis)
Purdon, Washey (Gray)
Pursell, Nancy E. (Lee)

Ragan, M.A. (Floyd)
Ramsey, Sarah A. (Beauchamp)
Randle, Syntry (Hill)
Ray, R.J. (Combs)
Rayburn, Ann (Montgomery)
Rayburn, E.C. (Snow)
Rayburn, L.A. (Durham)
Rayburn, Mollie (Pernell)
Rea, M.A.E. (Salman)
Rea, S.E.S. (Gregory)
Reader, M.E. (Reeder)
Reagh, M.F. (Reagh)
Real, Charlotte (Austin)
Real, Jane (Gay)
Reed, J.S. (Rowan)
Reed, Jane C. (Pritchard)
Reed, Julia (Broom)

BRIDE

Reed, Mary F. (Bennett)
Reed, Mollie O. (Chapman)
Reed, N.C. (Gentry)
Reeder, L.E. (Stranger)
Reeder, Lizzie (Britt)
Reel, Elizabeth (Singleton)
Reel, Susan (Griffin)
Reid, Dorah (Allan)
Richie, L.C. (Dillard)
Rivers, A.L. (Morris)
Robards, E.J. (Luke)
Robbins, E.J. (Robbins)
Roberson, Agnes (Bramlitt)
Roberson, Virginia (Whitlow)
Roberts, Barthena (McDowell)
Roberts, Mary V. (Horton)
Robertson, Jane (Edwards)
Robertson, Lucinda J. (Williams)
Robinson, Martha E. (Henderson)
Robinson, N.L. (Fuqua)
Robinson, S.A. (Branan)
Robinson, S.C. (Vaughn)
Rodgers, A.M.S. (Warren)
Rodgers, C.M. (Goodwin)
Rodgers, E.T. (Poe)
Rodgers, Eloise B. (Knox)
Rodgers, J.L. (Jones)
Rodgers, Josephine (Cobb)
Rodgers, Martha T. (Haney)
Rodgers, Mary (Jones)
Rodgers, S.A. (Souter)
Rodgers, Sallie A. (McGary)
Rodgers, Sarah (Whitlow)
Rodgers, Sarah J. (Griffin)
Rood, Mary E. (St John)
Rook, Thursey (Silvey)
Rogers, Gillie (Bell)
Roland, Narcissa (Brown)
Ross, M.E. (Thornton)

Rowan, N.J. (Simmons)
Roy, Harriet (matthews)
Roye, M.M. (Crenshaw)
Rucker, M.J. (Powell)
Ruod (?), M.E. (Alsup)
Rush, Maude (Freeman)
Rush, Mollie (Freeman)
Russell, F.D. (Wilder)
Russell, Kansas (Owen)

BRIDE

Russell, M.F. (Jones)
Russell, Martha (Milam)
Russell, Martha E. (Wilkinson)
Russell, Nancy A. (Johnson)
Rutledge, Eliza (Abernathy)
Russell, R.A. (King)
Rutledge, Mary V. (Whitten)

Saint, Margaret (Farror)
Salman, Henrietta (Turner)
Salman, P.A. (Turner)
Salmon, Bettie (Phillips)
Salmon, C.L. (Lewellen)
Salmon, Mary (Davis)
Sanders, C. (Hendrix)
Sander, Eliza A. (Seymore)
Sanders, Nancy (Mallory)
Sanders, Sarah (Pinson)
Sappington, Nelly (P.....)
Sansing, E.H. (Phillips)
Sartain, Mary Jane (Sullivan)
Sattawhite, Matilda (Riley)
Sawyers (?), A.E. (Wheeler)
Schoggens, Jeffie (Milam)
Scott, Caledonia (Head)
Screws, Josephine (Odell)
Seale, Mary (Seale)
Seales, Mary (Orr)
Seats, Fanny (Smith)
Seats, Mattie (Smith)
Sewell, Adeline (Owens)
Shannon, Harriet (Bramlett)
Shawver, Harriet (Smith)
Shelton, Frances (King)
Shelton, M.C. (Fleming)
Shettles, Sallie (Baker)
Shileds, Joshie (Bradon)
Shipman, Cora (Goodman)
Short, Melvina (Duncan)
Sibley, Serina (Franklin)
Silvan (?), N.E. (Pitts)
Simons, Becky (Simmons)
Simmons, E.L. (Johnson)
Simmons, Emma (Garrett)
Simmons, J.A. (Jackson)
Simmons, M.C. (Jenkins)
Simmons, M.R. (Tate)
Simpson, Emeline (Peters)
Simpson, M.C. (Fortune)
Sims, Mollie C. (Caldwell)

BRIDE

Skinner, L.E. (Clements)
Skinner, L.F. (Clements)
Skinner, Martha E.M.F. (Coats)
Skinner, Mary Jane (Pritchard)
Sledge, G.A. (Purnell)
Sledge, Julia (Blackstock)
Sledge, Pamela (Tallant)
Smith, Aelesia (Smith)
Smith, D.R. (Jackson)
Smith, E.C. (Pitts)
Smith, E.V. (Haney)
Smith, Elizabeth K. (Bennett)
Smith, Frances (Tapley)
Smith, H.E. (Tutor)
Smith, Harriet (Griffin)
Smith, Mrs. M. (Harris)
Smith, Lucinda (Tutor)
Smith, M.J. (Swafford)
Smith, M.R. (Baker)
Smith, Mary C. (McCarver)
Smith, Mary J. (Watts)
Smith, Mary J. (Otha)
Smith, N.J. (Hattox)
Smith, S.C. (Owens)
Smith, Sarah A.E. (Huglett)
Smith, Sarah J. (Brown)
Smith, T.B. (Hill)
Sneed, Mary (Russell)
Sneed, Mattie (Avent)
Sneed, S.L. (Russell)
Snipes, M.R. (Dyer)
Souter, laura (Vann)
Souter, Nannie (Wood)
Souter, Sallie (Phifer)
Spence, Jane A. (Roalin)
Spence, Sarah (Kelley)
Spencer, Florence M. (Todd)
Spencer, M.A. (Woodward)
Stark, E.J. (Perry)
Staggs, Amanda (Heatlp?)
Stamphill, Lugany (Gains)
Stamphill, Elizabeth (Brumett)
Starks, George Ann (Neel)
Starkey, Catharine (Coker)
Steel, Lizzie (Johnson)
Stegall, Elina (Collier)
Stegall, M.C. (Oakes)
Stegall, M.H. (Nixon or Newsom)
Stegall, M.L. (Donaldson)
Skinner, Love Ann (Stokes)

Stegall, Margaret C.M. (Jenkins)
Stegall, Sarepta (Carson)
Stephens, Hannah (Golding)
Stephens, Elizabeth (Linsey)
Stevenson, A.G. (Allsup)
Steward, F.D. (Douglass)
Stewart, Deliah (Staggs)
Stewart, G.E. (Clark)
Stewart, L.E. (Sims)
Stewart, M.C. (Abernathy)
Stewart, Mary (Hitchcock)
Stewart, Mary J. (Stewart)
Stewart, R.V. (Douglass)
Stewart, S.A. (Douglass)
Stewart, Sara J. (Tutor)
Stokes, H. (McCoy)
Stokes, Sallie (Price)
Strain, M.E. (Hoyle)
Street, M.A. (Moore)
Strube, Mary S. (McNeil)
Sudduth, Cate (Grant)
Sudduth, F.C. (Johnson)
Suggs, Della (Stepp)
Suggs, Jane C. (Hignite)
Suggs, Sara (Miller)
Sulivan, Sarah (Geter)
Sullivan, Ann (McNutt)
Sullivan, H.I. (Jeter)
Sullivan, M.E. (Hardin)
Surratt, Minny (McBride)
Svett (or Scott), E.H. (Mauldin)
Swafford, L.M. (Nelson)
Swafford, M.E.D. (Wells)
Swaim, B.J. (Bevill)
Swaim, Sarah E. (McGregor)
Swaim, Mrs. Violet (Tutor)
Swain, Mrs. M.C. (Bryant)
Swain, S.E. (Tutor)
Swindle, Dorris (Morgan)
Swindle, Mallasie (Brooks)
Swindle, Rebecca (Winfield)
Swindle, Rebecca (Dillard)

Tallant, Clarentine (Fooshee)
Tallant, Dalia (Fooshee)
Tallant, Josephine (Hutcherson)
Tallant, Martha A.E. (Tallant)
Tallant, Minerva (Sledge)
Tallant, S.V. (Tutor)

Tallie, Sallie (Anderson)
Tapley, Ellen R. (Cobb)
Taylor, Caty (Fields)
Taylor, M. (Owen)
Taylor, M.F. (Oriley)
Taylor, Mary S. (Ray)
Tedford, M.J. (Jones)
Teeter, Sarah M. (Smith)
Terrell, Mrs. M.M. (Daniel)
Terry, Mrs. Martha (Black)
Thomas, Eliza (Harris)
Thomas, P.A. (Montgomery)
Thomas, Sarah (Williams)
Thompkins, Nancy A. (Griffin)
Thompson, Anna (Aaron)
Thompson, Sallie (Homan)
Thornton, E.A. (Dickson)
Thornton, F.E. (Rodgers)
Thornton, Frances E. (Hattox)
Thornton, Malissa (Breye)
Thornton, Martha (Ross)
Thornton, N.A. (Patterson)
Thornton, S.C. (Rodgers)
Tigert, Sarah D. (Mayers)
Tindall, N.A. (Nichols)
Todd, Mary (Clark)
Todd, Mary E. (Dyson)
Todd, Mary E. (Dillard)
Todd, S.F. (Hampton)
Tribble, S.E. (Hale)
Trott, Anna B. (Walker)
Tunnell, Mary C. (Hood)
Turner, C.E. (Deaton)
Turner, M.T. (Albritton)
Turner, Nancy (Archer)
Turner, Sarah (Franklin)
Tuter, S.E.H. (Montgomery)
Tutor, Angeline (Westmoreland)
Tutor, Louisa (Hutchinson)
Tutor, M.A. (Hutchinson)
Tutor, Mary (McGregor)
Tutor, Mary (McGregor)
Tutor, N.J. (Herring)
Tutor, S.C. (Rea)
Tutor, Rebecca H. (Fooshee)
Tyer, C.A. (Major)
Tyer, M.H. (King)

Vance, Hester (Morrison)
Vance, Hester E. (Hardin)
Vance, Laura (Sullivan)
Vance, Margaret J. (Swaim)
Vassaur, Emma (Roberson)
Vaughn, Adaline (Dillard)
Vaughn, C.M. (Nixon)
Vaughn, Frances (McNeil)
Vaughn, M.J. (Laprade)
Vaughn, M.L. (McCoy)
Vaughn, Nancy Ann (Dillard)
Vaughn, S.F. (Bynum)
Venson, Tempa (Kelley)
Vinson, Martha S. (Hardy)
Vinson, N.E. (Robinson)
Vinson, Prudy (Williams)

Waddell, M.E. (Pearsell)
Wages, Martha J. (Miller)
Wages, Sallie (Griffin)
Wagner, Alice (Donaldson)
Wait, Mary F. (McHugg)
Waite, Rebecca (Goode)
Walden, Callie (Abernathy)
Waldo, Aria (Rodgers)
Walker, Catherine (Bowen)
Walker, Emily (Hudson)
Walker, Eliza (Griffin)
Walker, J.M. (Bowen)
Walker, Percilla (Gilsman)
Wallace, Josephine (Hood)
Wallace, Nancy (Reid)
Wallace, Sallie (Nabors)
Walls, Martha J. (Coker)
Walls, Rebecca (Ange)
Ward, Frances (Carlisle)
Wardlaw, E. (Hodges)
Wardlaw, F.P. (Nance)
Wardlaw, Florence (Hodges)
Wardlaw, Mary L. (McDonald)
Wardlaw, Rachel (Daggett)
Ware, Amanda (Williams)
Warner, Elizabeth (Bolton)
Warren, Martha (Mitchell)
Warren, Mary A. (Webb)
Warren, Permila (Lewis)
Warren, R.F. (Dowdy)
Washington, Ella (Bigha?)
Washington, Lucy (Murphy)
Washington, M.E. (Tutor)

Wave, Hattie (Hearn)
Weatherall, E.V. (Callaway)
Weatherall, Emma (Medford)
Weatherall, J.W. (Huntsman)
Weatherall, Margaret (Ellison)
Weatherall, Mollie R. (Haney)
Weaver, Caroline (Caldwell)
Weaver, Susan (Clayton)
Webster, B.F. (Rowzee)
Wedden, C.A. (Bridges)
Welch, Mary J. (Potter)
Wells, Malinda (Robins)
Wells, Mary (Parker)
Wells, Mary (Bevil)
Wells, Millie (Barksdale)
Wessinger, M.L. (White)
West, E.C. (Johnson)
West, Fannie (Baker)
Westmoreland, B.A. (Tutor)
Wetherford, Jane (Baker)
White, A.E. (Campbell)
White, Catie (Johnston)
White, Elizabeth (Ezell)
White, Jodie (Grisham)
White, Kate (Watts)
White, M.J. (Spencer)
White, N.J. (McLure)
White, O.F. (Walden)
White, Sarah (Waters)
Whitley, M.C. (Pannell)
Whitley, M.J. (McKinney)
Whitten, M.A. (Miears)
Whitten, Mrs. M.L. (PItts)
Whitworth, Mary (Gray)
Widener, Mary Jane (Hoke)
Winggington, Harriet (Young)
Wilber, E.J. (Coggins)
Wilder, A.E. (Hughey)
Wilder, Jane (Russell)
Wilder, M.J. (Wilbanks)
Wilder, N.R. (Cruse)
Wiley, America (Thornton)
Wiley, J.J. (Williams)
Wiley, Martha L. (Hood)
Wilie, Jeannette (Morrison)
Wilkins (or Williams?), Jennie (Cannon)
Wilks, M.A. (Brooks)
Willard, Alice (Sneed)
Willard, Sarah (Smith)

Williams, Mrs. E. (Phillips)
Williams, Mrs. E.J. (Fowler)
Williams, Ellen (Wallis)
Williams, Jane (Gaines)
Williams, Julia (Phillips)
Williams, M.A. (Hale)
Williams, Masury (Kyle)
Williams, M.E. (Conn)
Williamson, Mary (Bishop)
Wilson, Bettie (Leland)
Wilson, M.F. (Ward)
Wilson, Martha M. (Russell)
Wilson, N.J. (White)
Wilson, Narcissa (Roberson)
Withers, N.A. (Bratton)
Witherspoon, Ella (Hatcher)
Witherspoon, Millie (Mills)
Winn, C.A. (Nelson)
Witt, A.A. (Phillips)
Witt, M.B. (Tate)
Wood, Annie G. (Bevill)
Wood, C.V. (Galloway)
Wood, Emma (Taylor)
Wood, Fannie D. (Bevell)
Wood, Francis J. (Wood)
Wood, M.L. (Gafford)
Wood, R.A. (Shelton)
Wood, S.E. (Fleming)
Wood, Mrs. S.E. (Crawford)
Word, I.P. (Wells)
Worthy, Susanah (Winn)
Wosten, M.C. (Murphy)
Wren, Sarah J. (Turner)
Wyn, Frances (Deen)
Wynn, L.J. (Thornton)

York, T.E. (Smith)
Young, Alice (Shields)
Young, E.M. (Hapaway)
Young, Martha E. (Smith)
Young, Mary E. (Parrish)
Young, Sarah (Robbins)
Young, Rebecca (Jones)
Youngblood, H.E. (Faughn)
Youngblood, R.E. (Ellett)
Youngblood, Sallie (Harris)
Youngblood, Sarah (Griffin)

.......non, Sarah A.E. (L....)
[Micro-film too dark to read name]

PONTOTOC COUNTY, MISSISSIPPI

MARRIAGES

1880 - 1886

COMPILED BY

HAZLE BOSS NEET
207 NORTH MAIN
PONTOTOC, MISSISSIPPI 38863

PAGE	GROOM	BRIDE	DATE	
275	Abernethy, J.U.	Miss M.F. Anderson	27 May 1883	
411	Abry (Abney?), F.S.	Miss V.A. Alexander	30 Dec 1886	
256	Adams, A.C.	Mary H. Lilley	7 Apr 1883	
532	Adams, G.H.	Lou Johnson	28 Feb 1886	
343	Adams, G.T.	Clorris Carruth	33 Mar 1884	
480	Adams, J.Q.	Mrs. Russena Vasser	1 Nov 1885	
186	Alexander, Berry	Mary Ratliff	9 Aug 1887	
387	Allen, J.A.	Mollie Spence	12 Nov 1884	
82	Alsup, L.E. (Lemuel)	Ella Alsup	17 Jan 1881	
517	Anderson, Bowen	Miss M.S. Shirley	6 Jan 1886	
327	Anderson, B.F.	Miss N.A. Hodges	26 Dec 1883	(BO)
360	Anderson, G.N.	Marthy Mills	10 Dec 1884	
569	Anderson, James B.	Corra Henderson	18 Nov 1886	

[License dated 18 Nov. 1886 but no date for ministers return even tho he signed]

241	Anderson, W.M.	Miss M.J. Surratt	31 Dec 1883	

]Consent: Father, W.F. Surrett]

551	Andrews, W.H.	Mattie Savery	7 Jan 1886	
96	Arnold, Hugh M.	Allie Johnson	17 Mar 1881	
440	Arnold, W.C.	Mary Lower	12 Mar 1885	
132	Archer, R.H.	Miss M.E. Butler	15 Nov 1881	
567	Archey, John M.	Pauline Westmoreland	13 Nov 1886	

[Parents: T.Y. Archey and Jerome Wetmoreland)]

83	Austin, J.A.	Miss Lillie Martin	26 Jan 1881	
389	Ayers, J.W.	Miss L.L. Bumgardner	15 Nov 1884	
524	Baggett, A.T.	Miss M.A. Falkner	20 Jan 1886	
146	Baker, A.J.	Malissa Hitt	20 Dec 1881	
232	Baker, James	Luella Wellerford	24 Dec 1882	
338	Baker, M.S.	Miss E.J. Duncan	13 Feb 1884	

]Consent: Mother, Carrie Duncan]

472	Baker, W.W.	Miss M.J. Johnson	11 Oct 1885	
347	Ball, Joe	Frances Elizabeth Brown	17 Apr 1884	
238	Barksdale, W.D.	Miss A.E. Purvine	28 Dec 1882	
431	Barnes, J.W.	Maggie Martin	25 Feb 1885	
336	Barron, W.H.	Miss H.A. Miller	26 Jan 1884	
155	Beason, Clayton	Emma Johnson	26 Jan 1882	
207	Beavers, J.W.	Miss S.E. Crawford	22 Oct 1882	
87	Beavers, John E.	Bettie Gillum	6 Feb 1881	
322	Beckham, A.W.	Miss E.L.A. Cochran	20 Dec 1883	
43	Beckham, S.W.	Miss Jodie Cass	17 Nov 1880	
131	Bell, A.B.	Miss M.J. Seales	10 Nov 1881	
577	Bell, J.M.	Cornelia Wells	30 Nov 1886	
441	Belyen, J.G.	Miss S.E. Sullivan	22 Mar 1885	
16	Belyen, J.H.	Harriet C. Todd	1 Sept 1880	
270	Benjamin, Henry	Fannie Carwile	24 Apr 1883	(LO)
29	Bennett, A.B.	Miss R.J. McNeely	10 Oct 1880	

[License says 1888]

[LO] - License Only

No.	Groom	Bride	Date	
544	Bennett, W.S.	Malisie Sanders	20 Jan	1886
	[Parents: W.H. and B.D. Sanders]			
426	Berry, Will M.	Zoe C. Bell	28 Jan	1885
392	Betts, J.B.	Miss L.J. Hadley	3 Dec	1884
198	Betts, J.T.	Lorena Ivy	27 Sept	1882
148	Betts, T.H.	Belle King	1 Jan	1882
312	Bevil, W.B.	Lee Ann Gordon	3 Dec	1883
404	Bigham, J.J.	Beckie Browning	27 Dec	1884
143	Bigham, W.D.	Ellen Crausby	22 Dec	1881
315	Birchfield, B.R.	Miss M.A. Heartgraves	6 Dec	1883
508	Black, J.D.	Mattie Bigham	29 Dec	1885
333	Black, Jasper	Mary Smith	9 Jan	1884
254	Black, M.B.	Martha Johnson	29 Jan	1883
530	Black, T.R.	Miss S.F. Holimon	25 Feb	1886
1	Bolton, C.W.	Mary Bell	15 June	1880
597	Bolton, Jake	Ella Land	22 Dec	1886
191	Bolton, W.D.	Pattie A. Fontaine	27 Aug	1882
556	Bost, B.E.	Miss E.L. George	14 Sept	1886
491	Bost, W.W.	Ivy George	19 Nov	1885
	[License: Evy George)			
510	Bowen, J.E.	Luella Kelly	5 Jan	1886
	[Consent: Catharn Bowen and T.P. Kelly]			
393	Bowles, N.A.	Miss L.E. Davis	11 Dec	1884
574	Bradford, N.W.	Miss E.L. Baskin	24 Dec	1886
21	Braley, W.T.	Miss M.L. Frierson	22 SEpt	1880
521	Bramlett, H.T.	Ida Y. Whitlow	14 Jan	1886
9	Bramlett, J.A.	Miss N.B. Grizzell	16 Aug	1880
468	Bramlett, J.M.	Miss M.J. Sullivan	25 Sept	1885
295	Bramlitt, S.C.	Hattie Vaughn	20 Sept	1883 (LO)
313	Bramlitt, T.W.	Miss V.V. Pannell	5 Dec	1883
115	Brandon, W.W.	Miss E.R. Holcomb	13 Oct	1881
153	Bratton, C.T.	Miss J.A. Tutor	12 Jan	1882
421	Bratton, J.N.	Miss S.A. Sledge	11 Jan	1885
388	Bray, C.S.	Miss E.E. Howard	16 Nov	1884
268	Broom, J.L.	Mrs. Elizabeth Hensley		
	[Returned - Not executed]			
414	Brown, C.A.	Ella Porter	7 Jan	1885
218	Brown, D.H.	Amanda Brown	27 Nov	1882
195	Brown, G.R.	Lula Creag	14 Sept	1882
161	Brown, H.N.	Nancy Zackary	29 Jan	1882
167	Brown, J.O.	Miss M.A. McKnight	26 Feb	1882
179	Brown, J.W.	Miss L.L. Knight	2 July	1882
427	Brown, James R.	Miss E.A. Kelly	8 Feb	1885
72	Brown, R.P., Jr.	Miss E.C. Stegall	9 Jan	1881
459	Brown, T.J.	Miss L.O. Lambert	2 Aug	1885
231	Brown, W.L.	Miss A.A. Wilder	26 Dec	1882
295	Browning, E.H.	Miss N.J. Swords	16 Oct	1882
	[E.G. Browning on license]			
405	Browning, J.E.	Joanna Bigham	24 Dec	1884
593	Browning, Martin	Bessie Sparks	23 Dec	1886

568	Browning, Martin	Bettie Sparks	18 Dec	1886 (LO)
557	Browning, T.B.	Miss C.Y. Warren	17 Sept	1886
110	Bryant, George J.	Mary Lake	26 Aug	1881
216	Buchanan, J.D.S.	Miss B.F. High	16 Nov	1882
138	Bullard, H.C.	Miss R.A. Lesley	1 Dec	1881
278	Burks, Henry	Sarah M. Wilmouth	26 June	1883
197	Burks, J.A.	Amanda Pilcher	17 Sept	1882
558	Burks, J.H.	Miss N.J. Gaines	7 Oct	1886
349	Burks, Reubin	Miss D.J. Miles	12 June	1884
498	Busby, R.L.	Miss C.F. Waldrop	27 Nov	1885
12	Russa, J.A.	Jones, Fannie C.	22 Aug	1880
352	Caldwell, J.C.	Miss L.A. Staton	22 Jan	1884
56	Caldwell, J.R.	Martha Jane Gambrell	16 Dec	1880
553	Calek, Cole (C.N.)	Sendia Staggs		
326	Calloway, R.B.	Miss F.J. Stegall	27 Dec	1883

[Bond says Francis Stegall]

200	Calloway, R.C.	Alice Worsham	24 Sept	1882
512	Calloway, W.F.	Georgie O'Neal	3 Jan	1886
400	Campbell, A.C.	Lou Ferrell	17 Dec	1884
10	Campbell, W.D.	Miss C.A. McCoy	18 Aug	1880
447	Campbell, W.R.	Miss S.F. Homan	30 Aug	1885
136	Card, W.A.	Miss M.F. Tutor	24 Nov	1881
434	Carlock, W.M.	Miss C.I. Surrant	25 Feb	1885 (LO)
257	Carnes, T.R.	Rosa Parker	1 Feb	1883
436	Carpenter, D.G.	Miss M.E. Owen	3 Mar	1885
33	Carr, Newton	Mrs. E.F. Boatman	24 Oct	1880
325	Carr, R.S.	Anna Ingram	22 Dec	1883 (LO)
354	Carter, J.M.	Mary S. Rau	10 July	1884
384	Carwild, George	Emerline Grisham	6 Nov	1884
248	Carwile, W.S.	Miss M.E. Grisham	13 Feb	1883
494	Champion, J.J.	Miss S.J. Drewrey	26 Nov	1885
119	Clark, F.M.	Mollie Rice	4 Oct	1881
522	Clark, George	Cassie T. Singleton	17 Jan	1886
301	Clark, J.M.	Miss M.E. Givhan	31 Oct	1883
345	Clements, D.F.	Miss M.F. Joens	20 Mar	1884
550	Coker, Robt	Mrs. M.E. Davis	6 Aug	1886

[Consent: G.W. Coker]

342	Collier, G.M.	Cordella West	10 Mar	1884
149	Collins, John L.	Alice Bibby	28 Dec	1881
380	Combs, J.M.	Miss M.E. Kelly	24 Oct	1884
222	Conlee, E.C.	Miss N.L. Malone	29 Nov	1882
285	Cooper, Thomas	Jennie McClellen	14 Aug	1883

[License reads Jennie Sledge]

583	Cox, John	Miss Laionia Lowery	8 Dec	1886

[Consent: W.T. Lowery]

372	Cox, L.Y.	Miss C.C. Jones	12 Oct	1884
127	Cox, Stephen	Miss Jimmie Sullivan	3 Nov	1881
124	Crausby, A.H.	Miss M.E. Scott	23 Oct	1881

[Augustus Harrison Crausby]

502	Creed, J.C.	Miss L.F. Griffin	2 Dec 1885	
133	Cromwell, W.A.	Miss M.E. McCharen	17 Nov 1881	
36	Cruse, J.M.M.	Mollie Gregory	18 Oct 1880	
507	Cummings, A.F.E.	Minnie Caldwell	23 Dec 1885	
552	Cummings, J.M.	Mrs. Modie Dunn	12 Aug 1886	
585	Daniel, J.C.	Frealon Lamon	23 Dec 1886	
13	Davis, Allen	Mrs. R.C. Hardin	25 Aug 1880	
469	Davis, John	Mollie McCullough	27 Sept 1885	
525	Davis, U.N.	Miss C.I. Little	24 Jan 1886	
420	Davis, W.J.	Miss L. Little	11 Jan 1885	
561	Davis, W.R.	Miss A.L. McCullough	7 Oct 1886	
42	Davis, Wm A.	Sophronia Nix	18 Nov 1880	
303	Day, M.C.	Miss A.L. Miller	18 Nov 1883	
70	Deavenport, D.G.	Janie C. Crawford	14 Dec 1880	
297	DeJerrott, C.H.	Mrs. J.A. McEachern	2 Oct 1883	(LO)
467	Dickson, W.P.	Miss F.S. Shannon	25 Sept 1885	

[Bond - Dixon]

188	Dillard, A.R.	Nannie Russell	20 Aug 1882	
68	Dillard, W.H.	Miss Annie Weaver	30 Dec 1880	

[Consent for Annie Weaver by parents Ransom and Susan Clayton]

449	Dillard, W.N.	M.A. Shettles	19 May 1885	
572	Dison, w.R.	Nannie Setzler	2 Dec 1886	
437	Doulgas, R.L.	Mrs. L. Hutchison	10 Mar 1885	

[License reads Miss.]

280	Dover, E.A.	Miss N.J. (Franklin	11 July 1883	
28	Dover, W.H.	Miss M.J. Hellums	7 Oct 1880	
95	Dues, Walter	Mollie V. Edwards	13 Mar 1881	
54	Duke, W.J.	Miss A.N. Collins	16 Dec 1880	
269	Duncan, A.G.	Miss S.A. Owen	19 Apr 1883	
292	Duncan, J.T.	Miss R.P. Vaughn	6 Aug 1883	(LO)
546	Duncan, M.L.	Miss W.B. Wait	27 June 1886	

[Parent of Miss W.B. Wait - A.M. Vinson]

126	Dyson, L.W.	Miss F.E. Ellis	26 Oct 1881	
363	Echols, A.P.	Mollie Davis	29 Aug 1884	(LO)
484	Echols, J.W.	Miss M.A. Wood	11 Nov 1885	
193	Edington, Ethel N.	Fannie M. Flarherty	7 Sept 1882	
84	Edington, G.E. (H?)	Miss L.T. Jones	5 Feb 1881	
394	Edington, R.W.	Miss E.H. Moore	10 Dec 1884	
598	Edwards, Joe	Miss M.A. Rackley	23 Dec 1886	
586	Eelbeck, F.C.	Lou H. Givhan	15 Dec 1886	
361	Ellis, John U.	Mary Crasby (Crosby?)	21 Aug 1884	
288	Falkner, Jasper	Dora E. Abernathy	26 Aug 1883	
401	Farrer, J.F.	Lula Widener	18 Dec 1884	

[Consent: G.W. and Virginia Widener]

93	Faulkner, A.S.	Miss C.A. Simpson	3 Mar 1881	
575	Faulkner, N.	Miss S.E. Sibley	23 Nov 1886	

116	Ferguson, R.S.	Miss Grenada Bushilon	15 Sept	1881

[Consent for Grenada - N. Shirley, Guardian]

592	Ferguson, W.H.	Lena Skinner	23 Dec	1886	
194	Fields, H.E.	Parilee Russell	10 Sept	1882	
236	Fields, J.F.	Miss L.M. Laprade	21 Dec	1882	
219	Flaherty, H.A.	Ida Waddell	23 Nov	1882	
226	Flaherty, W.M., Jr.	Rebecca Lower	7 Dec	1882	
463	Franks, E.L.	Miss A.E. Perry	11 Aug	1885	
20	Frierson, A.A.	Miss B.E. Westmoreland	22 Sept	1880	
540	Gains, R.W.	Miss M.E. Kelly	21 Apr	1886	
390	Gardner, J.L.	Miss A.E. Wells	25 Nov	1884	
493	Gay, C.L.	Miss T.V. Warren	17 Nov	1885	
213	Giddens, J.W.	Miss M.L. White	2 Nov	1882	
483	Gilder, G.N.	Ida Simmons	8 Nov	1885	
51	Gilder, R.H.	Miss M.J. Thornton	9 Dec	1880	
253	Gillespie, J.D.	Miss H.C. Briggs	4 Feb	1883	
262	Gilmer, J.M.	Mollie Neely	1 Mar	1883	
403	Gilmer, J.W.	Miss M.E. Lowry	24 Dec	1884	
505	Ginn, R.J.	Miss E.F. Atkins	31 Dec	1885	
264	Givhan, W.W.	Maggie Cates	7 Mar	1883	
337	Glover, Lee	Martha McWhirter	3 Feb	1884	
229	Goggans, James T.	Carrie C. Dunn	13 Dec	1882	
444	Goggans, Sulee	Dolly Perry	26 Mar	1885	
223	Godfrey, T.P.	Mary Baker	30 Nov	1882	
106	Godfrey, W.H.	Miss M.V. Priesh	11 Aug	1881	
370	Goldman, Wiley	Annie Hubbard	5 Oct	1884	
375	Gooch, W.A.	Miss M.F. Bigham	16 Oct	1884	
265	Goodman, J.J.	Mollie E. Pitts	6 Mar	1883	
203	Goodwin, J.F.	Miss V.C. Fowler	12 Oct	1882	
202	Goodwin, J.T.	Miss L.M. Mask	1 Oct	1882	
496	Grafton, A.F.	Ellen Steel	1 Dec	1885	
365	Grant, L.D.	Miss R.L. Freeman	10 Sept	1884	
182	Grant, W.J.	Miss N.M. Freeman	1 Aug	1882	
499	Green, G.W.	Miss Sallie Malone	26 Nov	1885	

[Sallie, age 22, consent by parents James Meeks and wife]

215	Gregory, S.B.	P.D. Kelley	5 Nov	1882	
402	Grisham, J.I. (Isaac)	Miss M.L. McDonald	18 Dec	1884	
27	Grisham, John	Rebecca Carwile	7 Oct	1880	
538	Guinn, L.H.	Miss Willie P. Givhan	31 Mar	1886	
428	Guinn, W.W.	Miss B.E. Sadler	17 Feb	1885	
353	Guthrie, J.W.	Miss M.B. Long	15 June	1884	
53	Hadley, Joseph	S.E. Lower	12 Dec	1880	
366	Hall, Monroe	Mattie Burks	20 Sept	1884	(LO)
490	Hall, W.H.	Miss Lizzie Pitts	19 Nov	1886	
477	Hamilton, Evans	Fannie Tallant	25 Oct	1885	
37	Hamilton, J.P.	Miss Doney Waldrop	20 Oct	1880	(LO)
86	Haney, Jesse F.	Miss L.L. Weatherall	3 Feb	1881	

501	Haney, R.L.	Miss E.C. Taylor	29 Nov	1885
520	Haney, S.K.	Miss A.M. Brown	17 Jan	1886
514	Hanna, A.T.	Miss S.M. Miller	4 Jan	1886
105	Hanson, J.J.	F.E. Pilcher	6 Aug	1881
156	Harden, A.C.	Martha Stegall	18 Jan	1882
277	Harmon, Gilbert	Georgia Ann Jaco	26 June	1883
542	Harmon, Wright	Miss Morgan Moore	20 May	1886
554	Harris, J.V.	Julia L. Leaggett	25 Aug	1886
129	Harris, T.M.	Miss Sinne Alsup	9 Nov	1881
111	Harrison, A.P.	Belle S. Forman	29 Aug	1881
471	Harrison, W.H.	Miss V.R. Herndon	8 Oct	1885
135	Hawkins, E.W.	Miss N.J. Rodgers	23 Nov	1881
594	Hellums, L.R.	Miss E.L. Freeman	26 Dec	1886

[License - Evaena Freeman]

3	Helms, A.L.	Miss M.L. Shannon	1 July	1880
286	Henderson, J.C.	Miss A.L. Milam	11 Sept	1883

[Licnese reads Anna Milam, consent by father J.W. Milam]

271	Henderson, J.M.	Lillie Brooks	26 Apr	1883

]License reads Dr. Henderson]

140	Herd, Wm	Sallie Cummings	1 Dec	1881
368	Herring, J.W.	Miss S.A. Walker	28 Sept	1884
386	Hill, E.R.	Alice Gates	13 Nov	1884
41	Hill, Henry	Beulah, E. Garner	11 Nov	1880

[License reads 1881. Consent by mother Mrs. Ella Hill]

177	Hill, S.G.	Mrs. E.D. Saunders	10 May	1882	
272	Hill, W.H.	Miss M.P. Moore	1 May	1883	
357	Hinton, W.C.	Mattie Lower	27 July	1884	
324	Hodges, J.T.	Lula Webb	19 Dec	1883	(LO)

[Consent by parent S.D. Webb]

69	Hodges, Wm	Miss M.A. Carpenter	6 Jan	1881	
152	Holditch, J.D.	Alice Crausby	12 Jan	1882	
210	Holley, J.B.	Ellen White	22 Oct	1882	
495	Holliday, F.V.	Sallie Mayo	26 Nov	1885	
543	Homans, Sam	Ellen Cambell	12 June	1886	
240	Hooker, J.C.	Miss P.A. Patterson	26 Dec	1882	
23	Horton, G.G.	Mrs. N.C. Andrews	6 Oct	1880	
450	Horton, H.C.	Miss M.E. Hardin	24 May	1885	
433	Howard, W.A.	Miss M.A. Rush	25 Feb	1885	
578	Howell, J.D.	Miss S.E. Jones	30 Nov	1886	(LO)
113	Howell, W.A.	Susan Mauldin	1 Sept	1881	
284	Howell, W.M.	Martha Campbell	5 Aug	1883	
108	Hudson, C.W.	Miss R.J. Wait	23 Aug	1881	
206	Hudson, J.W.	Lizzie W. Bardee	18 Oct	1882	
176	Hudson, John H.	Mary F. Watts	11 May	1882	
24	Hubbard, A.C.	Miss M.F. Jackson	3 Oct	1880	
304	Hubbard, John H.	Miss S.E. Flemming	31 Oct	1883	
476	Huffstickler, C.	Miss V.A. Lovings	28 Oct	1885	
442	Huffstickler, W.B.	Callie Lovings	22 Mar	1885	

581	Inmon, T.J.	Miss S.E. Bolen	9 Dec	1886	
587	Inmon, Will	Cinthia Shanon	16 Dec	1886	
348	Jackson, George	Zoe Lawson	3 May	1884	
335	Jackson, J.E.	Miss M.M. Hickey	22 Jan	1884	
79	Jamison, W.A.	Miss M.C. Taylor	21 Jan	1881	
187	Jacob, A.J.	Lizzie Waldo	11 Aug	1882	
118	Jeeter, Wm J.	Julia Lovings	29 Sept	1881	
92	Jennings, George	Miss A.E. Rowland	3 Mar	1881	
25	Jernigan, R.S.	Miss D.J. Gregory	6 Oct	1880	
	[Certificate reads B.L. Gregory]				
346	Johnson, A.N.	Mollie Coats	4 Apr	1884	(LO)
413	Johnson B.F.	Miss M.J. Stegall	31 Dec	1885	
381	Johnson, C.W.	Mattie Cummings	30 Oct	1884	
497	Johnson, L.B.	Miss L.A. Brown	24 Nov	1885	
377	Johnson, L.H.	E.A. Hooper	19 Oct	1884	
184	Johnson, S.J.	E.R. Garnett	6 Aug	1882	
94	Johnson, W.F.	Miss L.A. Todd	4 Mar	1881	
274	Johnson, W.G.	Mrs. Bettie Owens	20 May	1883	
97	Johnston, R.N.	Cora McClarty	20 Mar	1881	
259	Jones, A.J.	Sallie Patterson	7 Feb	1883	
519	Jones, J.N. (Neely)	Miss N.Y. Wood	12 Jan	1886	
311	Jones, John N.	Miss T.E. Purdon	2 Dec	1883	
504	Jones, Marvin	Mollie Sappington	17 Dec	1885	
251	Jordan, A.F.	Miss L.A. Sneed	30 Jan	1883	
328	Kelly, F.W.	Mattie J. Scott	29 Dec	1881	(LO)
	[Consent: L.P. Scott]				
318	Kelly, J.J.	Miss L.A. Caldwell	15 Dec	1883	
535	Kelly, R.P.	Miss S.J. Caldwell	24 Mar	1886	
570	Kelly, S.P.	Lou Moore	24 Nov	1886	
5	Kelly, W.	Sophronia Gregory	25 July	1880	
590	Kemp, D.B.	Miss M.M. Allen	16 Dec	1886	
	[Bond reads Camp]				
235	Kidd, A.L.	Miss G.A. Browning	22 Dec	1882	
	[Returned - Not Executed]				
249	Kidd, J.E.	Katy Harris	21 Jan	1883	
175	King, W.A.	Miss N.A. Moore	14 May	1882	
266	Koon, J.M.	Mrs. V.A. Roach	13 Mar	1883	
	[License reads Miss]				
81	Kyle, J.A.	Miss G.V. Beard	25 Jan	1881	
438	Lamar, E.P.	Miss S.J. Dickson	11 Mar	1885	
102	Lamb, E.D.	Hattie McCarmie	23 July	1881	
412	lauderdale, C.C.	Manie Pyle	1 Jan	1885	
147	Lauderdale, L.G.	Liddie Miller	29 Dec	1881	
220	Lawrence, N.L.	Mary E. Rodgers	12 Dec	1882	
162	Lee, James F.	Miss S.M. Washington	26 Feb	1882	

#	Groom	Bride	Date	
382	Lemons, R.C.	Ola Wells	27 Nov	1884
165	Lewelling, W.J.	Miss H. Harrison	15 Feb	1882
	[Also spelled Lewellen on this page]			
323	Lilley, M.D.	Lanie Wilson	20 Dec	1883
145	Lilley, W.D.	Miss T.B. Stone	21 Dec	1881 (LO)
541	Linsley, J.E.	Mrs. M.H. Tutor	9 May	1886
180	Little, B.B.	Miss S.B. Clements	9 July	1882
128	Little, W.R.	Miss A.C. Bland	6 Nov	1881
356	Long, George	Mary Pritchard	23 July	1884
329	Long, J.K.	Miss L.J. Stokes	30 Dec	1883
134	Long, J.M.	Nannie Simpson	16 Nov	1881
562	Longest, C.J.	Miss S.C. Baker	13 Oct	1886
78	Lowery, S.R.	Miss E.C. Armstrong	20 Jan	1881
2	Lowery, Wm	Mary Wagner	25 June	1880
130	Lowry, Dr. G.W.	Miss L.E. Anderson	10 Nov	1881
555	Lucus, J.J.	Mary Orr	12 Sept	1886
258	Lyon, W.H.	Lizzie Pitts	8 Feb	1883
142	McAlister, W.M.	Annie Garrett	22 Dec	1881
523	McCammon, J.M.	Miss L.Y. Dillard	19 Jan	1886
456	McCarney, J.E.	Ida Harmon	13 July	1885
212	McChearn, R.E.	Mary Martin	1 Nov	1882
71	McCleskey, J.M.	Miss N.S. McCullough	9 Jan	1881
551	McClure, John	Miss S.E. Hill	8 Aug	1886
48	McCord, W.N.	Miss M.E. Medlock	11 Dec	1880
66	McCoy, J.E.	Annie Williams	30 Dec	1880
172	McCoy, S.S.	Miss J.L. Simpson	30 Mar	1882
564	McCutchen	Mary Cooper	9 Nov	1886
506	McEachern, J.W.	Miss J.A. Wood	23 Dec	1885
406	McElvaney, C.B.	Miss M.F. Norwood	25 Dec	1884
114	McElvaney, Wm R.	Miss M.J. Smith	4 Sept	1881
383	McGregory, W.F.	Marthy Carpenter	4 Nov	1884
50	McJunkin, W.D.	Mary E. McJunkin	14 Dec	1880
104	McKinney, J.B.	Amanda Inmon	11 Aug	1881
209	McKnight, D.W.	Miss M.E. Bowen	22 Oct	1882
371	McNeely, J.A.	Miss H.C. Cooper	7 Oct	1884
7	McVay, Thomas	Josie McDonald	10 Aug	1880
298	McWhirter, B.L.	Bettie Rodgers	7 Oct	1883
	[License reads Robt L. McWhirter]			
511	McWhirter, J.M.	S.E. Johnson	3 Jan	1886
75	McWhirter, J.T.	Emma Owen	13 Jan	1881
18	Maddox, Green, Jr.	Mrs. Donie Surratt	1 Sept	1880
	[Consent by father Green Maddox, Sr.]			
166	Mahew, J.A.	Miss S.A. Jones	27 Feb	1882
451	Maness, James M.	Ella E. Edwards	31 May	1885
	[Consent by J.W. Edwards]			
559	Maness, Marshall	Emma Edwards	2 Oct	1886
479	Martin, M.D.	Ola Pickens	3 Nov	1885
260	Matthews, Jno A.	Mrs. S.A. Snider	15 Feb	1883

422	Maulding, H.C.	Annie Harwood	13 Jan	1885
47	May, G.W.	Alice Patton	4 Jan	1881
19	Mayfield, J.T.	Mary B. Huckabee	12 Sept	1880
276	Milam, G.W.	Lou Davis	26 June	1883
283	Mills, J.T.	Martha Kelly	22 July	1883
316	Minor Henry	Olivia Flaherty	13 Dec	1883
314	Minor, T.M.	Dora Harris	6 Dec	1883
443	Mitchell, C.B.	Sara W. White	25 Mar	1885
466	Mitchell, J.W.	Miss S.A. Sewell	20 Sept	1885
396	Montgomery, A.	Miss Francis Vaughn	11 Dec	1884
279	Montgomery, D.N.	Clarinna Pilcher	8 July	1883
123	Montgomery, J.C.	Miss N.A. Montgomery	-- Nov	1881
492	Montgomery, W.C.	Miss I.L. Bland	19 Nov	1885
242	Moody, W.H.	Miss M.H.A. Black	11 Jan	1883
		[License - Mrs. M.H.A. Black]		
399	Moore, W.D.	Sina Collins	17 Dec	1884
435	Morgan, R.L.	Miss N.A. Johnson	4 Mar	1885
453	Morrow, J.A.	Miss I.E. Hodges	23 June	1885
359	Moss, W.D.	Miss M.E.G. McKinney	6 Aug	1884
181	Murdock, Martin	Miss M.C. Stovall	11 July	1882
76	Nurphy, H.J.	Addie Gillespie	20 Jan	1881
62	Murphy, J.E.	Amelia E. Sanders	26 Dec	1880
32	Neely, W.F.	Miss M.B. Archer	14 Oct	1880
101	Neigh, J.L.	Miss L.P. Buchanan	21 July	1881
199	Nelson, Joshua A.	Martha Daniel	29 Jan	1882
474	Newson, W.H.	Miss H.G. Gates	15 Oct	1885
563	Northcut, W.J.	Jennie Burke	24 Oct	1886
534	Norwood, J.H.	Miss M.A. Carr	4 Mar	1886
330	Norwood, W.A.	Julia Parker	3 Jan	1883
261	Norwood, W.L.	Miss P.E. Carnes	28 Feb	1883
89	Overstreet, W.S.	Martha J. Gideon	16 Feb	1881 (LO)
73	Owen, J.B.	Mary E. Donaldson	12 Jan	1881
30	Palmer, C.M.	Sarah Brown	10 Oct	1880
418	Parks, B.	Miss S.E. Coward	13 Jan	1885
424	Patterson, Jas H.	Miss P.B. Barrington	20 Jan	1885
239	Patterson, W.N.	Hassie Newell	28 Dec	1882
547	Peachy, John	Mary Perden	4 July	1886
64	Pearson, J.W.	Dollie Taylor	23 Dec	1880
395	Peden, T.S.	Sophrona Callaway	17 Dec	1884
55	Pegues, E.C.	Mary E. Brown	14 Dec	1880
355	Petit, J.J.	Sarah J. Walls	14 July	1884
192	Pettit, Henry	Mary Frances Walls	2 Sept	1882
90	Pettit, Wm	Polly Walls	20 Feb	1881
589	Phillips, Y.N.	Margaret Kelly	15 Dec	1886
17	Pickens, W.S.	Miss M.L. Johnson	1 Sept	1880
183	Pilcher, James	Lucy A. Kidd	13 Aug	1882
40	Pitts, H.B.	Miss Dell Rootes	4 Nov	1880
247	Pitts, J.C.	Annie Lowry	14 Jan	1883
300	Pitts, M.B.	Belle Brown	24 Oct	1883

80	Pitts, R.S.	Miss N.A. Seale	20 Jan	1881	
429	Pitts, W.H.	Amanda Smith	17 Feb	1885	
190	Pittman, J.M.	Ada McNeely	24 Aug	1882	
107	Ponder, J.H.	Miss M.A. Carson	14 Aug	1881	
121	Ponder, W.C.	Miss E.A. Griffin	13 Oct	1881	
439	Porter, H.H.	Ella C. Allsup	7 Mar	1885	
173	Porter, Thos J.	Mary M. McDonald	2 Apr	1882	
309	Porter, Wm M.	Sarah E. Smith	19 Nov	1883	(LO)
98	Potter, J.D.	Annie J. Spencer	31 Mar	1881	
425	Pound, G.H.G.	Josie Jones	22 Jan	1885	
549	Powell, L.R.	Miss M.A. Price	1 Aug	1886	
299	Poyner, F.R.	Miss E.L. Drake	18 Oct	1883	
379	Poyner, J.B.	Miss L.J. Davis	22 Dec	1884	
245	Prather, A.H	Miss A.E. Miller	11 Jan	1883	
224	Price, J.M.	Lizzie Rodgers	5 Dec	1882	
464	Price, John	Miss N. Pitts	20 Aug	1885	
125	Price, John A.H.	Amanda J. Rawls	23 Oct	1881	
350	Price, T.J.	Sallie Crawford	11 June	1884	
432	Price, W.H.	Miss L.L. Perdon	26 Feb	1885	
243	Price, W.R.	Miss M.J. Munn	4 Jan	1883	
362	Pritchard, J.C.	Miss T.A. Mitchell	28 Aug	1884	
376	Rackley, E.	Miss M.J. Rutledge	19 Oct	1884	
170	Rackley, John	Jodie Rutledge	16 Mar	1882	
373	Ray, J.D.	Sallie Tucker	12 Oct	1884	
	[Parents consent: S.D. and H.O. Tucker]				
419	Rayburn, W.T.	Miss M.E. Maples	9 Jan	1885	
14	Rea, G.W.	M.L. Turner	24 Aug	1880	
458	Rea, G.W.	Miss M.B. Franklin	13 Aug	1885	
485	Rea, W.A.S.	Miss H.M. Westmoreland	15 Nov	1885	
340	Reigh, J.E.	Miss D.L. Ward	26 Feb	1884	
281	Reynolds, J.C.	Miss F.J. McKnight	19 July	1883	
460	Robins, L.B.	Miss N.E. Dowdy	2 Aug	1885	
117	Robins, N.F.	Miss J.A. Dillard	25 Sept	1881	
476	Roberson, L.R.	Ella Zinn	25 Oct	1885	
63	Roberson, Wm	Miss P.M. Bell	22 Dec	1880	(LO)
85	Roberts, J.N.	Laverna Robertson	1 Feb	1881	
528	Rockett, R.H.	Bettie Isbell	8 Feb	1886	
263	Rodgers, A.A.	Mrs. J.A.K. Taylor	6 Mar	1883	
302	Rodgers, Joseph	Mary Pitts	27 Oct	1883	(LO)
307	Rodgers, S.J.F.	Orlena Pound	15 Nov	1883	
385	Rodgers, W.F.	Ida B. Gregory	9 Nov	1884	
545	Rogers, J.A.	Miss Vada Setzler	22 June	1886	
	[Consent: B.F. Rodgers and V.J. Setzler]				
573	Roggers, J.S.	Belle Tate	25 Dec	1886	
	[Bond - J.S. Rodgers]				
46	Rowzee, J. Hamp	Miss Nettie F. Walker	2 Dec	1881	
103	Rucker, B.A.	Sallie Gilmore	2 Aug	1881	
410	Russell, D.F.	Miss M.A. Simmons	31 Dec	1884	
39	Russell, Jno A.	Sarah E. McCord	31 Oct	1880	

364	Russell, L.A.	Minnie Strange	3 Sept	1884
	[Consent: M.A. Strange]			
509	Russell, P.H.	Annie A. Neely	30 Dec	1885
339	Russell, W.V.	Mary Patterson	28 Feb	1884
500	Rutledge, J.H.	Mrs. N.E. McKnight	1 Dec	1885
208	Rutledge, J.M.	Miss F.E. Eubank	22 Nov	1882
67	Samphill, J.J.	Miss M.P. Staggs	30 Dec	1880
580	Sappington, H.D.	Marthy Brown	3 Dec	1886
230	Sappington, P.B.	Miss J.P. Archer	20 Dec	1882
358	Seales, W.M.	Mollie Hawkins	2 Aug	1884
448	Sewell, J.A.	Mary Strange	30 Apr	1885
	[Consent: Mrs. L.A. Sewell]			
49	Sewell, S.A.	Vesta Strange	9 Dec	1880
452	Setzler, G.M.	Miss O. Jones	9 June	1885
8	Shelton, C.P.	Miss L.E. Robertson	17 Aug	1880
45	Shelton, G.B.	Miss L.M.S. Peoples	24 Nov	1880
169	Sheperd, R.G.	Miss F.J. Hall	2 Mar	1882
112	Sherer, T.W.	Miss D.E. Rogers	31 Aug	1881
38	Sherer, W.J.	Miss Alice T. Rodgers	24 Oct	1880
174	Shettleworth, G.R.	Sarah Pitts	6 May	1882 (LO)
533	Sibley, J.L.	Annie Hensley	1 Mar	1886
273	Shirley, John	Miss G.A. McCarter	9 May	1883 (LO)
317	Simmons, J.A.	Miss S.A. Caldwell	17 Dec	1883
139	Simms, W.B.	Miss N.A. King	1 Dec	1881
351	Slaughter, G.W.	Miss M.C. Cooper	15 June	1884
57	Slaughter, P.H.	M.N. McCharen	16 Dec	1880
157	Slaughter, R.G.	Miss S.A. McNiel	24 Jan	1882
35	Sledge, J.W.	Addie Brock	17 Oct	1880
475	Smith, C.H.	Nancy Price	19 Oct	1885
369	Smith, J.B.	Miss F.E. Tutor	29 Sept	1884
516	Smith, Frank	Mary Reed	No Date	
	[NOTE: "This young ladie returned and does not want to marry Mr. Smith"]			
560	Smith, G.F.	Mattie Young	3 Oct	1886
164	Smith, J.W.	Mary C. Brown	16 Jan	1886
457	Smith, Joseph	Mary Owens	26 July	1885
	[License - Mary Owen]			
233	Smitherman, J.S.	Loana Jones	21 Dec	1882
252	Sneed, J.L.	Miss M.A. Robins	26 Jan	1883 (LO)
144	Snowden, Willie	Amelia Mayfield	19 Dec	1881
	[License dated, then a note stating "Error See Colored Docket".]			
122	Souter, J.T.	Miss E.B. Morphis	12 Oct	1881
74	Souter, M.W.	Mollie F. Price	17 Jan	1881
52	Souter, R.J.	Miss Dannie Scott	9 Dec	1880
109	Spears, J.A.	Virginia Sledge	18 Aug	1881
341	Sprouse, J.C.	Susie White	24 Feb	1884
486	Staggs, J.E.	Miss L.M. Baker	22 Nov	1885
473	Starling, L.C.	Carline Phillips	14 Oct	1885

160	Staten, L.M.	Miss M.A. Henry	29 Jan	1882	
290	Staten, W.A.	Mollie Givens	28 Aug	1883	(LO)
31	Stegall, M.B.	Miss L.L. Miears	17 Oct	1880	
294	Stegall, R.C.	Miss L.A. Kelly	13 Sept	1883	
407	Stegall, T.M.	Mary Camel	25 Dec	1885	
22	Stegall, W.H.	Mrs. M.A. Simmons	3 Oct	1880	
58	Stephens, D.B.	Miss A.J. Bass	19 Dec	1880	
527	Stephens, George	Rosanna Holditch	11 Feb	1886	
576	Stepp, G.W.	Miss M.E. Pegues	25 Nov	1886	
367	Stewart, J.M.	Miss M.P. Woods	7 Oct	1884	
217	Stovall, A.R.	Miss M.J. Hoke	19 Nov	1882	
461	Stovall, J.B.	Ida Crestman	9 Aug	1885	
571	Stowe, John	Anna Waldo	20 Nov	1886	
	[Bond - George Stowe]				
481	Strickland, N.	Miss M.J. Ayers	5 Nov	1885	
150	Sudduth, J.C.	Mrs. Susan Pound	5 Jan	1882	
158	Sudduth, H.P.	Miss N.A. Donaldson	19 Jan	1882	
310	Swain, C.M.	Miss M.Z. Bevill	27 Nov	1883	
332	Swindle, Joe	Susie Echols	2 Jan	1884	(LO)
331	Tallant, J.D.	Miss W.R. Smith	31 Dec	1883	(LO)
244	Taylor, J.B.	Miss G.E. Lowery	7 Jan	1883	
374	Terrell, A.Y.	Miss A.P. Scott	15 Oct	1884	
	[Bond - Amanda Scott]				
120	Thaxton, E.H.	Lena Thornton	4 Oct	1881	
234	Thomason, A.M.	Miss D.E. Pritchard	21 Dec	1882	
579	Thompson, R.S.	Ella Williams	2 Dec	1886	
151	Thornton, H.L.	J.D. Malissa Parham	10 Jan	1882	
566	Thornton, J.F.	Bettie Widener	13 Nov	1886	
282	Tramerls(?), Jospeh	Belle Waldo	18 July	1883	(LO)
214	Trice, W.W.	Sallie H. Wyley	8 Nov	1882	
	[Wilder W. Trice]				
334	Tucker, A.D.	Miss J.R. Caldwell	17 Jan	1884	
246	Tunnell, J.T.	Miss T.V. Hood	15 Jan	1883	
344	Turner, E.J.	Miss L.A. Tutor	15 Mar	1884	
267	Tutor, A.N.H.	Miss M.J.A. Rea	21 Mar	1883	
531	Tutor, G.F.	Allie Waldrop	3 Mar	1886	
565	Tutor, T.J.	Miss S.M. Gregory	11 Nov	1886	
378	Tutor, W.H.	Miss M.E. Linsley	19 Oct	1884	
65	Tweedle, J.M.	Mary M. KIng	27 Dec	1880	
88	Vaughan, J.H.	Ann Crawford	17 Feb	1881	
11	Vaughn, John R.	Mattie S. Winters	20 Aug	1880	
26	Vaughn, R.M.	Mrs. M.V. Horton	5 Oct	1880	
178	Waldo, A.J.	Sallie Smith	11 June	1882	
163	Waldo, J.P.	Susanna Miller	25 Feb	1882	
591	Waldrop, J.W.	Lillie Bell Skinner	23 Dec	1886	
423	Waldrop, W.F.	Miss L.E. Copper	20 Jan	1885	
	[Licnese - Miss L.E. Cooper]				

221	Wagner, W.H.	Miss E.A. GRay	22 Nov	1882	
201	Walker, Henry F.	Anlo Huntington	27 Sept	1882	
445	Walker, T.B.	Miss S.A.M. Holley	29 Mar	1885	
415	Walker, W.F.	Miss M.E. Hartley	10 Jan	1885	
306	Walker, W.R.	Miss S.H. Washington	12 Nov	1883	(LO)
255	Wall, J.D.	Jennie Arnold	31 Jan	1883	
	[License - Eugenia Arnold]				
584	Wallace, J.W.	Eliza Hood	12 Dec	1886	
391	Wallis, W.F.	Josie Simmons	27 Nov	1884	
536	Walls, E.V.	Adie Mathews	29 Mar	1886	
487	Walls, James R.	Allie Harris	14 Nov	1885	(LO)
	[Note reads: Miss Harris declines]				
250	Walls, Jno B.	Mary Jane Morphis	25 Jan	1883	
199	Walls, Joseph	Miss H.A. Mathis	19 Sept	1882	
196	Walls, W.P.	E.J. Chase	17 Sept	1882	
503	Ware, J.A.	Minnie Abbott	9 Dec	1885	
15	Warren, D.W.	Miss P.E. McCullough	26 Aug	1880	(LO)
289	Warren, W.B.	Miss L.A.O.A. James	28 Aug	1883	(LO)
61	Washington, J.P.	Miss J.O. Murphy	26 Dec	1880	
225	Watts, W.R.	Miss M.E. Reeder	2 Dec	1882	
482	Watson, Wells	Miss Sallie Johnson	7 Nov	1885	
	[License - Mrs. Sallie Johnson]				
513	Watters, T.L.	Mattie Y. Rackley	3 Jan	1886	
582	Weatherall, John T.	Annie Thomason	9 Dec	1886	
77	Weatherall, Wm A.	Callie Miller	19 Jan	1881	(LO)
228	Weatherall, W.A.	Maggie Barr	12 Dec	1882	
529	Weatherall, W.A.	Miss M.A. Arnold	25 Feb	1886	
171	Weaver, N.J.	Miss M.P. Laprade	26 Mar	1882	
465	Webb, Nathan	Miss L.T. Nickols	6 Sept	1885	
99	Webb, W.J.	Mrs. N.M. Keyes	12 June	1881	
100	Weems, Columbus	Alice Ralls	13 July	1881	
	[Consent: Father, H. Ralls]				
60	Welch, H.H.	Mrs. N.M. Harris	21 Dec	1880	
44	Wells, C.F.	Mollie Harris	25 Nov	1880	
308	Wells, C.F.	Kittie Wood	17 Nov	1883	(BO)
204	West, Alexander	Kate Brown	18 Oct	1882	
168	West, J.F.	Amanda Burks	28 Feb	1882	
305	Westmoreland, A.J.	Miss S.V.A. Rea	14 Nov	1883	
34	Westmoreland, J.W.	Mrs. Nancy Stepp	17 Oct	1880	
227	White, Eddie	Ida Grant	10 Dec	1880	
548	White, John	Bettie Allen	4 July	1886	
454	White, R.H.	Mollie Sullivan	12 July	1885	
446	White, T.W.	Cinthia Austin	23 Apr	1885	
4	Whiteside, W.B.	Miss Nancy M. Tutor	30 June	1880	
470	Whitten, J.L.	Miss A.E. Biggers	27 Sept	1885	
	[Consent: J.N. Whitten]	[Consent: Mrs. A.A. Biggers]			
430	Whitworth, H.R.	Miss H.B. Parker	19 Feb	1885	
185	Whitworth, T.M.	Miss M.V. Tutor	6 Aug	1882	
526	Wilbur, J.T.	Josie Smith	4 Feb	1886	

398	Wilder, R.P.	Miss A.A. Cox	17 Dec	1884
489	Wilder, S.A.	Miss E.A. Caldwell	19 Nov	1885
237	Wilder, W.H.R.	Miss S.F. Goggins	21 Dec	1882
588	Willard, J.M.	Miss N.M. Russell	23 Dec	1886
91	William, A.W.	Miss S.L. Robins	1 Mar	1881
296	Williams, B.D.	Clarinda Jones	27 Sept	1883
488	Williams, B.F.	Miss G.E. Swofford	18 Nov	1885
154	Williams, J.C.	Miss S.A. Pilcher	12 Mar	1882
409	Windfield, J.B.	Miss S.J. Smith	28 Dec	1884
6	Wingo, T.J.	Miss Bettie D. Hodges	5 Aug	1880
211	Witt, A.J.	Mattie Dixon	30 Oct	1882
291	Witt, W.R.	Cornilia Kennum	6 Sept	1883
462	Wood, J.W.	Miss S.D. Purvine	9 Aug	1885
189	Woodson, John W.	Attie White	20 Aug	1882
518	Wood, T.R.	Mattie Miller	12 jan	1886
319	Wood, W.H.	Miss L.R. Souter	20 Dec	1883
397	Wright, T.W.	Susie Malone	11 Dec	1884
539	Young, J.A.	Mary Smith	18 Apr	1886
137	Young, Wm	Annie Stockstill	23 Nov	1881
293	Yount, Thomas J.	Mrs. F.L. Smith	12 Sept	1883

BRIDE INDEX
SURNAME OF GROOM IN BRACKETS

Abbott, Minnie (Ware)
Abernathy, Dora E. (Falkner)
Alexander, V.A. (Abry or Abney?)
Allen, Bettie (White)
Allen, M.M. (Kemp, Camp)
Alsup, Ella (Alsup)
Alsup, Ella C. (Porter)
Alsup, Sinne (Harris)
Anderson, L.E. (Lowry)
Anderson, M.F. (Abernathy)
Andrews, N.C. (Horton)
Archer, M.B. (Neely)
Archer, J.P. (Sappington)
Armstrong, E.C. (Lowery)
Arnold, Jennie (Wall)
Arnold, M.A. (Weatherall)
Atkins, E.F. (Ginn)
Austin, Cinthia (White)
Ayers, M.J. (Strickland)

Baker, L.M. (Staggs)
Baker, Mary (Godfrey)
Baker, S.C. (Longest)
Bardee, Lizzie W. (Hudson)
Barr, Maggie (Weatherall)
Barrington, P.B. (Patterson)
Baskin, E.L. (Bradford)
Bass, A.J. (Stephens)
Beard, O.V. (Kyle)
Bell, Mary (Bolton)
Bell, P.M. (Robertson)
Bell, Zoe C. (Berry)
Betts, M.L. (Giddens)
Bevill, M.Z. (Swain)
Bibby, Alice (Collins)
Biggers, A.E. (Whitten)
Bigham, M.F. (Gooch)
Bigham, Joanna (Browning)
Bigham, Mattie (Black)
Black, M.H.A. (Moody)
Bland, A.C. (Little)
Bland, I.L. (Montgomery)
Boatman, Mrs. E.F. (Carr)
Bolen, S.E. (Inmon)
Booth, Sallie (Waldo)
Bowen, M.E. (McKnight)
Briggs, H.C. (Gillespie)

Brock, Addie (Sledge)
Brooks, Lillie (Henderson)
Brown, A.M. (Haney)
Brown, Amanda (Brown)
Brown, Belle (Pitts0
Brown, Frances Elizabeth (Ball)
Brown, Kate (West)
Brown, Marthy (Sappington)
Brown, Mary C. (Smith)
Brown, Mary E. (Pegues)
Brown, L.A. (Johnson)
Brown, Sarah (Palmer)
Browning, Beckie (Bigham)
Browning, G.A. (Kidd)
Buchanan, L.P. (Neigh)
Bumgardner, L.L. (Ayers)
Burks, Amanda (West)
Burks, Jennie (Northcut)
Burks, Mattie (Hall)
Bushilon, Grenada (Ferguson)
Butler, M.E. (Archer)

Caldwell, e.A. (Wilder)
Caldwell, J.M. (Tucker)
Caldwell, Minnie (Cummings)
Caldwell, L.A. (Kelly)
Caldwell, S.J. (Kelly)
Caldwell, S.A. (Simmons)
Callaway, Sophronia (Peden)
Cambell, Ellen (Homans)
Camel, Mary (Stegall)
Campbell, Martha (Howell)
Carnes, P.E. (Norwood)
Carpenter, M.A. (Hodges)
Carpenter, Marthy (McGregory)
Carr, M.A. (Norwood)
Carruth, Clorris (Adams)
Carson, M.A. (Ponder)
Carwile, Fannie (Benjamin)
Carwile, Rebecca (Grisham)
Cass, Jodie (Beckham)
Cates, Maggie (Givhan)
Chase, E.J. (Walls)
Clements, S.B. (Little)
Coats, Mollie (Johnson)
Cochran, E.L.A. (Beckham)
Collins, A.N. (Duke)

Collins, Sina (Moore)
Cooper, H.C. (McNeely)
Cooper, L.E. (Waldron)
Cooper, M.C. (Slaughter)
Cooper, Mary (McCutchen)
Copper (Cooper?), L.E. (Waldrop)
Coward, S.E. (Parks)
Cox, A.A. (Wilder)
Crausby, Alice (Holditch)
Crausby, Ellen (Browning)
Crawford, Ann (Vaughan)
Crawford, Janie C. (Deavenport)
Crawford, S.E. (Beavers)
Crawford, Sallie (Price)
Creag, Lula (Brown)
Crestman, Ida (Stovall)
Crosby (Crasby?), Mary (Ellis)
Cummings, Mattie (Johnson)
Cummings, Sallie (Herd)

Daniel, Martha (Nelson)
Davis, L.E. (Bowles)
Davis, L.J. (Poyner)
Davis, Lou (Milam)
Davis, M.E. (Coker)
Davis, Mollie (Echols)
Dickson, S.J. (Lamar)
Dillard, J.A. (Robins)
Dillard, L.Y. (McCammon)
Dixon, Mattie (Witt)
Donaldson, Mary E. (Owen)
Donaldson, N.A. (Sudduth)
Dowdy, N.E. (Robins)
Drake, E.L. (Poyner)
Drewry, S.J. (Champion)
Duncan, E.J. (Baker)
Dunn, Carrie C. (Coggans)
Dunn, Modie (Cummings)

Echols, Susie (Swindle)
Edwards, Ella (Maness)
Edwards, Emma (Maness)
Edwards, Mollie V. (Dues)
Ellis, f.E. (Dyson)
Eubanks, F.E. (Rutledge)

Falkner, M.A. (Baggett)
Ferrell, Lou (Campbell)
Flaherty, Oliva (Minor)
Flarherty, Fannie M. (Eddington)
Flemming, S.E. (Hubbard)

Fontaine, Pattie A. (Bolton)
Forman, Belle S. (Harrison)
Fowler, V.C. (Goodwin)
Freeman, E.L. (Hellums)
Freeman, N.M. (Grant)
Freeman, R.L. (Grant)
Franklin, M.B. (Rea)
Franklin, N.J. (Dover)
Frierson, M.L. (Braley)

Gaines, N.J. (Burke)
Gambrell, Martha Jane (Caldwell)
Garner, Beulah (Hill)
Garnett, E.R. (Johnson)
Garrett, Annie (McAlister)
Gates, Alice (Hill)
Gates, H.G. (Newson)
George, E.L. (Bost)
George, Ivy (Bost)
Gideon, Martha J. (Overstreet)
Gillespie, Addie (Murphy)
Gilmore, Sallie (Rucker)
Gillum, Bettie (Beavers)
Givhan, Lou H. (Eelbeck)
Givhan, M.E. (Clark)
Givhan, Willie P. (Guinn)
Givens, Mollie (Staten)
Coggins, S.F. (Wilder)
Gordon, Lee Ann (Bevil)
Grant, Ida (White)
Gray, E.A. (Wagner)
Gregory, D.J. (Jernigan)
Gregory, Ida B. (Rodgers)
Gregory, Mollie (Cruse)
Gregory, S.M. (Tutor)
Gregory, Sophronia (Kelly)
Griffin, E.A. (Ponder)
Grisham, Emerline (Carwild)
Griffin, L.F. (Creed)
Grisham, M.E. (Carwile)
Grizzell, N.B. (Bramlett)

Hadley, L.J. (Betts)
Hall, F.J. (Shephard)
Hardin, M.E. (Horton)
Hardin, Mrs. R.C. (Davis)
Harmon, Ida (McCarney)
Harris, Allie (Walls)
Harris, Dora (Minor)
Harris, Katy (Kidd)
Harris, Mollie (Wells)

Harris, N.M. (Welch)
Harrison, H. (Lewelling)
Hartley, M.E. (Walker)
Hawkins, Mollie (Seales)
Heartgraves, M.A. (Birchfield)
Henderson, Corra (Anderson)
Hellums, M.J. (Dover)
Henry, M.A. (Staten)
Hensley, Annie (Sibley)
Hensley, Mrs. Elizabeth (Broom)
Herndon, V.R. (Harrison)
Hickey, M.M. (Jackson)
High, B.F. (Buchanan)
Hill, S.E. (McClure)
Hitt, Malissa (Baker)
Holcomb, E.R. (Brandon)
Hodges, Bettie D. (Wingo)
Hodges, I.E. (Morrow)
Hodges, N.A. (Anderson)
Holditch, Rosanna (Stephens)
Hoke, M.J. (Stovall)
Holiman, S.F. (Black)
Holley, S.A.M. (Walker)
Homan, S.F. (Campbell)
Hood, Eliza (Wallace)
Hood, T.V. (Turner)
Hooper, E.A. (Johnson)
Horton, Mrs. M.V. (Vaughn)
Howard, E.E. (Bray)
Hubbard, Annie (Goldman)
Huckabee, Mary B. (Mayfield)
Huntington, Anlo (Walker)
Hutchison, Mrs. L. (Douglas)

Ingram, Anna (Carr)
Inmon, Amanda (McKinney)
Isbell, Bettie (Rockett)
Ivy, Lorena (Betts)

Jaco, Georgia Ann (Harmon)
Jackson, M.F. (Hubbard)
James, L.A.O.A. (Warren)
Joens, M.F. (Clements)
Johnson, Allie (Arnold)
Johnson, Emma (Beason)
Johnson, Lou (Adams)
Johnson, M.J. (Baker)
Johnson, M.L. (Pickens)
Johnson, Martha (Black)
Johnson, N.A. (Morgan)
Johnson, S.E. (McWhirter)

Johnson, Mrs. Sallie (Watson)
Jones, C.G. (Cox)
Jones, Clarinda (Williams)
Jones, Fannie C. (Bussa)
Jones, Josie (Pound)
Jones, L.T. (Edington)
Jones, Loana (Smitherman)
Jones, O. (Setzler)
Jones, S.A. (Mahew)
Jones, S.E. (Boswell)

Kidd, Lucy A. (Pilcher)
King, Belle (Betts)
King, Mary M. (Tweedle)
King, N.A. (Simms)
Knight, L.L. (Brown)
Kelly, P.D. (Gregory)
Kelly, E.A. (Brown)
Kelly, M.E. (Combs)
Kelly, M.E. (Gains)
Kelly, Luella (Bowen)
Kelly, Margaret (Phillips)
Kelly, Martha (Mills)
Kelly, L.A. (Stegall)
Kennum, Cornelia (Witt)
Keyes, Mrs. N.M. (Webb)

Lake, Mary (Bryant)
Lambert, L.O. (Brown)
Lemon, Frealon (Daniel)
Land, Ella (Bolton)
Laprade, L.M. (Fields)
Laprade, M.P. (Weaver)
Lawson, Zoe (Jackson)
Leaggett, Julia L. (Harris)
Lesley, R.A. (Bullard)
Lilley, Mary H. (Adams)
Linsley, M.E. (Tutor)
Little, C.I. (Davis)
Little, L. (Davis)
Long, M.B. (Guthrie)
Lower, Mary (Arnold)
Lower, Mattie (Hinton)
Lower, Rebecca (Flarherty)
Lower, S.E. (Hadley)
Lowery, G.E. (Taylor)
Lowery, Laionia (Cox)
Lowry, Annie (Pitts)
Lowry, M.E. (Gilmer)

McCarmie, Hattie (lamb)

McCarter, G.A. (Shirley)
McCharen, M.E. (Campbell)
McCharen, M.N. (Slaughter)
McClarty, Cora (Johnston)
McClellon, Jennie (Cooper)
McCord, Sarah E. (Russell)
McCoy, C.A. (Campbell)
McCullough, A.L. (Davis)
McCullough, Mollie (Davis)
McCullough, N.S. (McCluskey)
McCullough, P.E. (Warren)
McDonald, Josie (McVay)
McDonald, M.L. (Grisham)
McDonald, Mary M. (Porter)
McEachern, Mrs. J.A. (DeJerrett)
McJunkin, Mary E. (McJunkin)
McKinney, M.E.G. (Moss)
McKnight, F.J. (Reynolds)
McKnight, M.A. (Brown)
McKnight, N.E. (Rutledge)
McNeely, Ada (Pittman)
McNeely, R.J. (Bennett)
McNiel, S.A. (Slaughter)
McWhirter, Martha (Glover)

Malone, N.L. (Conlee)
Malone, Sallie (Green)
Malone, Susie (Wright)
Maples, M.E. (Rayburn)
Martin, Lillie (Austin
Martin, Maggie (Barnes)
Martin, Mary (McChearn)
Mask, L.M. (Goodwin)
Mathews, Adie (Walls)
Mathis, H.A. (Walls)
Maulden, Susan (Howell)
Mayfield, Amelia (Snowden)
Mayo, Sallie (Holliday)
Medlock, M.E. (McCord)
Miears, L.L. (Stegall)
Milam, A.L. (Henderson)
Miles, D.J. (Burks)
Miller, A.E. (Prather)
Miller, A.L. (Day)
Miller, Callie (Weatherall)
Miller, H.A. (Barron)
Miller, Liddie (Lauderdale)
Miller, Mattie (Wood)
Miller, S.M. (Hanna)
Miller, Susanna (Waldo)
Mills, Marthy (Anderson)

Mitchell, T.A. (Pritchard)
Montgomery, N.A. (Montgomery)
Moore, E.H. (Edington)
Moore, Lou (Kelly)
Moore, M.P. (Hill)
Moore, Morgan (Harmon)
Moore, N.A. (King)
Morphis, E.B. (Souter)
Morphis, Mary Jane (Walls)
Munn, M.J. (Price)
Murphy, J.O. (Washington)

Neely, Annie A. (Russell)
Neely, Mattie (Crausby)
Neely, Mollie (Gilmer)
Newell, Hassie (Patterson)
Nichols, L.T. (Webb)
Nix, Sophronia (Davis)
Norwood, Annie (Maulding)
Norwood, M.F. (McElvaney)

O'Neal, Georgie (Calloway)
Orr, Mary (Lucus)
Owen, M.E. (Carpenter)
Owen, S.A. (Duncan)
Owens, Mrs. Bettie (Johnson)
Owen, Emma (McWhirter)
Owens, Mary (Smith)

Pannell, V.V. (Bramlitt)
Parham, J.D. Malissa (Thornton)
Parker, H.S. (Whitworth)
Parker, Julia (Norwood)
Parker, Rosa (Carnes)
Patterson, Mary (Russell)
Patterson, P.A. (Hooker)
Patterson, Sallie (Jones)
Patton, Alice (May)
Pegues, M.E. (Stepp)
Perden, Mary (Peachy)
Perdon, L.L. (Price)
Peoples, L.M.S. (Shelton)
Perry, A.E. (Franks)
Perry, Dolly (Goggans)
Phillips, Carline (Starling)
Pickens, Ola (Martin)
Pilcher, Amanda (Burks)
Pilcher, Clarinna (Montgomery)
Pilcher, F.E. (Hanson)
Pilcher, S.A. (Williams)
Pitts, Mollie E. (Goodman)

Pitts, Lizzie (Hall)
Pitts, Lizzie (Lyon)
Pitts, Mary (Rodgers)
Pitts, N. (Price)
Pitts, Sarah (Shettleworth)
Porter, Ella (Brown)
Pound, Orlena (Rodgers)
Pound, Mrs. Susan (Sudduth)
Price, M.A. (Powell)
Price, Mollie F. (Souter)
Price, Nancy (Smith)
Priesh, M.V. (Godfrey)
Pritchard, D.E. (Thompson)
Pritchard, Mary (Long)
Purdon, T.E. (Jones)
Purvine, A.E. (Barksdale)
Purvine, S.D. (Wood)
Pye, Nanie (Lauderdale)

Rackley, M.A. (Edwards)
Rackley, Mattie Y. (Watters)
Ralls, Alice (Weems)
Ratliff, Mary (Alexander)
Rau, Mary S. (Carter)
Rawls, Amanda J. (Price)
Rea, M.J.A. (Tutor)
Rea, S.V.A. (Westmoreland)
Reed, Mary (Smith)
Reeder, M.E. (Watts)
Rice, Mollie (Clark)
Roach, Mrs. V.A. (Koon)
Rodgers, Alice T. (Sherer)
Rodgers, Bettie (McWhirter)
Rodgers, Lizzie (Price)
Rodgers, Mary E. (Lawrence)
Rodgers, N.J. (Hawkins)
Roberson, L.E. (Shelton)
Robertson, Laverna (Roberts)
Robins, M.A. (Sneed)
Robins, S.L. (William)
Rogers, D.E. (Sherer)
Rootes, Dell (Pitts)
Rowland, A.E. (Jennings)
Rush, M.A. (Howard)
Russell, N.M. (Willard)
Russell, Nannie (Dillard)
Russell, Parilee (Fields)
Rutledge, Jodie (Rackley)
Rutledge, M.J. (Rackley)

Sadler, B.E. (Guinn)

Sanders, Amelia E. (Murphy)
Sanders, Malisie (Bennett)
Sappington, Mollie (Jones)
Saunders, Mrs. E.D. (Hill)
Savery, Mattie (Andrews)
Scott, A.P. (Terrell)
Scott, Dannie (Souter)
Scott, M.E. (Crausby)
Scott, Mattie J. (Kelly)
Seale, N.A. (Pitts)
Seales, M.J. (Bell)
Setzler, Nannie (Dison)
Setzler, Vada (Rogers)
Sewell, S.A. (Mitchell)
Shannon, F.S. (Dickson)
Shannon, M.L. (Helms)
Shanon, Cinthia (Inmon)
Shettles, M.A. (Dillard)
Shirley, M.S. (Anderson)
Simmons, Ida (Gilder)
Simmons, Josie (Wallis)
Simmons, Mrs. M.A. (Stegall)
Simmons, M.A. (Russell)
Sibley, S.E. (Faulkner)
Simpson, C.A. (Faulkner)
Simpson, J.L. (McCoy)
Simpson, Nannie (Long)
Singleton, Cassie T. (Clark)
Skinner, Lillie Bell (Waldrop)
Skinner, Lena (Ferguson)
Sledge, Jennie (Cooper)
Sledge, S.A. (Bratton)
Sledge, Virginia (Spears)
Smith, Amanda (Pitts)
Smith, F.L. (Yount)
Smith, Josie (Wilbur)
Smith, M.J. (McElvaney)
Smith, Mary (Black)
Smith, Mary (Young)
Smith, N.R. (Tallant)
Smith, S.J. (Winfield)
Smith, Sarah E. (Porter)
Sneed, L.A. (Jordan)
Snider, Mrs. S.A. (Matthews)
Souter, L.R. (Wood)
Sparks, Bessie (Browning)
Sparks, Bettie (Browning)
Spence, Mollie (Allen)
Spencer, Annie J. (Potter)
Staggs, M.P. (Samphill)
Staggs, Sendia (Calek)

Staten, L.A. (Caldwell)
Steel, Ellen (Crafton)
Stegall, E.C. (Brown)
Stegall, Fannie J. (Calloway)
Stegall, M.J. (Johnson)
Stegall, Martha (Harden)
Stepp, Mrs. Nancy (Westmoreland)
Stockstill, Annie (Young)
Stokes, L.J. (Long)
Stone, I.B. (Lilley)
Stovall, M.C. (Murdock)
Strange, Mary (Sewell)
Strange, Minnie (Russell)
Strange, Vesta (Sewell)
Sullivan, Jimmie (Cox)
Sullivan, M.J. (Bramlett)
Sullivan, Mollie (White)
Sullivan, S.E. (Belyen)
Surrant, C.I. (Carlock)
Surratt, Mrs. Donie (Maddox)
Surratt, M.J. (Anderson)
Swofford, G.E. (Williams)
Swords, N.J. (Browning)

Tallant, Fannie (Hamilton)
Tate, Belle (Roggers)
Taylor, Dollie (Pearson)
Taylor, E.C. (Haney)
Taylor, J.A.K. (Rodgers)
Taylor, M.C. (Jamison)
Thomason, Annie (Weatherall)
Thornton, Lena (Thaxton)
Thornton, M.J. (Gilder)
Todd, Harriet C. (Belyen)
Todd, L.A. (Johnson)
Tucker, Sallie (Ray)
Turner, M.L. (Rea)
Tutor, F.E. (Smith)
Tutor, J.A. (Bratton)
Tutor, M.F. (Card)
Tutor, Mrs. M.H. (Linsley)
Tutor, M.V. (Whitworth)
Tutor, Nancy M. (Whitesides)

Vasser, Mrs. Russena (Adams)
Vaughn, Francis (Montgomery)
Vaughn, Hattie (Bramlitt)
Vaughn, R.F. (Duncan)

Waddell, Ida (Flaherty)
Waldo, Anna (Stowe)
Waldo, Belle (Tramerls ?)

Waldo, Lizzie (Jacobs)
Waldrop, Allie (Tutor)
Waldrop, C.F. (Busby)
Waldrop, Doney (Hamilton)
Wagner, Mary (Lowery)
Wait, R.J. (Hudson)
Wait, W.B. (Duncan)
Walker, Nettie F. (Rowzee)
Walker, S.A. (Herring)
Walls, Mary Frances (Pettit)
Walls, Polly (Pettit)
Ward, D.L. (Reigh)
Warren, C.Y. (Browning)
Warren, T.V. (Gay)
Washington, S.H. (Walker)
Washington, S.M. (Lee)
Watts, Mary F. (Hudson)
Weatherall, L.L. (Haney)
Weaver, Annie (Dillard)
Webb, Lula (Hodges)
Wellerford, Luella (Baker)
Wells, A.E. (Gardner)
Wells, Cornelia (Bell)
Wells, Ola (Lemons)
Wells, Sarah J. (Petit)
West, Cordelia (Collier)
Westmoreland, B.E. (Frierson)
Westmoreland, H.M. (Rea)
Westmoreland, Pauline (Archey)
White, Attie (Woodson)
White, Ellen (Holley)
White, Sara W. (Mitchell)
White, Susie (Sprouse)
Whitlow, Ida Y. (Bramlett)
Widener, Bettie (Thornton)
Widener, Lula (Farrar)
Wilder, A.A. (Brown)
Wilmouth, Sarah M. (Burks)
Williams, Annie (McCoy)
Williams, Ella (Thornton)
Wilson, Lanie (Lilley)
Winters, Mattie S. (Vaughn)
Wood, J.A. (McEachern)
Wood, Kittie (Wells)
Wood, N.A. (Echols)
Woods, M.P. (Stewart)
Wood, N.Y.C. (Jones)
Worsham, Alice (Calloway)
Wyley, Sallie H. (Trice)

Young, Mattie (Smith)

Zackery, Nancy (Brown)
Zinn, Ella (Roberson)

MARRIAGE BOOK - 1887 - 1891

PONTOTOC, MISSISSIPPI

INDEXED BY

HAZLE BOSS NEET
207 NORTH MAIN
PONTOTOC, MISSISSIPPI 38863

PAGE	GROOM	BRIDE	DATE	
452	Adams, J.G.	Sary M. Young	24 July 1891	
82	Adkins, E.C.	Mattie Whitlow	5 Dec !887	
433	Adkinson, G.F.	Miss M.C. Bell	5 Apr 1891	
260	Alexander, Berry	Lucia Brown	7 July 1889	
250	Allred, James	Bettie Mann	23 May 1889	
429	Anderson, Charles	Miss T.A. Kelly	15 Mar 1891	
297	Anderson, J.F.	Lorena Black	11 Dec 1889	
15	Anderson, J.T.	Miss M.S. Camp	10 Jan 1887	
	[License - M.E. Camp]			
5	Andrews, J.C.	Miss A.B. Swords	26 Dec 1886	
127	Archey, D.G.	Annie Anderson	20 Feb 1888	(BO)
76	Austin, J.D.	Miss M.C. Holly	27 Nov 1887	
149	Austin, W.F.	Helen M. Lilley	12 July 1888	
3	Austin, W.L.	Miss M.A. Grist	27 Dec 1886	
61	Baker, Charlie	Giona Browning	15 Sept 1887	
488	Baker, W.Y.	Miss R.A. Spears	10 Dec 1891	
289	Barclay, N.P.	Sue M. Roots	21 Nov 1889	
394	Barnes, John	Miss C.A.L. McCormick	25 Dec 1890	
43	Barnett, James M.	Mrs. Sue M. Powell	12 July 1887	
	[Licnese reads Miss Sue]			
169	Beeson, C.J.	Bettie Savely	21 Oct 1888	
196	Belk, S.M.	Mrs. C.E. Gilpen	18 Dec 1888	
143	Bell, Ben M.	Mattie Gideon	12 June 1888	
478	Benjamin, J.E.	Miss M.L. Dillard	15 Nov 1891	
58	Berry, J.T.B.	Jessie I. Brooks	14 Sept 1887	
521	Black, J.D.	Alice Craig	10 Jan 1892	
518	Black, J.R.	Nannie Craig	3 Jan 1892	
215	Black, R.L.	M.C.P. Pannell	10 Jan 1889	
	[Consent: E.M. Pannell, Father]			
221	Black, T.W.	Lucie Holloman	23 Jan 1889	
165	Blair, G.L.	Minnie Wood	23 Sept 1888	
372	Blakely, G.B.	Miss A.M. Wooley	29 Nov 1890	(BO)
107	Blaylock, W.R.	Rosa Miller	11 Jan 1888	
457	Bockman, Hosea	Miss M.E. Pappasan	23 Aug 1891	
470	Bockman, W.H.	Sadie Addams	14 Oct 1891	(LO)
382	Bouchillon, H.B.	Miss O.P. Tutor	24 Dec 1890	
317	Bouchillon, J.T.	Miss M.A. McGregor	25 Jan 1890	
336	Bowen, D.W.	Addie Russell	1 June 1890	
	[Consent: J.A. Russell]			
40	Bowen, S.A.	Miss M.E. Bratton	26 June 1887	
238	Bowles, J.C.	Sallie Johnson	26 Mar 1889	
38	Box, George	Zella Hill	2 June 1887	
282	Box, L.J.	Miss L.A. Thornton	30 Oct 1889	
228	Bramlett, A.S.	Ella Bolen	29 Jan 1889	
95	Bramlett, N.T.	Emma Whitlow	22 Dec 1887	
417	Brandon, I.N.	Etta G. Pitts	22 Feb 1891	
230	Brandon, W.J.	Miss S.E. Lambert	7 Feb 1889	

(LO) - License Only   (BO) - Bond Only

PAGE	GROOM	BRIDE	DATE		
502	Brassfield, J.H.	Dora Bramlett	20 Dec	1891	
13	Bratton, L.P.	Callie Jones	6 Jan	1887	
128	Bray, D.G.	Josephine Washington	26 Feb	1888	
8	Bray, J.S.	Miss F.D. Henry	16 Jan	1887	
469	Bray, W.T.	Miss S.A. Wilson	15 Oct	1891	
154	Brazil, R.L.	Annie Kelly	12 Aug	1880	
	[Consent: N.C.Kelly, Father]				
186	Bristol, J.A.	Miss A.L. Harvson(?)	9 Dec	1888	
223	Brown, A.G.	Antnet Johnson	23 Jan	1889	
265	Brown, L.J.	Mattie Johnson	15 Aug	1889	
517	Brown, D.M.	Melia Murphy	31 Dec	1891	
435	Brown, F.J.	Miss E.G. Roye (Ella)	15 Apr	1891	
287	Brown, J.W.	Minnie Thomason	13 Nov	1889	
239	Brown, James	Etta Crawford	27 Mar	1889	
302	Brown, Z.R.	Miss M.L. Reeder	19 Dec	1889	(BO)
513	Browning, J.M.	Julia Baker	30 Dec	1891	
80	Bryant, T.A.	Miss M.C. Westmoreland	30 Nov	1887	
348	Buchannon, V.B.	Anna Bevil	28 Aug	1890	
343	Bullard, John	Ruthie Warren	3 July	1890	
164	Burchfield, J.E.	Miss S.C. Buckley	19 Sept	1888	
115	Burk, S.E.	Jennie Weeks	22 Jan	1888	
402	Burnett, O.C.	Lena Rowan	4 Jan	1891	
510	Bynum, John L.	Jennie Ball	24 Dec	1891	
273	Caldwell, G.W.	Nannie Campbell	22 Sept	1889	
177	Caldwell, J.C.	Fannie J. Aycock	26 Nov	1888	
421	Caldwell, J.D.	Lula Vaughn	25 Feb	1891	
83	Caldwell, John W.	Ida B. McCoy	8 Dec	1887	
	[Consent: Wm McCoy, Father]				
524	Caldwell, S.O.	Miss L.C. Simmons	10 Jan	1892	
75	Calloway, J.R.	Miss L.D. Crawford	23 Nov	1887	
507	Calloway, J.R.	Mandie Haney	24 Dec	1891	
	[Bond reads Maudie Haney]				
217	Calloway, R.L.	Miss A.L. Brown	9 Jan	1889	
133	Camp, C.S.	Miss W.E. Allen	18 Mar	1888	
188	Campbell, J.T.	Mrs. Emma Pegues	12 Dec	1888	
284	Cantriel, J.W.	Birthie Morgan	15 Nov	1889	
33	Carr, J.R.	Miss E.M. Hill	17 Apr	1887	
	[Consent: J.D. Hill, Father]				
71	Carter, R.L.	Lucy Tutor	13 Nov	1887	
419	Carter, W.C.	Mattie A. Rodgers	26 Feb	1891	
26	Carter, W.L.	Annie Park	14 Mar	1887	
253	Cartwright, C.W.	Annie E. Castleberry	4 June	1889	
27	Carwile, J.E.	Miss M.A. Grice	17 Mar	1887	
213	Cates, T.J.	Miss F.E. Gilmer	1 Jan	1889	
134	Chaney, John	Mrs. Emma Britt	20 Mar	1880	
388	Chaney, William	Zuenadora Winfield	21 Dec	1890	
520	Clark, Tilson	Miss M.F. Caldwell	11 Jan	1892	

PAGE	GROOM	BRIDE	DATE	
73	Clayton, J.S.	Emma Watts	20 Nov 1887	
	[Consent by Parents - Frank and Marthy Watts]			
474	Cobb, W.E.	Miss C.J. Simpson	1 Nov 1891	
499	Cobb, W.W.	Miss M.L. Buchanan	27 Dec 1891	
231	Coker, Virdie	Lou Todd	10 Feb 1889	
	[Consent by S.E.J. Coker] [Consent by Elizabeth Todd]			
318	Collier, R.B.	Nora E. Combs	23 Jan 1890	
100	Conlee, James H.	Pennie Simpson	27 Dec 1887	
	[Consent by father - C.J. Simpson]			
219	Cook, J.D.	Mary Todd	12 Jan 1889	
	[Consent by father W.M. Cook] [Consent by mother P.A. Todd]			
430	Cooper, G.W.	Miss N.E. Murphy	19 Mar 1891	
16	Cooper, J.W.	Miss M.E. Kidd	10 Jan 1887	
170	Cooper, John W.	Clemma Carter	21 Oct 1888	
426	Cooper, M.H.	Miss E.M. Stegall	6 Mar 1891	
167	Cooper, R.A.	Analou Berry	16 Oct 1888	
410	Cowsert, J.R.	Della Hill	31 Jan 1891	(BO)
511	Craig, M.S.	Miss F.E. Ball	27 Dec 1891	
67	Crane, M.L.	Miss C.A. Russell	13 Nov 1887	
114	Craw, J.W.	Miss B.C. McNeely	21 Jan 1888	
338	Crawley, E.E.	Della Williams	4 June 1890	
386	Crawson, F.S.	Miss Y.A. Card	21 Dec 1890	
322	Cunningham, Samuel	Susie Morgan	10 Feb 1890	(BO)
195	Cummings, A.B.B.	Miss M.C. Evans	20 Dec 1888	
465	Cummings, D.R.	Maggie Dunn	13 Sept 1891	
106	Cummins, Lafayette	Miss A.M. Whitesides	5 Jan 1888	
	[Consent by father W.B. Whitesides]			
485	Daniel, J.E.	Miss E.L. Tallant	3 Dec 1891	
42	Daniel, T.A.	Mrs. Mary Vance	6 July 1887	
271	Davis, Adney	Mollie Horton	8 Sept 1889	
229	Davis, J.D.	Julia McCoby	3 Feb 1889	
120	Davis, Robert	Miss M.E. Chaney	2 Feb 1888	
311	Denton, W.J.	Sallie Willard	14 Jan 1890	
392	Dillard, B.M.	Miss N.L. Fontaine	23 Dec 1890	
125	Dillard, J.D.	Margaret Fuller	22 Feb 1888	
156	Dillard, J.D.	Mattie Stegall	19 Aug 1888	
515	Dillard, J.L.	Laula Thompson	30 Dec 1891	
232	Dillard, W.P.	Emma Laprade	13 Feb 1889	
291	Dison, G.W.	Miss M.J. Nowlin	24 Nov 1889	
	[Bond reads Dyson]			
349	Donaldson, J.J.	Miss M.D. Souter	4 Sept 1890	
	[License reads Mrs. M.D. Souter]			
288	Douglas, T.J.	Miss L.M. Herndon	17 Nov 1889	
344	Douglas, W.O.	Ella Taylor	7 July 1890	
456	Drake, W.P.	Miss A.L. Crawford	20 Aug 1891	
280	Drewey, J.G.	Miss A.A. Waits	24 Oct 1889	

PAGE	GROOM	BRIDE	DATE	
463	Duncan, G.W.	Miss B.E. Sullivan	2 Sept 1891	
31	Dunlap, J.B.	Miss V.B. Buchanan	31 Mar 1887	
263	Durham, A.J.	Susanna Douglas	9 Aug 1889	
56	Durham, Wm M.	Miss E.O.M. Rayburn	7 Sept 1887	
94	Dye, W.A.	Mrs. S.A. Rye	22 Dec 1887	
162	Echols, Jno E.	Ollie Harmon	13 Sept 1888	
175	Echols, W.E.	Maloney Staggs	12 Nov 1888	
315	Edwards, J.R.	Miss J.F. Strain	19 Jan 1890	
		[License: Miss J.F. Stroupe]		
104	Ellis, B.R.	Miss G.A. Daggett	15 Jan 1888	
		[Bond: Grace Anna Daggett]		
413	Ellis, J.O.	Miss D.B. Brown	16 Feb 1891	(BO)
497	Emis, N.B.	Miss Alter Lovins	14 Dec 1891	
408	Evans, J.L.	Nannie Lawor	29 Jan 1891	
482	Evans, P.	Miss N.P. Sparks	29 Nov 1891	
368	Farar, D.A.	Miss A.H. Owen	22 Nov 1890	
70	Ferguson, B.F.	Miss F.A. Fuller	9 Nov 1887	
352	Ferguson, B.F.	Miss S.E. White	19 Sept 1890	
295	Ferguson, E.E.	Emma Lewelling	6 Dec 1889	(BO)
136	Ferrell, N.P.	Etna Purvis	5 Apr 1888	
187	Fields, E.G.	Nannie Cruse	12 Dec 1880	
10	Fields, W.M.	Miss L.J. Cruse	6 Jan 1887	
342	Fitzpatrick, J.A.	Lela E. Teeter	26 June 1890	
256	Fleming, A.F.	Miss R.E. Parrish	9 June 1889	
432	Fleming, Wm J.	Corrie Milam	22 Mar 1891	
385	Foster, J.C.	Miss F.L. Barr	18 Dec 1890	
173	Foster, R.L.	Miss A.C. Smitherman	8 Nov 1888	
35	Fowler, Milus	Mrs. M.E. Land	12 May 1887	
309	Franks, L.W.	Miss R.J. Anderson	9 Jan 1890	
529	Gafford, W.F.	Miss F. Todd	28 Jan 1892	
218	Galloway, J.T.	Miss H.E. Baylass	6 Jan 1889	
359	Galloway, T.E.	Miss O.M. Holloway	30 Oct 1890	(BO)
298	Galloway, W.T.	Miss Willie A. Tate	17 Dec 1889	
109	Gambrell, J.H.	Ida H. Milam	12 Jan 1888	
327	Garrett, J.T. (I?)	Miss E.A. Harrison	20 Feb 1890	
267	Garrison, W.A.	Nattie S. Winters	29 Aug 1889	
		[Consent: S.P. Winters]		
141	Gentry, J.W.	Minnie Lee	21 May 1888	
65	Gentry, Wm H.	Miss D.J. Brown	4 Oct 1887	
4	Gilder, B.B.	Rachiel Johnson	30 Dec 1886	
145	Gillespie, J.D.	Miss H.L. Furguson	28 June 1888	
189	Gillmore, J.W.	Maggie Billingsly	12 Dec 1880	
241	Gilmer, J.C.	Miss M.F. Lowry	10 Apr 1889	
180	Goldman, W.M.	Miss O.J. Hubbard	25 Nov 1888	
85	Goggans, J.S.	Miss E.C. Jones	8 Dec 1887	
44	Garmon, Albert	Louisa Bryant	12 July 1887	

PAGE	GROOM	BRIDE	DATE	
443	Gorman, B.E.	Docia Ray	9 June 1891	
199	Gorman, R.A.	Irene E. Gilmer	25 Dec 1888	
183	Gordon, W.A.	Corrie Johnson	27 Dec 1888	
364	Graham, E.N.	Dora L. Simmons	13 Nov 1890	
47	Greenwood, W.R.	Mattie Miller	21 July 1887	
63	Gregory, J.D.	Miss P.B. Tutor	25 Sept 1887	
88	Gregory, J.F.	Miss J.J. Potter	18 Dec 1887	
330	Gregory, R.C.	Josephine Jones	16 Mar 1890	
34	Gregory, S.J.	Winnie Jernigan	28 Apr 1887	
310	Griffin, A.T.	Mary Swords	12 Jan 1890	
60	Griffin, G.I.	Belle Simmons	13 Sept 1887	

[Consent by father Jas. Griffin, Sarepta, Miss. and Jack Simmons, Randolph, Miss. Note at bottom of page "License returned, not executed."]

PAGE	GROOM	BRIDE	DATE	
57	Grisham, J.W.	Fannie Gay	23 Oct 1887	
431	Griffin, Lee	Cora Hutch	22 Mar 1891	
96	Griffin, W.F.	Betty Smith	22 Dec 1887	
357	Griffin, W.H.	Miss S.M. Price	16 Oct 1890	
264	Grisham, Jim	Susie Benjamin	14 Aug 1889	
399	Grisham, P.H.	Bessie F. Pyle	30 Dec 1890	
153	Hair, J.I.	Miss M.J. Blunt	4 Aug 1888	(BO)
393	Hale, T.J.	Minnie Sanders	1 Jan 1891	
110	Haley, Oliver	Miss Bunch Young	13 Jan 1888	

[Consent by father John Haley, Egypt, Miss.]

PAGE	GROOM	BRIDE	DATE	
18	Hamilton, J.W.	Fannie Williams	19 Jan 1887	

[License - Fannie Wilson]

PAGE	GROOM	BRIDE	DATE	
152	Hampton, Bakter	Miss L.V. McNeely	5 Aug 1888	
383	Hampton, R.M.	Miss M.L. Priest	21 Dec 1890	
118	Haney, H.J.	Miss G.A. Jackson	26 Jan 1888	
247	Haney, J.B.	Mary Seals	2 May 1889	
498	Haney, S.E.	Miss M.E. Seals	13 Dec 1891	
281	Hardin, H.Y.	Miss Willie Jinkins	29 Oct 1889	
346	Harmon, J.W.	Miss J.A. McAlister	13 Aug 1890	
211	Harrison, Frank	Ada Sanders	31 Dec 1888	
147	Harrison, W.T.	Ada Powell	28 June 1888	
268	Hartly, B.H.	Miss M.J. Suell	29 Aug 1889	
304	Hawkins, T.H.	Mary Warren	26 Dec 1889	
184	Helums, J.M.	Miss Parlee WAlker	6 Dec 1888	
255	Hellums, W.P.	Miss L. Onsberry	8 June 1889	
90	Henderson, G.W.	Ida Wood	22 Dec 1887	
254	Henderson, James	Miss Jessie West	7 June 1889	
148	Hendrick, S.B.	Miss F.J. Osborn	30 June 1888	(BO)
62	Henry, R.L.	Miss S.M. Lee	18 Sept 1887	

[License - Mrs. S.M. Lee]

PAGE	GROOM	BRIDE	DATE	
503	Herndon, Oscar	Miss Syrena Swain	23 Dec 1891	
97	Herndon, W.F.	Miss M.D. Tutor	25 Dec 1887	
163	Hester, Joseph	Josephine McKinney	18 Sept 1888	

PAGE	GROOM	BRIDE	DATE	
461	Hester, Mose	Lula McNice	26 Aug	1891
55	Hester, Wiley	Mary Reed	21 Aug	1887
89	High, D.B.	Nannie Stovall	25 Dec	1887
396	High, J.H.	Clarra Stovall	28 Dec	1890
458	Hightower, John	Bettie Stovall	23 Aug	1891
337	Hill, J.D.	Miss I.E. Cristman	8 June	1890
220	Hill, J.T.	Florence Weaver	20 Jan	1889
101	Hill, R.A.	Mattie Jones	25 Dec	1887
319	Hitchcock, J.B.	Bettie Jones	26 Jan	1890
30	Hitchcock, W.J.	Stella Douglas	23 Mar	1887
240	Hodges, B.F.	Miss F.E. Poke	2 Apr	1889
391	Hodges, J.B.	Ida Mitchell	23 Dec	1890
380	Holloway, E.M.	Leenia McGregor	21 Dec	1890
381	Holloway, R.M.	Mattie McGregor	21 Dec	1890
362	Holly, W.R.	Miss M.E. Wilson	9 Nov	1890
473	Holt, W.T.	Modena Lyons	29 Oct	1891
252	Horton, W.C.	Jane Long	3 June	1889
451	Houpt, F.S.	Mattie Bolen	19 July	1891
504	Howell, W.M.	Miss M.C. McCoy	25 Dec	1891
160	Hubbard, J.B.	Miss R.J. Flemming	2 Sept	1888
245	Hughes, C.T.	Mattie Spencer	7 May	1889
244	Humphries, L.	Sarah Surratt	28 Apr	1889
126	Huntington, W.M.	Miss Jessie Carr	22 Feb	1888
146	Hutchins, Abner	Sallie Ray	27 June	1888
303	Ivy, C.A.	Nora Fowler	28 Dec	1889
45	Jackson, J.E.	Miss Annie Haney	17 July	1887
341	Jeeter, T.J. [Bond - Jeter]	Maggie Bolen	26 June	1890
455	Jenkins, J.A.	Annie Carr	23 Aug	1891
225	Jernigan, W.J.	Ida H. Edwards	27 Jan	1889
12	Johnson, E.D.	Miss M.E. Montgomery	6 Jan	1887
74	Johnson, C.A.	Mollie Stewart	20 Nov	1887
369	Johnson, J.L.	Helen Rutledge	27 Nov	1890
496	Johnson, J.L.	Miss C.B. Whitworth	20 Dec	1891
151	Johnston, A.A.	Mattie L. Simmons	2 Aug	1888
197	Jones, J.H.	Eviline Harrison	18 Dec	1888
294	Jones, Lawrence	Mamie Henderson	8 Dec	1889
466	Joyner, J.C.	Ally Weeden	27 Sept	1892
345	Kelly, G.W. [Consent: W.A. Jackson]	Miss M.F. Jackson	7 July	1890
331	Kelly, Geo	Jane Decanter	16 Mar	1890
270	Kelly, J.H.	Etta Cobb	31 Aug	1889 (BO)
258	Kelly, R.E.	Emma Bowen	27 June	1889
98	Kelley, W.D.	Joanna Tutor	1 Jan	1888
301	King, J.H.	Miss C.E.A. Vandiver(?)	18 Dec	1889 (BO)
139	King, Jas D.	Miss S.C. Pickens	13 May	1888

PAGE	GROOM	BRIDE	DATE	
117	Kirby, C.C.	Miss Willie Worsham	2 Feb	1888
93	Kitchens, W.B.	Florence Simmon	21 Dec	1887
78	Kitchens, W.D.	Florence Simmons	26 Nov	1887

[Consent by father W.M. Simmons. Note reads "Returned Not Esecuted"]

PAGE	GROOM	BRIDE	DATE	
119	Kyle, J.A.	Luna Glenn Russell	30 Jan	1888 (BO)
194	Kyle, T.F.	Miss J.C. Bass	15 Dec	1888
275	Lambert, P.C.	Essie Humphries	28 Sept	1889

[Bond Only - Returned Not Executed]

PAGE	GROOM	BRIDE	DATE	
335	Lancaster, W.A.	Miss N.E. Henry	24 May	1890
121	Land, S.L.	Miss E.P. Aycock	7 Feb	1888

[Consent: A.J.Aycock]

PAGE	GROOM	BRIDE	DATE	
447	Langston, D.C.	Miss T. Etta Davis	24 June	1891
216	Laprade. J.F.	Miss Jane Martin	8 Jan	1889
407	Lauderdale, J.F.	Miss Annie Mills	25 Jan	1891
355	Lewelling, W.J.	Mary Jame Miller	5 Oct	1890

[License - Miss M.J. Wilder]

PAGE	GROOM	BRIDE	DATE	
468	Leweling, W.J.	Miss L.C. Leweling	12 Oct	1891
116	Little, B.B.	Miss Catherine Kelly	25 Jan	1888
105	Little, J.T.	Cintha Chapman	4 Jan	1888
323	Livingston, W.T.	Emma Caldwell	11 Feb	1890 (BO)
226	Lofton, E.J.	Elizabeth Snider	24 Jan	1889
113	Longest, J.W.	Cora Crawford	24 Jan	1888
185	Lovell, B.M.	Miss M.E. Pyle	9 Dec	1888
477	Lower, J.C.	Mattie Jackson	11 Nov	1891
193	Lower, J.H.	Miss N.E. Thompson	16 Dec	1888
495	Lowry, E.G.	Jennie M. Jenkins	15 Dec	1891
108	Lowry, J.M.	Miss M.Y. O'Neal	12 Jan	1888
69	Lowry, John	Laura Parrish	5 Nov	1887
379	Lyon, J.R.	Annie Mayo	18 Dec	1890
472	McAlister, W.W.	Miss S.D. Nelson	25 Oct	1891
224	McCarver, B.F.	Sallie Bigham	24 Jan	1889
490	McCarver, E.R.	Dovie Farris	10 Dec	1891
527	McCarver, R.V.	Mattie Nuson (Nelson?)	16 Jan	1892
39	McCord, J.N.	Miss Addie Miller	8 June	1887
192	McCord, J.T.	Miss Ida Burson	20 Dec	1888
367	McCormick, H.J.	Miss E.P. Lantrip	19 Nov	1890
277	McClarty, P.L.	Annie Black	3 Oct	1889
373	McCoy, J.M.	Miss G.A. Shelton	3 Dec	1890
11	McCoy, John T.	Miss Janey Pitts	5 Jan	1887

[License - Jennie PItts]

PAGE	GROOM	BRIDE	DATE	
227	McCoy, S.P.C.	Abella Milam	27 Jan	1889
233	McCoy, W.T.	Loula J. Milam	13 Feb	1889
138	McCraw, J.W.	Miss S.C. Langley	17 May	1888
68	McCullough, H.G.	Miss Willie Webb	2 Nov	1887
158	McCullough, T.G.	Miss S.M. Higgins	10 Aug	1888
86	McDaniel, Charlie	Lillian Drake	15 Dec	1887

PAGE	GROOM	BRIDE	DATE	
206	McElbaney,	Miss F.L. Robbins	27 Dec 1888	
350	McElbany,	Miss M.P. Hill	7 Sept 1890	
178	McGaugly, F.C.	Beulah Lilly	28 Nov 1888	
324	McGill, L.C.	Miss A.B. Simons	12 Feb 1890	
	[Bond - Almeter B. Simons]			
389	McGraw, C.A.	Virona Parrish	20 Dec 1890	
449	McGreger, J.M.	Miss L.C. Jones	1 July 1891	
	[Note - No Certificate Returned With License]			
22	McGregor, A.H.	Mrs. M.A. Carnes	11 Feb 1887	
37	McGregor, J.W.	Fannie Watson	29 May 1887	
425	McGregor, S.Y.	Georgia James	5 May 1891	
397	McGregor, W.R.	Emma James	27 Dec 1890	
	[Bond reads Emma Jeans]			
307	McGregor, William Henry	Emily Orange Carpenter	8 Jan 1890	
526	McKnight, J.W.	Miss F.I. Pitts	14 Jan 1892	
420	McKnight, S.B.	Fannie Scott	23 Mar 1891	
214	McMillon, Peter	Anna Wilder	19 Jan 1890	
36	McNeil, G.N.	Sallie Dixon	25 May 1887	
	[License - Sallie Dickson]			
400	McWhirter, J.T.	Miss M.H. Watts	1 Jan 1891	
77	Marshall, J.M.	Fannie Wadkins	27 Nov 1887	
406	Martin, O.J.	Nannie B. Conlee	22 Jan 1891	
157	Mask, Warren	Fannie Barrett	23 Aug 1888	
530	Maxcy, J.H.	Amanda Thompson	28 Jan 1892	
532	May, B.F.	Sallie Garrison	12 Apr 1892	
442	Mayo, J.M.	Myrtle, Buchanan	4 June 1891	
398	Midlock, J.A.	S. Anne Dillard	28 Dec 1890	
411	Miller, A.T.	Miss R.S. Christman	3 Feb 1891	(BO)
132	Miears, J.P.	Ida Crum	11 Mar 1888	
140	Miller, J.A.	Caroline Houpt	17 May 1888	
179	Miller, J.A.	Carline Houpt	17 May 1888	
	[X marked through page]			
203	Miller, T.J.	Miss M.J. Blunt	20 Dec 1888	(BO)
28	Miller, W.H.	Miss N.M. Anderson	20 May 1887	
236	Miller, W.T.	Fannie Cantrell	15 Feb 1889	
423	Mills, J.L.	Miss L.S. Buchanan	1 Mar 1891	
436	Minyard, J.J.	Annie Lane	16 Apr 1891	
248	Mitchell, C.B.	Mrs. Pauline Patterson	16 May 1889	
190	Mitchell, Charles D.	Mamie C. Herron	12 Dec 1888	
375	Mitchell, J.P.	Miss M.E. Johnson	6 Dec 1890	(BO)
9	Mize, J.A.	Allice Murphy	5 Jan 1887	
441	Montgomery, J.C.	Marthy Parrish	27 May 1891	
144	Montgomery, T.A.	Miss M.A. Little	16 June 1888	
	[Bond and License - No Minister's return]			
360	Montgomery, W.A.J.	Irene McCharen	3 Nov 1890	(BO)
428	Moorland, W.B.	Mollie Kellie	22 Mar 1891	

PAGE	GROOM	BRIDE	DATE	
464	Morman, Frank	Lennie Gaines	9 Sept	1891
	[Consent: R.W. Gains]			
519	Morphis, Marion	Miss M.A. Glover	3 Jan	1892
200	Morphis, John C.	Sadie B. Clark	20 Dec	1888
328	Morphis, J.M.	Elizabeth McWhirter	23 Feb	1890
489	Morphis, W.R.	Miss M.J. Cannon	10 Dec	1891
207	Morrison, C.T.	Miss M.E. Parrish	27 Dec	1888
404	Morrison, L.M.	Nancy Weeks	13 Jan	1891 (BO)
222	Murphy, W.L.	Miss B.L. Grist	22 Jan	1889
459	Munn, J.A.	Miss M.A. Jones	25 Aug	1891
424	New, Ed	Susie Cunningham	1 Mar	1891
198	Nichols, R.B.	Jennie Brandon	20 Dec	1888
365	Nix, J.T.	Miss L.G. Lesly	13 Nov	1890
182	Nowlin, G.M.	Miss M.R. Owen	2 Dec	1888
494	Nowlin, W.H.	Miss L.A. Dillard	20 Dec	1891
159	Oden, W.M.	Miss A.E. Thompson	2 Dec	1888
278	Osborn, Sam	Miss L.A. Montgomery	6 Oct	1889
316	Owen, B.D.	Miss G.A. McWhirter	23 Jan	1890
235	Owen, Ben	Frances Ginn	14 Feb	1889
131	Owens, C.H.	Miss A.S.A. Kidd	8 Mar	1880
174	Palmer, C.E.	Emma Tutor	11 Nov	1888
366	Parks, J.R.	Miss M.E. Coward	15 Nov	1890
321	Parrish, H.W.	Pink Sappington	9 Feb	1890
440	Parrish, J.F.	Miss A.L. Smith	25 May	1891
390	Parrish, W.L.	Etta Harvey	20 Dec	1890 (BO)
237	Patterson, C.M.	Lizzie Mooney	24 Mar	1889
506	Patterson, M.A.	Mrs. L.V. Pittman	27 Dec	1891
249	Patterson, Z.K.	Minnie Scott	19 May	1889
279	Payne, James I.	Emma Potter	17 Oct	1889
111	Pearson, W.H.	Laudie Miller	20 Jan	1888
434	Peeden, J.S.	Jennie Anderson	12 Apr	1891
246	Pegues, W.E.	Miss M.W. Leed	1 May	1889
99	Petit, W.F.	Miss H.C. Gillespie	28 Dec	1887
405	Pitts, B.R.	Corrie Caldwell	22 Jan	1891
312	Pitts, H.L.	Iola Ellis	16 Jan	1890
505	Pittman, H.W.	Miss M.V. Owen	24 Dec	1891
293	Polk, S.M.	Bettie Mitchell	5 Dec	1889
476	Pope, R.L.	Lanla Ray	11 Nov	1891
20	Pope, T.J.	Ellen Ray	26 Jan	1887
	[License - Ella RAy]			
487	Porter, N.B.	Miss M.L. Sibley	1 Dec	1891
467	Pound, C.A.D.	Miss N.E. Faulkner	7 Oct	1891
450	Prude, R.L.	Obenna Deason	12 July	1891
371,	Prude, T.P.	Miss M.A. Davidson	27 Nov	1890
356	Purden, Jeff W.	Lucinda Price	7 Oct	1890
210	Purvis, R.R.	Ada Whitlow	30 Dec	1888

PAGE	GROOM	BRIDE	DATE	
361	Putt, J.J.	Emma Smith	6 Nov 1890	
320	Raines, Woodland	Sallie Bonds	2 Feb 1890	
438	Rayburn, M.D.	Cora L. Hampton	12 May 1891	
528	Reeder, S.L.	Lula E. Mounce	20 Jan 1892	
395	Rice, P.E.	Carrie Arnold	24 Dec 1890	
285	Richie, W.J.	Mollie Brown	5 Nov 1889	
514	Ridge, Harvy	Annie Sanders	25 Dec 1891	
412	Riley, C.H.	Miss F.A. Ingram	8 Feb 1891	
	[Consent: G.W. Riley]			
205	Robbins, F.L.	Lewella Robbins	24 Dec 1888	(BO)
	[This page marked out with an X]			
376	Robbins, G.W.	Miss E.L. Pittman	11 Dec 1890	
358	Robbins, O.W.	Miss S.M. Todd	26 Oct 1890	
439	Roberson, Thos J.	Mary Irene Bolton	20 May 1891	
334	Roberts, W.W.	Clora Castleberry	30 Apr 1890	
29	Robbins, H.A.	Miss M.E. Warren	27 Mar 1887	
181	Rodgers, C.H.	Miss E.B. Patterson	2 Dec 1888	
523	Rodgers, I.N.	Miss S.A. Harrison	13 Jan 1897	(BO)
292	Rodgers, J.A.	Mary Newell	21 Dec 1889	
437	Rodgers, J.W.	Miss H.A. McFarland	26 Apr 1891	
	[Bond - Hattie A. McFarland]			
257	Rogers, Henry	Callie Clifton	16 June 1889	
	[Consent - M.W. and E.F. Clifton of Toccopola]			
471	Roper, T.A.	Mrs. M.A. Miers	18 Oct 1891	
313	Rosemand, B.L.	Margaret Martin	16 Jan 1890	
484	Ross, M.F.	Miss M.J. Graham	3 Dec 1891	
409	Rush, James	Dora McCullough	28 Jan 1891	
	Consent: W.F. McCullough]			
150	Russell, J.A.	Rachel Hattox	26 July 1888	(LO)
124	Russell, M.S.	Miss T.E. Nobles	18 Feb 1880	
103	Rutledge, J.R.	Lula Todd	27 Dec 1887	
	[This license was started but no date. No ministers signature on return]			
418	Rutledge, W.A.	Miss N.E. Watts	26 Feb 1891	
23	Salmon, J.H.	Anna B. Pickens	6 Feb 1887	
243	Samples, H.W.	Miss R.F. Donaldson	1 May 1889	
123	Saunders, C. (Camisas)	Mattie Hall	7 Feb 1880	
	[License - Sanders. Father: A.R. Sanders]			
129	Sanders, Henry	Miss J.C. Frazer	22 Feb 1888	
52	Sawyer, James	Mrs. M.J. McKinney	14 Aug 1887	
	[License - Miss M.J. McKinney]			
416	Seale, Marlin	Beula Jackson	19 Feb 1891	
378	Seals, W.H.	Mollie Mahan	10 Dec 1890	
72	Shannon, L.Y.	Miss M.B. Wells	17 Nov 1887	

PAGE	GROOM	BRIDE	DATE	
354	Shearer, W.A.J.	Julia Dickson	24 Sept	1890
300	Shelton, J.W.	Miss W.P. Alexander	18 Dec	1889
53	Shettles, G.R.	Rebecca Goggans	14 Aug	1887
446	Shockley, F.M.	Ara Clayton	16 June	1891
54	Short, John	Linnie Pritchard	24 Aug	1887
460	Simmons, C.B.	Miss L.J. McNeece	26 Aug	1891
	[Bond - Laura Jane McNeece]			
166	Simmons, G.M.	Jennie Kitchens	30 Sept	1888
242	Simmons, John D.	Leuella West	18 Apr	1889
516	Simmons, Marvin	Eliza Wilson	27 Dec	1891
79	Sledge, H.B.	Delia Montgomery	1 Dec	1887
387	Smith, C.P.	Emma C. Bell	22 Dec	1890
306	Smith, J.A.	Miss G.A. Austin	26 Dec	1889
161	Smith, W.T.	Miss Lee Young	9 Sept	1888
46	Smitherman, V.A.	Sallie Miller	20 July	1887
112	Souter, O.B.	Laudie Wood	22 Jan	1888
91	Spears, C.C.	Miss F.E. Simpson	25 Dec	1887
491	Spears, T.J.	Miss Reni Hale	10 Dec	1891
374	Spence, John R.	Miss M.A. Sanders	7 Dec	1890
	[Consent: M.E. Sanders]			
283	Staton, J.W.	Miss Francis Franklin	15 Nov	1889
19	Staggs, J.T.	Miss M.J. Mills	19 Jan	1887
214	Stepp, James	Lou Goggans	3 Jan	1889
325	Stepp, W.J.	Alice Kelly	13 Feb	1890
48	Stewart, J.M.	Evaline McCarter	20 July	1887
363	Stewart, John	Annie Parrish	12 Nov	1890
296	Stovall, W.B.	Miss L.L. Lemons	8 Dec	1889
51	Strain, James	Fannie Wilson	11 Aug	1887
170	Strong, J.H.	Miss L.B. Shirley	25 Nov	1890
481	Sudduth, A.L.	Minnie Sudduth	17 Nov	1891
176	Sullivan, J.E.	Hattie Bleyew (?)	18 Nov	1886
454	Sullivan, M.E.	Miss E.E. Manins	7 Aug	1891
2	Swaim, C.F.	Miss A.B. Bevil	23 Dec	1886
299	Swaim, L.P.	Miss L.E. Hellums	17 Dec	1889
512	Swim, Matthew	Miss Lee Whitworth	3 Jan	1892
25	Swindle, Jim	Anna Little	2 Mar	1887
122	Swords, J.J.	Miss M.A. Rodgers	2 Dec	1888
	[Bond dated 1 Feb 1888]			
305	Tate, J.E.	Miss M.B. Witt	23 Dec	1889 (BO)
333	Taylor, C.P.	Cora May Phillips	12 Apr	1890
401	Taylor, H.C.	Alice Lewellen	4 Jan	1891
49	Terrell, J.M.	Miss P.P. Sledge	17 Aug	1887
262	Terrell, M.T.	Ednie Black	31 July	1889
308	Thomas, M.L.	Miss M.I. Wood	9 Jan	1890
66	Thomas, W.F.	Miss S.A. Warren	10 Oct	1887
353	Thompson, B.H.	Lora E. Bolton	23 Sept	1890
332	Thornton, Frank	Martha Keanon	7 Apr	1890

PAGE	GROOM	BRIDE	DATE	
525	Thornton, J.W.	Miss H.B. Wooten	14 Jan	1892
276	Todd, C.H.	Miss N. Cook	2 Oct	1889
480	Todd, J.M.	Dora E. Orr	15 Nov	1891
234	Todd, R.L.	Miss S.B. Lowry	13 Feb	1889
261	Towlison, William	Miss M.J. Pannell	3 July	1889
414	Tutor, E.A.	Miss E.A. Hamilton	19 Feb	1891

[Bond states Miss Hamilton as C.A. Hamilton]

PAGE	GROOM	BRIDE	DATE	
81	Tutor, E.C.	Lula Ferguson	28 Dec	1887
202	Tutor, C.C.	Ballas Herndon	23 Dec	1888
64	Tutor, L.L.	Miss S.A. Gregory	2 Oct	1887
340	Tutor, J.T.	Della Herdon	19 June	1890
384	Tucker, J.O.	Dora Gillstrap (?)	18 Dec	1890
14	Tucker, V.B.	Miss L.E. Stephens	9 Jan	1887
351	Tully, J.F.	Lena Russell	14 Sept	1890
453	Turner, E.C.	Miss P.L.D. Wilson	2 Aug	1891
531	Underwood, R.S.	Annie Gillespie	14 Feb	1892
204	Vance, S.A.	Miss S.M. Burks	23 Dec	1888
448	Vaughn, A.L.	M.A. Montgomery	28 Aug	1891
24	Vaughn, H.F.	Miss M.E. Hensley	15 Feb	1887
444	Vaughn, J. Lewis	Bettie Newell	8 July	1891
377	Vaughn, W.P.	Dena Sibly	11 Dec	1890
486	Walker, J.S.	Belle McWhirter	26 Nov	1891
59	Wall, J.B.	Lenna H. Tutor	25 Sept	1887

[Consent - W.A.J. Wall, father.   Consent - Henwell Tutor
Both from Randolph, Mississippi]

PAGE	GROOM	BRIDE	DATE	
266	Walls, H.P.	Susie Petit	15 Aug	1889
501	Ward, J.L.	Miss N.J. Hutchinson	20 Dec	1891
329	Warren, J.A.	Bell Mahan	11 Mar	1890
7	Warren, J.D.	Miss M.P. Faver	2 Jan	1887
171	Warren, J.P.	Lounena Wilson	27 Oct	1888
172	Warren, J.R.	Miss E.W. McNeely	28 Oct	1888
201	Warren, L.L.	Miss L.M. Nowlin	23 Dec	1880
84	Warren, W.T.	Miss T.E. Williams	8 Dec	1887
1	Warren, W.C.	Miss S.C. Pannell	5 Jan	1887
212	Watts, R.C.	Miss S.C. Owen	3 Jan	1889

[Minister's Return - R.L. Watts]

PAGE	GROOM	BRIDE	DATE	
326	Watts, Thomas F.	Annie Wilder	19 Feb	1890
21	Weatherall, C.L.	Jennie Rogers	20 Jan	1887
422	Weatherall, W.W.	Julia E. Lowry	26 Feb	1891
41	Webb, J.C.	Ellen McCullough	4 July	1887
92	Weeks, S.M.	Miss G. Grisham	22 Dec	1887
500	Wells, B.G.	Etta Lee Bullard	18 Dec	1891
87	Wells, G.W.	Miss D.S. Smitherman	1 Jan	1888
479	Wells, J.F.	Miss I.M. Hardin	19 Nov	1891
272	Wells, L.D.	Ida K. Stark	8 Sept	1889
475	Wells, R.A.	Maggie Smitherman	8 Nov	1891

PAGE	GROOM	BRIDE	DATE	
6	Westmoreland, W.W.	Miss M.C. Herrington	29 Dec 1886	
208	Wheeler, W.M.	Amanda Brown	27 Dec 1886	
209	White, A.B.	Nannie Harrison	1 Jan 1889	
403	Whitlow, C.W.	Lois Fuqua	15 Jan 1891	
135	Whitlow, J.S.	Sudie Hobson	22 Mar 1888	
102	Whitten, J.A.	Maggie Hendricks	29 Dec 1887	
142	Whitworth, C.C.	Lizzie Whitworth	31 May 1888	
339	Wilder, J.H.	Miss S.N. Swords	8 June 1890	
274	Wilder, L.R.	Miss S.A. Fields	19 Sept 1889	
191	Wilder, W.H.	Miss S.C. Swords	13 Dec 1888	
290	Williams, T.H., Jr.	Miss S.E. Springer	24 Nov 1889	
130	Wingo, H.C.	Miss M.J. Hinton	1 Mar 1888	
347	Wilson, A.N.	Mrs. H.A. Pitts	21 Aug 1890	
137	Wilson, M.D.L.	Mollie Key	21 Apr 1888	
251	Wilson, R.L.	Miss J.I. Todd	25 May 1889	
415	Wilson, W.H.	Fannie Gillilard	18 Feb 1891	
17	Wood, C.B.	Miss D.J. Jackson	16 Jan 1887	
168	Wood, J.C.	Lizzie Sims	18 Oct 1888	
286	Wood, T.J.	Miss H.E. Johnson	11 Nov 1889	(BO)
32	Wood, W.W.	Miss F.M. Williams	7 Apr 1887	
50	Wooten, J.L.	Cordia Martin	10 Aug 1887	
483	Young, J.C.	Alice Wilson	26 Nov 1891	
155	Zackery, J.I.	Margaret Donald	20 Dec 1888	

BRIDE INDEX
GROOMS SURNAME IN BRACKETS

Addams, Sadie (Brockman)
Alexander, Miss W.P. (Shelton)
Allen, Miss W.E. (Camp)
Anderson, Annie (Archer)
Anderson, Jennie (Peeden)
Anderson, Miss N.M. (Miller)
Anderson, Miss R.J. (Franks)
Arnold, Carrie (Rice)
Austin, Miss G.A. (Smith)
Aycock, Miss E.P. (Land)
Aycock, Fannie J. (Caldwell)

Baker, Julia (Browning)
Ball, Miss F.E. (Craig)
Ball, Jennie (Bynum)
Barr, Miss F.L. (Foster)
Barrett, Fannie (Mask)
Bass, Miss J.C. (Kyle)
Bayless, Miss H.E. (Galloway)
Bell, Emma C. (Smith)
Bell, Miss M.C. (Atkinson)
Benjamin, Susie (Grisham)
Berry, Analou (Cooper)
Bevil, Anna (Buchanan)
Bevill, Miss A.B. (Swaim)
Bigham, Sallie (McCarver)
Billingsly, Maggie (Gilmore)
Black, Annie (McClarty)
Black, Ednie (Terrell)
Black, Lorena (Anderson)
Belyew(?), Hattie (Sullivan)
Blunt, Miss M.J. (Hair)
Blunt, Miss M.J. (Miller)
Bolen, Ella (Bramlett)
Bolen, Maggie (Jeeter)
Bolen, Mattie (Houpt)
Bolton, Lora E. (Thompson)
Bolton, Mary Irene (Robertson)
Bonds, Sallie (Raines)
Bowen, Emma (Kelly)
Bramlett, Dora (Brassfield)
Brandon, Jennie (Nichols)
Bratton, Miss M.E. (Bowen)
Britt, Mrs. Emma (Chaney)
Brooks, Jessie I. (Berry)
Brown, Miss A.L. (Calloway)
Brown, Amanda (Wheeler)
BRown, Miss D.B. (Ellis)

Brown, Lucia (Alexander)
Brown, Mollie (Richie)
Brown, Miss D.J. (Gentry)
Browning, Giona (Baker)
Bryant, Louisa (Garmon)
Buckley, Miss S.C. (Burchfield)
Bullard, Etta Lee (Wells)
Burks, Miss S.M. (Vance)
Burson, Ida (McCord)
Buchanan, Miss L.S. (Mills)
Buchanan, Miss M.L. (Cobb)
Buchanan, Myrtle (Mayo)
Buchanan, Miss V.B. (Dunlap)

Caldwell, Corrie (Pitts)
Caldwell, Emma (Livingston)
Caldwell, Miss M.F. (Clark)
Camp, Miss M.S. (Anderson)
Campbell, Nannie (Caldwell)
Cantrell, Fannie (Miller)
Cannon, Miss M.J. (Morphis)
Carnes, Mrs. M.A. (McGregor)
Carpenter, Emily Orange (McGregor)
Carr, Annie (Jenkins)
Carr, Jessie (Huntington)
Carter, Clemma (Cooper)
Castleberry, Annie E. (Cartwright)
Castleberry, Clora (Roberts)
Chaney, Miss M.E. (Davis)
Chapman, Cintha (Little)
Christman, Miss R.S. (Miller)
Clark, Sadie B. (Morphis)
Clayton, Ara (Shockley)
Clifton, Callie (Rodgers)
Cobb, Etta (Kelly)
Conlee, Nannie B. (Martin)
Conlee, Nora E. (Collier)
Cook, Miss N. (Todd)
Coward, Miss M.E. (Parks)
Craig, Alice (Black)
Craig, Nannie (Black)
Crawford, Miss A.L. (Drake)
Crawford, Cora (Longest)
Crawford, Etta (Brown)
Crawford, Miss L.D. (Calloway)
Cristman, Miss I.E. (Hill)
Crum, Ida (Miears)
Cruse, Miss L.J. (Fields)

Cruse, Nannie (Fields)
Cunningham, Susie (New)

Daggett, Miss G.A. (Ellis)
Davis, T. Etta (Langston)
Davidson, Miss M.A. (Prude)
Deason, Obenna (Prude)
Decanter, Jane (Kelly)
Dickson, Julia (Shearer)
Dillard, S. Anna (Midlock)
Dillard, Miss L.A. (Nowlin)
Dillard, Miss M.L. (Benjamin)
Dixon, Sallie (McNeil)
Donald, Margaret (Zackery)
Donaldson, Miss R.F. (Samples)
Douglas, Stella (Hitchcock)
Douglas, Suanna (Durham)
Drake, Lillian (McDaniel)
Dunn, Maggie (Cummings)

Edwards, Ida H. (Jernigan)
Ellis, Iola (Pitts)
Evans, Miss M.C. (Cummings)

Farris, Dovie (McCarver)
Faver, Miss M.P. (Warren)
Faulkner, Miss N.E. (Pound)
Ferguson, Lula (Tutor)
Fields, Miss S.A. (Wilder)
Flemming, Miss R.J. (Hubbard)
Fontaine, Miss N.L. (Dillard)
Fowler, Nora (Ivy)
Franklin, Francis (Staton)
Frazer, Miss J.C. (Sawyer)
Fuller, Miss F.A. (Ferguson)
Fuller, Margaret (Dillard)
Furguson, Miss H.L. (Gillespie)
Fuqua, Lois (Whitlow)

Gains, Lennie (Morman)
Garrison, Sallie (May)
Gay, Fannie (Grisham)
Gideon, Mattie (Bell)
Gillespie, Annie (Underwood)
Gillespie, Miss H.C. (Petit)
Gilliland, Fannie (Wilson)
Gillstrap (?), Dora (Tucker)
Gilmer, Miss F.E. (Cates)
Gilmer, Irene E. (Gorman)
Gilpen, Miss C.E. (Belk)
Ginn, Frances (Owen)

Glover, Miss M.A. (Morphis)
Goggans, Lou (Stepp)
Goggans, Rebecca (Shettles)
Graham, Miss M.J. (Ross)
Gregory, Miss S.A. (Tutor)
Grice, Miss M.A. (Carwile)
Grisham, Miss G. (Weeks)
Grist, Miss B.L. (Murphy)
Grist, Miss M.A. (Austin)

Hale, Reni (Spears)
Hall, Mattie (Saunders)
Hamilton, Miss E.A. (Tutor)
Hampton, Cora L. (Rayburn)
Haney, Annie (Jackson)
Haney, Maudie (Calloway)
Hardin, Miss I.M. (Wells)
Harmon, Ollie (Echols)
Harrison, MIss E.A. (Garrett)
Harrison, Evilene (Jones)
Harrison, Nannie (White)
Harrison, Miss S.A. (Rodgers)
Harvey, Etta (Parrish)
Harvson (?), Miss A. (Bristol)
Hattox, Rachel (Russell)
Hellums, Miss L.E. (Swaim)
Henderson, Mamie (Jones)
Hendricks, Maggie (Whitten)
Henry, Miss N.E. (Lancaster)
Henry, Miss F.D. (Bray)
Hensley, Miss M.E. (Vaughn)
Herrington, Miss M.C. (Westmoreland)
Herdon, Della (Tutor)
Herndon, Ballas (Tutor)
Herndon, MIss L.M. (Douglas)
Herron, Mamie C. (Mitchell)
Higgins, Miss S.M. (McCullough)
Hill, Della (Cowsert)
Hill, Miss E.M. (Carr)
Hill, MIss M.P. (McElbany)
Hill, Zella (Box)
Hinton, Miss M.J. (Wingo)
Hobson, Sudie (Whitlow)
Holloman, Lucie (Black)
Holloway, Miss O.M. (Galloway)
Holly, Miss M.C. (Austin)
Horton, Mollie (Davis)
Houpt, Carline (Miller)
Houpt, Caroline (Miller)
Hubbard, Miss O.J. (Goldman)
Humphries, Essie (Lambert)

Hutch, Cora (Griffin)
Hutchison, Miss N.J. (Ward)

Ingram, Miss F.A. (Riley)

Jackson, Beula (Seale)
Jackson, Miss D.J. (Wood)
Jackson, Miss G.A. (Haney)
Jackson, Miss M.F. (Kelly)
Jackson, Mattie (Lower)
James, Emma (McGregory)
James, Georgia (McGregor)
Jenkins, M. (Lowry)
Jernigan, Winnie (Gregory)
Jinkins, MIss Willie (Hardin)
Johnson, Antnet (Brown)
Johnson, Corrie (Gordon)
Johnson, Miss H.E. (Wood)
Johnson, Miss M.E. (Mitchell)
Johnson, Mattie (Brown)
Johnson, Rachiel (Gilder)
Johnson, Sallie (Bowles)
Jones, Bettie (Hitchcock)
Jones, Callie (Bratton)
Jones, Miss E.C. (Goggans)
Jones, Josephine (Gregory)
Jones, MIss L.C. (McGregor)
Jones, Miss M.A. (Munn)
Jones, Mattie (Hill)
Keanon, Martha (Thornton)
Key, Mollie (Wilson)
Kellie, Mollie (Moorland)
Kelly, Annie (Brazil)
Kelly, Alice (Stepp)
Kelly, Catherine (Little)
Kelly, MIss T.A. (Anderson)
Kidd, Miss A.S.A. (Owen)
Kidd, Miss M.E. (Cooper)
Kitchens, Jennie (Simmons)

Lambert, Miss S.E. (Brandon)
Land, Mrs. M.E. (Fowler)
Lane, Annie (Minyard)
Langley, Miss S.C. (McCraw)
Lantrip, Miss E.P. (McCormick)
LaPrade, Emma (Dillard)
Lawor, Nannie (Evans)
Lee, Minnie (Gentry)
Lee, Miss S.M. (Henry)
Leed, Miss M.W. (Pegues)
Lemons, Miss L.L. (Stovall)

Lesly, Miss L.Q. (Nix)
Lewellen, Alice (Taylor)
Leweling, Miss L.C. (Leweling)
Lewelling, Emma (Ferguson)
Lilley, Helen M. (Austin)
Lilly, Beulah (McGaughly)
Little, Miss M.A. (Montgomery)
Little, Anna (Swindle)
Long, Jane (Horton)
Lowry, Julia A. (Weatherall)
Lowry, Miss M.F. (Gilmer)
Lowry, Miss S.B. (Todd)
Lovins, Miss Alter (Emis)
Lyons, Modena (Holt)

McAlister, Miss J.A. (Harmon)
McCarter, Evaline (Stewart)
McCharen, Irene (Montgomery)
McCoby, Julia (Davis)
McCormick, Miss C.A.L. (Barnes)
McCoy, Ida B. (Caldwell)
McCoy, Miss M.C. (Howell)
McCullough, Dora (Rush)
McCullough, Ellen (Webb)
McFarland, Miss H.A. (Rodgers)
McNice, Lula (Hester)
McNeely, Miss B.C. (Craw)
McNeely, MIss E.W. (Warren)
McNeely, Miss L.V. (Hampton)
McGregor, Leenia (Holloway)
McGregor, Miss M.A. (Bouchillon)
McGregor, Mattie (Holloway)
McKinney, Josephine (Hester)
McWhirter, Belle (Walker)
McWhirter, Elizabeth (Morphis)
McWhirter, MIss G.A. (Owen)

Mahan, Bell (Warren)
Mahan, Mollie (Seals)
Manins, Miss E.E. (Sullivan)
Mann, Bettie (Allred)
Martin, Cordia (Wooten)
Martin, Jane (LaPrade)
Martin, Margaret (Rosemond)
Mayo, Annie (Lyon)
Miears, Mrs. M.A. (Roper)
Milam, Abella (McCoy)
Milam, Corrie (Fleming)
Milam, Ida H. (Gambrell)
Milam, Loula J. (McCoy)
Miller, Addie (McCord)

Miller, Mary Jane (Lewelling)
Miller, Mattie (Greenwood)
Miller, Laudie (Pearson)
Miller, Rosa (Blaylock)
Miller, Sallie (Smitherman)
Mills, Annie (Lauderdale)
Mills, Miss M.J. (Staggs)
Mitchell, Bettie (Polk)
Mitchell, Ida (Hodges)
Montgomery, Delia (Sledge)
Montgomery, Miss L.A. (Osborn)
Montgomery, M.A. (Vaughn)
Montgomery, Miss M.E. (Johnson)
Mooney, Lizzie (Patterson)
Morgan, Birthie (Cantriel)
Morgan, Susie (Cunningham)
Mounce, Lula E. (Reeder)
Murphy, Allice (Mize)
Murphy, Melia (Brown)
Murphy, Miss N.E. (Cooper)

Nelson, Miss S.P. (McAlister)
Newell, Bettie (Vaughn)
Newell, Mary (Rodgers)
Nobles, Miss T.E. (Russell)
Nowlin, Miss M.J. (Dison)
Nowlin, Miss L.M. (Warren)
Nuson, Mattie (McCarver)

O'Neal, Miss M.Y. (Lowry)
Onsberry, Miss L. (Hellums)
Orr, Dora E. (Todd)
Osborn, Miss F.J. (Hendricks)
Owen, Miss A.H. (Farar)
Owen, Miss M.R. (Nowlin)
Owen, Miss M.V. (Pittman)
Owen, Miss S.C. (Watts)

Pannell, M.C.P. (Black)
Pannell, Miss M.J. (Towlison)
Pannell, Miss S.E. (Waters)
Pappasan, Miss M.E. (Bockman)
Park, Annie (Carter)
Parrish, Annie (Stewart)
Parrish, Laura (Lowry)
Parrish, Miss M.E. (Morrison)
Parrish, Marthy (Montgomery)
Parrish, Miss R.E. (Fleming)
Parrish, Virona (McGraw)
Patterson, MIss E.B. (Rodgers)
Patterson, Mrs. Pauline (Mitchell)

Pegues, Mrs. Emma (Campbell)
Petit, Susie (Walls)
Phillips, Cora May (Taylor)
Pickens, Anna B. (Salmon)
Pickens, Miss S.C. (King)
Pittman, Mrs. L.V. (Patterson)
Pitts, Etta G. (Brandon)
Pitts, Miss H.A. (Wilson)
Pitts, Janey (McCoy)
Poke, Miss F.E. (Hodges)
Porter, Emma (Payne)
Porter, Miss J.J. (Gregory)
Potts, Miss F.E. (McKnight)
Powell, Ada (Harrison)
Powell, Mrs. Sue M. (Barnett)
Price, Lucinda (Purdon)
Price, Miss S.M. (Griffin)
Priest, Miss M.L. (Hampton)
Pritchard, Linnie (Short)
Purvis, Etna (Ferrell)
Pyle, Bessie F. (Grisham)
Pyle, Miss M.E. (Lovell)

Ray, Docia (Gorman)
Ray, Ellen (Pope)
Ray, Lanla (Pope)
Ray, Sallie (Hutchins)
Rayburn, Miss E.O.M. (Durham)
Reed, Mary (Hester)
Reeder, Miss M.L. (Brown)
Robbins, Miss F.L. (McElbaney)
Robbins, Lewella (Robbins)
Rodgers, Miss M.A. (Swords)
Rodgers, Mattie A. (Carter)
Rogers, Jennie (Weatherall)
Roots, Sue M. (Barkley)
Roye, Miss E.G. Ella (Brown)
Rowan, Lena (Burnett)
Russell, Addie (Bowen)
Russell, Miss C.A. (Crane)
Russell, Lena (Tully)
Russell, Luna Glen (Kyle)
Rutledge, Helen (Johnson)
Rye, Mrs. S.A. (Dye)

Sanders, Ada (Harrison)
Sanders, Annie (Ridge)
Sanders, Miss M.A. (Spence)
Sanders, Minnie (Hale)
Sappington, Pink (Parrish)
Savely, Bettie (Beeson)

Scott, Fannie (McKnight)
Scott, Minnie (Patterson)
Seals, Miss M.E. (Haney)
Seals, Mary (Haney)
Shelton, Miss G.A. (McCoy)
Shirley, Miss L.B. (Strong)
Sibley, Dena (Vaughn)
Sibley, Miss M.L. (Porter)
Simmons, Belle (Griffin)
Simmons, Dora L. (Graham)
Simmons, Florence (Kitchens)
Simmon, Florence (Kitchens)
Simmons, Mattie L. (Johnston)
Simmons, Miss L.C. (Caldwell)
Simons, Miss A.B. (McGill)
Simpson, Miss C.J. (Cobb)
Simpson, Miss F.E. (Spears)
Simpson, Pennie (Conlee)
Sims, Lizzie (Wood)
Sledge, Miss M.J. (Shirley)
Sledge, Miss P.P. (Terrell)
Smitherman, Miss A.C. (Foster)
Smitherman, Miss D.S. (Wells)
Smitherman, Maggie (Wells)
Smith, Miss A.L. (Parrish)
Smith, Betty (Griffin)
Smith, Emma (Putt)
Snider, Elizabeth (Lofton)
Souter, Miss M.D. (Donaldson)
Sparks, Miss N.P. (Evans)
Spears, R.A. (Baker)
Spencer, Mattie (Hughs)
Springer, Miss S.E. (Williams)
Staggs, Maloney (Echols)
Stark, Ida K. (Wells)
Stegall, Miss E.M. (Cooper)
Stegall, Miss E.M. (Cooper)
Stephens, Miss L.E. (Tucker)
Stewart, Mollie (Johnson)
Stovall, Clarra (High)
Stovall, Nannie (High)
Strain, Miss J.E. (Edwards)
Sudduth, Minnie (Sudduth)
Suell, Miss M.J. (Hartley)
Sullivan, MIss B.E. (Duncan)
Surratt, Sarah (Humphries)
Swain, Syrena (Herndon)
Swords, Miss A.B. (Anderson)
Swords, Mary (Griffin)
Swords, Miss S.C. (Wilder)
Swords, Miss s.N. (Wilder)

Tallant, Miss E.L. (Daniel)
Tate, Miss Willie A. (Galloway)
Taylor, Ella (Douglas)
Teeter, Lela E. (Fitzpatrick)
Thomason, Minnie (Brown)
Thompson, Miss E.A. (Oden)
Thompson, Amanda (Maxey)
Thompson, Laula (Dillard)
Thompson, Miss N.E. (Lower)
Thornton, Miss L.A. (Box)
Todd, Miss F. (Gafford)
Todd, Miss J.I. (Wilson)
Todd, Lou (Coker)
Todd, Lula (Rutledge)
Todd, Mary (Cook)
Todd, Miss S.M. (Robbins)
Tutor, Emma (Palmer)
Tutor, Joanna (Kelly)
Tutor, Lenna H. (Wall)
Tutor, Lucy (Carter)
Tutor, Miss M.D. (Herndon)
Tutor, Miss O.FP. (Bouchillon)
Tutor, Miss P.B. (Gregory)

Vance, Mrs. Mary (Daniel)
Vandiver(?), Miss C.E.A. (King)
Vaughn, Lula (Caldwell)

Wadkins, Fannie (Marshall)
Waits, Miss A.A. (Drewey)
Walker, Parlee (Helums)
Warren, Miss M.E. (Robbins)
Warren, Mary (Hawkins)
Warren, Ruthie (Bullard)
Warren, MIss S.A. (Thomas)
Washington, Josephine (Bray)
Watson, Fannie (McGregor)
Watts, Emma (Clayton)
Watts, Miss M.H. (McWhirter)
Watts, Miss N.E. (Rutledge)
Weaver, Florence (Hill)
Webb, Willie (McCullough)
Weeden, Ally (Joyner)
Weeks, Jennie (Burk)
Weeks, Nancy (Morrison)
Wells, Miss M.B. (Shannon)
West, Jessie (Henderson)
West, Luella (Simmons)
Westmoreland, Miss M.C. (Bryant)
Whitlow, Ada (Purvis)
Whitlow, Emma (Bramlett)

Whitlow, Mattie (Adkins)
Whitworth, MIss C.B. (Johnson)
Whitworth, Lee (Swim)
Whitworth, Lizzie (Whitworth)
White, Miss S.E. (Ferguson)
Whitesides, Miss A.M. (Cummins)
Wilder, Annie (Watts)
Wilder, Anna (McMillen)
Willard, Sallie (Denton)
Williams, Della (Crawley)
Williams, Miss F.M. (Wood)
Williams, Fannie (Hamilton)
Williams, Miss T.E. (Warren)
Winfield, Zuenadora (Chaney)
Wilson, Alice (Young)
Wilson, Eliza (Simmons)
Wilson, Fannie (Strain)
Wilson, Lounena (Warren)
Wilson, Miss M.E. (Holly)
Wilson, MIss P.L.D. (Turner)
Wilson, Miss S.A. (Bray)
Winters, Mattie S. (Garrison)
Witt, Miss M.B. (Tate)
Wood, Ida (Henderson)
Wood, Laudie (Souter)
Wood, Miss M.I. (Thomas)
Wood, Minnie (Blair)
Wooley, Miss A.M. (Blakely)
Wooten, H.B. (Thornton)
Worsham, Willie (Kirby)

Young, Miss Bunch (Haley)
Young, Lee (Smith)
Young, Sary M. (Adams)

www.ingramcontent.com/pod-product-compliance
Lightning Source LLC
Chambersburg PA
CBHW081131170426
43197CB00017B/2825